Edwina Currie has been an MP since 1983. She was a Minister in Margaret Thatcher's government from 1986 to 1988 and turned down John Major's invitation to return to office in 1992. She was a Conservative candidate in the 1994 European elections and is married with two daughters. Her first novel, *A Parliamentary Affair*, was an international bestseller.

'Intense sex and political manipulation in a steamy tale'
Today

'Leaves you wondering how much could, or indeed has, happened'
The Sun

'The perfect way to relax with a rattling good read'
Independent on Sunday

'An extremely timely and graphic novel – an uncomfortable amalgam of truth and fiction'
Independent Magazine

'Spot on . . . good passages of observation and interesting sidelights on parliamentary life'
Daily Telegraph

'A steamy tale of scandal and seduction, erotic escapades and political intrigue, set in the hallowed corridors of Westminster'
Glasgow Daily Record

EDWINA CURRIE

A Woman's Place

Hodder & Stoughton

Currie, Edwina
Woman's Place
I. Title
823.914 [F]

ISBN 0 340 66580 7

Typeset by Hewer Text Composition Services, Edinburgh
Printed and bound in Great Britain by
Mackays of Chatham PLC

Hodder and Stoughton
A Division of Hodder Headline PLC
338 Euston Road
London NW1 3BH

For my mother, Pese Cohen, born 22 January 1912

Author's Note

This is a novel about modern British political life, today and in the near future. I have tried to make it as authentic as possible, to convey some insight how we live and work. So the background is realistic and I have even taken the liberty of fleshing it out with some real people, under their real names. But my plot and my central characters are all completely imaginary and no reference is intended to the real people holding their offices at the times in question, or to any other person.

Edwina Currie
London, February 1996

One is certainly not free to write on any subject. One does not choose one's subject, but is chosen by it.

Gustave Flaubert

It can take a long time to accept that celebrity is merely a different form of loneliness.

Arthur Miller

Who's Who

Some of the people in this book will be found in current or recent editions of *Who's Who*, *The Times Guide to the House of Commons* and *Vacher's Parliamentary Companion*. The following, however, appear unaccountably to have been omitted.

BAMPTON, EDWARD, MP. Born 1946 in Yorkshire. Minister of State, Home Office. Educated Huddersfield Grammar School. Stubbs Fine Cloths 1962–73. Chairman and Managing Director, Bampton Engineering Ltd, 1974–86. Elected (Cons.) for Hebden Bridge 1983. Campaigned for John Major 1990, 1995. Parliamentary Under-Secretary, Ministry of Defence, 1992–3. Married 1969 Jean; two *d*. Clubs: Kirklees Conservative Club, Huddersfield Royal British Legion, Yorkshire Cricket. Recreations: bird-watching, real ale.

CHADWICK, MARTIN. Civil servant. Born 1952. Educated Shrewsbury and Jesus College, Oxford. Son of Sir Matthew Chadwick, CB, KCMG, former Perm Sec at the Home Office. Married with two children. Current residence: Sittingbourne, Kent. Club: Athenaeum. Recreations: writing Latin verse, collecting ties.

DICKSON, ROGER, MP. Born 14 Feb 1952. Secretary of State for the Environment. Educated Wandsworth Comprehensive School, London; Associate of the Institute of Bankers 1975; MA in Administration and Politics, the Open University, 1982. Tarrants Bank 1968–75. Chairman, Dickson and Associates 1975–87. Contested Hammersmith (Cons.) 1979, returned for North-West Warwickshire 1983. PPS, Dept of Trade and Industry 1987. Whip 1990, Senior Whip 1992. Minister of State, Department of the Environment, promoted Secretary of State on resignation of Sir Nigel Boswood, *q.v.* Married 1980 the Hon. Caroline Tarrant, *d.* of Lord Tarrant *q.v.*; three children. Clubs: Carlton, St Stephen's. Recreations: home, family, taking risks.

FERRIMAN, FREDERICK, MP. Born 1934. Educated Marlborough, Christ Church, Oxford; MA 1955, third class (Greats). Farmer and company director. First elected 1974 (Cons.) for Northampton West. Chairman, secretary or treasurer of various Conservative backbench and all-party parliamentary committees and groups. Member national council, Freedom Association, 1988–   . Member, Public Accounts Committee, Committee of Privileges. Gave extensive evidence to the Nolan Committee on Standards in Public Life. Clubs: Carlton, White's, Cecil, IOD. Recreations: politics and business.

HARRISON, DEREK, MP. Born 1961. PPS to Ted Bampton MP *q.v.* 1993–   . Educated Hatfield School and the University of Kent at Canterbury (BA, Accounting). Research Assistant to Edwina Currie MP 1989–90. Conservative Central Office, family issues desk, 1990. Research Officer, Adam Smith Institute, 1991–92. Elected 1992 (Cons.) Cotswolds North. Unmarried. Clubs: Carlton, Brooks's. Recreations: bridge, country pursuits, reading, not walking.

LAIDLAW, FREDERICK, MP. Born 29 March 1972 in Milton, Hampshire. Educated Hambridge Secondary School, Southampton University (BSc in Business Administration). Sales Executive, Bulstrode and Co, 1992–6. Elected (Cons.) for Milton and Hambridge, Hants. Unmarried. Clubs: none. Recreations: keeping my head above water.

QUIN, KEITH, MP. Born 1952 in Manchester. Educated Bury Grammar School and Hull University (BA Hons History). Lecturer in sociology and trade union history, Kingston upon Hull College of Further Education (now the University of Humberside) 1972–83. Elected (Lab.) Manchester Canalside 1983. Married to Councillor Mrs Edith Quin JP; no children. Member various backbench Labour and all-party groups. Recreations: conservation of endangered species.

STALKER, ELAINE, MP. Née Johnson. Born 13 October 1956. Educated King Edward's High School for Girls, Barham, and Barham University (BA Hons, History and Politics). Voluntary worker, mental handicap projects, and part-time tutor, Open University, 1982–92. Member Barham City Council 1985–91, deputy leader Conservative group. Elected (Cons.) Warmingshire South 1992. Married 1977 Michael Stalker, senior pilot with British Airways; marriage *diss* 1995.

One *d.*, Karen, born 1978. Clubs: none. Recreations: family, home, domestic arts.

YORK, ANTHONY, MP. Born 1 August 1963. Educated Haileybury and Christ Church, Oxford (History). Executive, Nick Leeson and Sons, New York, (international dealers) 1990–2. Rothschild's 1992–5 (assistant to Norman Lamont MP). Director, York and Sons Ltd, Avon, 1988– . Member executive cttee, Friends of Friendless Churches. Returned (Cons.) for Newbury. Unmarried. Clubs: Marylebone Cricket Club, RAC, Royal Dorset Yacht. Recreations: sport, music, travel.

Chapter One

The State Opening of the new Parliament, the very grandest of official occasions, was finally under way.

London seemed cleaner, younger, as if full of hope at this new beginning. By ten o'clock traffic had been halted on the route and sawdust scattered for the horses. Flags fluttered from hastily erected white and gold poles. Crash barriers by Buckingham Palace, the Mall, around Parliament Square and along Whitehall kept crowds of many nationalities in check as they clutched cameras, guidebooks, umbrellas and lunch. Police and guardsmen squared their shoulders under close-fitting black or red tunics, their breastplates and bayonets flashing in the sun.

Elaine Stalker hurried towards the House of Commons. Not for the first time she was struck by how different it was compared to a normal day. In place of traffic noise the lilt of martial music came fitfully on the breeze. Far off she could hear the tramp of hard boots from the barracks on Birdcage Walk accompanied by jingling harness and champing horses and the intermittent bark of commands. It was as if the air were charged with extra oxygen, just because the Queen was on her way.

Elaine had not expected to be pushing past camcorder-toting tourists and heading for her rightful seat on the green benches. In South Warmingshire the election had been so close that throughout the campaign she had steeled herself for defeat. She had even made tentative but discreet inquiries about a proper job afterwards. Some days during the campaign had been no more than a series of hostile encounters with disgruntled electors and a sneering press; the hours of election night as the votes were silently counted were a torture. It was a shock, therefore, to win by a margin of 2,503 – a whisker in an electorate of 75,000 but, as Churchill had once pointed out, for a majority one was enough. Photographs taken on the night showed her disbelieving face, as if about to protest that the returning officer had made a mistake. What a pity she had had no one to celebrate with, no husband on her arm.

1

That her success was shared by the government and party of which she was a member was an even bigger surprise, not least to its own adherents. Opinion polls had been pessimistic almost to the final day. At the last moment, however, the challengers had made several useful errors. The worst was the Opposition Party rally in Newcastle the Thursday before the poll at which to loud fanfares the leading protagonists were introduced as Cabinet Ministers, as if the election were already won. The voters observed grimly that their own role in the matter seemed of small account, and duly voted for the devil they knew.

Elaine felt weak with amazement, but weary. After her first contest her main emotion had been euphoria but that had soon ebbed away amid late nights, failed ambitions and muddled relationships. Dead ends had beckoned, of which the most significant had been her long affair with a government Minister, Roger Dickson. Nothing whatever had come of it, unless being older and wiser counted; but it had ruined her marriage and changed her life. It had not affected him, her erstwhile lover. Roger had avoided both discovery and contrition and now sat confidently on the front benches. Just as she would expect, she mused, in a House so exclusively male. Her reflections made her smile wryly, even as she paused to acknowledge several members of the public who recognised and stopped her.

She pushed past a group of pupils from Westminster School who by tradition stood in everyone's way on the narrow pavement opposite the sovereign's entrance to Victoria Tower. As she waited to cross the road Big Ben struck ten-thirty. She glanced up and nodded, greeting the glittering clock tower as an old acquaintance.

'Good morning. Isn't it exciting?'

A dark-haired young man was at her side. He held out his hand in greeting. Elaine squinted up at him: it was a pest, being a woman at Westminster and so much shorter than her colleagues. This chap must be six foot one, and at a guess not yet twenty-five years old.

'Hello. Aren't you Fred Laidlaw – the victor at Milton and Hambridge? Congratulations, and welcome.'

Her slim companion grinned shyly. 'Yes, that's right. Not with the same endorsement as Nigel Boswood at the last general election, of course, but it's a great relief to have taken it back from the Liberals after that awful by-election.'

'Glad to have you on board.' Elaine was amused at how easy it was to slip back into Westminsterese, the boys' public school style of the back corridors. 'Without your success and a few others like it we'd have been heading for the wilderness. As it is, this Parliament could be unpleasantly like the last one, with our majority too close for comfort.'

She took Fred's arm and pointed. 'The best place to see is by the entrance gates to our car park. Once the carriages have passed, those in the know run inside to the MPs' family room and watch it on TV.'

Fred looked disappointed. 'I thought I'd watch out here and then go into the Chamber.'

The musicians were coming nearer with the blast of a long-forgotten imperial march. Across the square grey-haired members of Huntingdon Women's Institute pulled out miniature Union Jacks to wave at the Queen. Big Ben was striking again; nearly time. A sergeant-major nearby opened his mouth, threw back his head and bellowed a command. Elaine and Fred instinctively stepped back.

'Look, there's Johnson.' The royal coach was preceded by a diverse selection of notables. One government whip, officially entitled Vice-Chamberlain to Her Majesty's Household, had duties which included sending the Queen every week a word-picture of the Commons to give colourful counterpoint to the Prime Minister's staider audiences. This year it was to be Gregory Johnson. In black tails and striped pants, with grey topper and gloves in hand, he peered down from a black and gold carriage drawn by four caparisoned white horses, for all the world like a male Cinderella going to the ball. He waved cheekily at them and bowed.

More coaches and several sleek Daimlers followed; the Chief Whips of the Lords and Commons whom the crowd, not knowing their faces, assumed to be flunkeys; detectives and princes large and small – no princesses this year – and ladies-in-waiting, their wary eyes on the Crown Jewels in silk-lined boxes. A dozen detectives were present too, though not obviously so, since they were for the most part dressed uncomfortably in livery as coachmen. At last came the Household Cavalry, whose deafening hooves made further conversation impossible, and finally the Irish State Coach with the Queen.

'Since you insist on being there in person, let's go.' Elaine grabbed Fred's hand and started to run, down inside the steep cobbled courtyard, through into Speaker's Court, up the Ministers' stairs to the back of the Speaker's Chair and thus to the Chamber, all before the Queen was yet out of her carriage.

Panting slightly, Elaine pushed Fred ahead of her. 'Don't sit down: go to the bar of the House, and when the front benches move off towards the Lords slide in behind. That way you'll be on telly and all your new constituents will see you.'

Fred grinned gratefully and turned to gaze about him.

The Chamber was packed. The Prime Minister and Opposition Leader conversed with colleagues on both sides. Not for years had any MP worn formal dress, but Greville Janner sported a rose in his buttonhole and Nick Soames had a carnation the same cheery hue as his cheeks. Elaine spotted Freddie Ferriman: unfairly, for he never worked at it, his majority had gone up again. Derek Harrison had also done well. There were new faces, some returned as Fred had been in seats lost in by-elections, such as Anthony York, who had won back Newbury. She caught a heart-stopping glimpse of Roger Dickson near the Prime Minister, but he was deep in conversation with the Chancellor and did not notice her.

Elaine and the Speaker were not the only women on duty. At the far end of the building the Queen patted a silvery-grey curl, gathered up her pearl-encrusted handbag and took a deep breath.

Lights dimmed as the great procession began. The Lords Chamber was packed to the gunwales and suffocatingly hot. Yeomen of the Guard and gentlemen ushers and equerries, Garter Kings of Arms and Heralds Extraordinary and Poursuivant filed in. With a rustle everyone stood: archbishops and peers in ermine and lace, peeresses in old tiaras and new frocks, ambassadors in vivid robes with sashes and decorations, judges in powdered wigs, the Lord Chancellor in floor-sweeping black and gold, and guests dressed to the nines and desperately nervous stuffed into the galleries on four sides: all stood hushed and waiting.

The lights went up dramatically as the Queen entered and moved slowly in her full-length gown up the steps to the throne.

'My Lords, pray be seated.'

Somebody was missing: the elected House, all 659 of them. The Lower House must be summoned. The Lord Chamberlain lifted a white wand as if to conduct an invisible orchestra. In the distance Black Rod, otherwise an amiable retired soldier of impeccable reputation, bowed, turned on his heel and, preceded by a couple of policemen trying to keep straight faces, headed for the Commons. A few yards away Fred was caught by the cameras with a besotted expression.

There, trivial tradition turned into constitutional propriety as the great doors were slammed in Black Rod's face. For the hereditary monarch is not allowed into the Commons, not since her ancestor three centuries ago tried to arrest five defiant MPs at the start of the civil war which cost him his life, and which asserted the supremacy of Parliament.

The Queen's messenger hammered ceremoniously on the door and was duly admitted. Madam Speaker stepped down and followed him; the Prime Minister linked with the Leader of the Opposition, Ministers with front-benchers, and all danced in a stately minuet towards Central Lobby.

Then the scramble started. Fred Laidlaw innocently filed behind the Chancellor and nobody dared impede him, such was his rapt determination. Elaine tried to tuck in behind but Tom Pendry nimbly beat her to it. She was swept along in the crush and barely kept her feet. For the next ten minutes at the bar of the Lords she had a fair view only of Pendry's pink scrubbed neck.

It wasn't the Queen's own speech, of course. It was written for her by the government, a list of well-trailed announcements. If occasionally inflections of the regal voice or a slight raising of an eyebrow might imply royal dislike, she could change none of it.

'My Lords and Members of the House of Commons, I pray that the blessing of Almighty God may rest upon your counsels.'

The Queen's face showed no emotion as she handed the speech to an obsequious Lord Chancellor who gingerly climbed backwards down the steps from the throne. Then she rose and was gone.

The crowd of Members broke up in a general hubbub and sauntered back to restaurants and bars, seeking spouses, collecting coats, greeting friends. The House would resume later for a five-day debate on the Gracious Speech, in reality on the government's future programme. Elaine, still mindful that cameras were rolling, strolled out into the Lobby.

Fred Laidlaw found himself a trifle uncertainly in Central Lobby. People took no notice of him, for as yet he was unknown. He could easily have been a Commons researcher or the son of one of the older Members.

'Well, if it isn't Fred.'

He spun round and saw a stocky man who was smiling at him in encouragement. Shyly Fred held out his hand, which was grasped with some warmth.

'Keith Quin. Labour, Manchester Canalside.'

Fred was nonplussed. He was fairly sure he wasn't supposed to fraternise with the Opposition on his first day. 'Mr ... er, Quin? You're Labour, aren't you? I'm Tory, I'm afraid . . .'

'Aye, lad. You won back that by-election seat, didn't you? I know about you. The Labour candidate you beat was my niece. She said you acquitted yourself fine. She didn't have a chance, of course, but it's necessary experience. She's after mine when I retire.' Quin gave a conspiratorial wink.

Fred was at a loss how to reply.

'Grand place, isn't it?' Quin gestured at the great lofted ceiling, its mosaics of the four patron saints agleam in the television lights. Marble statues of statesmen halted in frozen mid-sentence, here a Harcourt, there a Balfour, names which meant nothing whatever to an awed Fred. 'Like a ruddy cathedral. That's what it's supposed to be, see, a place of worship.'

'Who are we supposed to be worshipping?' Fred was genuinely curious.

'That's the question. Nye Bevan reckoned it was designed for the most conservative religion of all – ancestor worship.' Quin eyed him up and down. 'Come from an ordinary background, do you, lad? Aye, I thought so. Then remember what else Bevan said – that it's not your ancestors, or mine, that got worshipped in there. It's the buggers who kept 'em down in their place. People like us are here to change things, not preserve 'em in aspic. Whatever our party. Don't forget.'

It dawned on Fred that there existed a whole etiquette of which he was totally ignorant. He wondered if he should offer this man a drink, but before he could speak Quin pointed towards the Lords.

'There's somebody'll be glad to have a word with you, I'll be bound. One of the better sort. See you around.'

Fred turned to see a slightly bowed figure beckon him over. It was Lord Boswood, the former holder of his seat until scandal had forced his resignation two years earlier.

It had been a busy election for Nigel Boswood, with many appearances on television as a respected pundit. His reputation had been partially restored by a press which had found juicier quarry in the sex lives of current Ministers; former targets were old hat. He had missed the daily cut and thrust, yet he had also been heartily thankful that for the first time in over thirty years he was not himself a candidate. It was a young man's game.

As he greeted his successor Nigel Boswood felt nervous. With a struggle he remembered Fred as a gawky youth offering bursts of enthusiasm during university holidays. When on graduation with a degree in business administration no job had materialised, Fred had returned to his parents' home and made himself useful around the Conservative office. Soon an energetic Young Conservatives branch was up and running with Fred its star. In due course a businessman supporter took pity on the youngster and found him a minor management position; but it was clear that the boy had set his heart on politics. So here he was, an MP already, the youngest in the House.

Boswood sighed. There were far too many around like that for his taste, youngsters with no experience whatever who lived and died within the political process alone. Never been anywhere or done anything. Never held a proper job, never run a company, never had to struggle, not really. Not travelled much, except with student railcards across Europe; for this was the new generation which casually saw Berlin or Budapest or Prague as extensions of home and had no idea of the price paid in blood to make those places free, let alone accessible.

'Ah, young Laidlaw! How pleasant to see you. Enjoyed it today?'

'Sir Nigel . . . I mean, Lord Boswood . . .' Fred stammered. Another complicated encounter, his third of the day.

'Nigel,' said Boswood firmly. He put a hand on Fred's elbow. 'Now, as I didn't know I would see you, I have committed the cardinal error of not having booked a table for lunch. But I can offer you hospitality in the Peers' bar, and then I will take you, if you are not otherwise engaged and will permit, to the secret place where we'll find the best cuisine in the entire Palace of Westminster.'

'Oh – right.' Fred pricked up his ears. 'That sounds like an excellent idea. Where is it?'

'Not the Peers' guest room. That's still too full of terrible old English cooking – spotted dick and wet cabbage. Most of their lordships, for all we've forty years of life peerages behind us, are still hereditary: so nursery food predominates. No, we'll go to the Lords' staff dining room. They're the real aristocrats around here; they don't stint themselves.'

Up in the press gallery James Betts tapped out the last lines of his sketch for the *Globe* and finished off a cigarette.

Vitriol laced with sugar for the State Opening, naturally. Readers would recognise the description of the Prince of Wales as morose and bitter; should his mother live as long as *her* mother, His Royal Highness would be in his seventies before he came to the throne. Freedom from family ties had certainly increased the Prince's productivity as far as public engagements were concerned: now he had over 500 a year to his credit. That's what we pay them for, grunted Betts to the computer screen.

Pity Diana hadn't attended, though. Since her announced retirement from public life, her face had been seen peeking wistfully round corners at airports and ski resorts throughout the world. Betts would lay money that she'd be in the pages of *Hello!* again before the year was out, as her sister-in-law had before her, showing off once more why her husband was daft to prefer anyone else. Then there was that gorgeous designer wardrobe, the constant renewal of which demanded the oxygen of publicity. Why on earth would any company offer their beautiful clothes or the latest jewellery, or sell them to her at sharp discounts, if no new photographs were available for the cover of *Paris-Match*?

Betts bent to his task and added a few words about the more recognisable characters of the Commons, including the 'naughty boys', Mellor, Yeo and Hughes, confined to the back benches after losing the battle against the public pillory. Mellor at least had expected to be returned to office after the election, but his former friendship with the Prime Minister was far too distant. A twinge of cramp, which still came and went, reminded Betts of another miscreant, Roger Dickson. It had been moments before the planned confrontation of the man with a question about his own misbehaviour that Betts had collapsed with the stomach infection which would make him tremble whenever he saw eggs for the rest of his life. The question could yet be asked, any time. What was missing and had never resurfaced was the hard evidence, that letter written by Dickson to his girlfriend; without it, the man could deny the story for ever – and probably would. Some lucky beggars would always get away with it.

On the other hand, there was the lady herself. Betts sucked his teeth. Touching forty, certainly, but footloose and fancy free. Her husband had done a bunk with another dame – one could hardly blame him. And that daughter, Karen. Must be around eighteen now, a real looker. Two women, both with a taste for the trousers, he was certain. Both worth watching, carefully.

George Horrocks turned away from the television, put down his sherry and gratefully accepted a canapé from his sister-in-law. The smell of roast pork wafted tantalisingly from the kitchen. This was infinitely better than dull meals in his club surrounded by old bores; Betty was an excellent hostess and a civilised and intelligent person, more like an older sister.

Horrocks pushed his hair off his brow in an unconsciously boyish gesture. It was many years since he had left the army; although the wrong side of fifty he had kept himself fit. Tall and lanky, he could be taken for a much younger man, especially since he still had most of his hair, apart from a slowly increasing bald spot, luckily hidden from the mirror, at the back of his head. He did not mind that its fairness was sprinkled generously with silver. For George was no ladies' man, and was uncomfortable when a woman who spotted his qualities would try to flirt with him. All that, he felt, had been left behind long ago when Margaret had walked out on him. It was fortunate there had been no children.

'I confess I find it very watchable, Betty.'

Betty Horrocks bustled into the kitchen to serve the roast potatoes. 'It is grand, isn't it? Of course you could get more involved, George, if you wanted, when your year of office as Deputy Lord Lieutenant's over.'

George's expression was thoughtful. 'I might just do that.'

'And should you be in the least interested I could find you a job, one job in particular.'

Horrocks finished his sherry. 'Plotting again, Betty? What have you in mind?'

Betty Horrocks stood up, a dish of steaming peas in one hand and a bottle of 1990 Beaujolais Villages in the other. Smartly dressed and verging on the stout, she had been left prosperous in her widowhood. She motioned George to the dinner table. Since her husband had died, it gave her pleasure to look after his younger brother from time to time, especially when his burgeoning interest in the political world was available to be exploited.

'I wanted to talk to you about that. Our MP, Elaine Stalker, is a lovely person, an excellent constituency Member and a good woman. At least that's my point of view and as her Conservative Association chairman I know her better than most. What she lacks is a decent social life and nobody should be without that. I was wondering, if I were to introduce the pair of you properly, whether you wouldn't see your way . . .' Her voice tailed away as her courage failed her.

George was silent, his lips pursed. He did not like anybody to organise his life, as his sister-in-law was aware. But his eyes were not hostile. It dawned on Betty Horrocks that the same thought might already have occurred to him. She swallowed and tried again.

'. . . to maybe asking her out?'

*   *   *

'Oh, Jayanti darling, it makes me want to cry.'

'It is indeed a beautiful ceremony. We are very privileged to be able to watch it,' Jayanti Bhadeshia agreed cautiously. His wife's predilection for the Queen was a family joke. He was not, however, about to argue with her.

Pramila Bhadeshia was eating brightly coloured Indian sweets. She licked her fingers like a child before reaching for a linen napkin. 'The High Commissioner was there – did you see him? What's he done to deserve that, I'd like to know. Wriggled his way to it, that's what, giving money to the President's campaign. Here am I with royal blood in my veins and I cannot be there. It isn't right!'

Her husband sighed. His wife's conviction that she was descended from a nineteenth-century maharaja was subject to some dispute by the present incumbent's family. The increased dowry her father was obliged to give for her in order to support the claim, however, had been more than acceptable. 'If it upsets you, don't watch.'

'No, it does not upset me. It's that every Asian man present is a visitor. Nobody attends by right.'

'That is simply not possible at the moment. There are no Conservative Asian members of the House of Lords – only Shreela Flather, I was forgetting her. There's that fool from the LSE – Desai, isn't it? – but he's Labour; and one from the Chinese community – Baroness Lydia Dunn from Hong Kong. Maybe it's acceptable if they're female. Better chance for you, my dear, than for me, perhaps.'

Bhadeshia was trying to tease his wife but she would have none of it. An audible sniff came also from a tiny figure in a dark blue sari huddled in an armchair in the corner – her mother. With a sinking feeling he recognised the emergence of a hobby horse and prayed silently that this one would be short-lived.

His wife was a strong-minded character, one of the features he secretly liked best about her; he recognised that much of the driving force of their household, of its financial success and standing, came from her. It made her a superb businesswoman too. Had he married a quieter, more complaisant woman, he would have still been the owner of only one or two shops instead of a whole chain. The Bhadeshia name was becoming better known commercially back in East Africa too, which felt like sweet revenge. Certainly he would never have had thirty million pounds in shares and on deposit at the bank. That much of it had disappeared in the demise of the Bank of Commerce and

Credit International rankled deeply but he was nevertheless a man of substance. Yet that conferred obligations, of which fact his wife was never slow to remind him.

But when she developed an obsession nothing would calm her until her objective had either been achieved or been shown to be completely impossible, usually after the expenditure of large sums of hard-earned money. Take their house, with its swimming pool and lawns, its live-in maid and gardener. Pramila had decided she wanted to live near the huge Lakeside shopping complex, the biggest shopping mall in the country. 'It reminds me so much of New York,' she would say wistfully. Hendon was no longer grand enough; the Brent Cross shopping centre 'too poky'. A house in Essex big enough for themselves, their four growing children and Pramila's mother and sister was a thoroughly expensive proposition.

The business was not a bottomless treasure chest. On the contrary: the international side devoured cash, though the outlook this year was more promising. He had had to dip into the money put aside for his sister's dowry to keep the mortgage within reasonable limits. Discussion of Lakshmi's wedding had been postponed for a year or two yet, until depleted funds had been replaced. Then there were his own two daughters, Priya and Sabita, still in their teens. A wedding for one cost over £100,000 these days, while dowries didn't bear thinking about. And the boys – Amit was on the way to becoming a doctor, which meant years of college fees, and Varun wanted to go into business like his father. Not for him a cold Cash and Carry at all hours: he'd expect a handsome start in life. Bhadeshia groaned inwardly.

'You are not listening to me, Jayanti,' Pramila accused him with awesome accuracy.

'I hear you, my sweet. You are right, the British system is riddled with prejudice. But what am I, a simple Hindu businessman, able to do? We should be thankful we were allowed to come here in safety as children. Had we stayed in Uganda we would have been mincemeat for Amin's dogs. It is enough to live in peace unmolested.'

'That is a long time ago. Now we are British, and we are part of Britain.' An ominous note had entered her lilting voice.

Jayanti wondered gloomily what was to come next.

'There should be recognition. The moment has arrived.'

Pramila sat up straight and twitched her red sari with the *aanchal* draping her head, as if she were about to make an announcement. She waited till her husband was gazing at her expectantly.

11

'I am now listening, my dear. What have you in mind?'

'First answer me this. Aren't you the most respected Asian businessman in London and one of the most successful? Aren't you a donor to charities of every kind? Aren't you an active supporter of the Conservative Party, which has just won another election? Wasn't Margaret Thatcher a great admirer of yours? Didn't she once say she wished more English-born businessmen were like you?'

'Ye . . . yes.'

Pramila rose and went to the wall next to the mantelpiece. Despite the warmth of the day a coal-effect gas fire burned in the grate; the women of his family felt the cold in England. She pointed to a framed photograph showing herself and her husband, one on each side of the former Prime Minister, all in sparkling evening dress and smiling broadly.

'She would have looked after you, Jayanti. I know it. Now she cannot do it, you must push yourself.'

'Doing what?'

'You should be a member of the House of Lords – yes, you. You should be Lord Bhadeshia, and take your seat like Lord Young and Lord Jakobovitz and the other Jewish lords, whose high position in British society is guaranteed. My bones demand it. You would be brilliant, my darling, I know it.'

Bhadeshia felt weak. In the corner the eyes of his mother-in-law glittered, though the diminutive body had not budged.

'And you . . .?'

Pramila bent her head modestly, then smiled. 'I would be Lady Bhadeshia. At last.'

Once the House was adjourned Elaine had no more to do and felt flat. It was without question marvellous to be part of all this. Yet how weird the ceremony was, and how incongruous. How deceitful: a ruler who is not a ruler, in an imperial crown without an empire, in evening dress in broad daylight, reads a speech which is not a speech to Lords who cannot lord it and Commons who strongly believe themselves to be very uncommon indeed. The gold glisters, but real wealth and control lay neither in the wool of the medieval Woolsack nor in the jewels on Her Majesty's head but on computer screens recording foreign exchange and stock markets in Singapore and Tokyo, Frankfurt and Sydney. Down in Canary Wharf young dealers in red braces switched their attention back to the purchase and sale of Deutschmarks, dollars and yen, marking shares up and down in a dozen languages, thus deciding who would live in style this year and who pay more taxes, casually exercising power vastly greater than any wielded with such meticulous ceremony by either the feudal monarch and her doddering peers or by Members of her Parliament.

Chapter Two

'I don't believe this.'

Elaine stood in her tiny Commons office and gaped despairingly at the sackful of mail spilled out on the floor. She squatted down and, without yet opening the envelopes, began to sort it into piles: handwritten blue envelopes on one side with constituency postmarks on top and more distant letters underneath; and large brown envelopes on the other. Anything with a typed address went to the bottom of the heap. Ordinary pleaders for help would gain her attention first, today as ever.

'How many did you say came today?'

Diane Hardy, fifty-something, plump, bespectacled and efficient, a Commons secretary for twenty years, pulled her cardigan across her ample bosom and grimaced. 'Around two hundred. Much the same yesterday. Don't just stare at it all, Elaine – it won't vanish by itself. Here's a paper knife. Or, if you prefer, I can get a bit of clerical assistance – cost you around a fiver an hour, but some student'll be glad of it.'

'Maybe I can get Karen in, once her exams are over.'

Elaine riffled through an already opened heap of paper, mostly printed matter from the previous day's intake. With Mailsort computer programmes it was all too easy to address each missive personally to her, couched in the friendliest terms; it would be impossible to second-guess what was and wasn't significant.

Diane sensed Elaine's flattened spirits and indicated one folder of scrawled letters. 'There are compensations, you know. You have some nice fan mail. Lots of old gents. Mr Sutton as usual, and Mr Papps, and old Bill Rivers who is so sweet. And a new one: look at this – "Your victory was a special event which will have been welcomed by all right-thinking people. You are a very wonderful lady. Seeing you on television with your lovely smile warms the cockles of my heart. I should love to meet you face to face" – and so on. Goes on for ten pages.'

Elaine took the letter, examined it and giggled. 'Pity he's writing from Leicester Prison, then, isn't it? What's the name – ah, signs himself Graham Dunn. Send him an acknowledgement, but put him in the funny file, just in case.'

She would not have considered for one moment accepting the invitation to meet. Once, several years earlier, she had innocently arranged to have tea in a hotel with the besotted Sutton. He turned out to have lost his wife in mysterious circumstances and was apparently seeking a replacement. The obligation of courtesy towards constituents did not extend to fulfilling their every fantasy.

'What on earth are they writing about?' Elaine mused. 'I know it was a big surprise when we won, but they can't all be fans. Or furious.'

'They aren't. But now the election's over it's business as usual. "Please will you sign an Early Day Motion in protest against the culling of rabbits or to congratulate Luton Football Club on winning the cup or demanding the end of nuclear dumps in East Timor." That sort of thing.'

'I wasn't aware that Luton had won the cup,' Elaine answered faintly. 'And I haven't much idea where East Timor is. Why on earth should everyone assume that MPs are knowledgeable about everything? We're expected to churn out instant opinions – is that really what the punters want? Why can't politicians sometimes be permitted to say, "I don't know" – or even "I don't care" or "It's none of our concern"?'

Diane sniffed. Her considered view of the British public *en masse* was unrepeatable.

No votes were anticipated for several days, until the Queen's Speech debate was out of the way, and no Question Time for either the Prime Minister or anyone else. The House was therefore unusually quiet after the excitement of the State Opening. Older, wiser Members were on the plane to Tenerife; plenty of other occasions would offer themselves in the years ahead when late-night divisions, hour upon midnight hour, would push their voting record to the point where boasts to local newspapers would be in order.

It was also international conference time. The Foreign Secretary was in Geneva at another round of talks on what to do about Bosnia. In Cairo, Dr Boutros Boutros-Ghali, United Nations Secretary-General, was spreading his hands self-deprecatingly about the failure of the latest UN mission in Central Africa. The new US President, who had won her campaign on an entirely domestic ticket, was engrossed in the Oval Room of the White House in a discussion on the rape of American forests. The *Globe*'s political editor, faced with a half-empty Commons or an all-expenses paid trip, had plumped for Switzerland. At least on the plane one might expect a better class of risqué stories from this Foreign Secretary than from the chap he had replaced.

The troublemakers, the ambitious and the hangers-on never left Westminster. Thus it was that Jim Betts, standing in for his absent boss, was to be seen lounging in Members' Lobby against the bust of Ramsay MacDonald a few minutes before six in the evening.

His attention was caught as the thickset figure of Minister of State Edward Bampton pushed through the swing doors. Judging from his direction Bampton had come from the Smoking Room, where gossip was dispensed along with the doubles. From his expression he had heard unpleasant news.

Betts riffled quickly through his mental card-index. Bampton was a Yorkshireman and overweeningly proud of it. He was always good for a misogynist dig or an appeal to traditional preferences such as warm beer and smoky pubs. Nearing fifty and about average height – which meant he was shorter than the typical Tory MP – podgy and ruddy-faced, he wore on his sleeve a cheerful resentment at being downgraded and, as he saw it, overlooked by the party hierarchy. His post at the Home Office, where he held responsibility for prisons, was a minor position; his role boiled down to carrying the can whenever the privately employed escort service lost a dangerous prisoner. It was widely believed that, if Bampton had his way, most of the more violent guests of Her Majesty would never have seen the light of day again.

Betts interposed himself neatly between the man and his intended destination. It seemed likely that Bampton was heading straight for the whips' office on the other side of the Lobby with the intention of thumping the table and saying his piece. Once inside he would be soothed and patted, fed a large Teacher's and a little flattery and talked out of whatever was eating him. The time to strike was now.

'You look fed up, Ted, if you don't mind me saying so. What's the matter – the missus found out about the girlfriend?'

Bampton scowled at the banter. 'I don't go in for that sort of stuff, as you well know, Jim. That's for fools who can't keep their trousers up. But I can't say I'm a happy man.'

Betts hazarded a guess. 'There's a reshuffle in the offing. Details out tomorrow. Is that it?'

Bampton glanced around quickly and dropped his voice. 'Too

16

bloody right,' he muttered. 'Once again the best jobs have gone to wet-behind-the-ears smart alecs with posh accents and public school backgrounds. We might as well still be in the age of pocket boroughs.'

Bampton warmed to his theme. 'Don't the party realise that people like that go down like a lead balloon in my part of the country? What we need up north are real men, businessmen, who know what the world's about. Run a business, fought for customers, chased the debts, got the money in week by week to pay the wages. Fought off the creditors and the liquidators *and* knocked the competition for six to boot. I've done all that, but who cares? I tell you, if we had a few more of my sort in this place and in Cabinet, we'd have better decision-making at the top, and we might be popular in between elections as well.' He paused for breath.

Betts shrugged sympathetically. 'Got to be on the inside, haven't you? Mind you, look at Roger Dickson. He's a self-made man – I mean, he married money, but nobody died and left him anything. Came up the hard way and doing all right.'

Betts and several other journalists were floating Dickson's name as a means of initiating comment on potential candidates for the next leadership contest. Even though the party had won, nobody expected the current holder to last long. Musings about the possible next leader were standard fare, and meat and drink to Bampton.

'He'd be preferable to the idiot we've got at the moment, campaign winner or no.' The Yorkshireman glowered. 'Do you know the PM offered to come to my constituency during the campaign? We told him not to bother, he'd only cost us votes.' He checked himself: off-loading a few jewels of his deepest political thinking, while enjoyable, was risky. 'Now Dickson has something about him, I'll grant you that. Though he has enemies too – some people didn't like how he handled Environment. But he's done well this time. The Foreign Office, so I hear. Big move; puts him in a perfect position for the next contest, provided he watches his step.'

The leading article formed itself in Betts's mind. *Ministers and backbenchers welcomed Dickson's appointment . . . spurred talk of his chances . . . fresh-faced, replacing the jaded features of . . . reshuffle failed to dampen criticism of the Prime Minister . . . one senior backbencher inferred that the PM's reputation had suffered as a result . . .* Bampton's remarks on his current leader would be stored for future use.

'And what about yourself, Ted? Surely they haven't sidelined you yet again?'

'No – not exactly.' Bampton was wary. 'I'm a Minister of State, after all. Should be grateful for the opportunity to serve, I suppose. But I was hoping for a move up this time. In fact I'd been promised, after a manner of speaking, a chance at Trade and Industry. That's more in my line.'

Equanimity restored by the brief opportunity to let off steam, Ted patted Betts resignedly on the back.

'I suppose I'll have to be satisfied for the moment. Keep my mouth shut and carry on plotting, eh?'

Elaine took a deep breath, lifted the overflowing waste-paper bin towards her, carried the mess out into the corridor, emptied the lot into the brown carriers marked 'Paper only' and returned with it to her office. For the next hour, fortified by a weak gin and tonic from a chipped mug, she twice filled the bin and emptied it again from the disorderly heaps on her desk. One note pleased her, from a Labour MP asking her if she would occasionally pair with him. That might make life easier. The monitor announced that one of the new Members, Anthony York, was making what must be his maiden speech. She would not leave until everything was cleared.

It was several hours before the dark red plastic of the last in-tray reappeared, unsullied by any further missives. In a tired gesture of victory, Elaine wrote 'Empty!' on a slip of yellow paper and stuck it to the tray with Sellotape. It would serve to encourage her next time the sheer drudgery of Commons life threatened to overwhelm her.

The phone rang. To get some peace Elaine had diverted her calls. She frowned.

'Sorry to intrude, Mrs Stalker,' the operator apologised, 'but I have your daughter on the line. Will you take the call?'

Elaine's mood lightened immediately. 'Sure, put her on.'

A click, and a familiar voice was shouting in her ear.

'Yeah!' Karen squealed. 'That's it! Mum, I've finished. Had my last oral today. No more exams. I'm free!'

'Well done – but don't be too cocky. I mean, if you don't pass you may have to retake them next year.'

'Never – I'd rather *die*. But I will get them. In fact, I wanted to ask you, Mum. If my grades are high enough I'd like to accept that offer from the London School of Economics. I know the place is physically a dump, but the teaching's good and there are theatres and art galleries

18

and London night life and I could see something of you. What do you think?'

'You won't have the money for the night life, madam.' Elaine was deliberately prim. Now there was no father at home to lay down the law she felt the weight of responsibility for her only child. A thought occurred to her: 'Are you planning to live with me – is that it? Because honestly, Karen, I haven't room. The flat has only one bedroom, as you well know . . .'

'No, no. You'd cramp my style and I yours. But keep an eye open for digs for me, would you? Your name might make the difference.'

'Will do. Meanwhile, where are you off to now?'

'Nottingham. Mark's house – his parents are in America. We're invited to a big party – the whole weekend, the entire class – to celebrate the end of exams. And the end of our time at college together, so we'll all get maudlin and drunk. Should be *great*.'

Elaine reflected briefly on the unsuspecting householders who probably did not realise quite what Karen and her friends, well-meaning youngsters though they might be, could do to a property over forty-eight hours.

'Be careful. Remember what happened . . .' She did not add, '. . . last time you got drunk.' Karen had ended up in hospital having her stomach pumped and had nearly died of alcohol poisoning. Elaine had never found out exactly what had triggered the near-tragedy; and Karen would never tell her.

The girl's voice soothed. 'Don't worry – I'm more careful than most. I know I can't take it. But there was one more thing, Mum.' The voice took on a wheedling tone.

'Yes?'

'I'm skint. Can I have some money?'

He was trembling. It was worse once he had sat down, with everyone patting his shoulders, the nods of congratulation, the kindly if patronising remarks from the Labour Member opposite who followed. Anthony York ran a hand through his fair hair and could feel a rivulet of sweat trickle down his back. He bit his tongue and fought back a feeling close to tears.

Before this, his hardest moment had been the final selection at Newbury. Not many seats could be regarded as rock solid these days, but Newbury had been one of them until it had been lost in an unhappy by-election. Nevertheless the expectation of a substantial majority in more normal times and the beauty of the area had attracted a large contingent of would-be candidates. When Anthony's grave manner, impeccable reputation and distinguished appearance had fought off a dozen ex-MPs and two former Ministers squeezed from their seats by boundary changes, nobody was more surprised than he.

A maiden speech was a dramatic event – a great milestone in a politician's life, and a signpost to the future. The disappointment he felt in his own performance, therefore, was all the more acute. If ever he were to rise to great heights, today's amateurish phrases and ill-formed philosophy would be examined intently for clues as to his judgement, character and potential.

His parents, the editor of the local paper, the regional radio station – all would be waiting to hear from him. They would be at least curious, at best excited and proud. Perhaps he could buy a video of his performance, but doubted if he could bear to watch himself and learn, as he had been advised to do. The thought of being brought face to face with his own inadequacies made him cringe.

He wished profoundly he had done it better.

Edward Bampton pushed aside the ministerial red box and set himself to brood. Of course he ought to be grateful; the reshuffle could as easily have resulted in his being booted out. But the fact was he was bored and longed for a change. The Home Office job looked important on paper, gave him considerable clout in the government hierarchy and for anyone with a smidgen of interest in the criminal justice system would have been much prized. Indeed, there had been adverse comment when he, a non-lawyer, had been appointed to it three years before. Most of the barristers and solicitors who littered the Tory benches would have given their eye teeth to have spent the last hour with the set of ministerial files currently on his desk.

Yet for Bampton the adjournment debates he had to answer, the clauses he had to take through standing committees, the pointless criticism from irate backbenchers about the latest crime figures, the useless knowledge he had acquired on appeals and rights to silence, the endless decisions on immigration cases, any one of which made a lifetime's difference to an entire family, were insufficient. Faced by senior civil servants who were acknowledged international experts on all these subjects, he frequently felt out of place. The moment to complain to the whips had passed but his gut reaction was still deep impatience.

A soft tap came at the door; it opened to reveal Derek Harrison, tall and saturnine, standing hesitantly on the threshold.

Like most Ministers above the lowest rank, Bampton was entitled to a bag-carrier, a 'gofer' and general factotum. In true Westminster tradition the more lowly the post – and this one was unpaid – the grander the title. So Harrison was his Parliamentary Private Secretary, or PPS. Technically it was the first rung on the ministerial ladder; when a PPS was caught misbehaving his resignation would be reported as that of 'a member of the government'. The PPS was part of the ministerial team and attended meetings, other than the most confidential or high-powered, alongside his master. Often, however, the task boiled down to pouring the drinks and listening hard, then flattering his boss in the post-mortem afterwards.

Another part of the job involved the assiduous planting of useful questions with even more helpful supplementaries on ambitious back-benchers who aspired to become PPSs in their turn. On occasion a PPS might find himself mouthing his master's speech before a puzzled or irritated outside audience as he attempted to explain that due to unforeseen circumstances they would have to put up with him instead. That could be a neat opportunity in the right hands; but in the main the PPS acted as eyes and ears of his boss around Westminster, and as friend and confidant.

'I'm sorry – you're busy.' Harrison gestured at the still open box, its gold letters on red leather gleaming in the lamplight. 'Shall I come back later?'

'No, I'm done.' That wasn't strictly true but Bampton had had enough. 'Fancy a pint?'

'Sure.'

The boxes were locked and stacked on the desk. It was safe to leave them there; for the office, on the upper ministerial corridor, was guarded by police night and day.

The pair headed for the Kremlin, officially called the Strangers' Bar, down at Terrace level. Outside was windswept and damp, a typical English evening, but inside the place was smoky and packed.

Derek Harrison wrinkled his nose. His own preference would have been a quick dash across the road to the St Stephen's Club. Its elegant white interior, looking out towards St James's Park, was graced by many distinguished names from the party, exactly the sort an up-and-coming chap ought to know. The previous year it had been full of disgruntled ex-MEPs who had lost their seats; they tended to drown their sorrows in Slivovitz and Calvados to show off, but their conversation, peppered with references to Leipzig and Paris, intrigued and attracted Harrison. There would be a few businessmen, something in the City or doing well in imports. Their casual attitude to fifty-pound notes fascinated him most of all.

The Kremlin was buzzing as Members and hangers-on absorbed the implications of the reshuffle. The rumour factory had been so vigorous that the Prime Minister had decided to go ahead a day or two early. A copy of the Downing Street press notice lay soggy with beer froth on the bar and was consulted by all who passed.

Harrison lost sight of Bampton for a moment and found himself in a group of both Labour and Tory Members. He was instantly on his guard.

'I'd have thought he'd have been more radical.' Keith Quin lifted his pint glass, took a long swallow and smacked his lips ruminatively. 'Settled a few scores and that. After calling them right-wingers "bastards", you'd have thought he'd have got rid of a few. Instead he's put Hamilton in the Cabinet and promoted Lady Olga Maitland. She may have the biggest majority in the Commons now, but the thought of her in your whips' office . . .!'

Quin was trying to impress two new MPs, Harrison noted, both Conservatives. Fred Laidlaw, a half-pint of lager in his hand, was looking somewhat dazed: at a guess it was close to his bedtime. Anthony York, however, nursed a bitter lemon, which took some courage in this place. York had made his maiden speech. He was now one of the crowd and permitted such a modest eccentricity. Both newcomers, hesitant about concurring with their companion but unsure how to respond otherwise, turned in relief to Harrison.

The older man responded smoothly. 'On the contrary. The Prime Minister boxes clever with those he can't count on. That's why he's still on top despite all the criticism. He works on the Lyndon Johnson principle: "Better to have the beggar on the inside pissing out than on the outside pissing in."' The crudity made his listeners snicker.

Bampton motioned to Harrison from the other side of the bar. Obediently he detached himself and moved over, exchanging pleasantries on the way with both Labour and Conservative MPs. He made mental notes of several new faces, male and female, but he was pretty sure that the attractive fair-haired girl in a short skirt that revealed smooth thighs, perched on a bar-stool talking animatedly to Michael Brown, the victor at Brigg and Scunthorpe, was not an MP. She was pretty, and as she caught his eye smiled at him. He hesitated in passing; then an impatient look on Bampton's face forced him to press on.

'You keep your eyes to yourself,' Bampton chided as soon as they were together. 'I saw you give that lass the once-over. Trouble, that's all they are.'

'Just because you're happily married, Ted, doesn't mean that the rest of us are suited to monogamy.' Harrison was not angry; his sex-life was the subject of frequent gossip to which he was utterly impervious. 'As a confirmed bachelor, I have to spread it around a bit or it'll atrophy. Use it or lose it. Know what I mean?'

Bampton grunted. Despite his early background in the building trade he did not enjoy sexual banter. He had fallen for a woman only once, nearly thirty years before, courted her with old-fashioned charm, roses and chocolates and cards, married her on his twenty-third birthday and been faithful to her ever since. Their two daughters were the spitting image of their mother, large, gentle and humorous. He hoped they might some day marry men like himself and make them happy.

'Enough of that. What did you think of the reshuffle?'

Harrison made non-committal noises.

'Come on, Derek. You must have been expecting a move. You've been my PPS three years now, ever since I got this job. You did well, promoted so quickly in your first Parliament, but you mustn't get stuck now. I put in a good word for you, too. You should have been made up. Parliamentary Under-Secretary of State for National Heritage, something like that.'

Once again the grandeur of the title served to obscure the insignificance of the task, but all political life, Bampton knew, was what you made of it. Even as junior Minister in a low-grade department with a minute budget, a skilled and determined operator could make a name for himself. The description fitted Harrison perfectly; in fact, it would do for them both.

'The Prime Minister didn't have room for us this time,' Harrison suggested silkily. The Kremlin, he realised, had its advantages. The hubbub meant that private intrigues couldn't be overheard. The two men bent their heads together.

'Yeah, well, he may find there isn't much more room for *him*,' Bampton muttered darkly. 'There's talk, Derek. He can be challenged any time. When the moment comes we need to be ready.'

'You're not thinking . . .?'

'No, no. *I'm* not going to put up against him. But some fool will, and might get a surprisingly high vote. The PM will need to be warned. It gets really exciting if – and when – he stands down. He'll have to, sooner or later. Then the question is, which camp are we in? Whose wagon do we hitch ourselves to? If we get it wrong, we're out, but then that can happen any time anyway. If you don't have the favour of the boss you're nowhere. If we back the right horse, that's different – you'll be in, Derek, and I'll be tucking my little legs under that Cabinet table as President of the Board of Trade, where I belong.'

Neither was troubled by the mixed metaphors. To both men, vivid use of pictorial language, even if the pictures failed to follow on, was competent political style. And a cliché was a recognisable term used (or over-used) only by the Opposition.

'Do you have a view of who we should back?' Harrison had his own preferences, but Bampton had been in politics far longer.

'Well, let's see. Who is there? Ken Clarke will try and he must be the favourite. He wants it, he's keen and competent, and marginally less abrasive than he used to be. Portillo is the coming man, of course. Still a bit young and inexperienced, to my mind, and he's no friend of the likes of us. We don't make enough speeches about the immorality of public benefits for his taste. Pity about Michael Howard, but they simply won't have him because he's Jewish. You'd think he'd have spotted that a long time ago. Then there's Roger Dickson.'

Derek cradled his glass of white wine. It was almost empty, but he did not want to interrupt the exchange, especially as it was his turn to buy a round. 'You sound as if you've made up your mind, Ted.'

'Well – I like Dickson, to tell you the truth. He's a fresher face than our Kenneth, and in many ways more suited to the nineties. Ken's a grand chap with a fine record, but he often talks as if it's still the nineteen-fifties. He gets under the skin of my daughters, who tell me he's too old fashioned and macho for their taste. I can't quite see it. On the other hand they thoroughly approve of Dickson and say half the nation will fall in love with him – the feminine half, I hasten to add. Since women make up the majority of the electorate that can't be bad.'

'But what does he stand for?'

'Who knows . . . does it matter any more? The admen will decide. It's just that once they start on Roger Dickson they'll have plenty of high-quality material to work on. I reckon he's our man, and I'm going to start hinting so wherever I can.'

Harrison shrugged slightly and nodded; the inconclusive, insubstantial discussion matched his own feelings entirely. 'Time for another?' He pointed at his own empty glass.

Bampton downed the dregs of his beer and shook his head. 'No, I'm off home. Keep the old lady happy. See you tomorrow.'

Harrison watched him move across the room, greeting and chatting on the way, and out through the swing doors. Then he picked up both glasses and headed for the bar, where he inserted himself neatly between Michael Brown and his young lady companion. She turned and smiled at him again. Her face was oval, the skin light and smooth, the eyes blue and neatly made-up. Definitely worth further acquaintance.

'Now, Michael. What have we here? Don't tell me you're only interested in this young lady's political education. May I introduce myself? My name is Derek Harrison . . .'

'Welcome to the United Kingdom, Mr President. We hope you will have a most successful visit.'

'Yes, indeed. We are looking for improved relationships with your country. We need aid, and we are hoping for inward investment . . .'

President Mangaluso caught the bored expression on the Duke's face and realised that he was talking to the wrong person. Negotiations about money were not these days to be done with minor royalty but would have to wait until the meeting at the Foreign Office the next day. He pulled his robes around him in embarrassment and shivered; he wondered if the diminutive baroness now introducing herself as a 'lord in waiting', apparently a representative of the government, spent all her time meeting foreign dignitaries on chilly evenings at Victoria Station. She did not seem a very important person. He began to feel mildly irritated, then checked himself. Beggars couldn't be choosers.

Graciously the Duke urged him along the platform towards the waiting Rolls. A few flash bulbs popped; a straggling group of fellow countrymen waved tiny flags. He shook hands, grateful for the friendly faces.

'You should be ashamed to come here,' a voice growled.

The President froze, heart fluttering. Beside him a secret service man's hand slid inside his jacket.

'After what your country did – throwing all those poor people out. Murder and rape. Dispossession of all our goods. Have you come to apologise?'

Now the police officers were filtering into the crowd to identify the owner of the voice. It was not African, but not quite English either. East African Asian, perhaps, though Mangaluso could see no one who might fit that description.

'That was over twenty years ago. We have offered to pay compensation. We want people to return and start up their businesses again. We need them . . .' The quaver in his voice made it rise to a squeak.

The tall Duke and the tiny baroness positioned themselves one on each side and, taking their guest's elbows, propelled him gently into the car. As it moved away the President stared back into the crowd, fear on his face.

'Sorry about that,' remarked the Duke genially. 'Democracy, you know. I should take no notice.'

'That was the policy of my predecessor,' the President replied. His pulse was still racing. 'Did him no good, I am sorry to say.'

'Oh, really?'

'He ended up floating down the river past the presidential palace. My faction came to power last year in the first truly democratic elections since the British left. And now I have to persuade people like that' – he jerked his head back at the dispersing crowd – 'to forget the past and return. We are desperate for their business skills.'

'I'm sure we all wish you may succeed,' the baroness soothed.

'I have no choice,' the President muttered. 'In our country there is no House of Lords for ex-leaders, madam. Only the river, and the morgue.'

'Is anybody looking after you, Anthony? After your success this afternoon you should be making a grand entrance.'

Anthony York raised his head from the Press Association tapes in the corridor outside the Smoking Room. He wondered if it had been so obvious that he was nervous of entering the Members' Dining Room nearby on his own. He smiled gratefully at Elaine Stalker.

'So let's go in together. I should be delighted to bask in your reflected glory. And you might give me some good ideas about my own speech next week.'

Her gentle compliments settled his nerves. The two pushed through the doors and walked inside. The room was nearly full, and noisy. Elaine paused by two empty places at a long table near the window. 'May we join you?'

Two of the men made half-hearted attempts to rise to their feet but nobody else acknowledged that a woman was present. Elaine preferred it that way, but reflected with amusement that one of the Tory Members so studiously ignoring her had recently garnered modest headlines with a speech supporting a return to old-fashioned good manners – on the part of other people towards himself, no doubt.

'It will be a relief not to have quite so many late nights and heart-stopping votes, now we have a bigger majority,' Edward Bampton was saying. 'I'll have the roast beef, and make sure it's well done, please.'

'I'll have the same,' another voice chimed in. Fred Laidlaw was not about to risk arguing the merits of rare versus well-done meat with a Minister whose reputation for pugnacity ran before him. Not that he cared much either way.

The service was speedy though slapdash, the food surprisingly good, if modest in quantity. Bampton sent his plate back for an extra slice. Soon the talk turned to Anthony's achievement as anecdotes flew thick and fast about famous maiden speeches – John Major's in 1979, over-long and very boring, and Margaret Thatcher's as she moved a Private Member's Bill which, with typical persistence and luck, she piloted into law.

'Found somewhere to live yet?' Elaine was only a few years older than Anthony but felt almost motherly towards him.

'I'm staying with a relative at present but I'm looking for a house to buy, probably in Battersea.' That he could lay hands on the £200,000 required put Anthony into a different category even from many Tory MPs. 'My cousin Lachlan is coming over from America to study medicine at St Thomas's, but I could offer rooms to other colleagues. I intend it to be both comfortable and convenient for the House.'

'I'd be interested.' Fred was instantly eager. His initial searches for an affordable flat around Westminster had proved depressing. 'If the rent's reasonable, that is.'

'You'd be welcome. And maybe we could invite a nurse or two to join us; it would be nice to have some girls around. Not', he added hastily, seeing Elaine's expression, 'that I'd expect them to do housework or anything. I do believe in female equality. But I'd prefer a mixed house.'

'You'll get yourselves talked about, with women on the premises,' Bampton commented.

'I don't think so.' Anthony's manner was stiff. 'It would be a highly respectable establishment. I'd see to that.'

'When did you say this property would be ready?' Elaine asked thoughtfully. 'It might be perfect. You see I know somebody else who might be keen to join you . . .'

Away from its public areas the Palace of Westminster is a rabbit warren, a maze of narrow hallways, pockmarked stonework, unnumbered doors, dark staircases leading nowhere. Dead ends abound among the eleven hundred rooms and two miles of corridors. A sudden turn will reveal a broken photocopier littered with torn inky paper or a sackful of old memos or a bin stacked with tinned food for a blind man's dog. Among the twenty-four bars and restaurants is nowhere for the public to obtain a cup of tea; the river terraces will accommodate thousands on a summer evening yet the Chamber is not big enough to seat all the elected Members. From the roof garden to the underground rifle range, from the lofty room behind the clock face to the mouldering archives in Victoria Tower, its secret corners are known in their entirety to no one. All that its inmates can aspire to is a working knowledge of one small part, with fear and hazy ignorance about the remainder.

Through her affair with Roger Dickson, Elaine had become familiar with the ministerial area at the back of the Speaker's Chair. One set of stairs squeezed around a recently modernised lift and headed down into Speaker's Court, where Ministers' cars were parked by the Speaker's ornate doorway and where sick Members, brought in to vote to save Ministers' skins, could wait in their ambulances to be 'nodded through' by the whips.

Another route would have led Elaine upstairs and to Roger's ministerial room, where their last unhappy encounter had taken place. She would not be going there again. If it was true that Roger was moving to the Foreign Office then the choice would not be open to her, for he would decamp to that most magnificent of Whitehall buildings, where grand staircases and marble floors proclaimed the glories of empires only grudgingly given up and not yet forgotten. He deserved his success, but still the thought of the seal such a move would put to the end of their relationship – that the room above would be reallocated promptly to its next occupant, who would shift around the furniture and change the pictures – was deeply painful.

A third exit took her along a gloomy corridor past the offices of both the Home Secretary and the Leader of the House. At the latter the door was ajar. The sound of laughter floated out from a curtained inner room as glasses clinked. Being in charge of the management of the government's programme in the Commons without taking direct responsibility for any of its contents could be a grind or one of the most delightful jobs in the Cabinet, depending on the instincts of the holder, usually a senior figure on his way out.

Elaine doubted that such a description would ever attach to her. A government post, let alone the distant reaches of the Cabinet, seemed gone for good. When she had arrived at Westminster four years earlier her personal baggage had included much the same ambitions as most other young MPs'. There was no reason why not. As a university graduate and local councillor she had better intellectual equipment than most and more political experience than many. As a pretty young woman she obtained rather more than her share of media attention which rapidly made her familiar in the country, and thus, at least in theory, an asset to her party. Yet somehow nothing had worked out.

Maybe it had had something to do with her relationship, though she was reluctant to admit it. Not that she and Roger had been discovered: on the contrary, their discretion had been absolute and neither was likely to make an indiscreet remark in future out of what had been, she was sure, a true love affair. She was well aware that her original attraction to Roger had been a mixture of sex and politics. He had not been her equal but her whip. That meant he was in a position to advise and guide her, and in directly practical ways to *help*, by recommending her for promotion. Yet the call had never come. Perhaps the fear of discovery had held him back when he could have assisted her most, right at the start. He had been tremendously encouraging; but the near certainty remained that every time Roger Dickson's opinion had been sought he had suggested somebody else.

She walked on, briefcase in hand. There was nothing much in it except a Joanna Trollope novel to read before going to sleep. Despite living alone Elaine did not mean to drown her sorrows entirely in work. Too many Members forgot that the day would inevitably come when they would walk down these corridors for the last time; the outside world demanded a more balanced approach to life. She wondered how she might feel on that day herself . . .

'Hello, Elaine.'

As she came round a windowless corner a sensor switched on the ceiling light. She stopped dead.

'Roger! You startled me.'

He was taller than in her dreams, broader, more physical. The dark suit and plain shirt were as before but the flowered silk tie in blue and

29

gold hues was new, bought to hint at a modernity he probably didn't feel. He was carrying a red box in one hand, a folded newspaper in the other. She registered the short intake of breath, saw the flush mount on his cheeks, the effort he made to set his face into a pleasant but controlled expression. She could smell him – the Imperial Leather soap he used, but no aftershave, no perfume of any kind.

'Sorry. How are you, Elaine? You did splendidly to retain your seat. The polls were so against you.'

She took a small step backwards, to move away from his influence and retain some modicum of self-control. This was a struggle he must not see. If she wept for this man she must weep alone.

'And you are doing well, Roger. I am proud of you. Off to the Foreign Office – and where next, I wonder?'

'Oh, don't you start as well, Elaine. I've had my fill of stupid questions from journalists. It would be nice to retain a sense of my own ordinariness for a while longer. The standard reply, as you well know, is that there's no vacancy at Number Ten: period.'

Both laughed ruefully. It had been the anxiety about exposure in the over-heated British press which had forced Elaine to end their affair; but she recognised also that the private Roger was now buried so deep that she might as well have made love to a video-recording as seek to retain contact with the real person. It would be an age before he could abandon his official cover and return to normal life – and by then he might have forgotten all about her.

Suddenly Roger glanced up and down the corridor. Satisfied, he reached out, held her arm and spoke urgently.

'We meant something to each other once, Elaine, and not so long ago. You are a fine woman. I probably should have told you years ago that you mattered a great deal to me. I'm sorry, I'm not very good at this, but do think there is any chance . . . ?'

Elaine detached herself firmly from his grasp. She prayed her voice would not betray her.

'No, I don't think so, Roger. It's simply too dangerous. You know that. And now if you don't mind . . .'

His expression darkened. She turned away, unable to hold his gaze. It would have been so easy to touch his cheek, to invite him quickly back to her flat for coffee, to agree with him that such as themselves led charmed lives and that all they had to do was be ultra-careful.

'Then let me try another tack. I shall need a new PPS, as mine has been promoted, and am in a position to ask for whomever I want. If I ask for you, Elaine, would you say yes?'

A plum job. Bag-carrier to the Foreign Secretary; to move in the best Whitehall environment and with the most able civil servants and diplomats. To see the secret telegrams and faxes. To know what was really going on, not only in Britain but in Europe, the USA, the Far East, anywhere. She would learn a tremendous amount about government inside and out. Foreign travel galore, too. With Roger: an official, permitted intimacy which could lead to . . .

'No, Roger. Please don't. If I'm to make my way up the greasy pole I have to do it without special help. People would gossip, don't you see? It might show, somehow – the way I looked at you sometimes, or a comment you let slip. You're going to be Prime Minister some day, as I always predicted. That will be good for our country as well as wonderful for you. I'm not going to spoil it. Thank you, but please – find somebody else.'

Brusquely, face averted, she pushed past him, headed down the stairs and out into the night. Behind her the last bell rang to announce the end of business. A policeman shouted the traditional goodnight: 'Who goes home?'

Once alone Elaine walked rapidly, eyes unseeing, towards her empty flat.

Chapter Three

Elaine tucked her suitcase more tightly under her seat, murmured excuses for the umpteenth time at the last person who had tripped over it and eyed her empty polystyrene cup with regret. The packed train pulled out of Victoria Station on its way to Brighton. It was October: Party Conference time.

'I suppose we should be pleased it's only seven minutes late,' she remarked to Diane. 'Probably some colleague who insisted the train be held up for him.' As she spoke the jovial mass of the Party Chairman lurched against her arm and almost buried her in an expansive grey-flannelled bottom.

Their travelling companion heaved himself away. Elaine caught her secretary's eye. Both giggled. 'You were probably right,' Diane agreed good-humouredly. 'But I shouldn't say it so loudly next time. Spoil your chances of promotion.'

'What chances?' Elaine did not allow any bitterness to show. After more than four years in Parliament she understood only too well the machinations required to make progress: the compliments to be offered to Ministers at Question Time, the supportive presence throughout a tedious debate, the long hours in the Members' Dining Room and the Smoking Room as bores old and new exaggerated their latest triumphs – she had tried all that. From time to time the dearth of females and the sparkle they could bring to the front benches was remarked upon and her hopes would rekindle. Yet the macho style of the Commons, its male language and nuances – the whole dusty code of the place – militated against women.

It was, she murmured, enough that she had won again. It was a privilege even to be an MP.

'I do enjoy it; and I'm genuinely glad to have the job. D'you remember what John Smith said a day or two before he died – what everyone wanted as his epitaph? "Give us the chance to serve." Well, I feel like that.'

Diane raised an eyebrow. She was present in her own right as an officer

32

of Battersea Conservatives. To save money the two had decided to rent a holiday flat together on the seafront. It would not do to bicker. On the other hand, her employer needed to be in feisty mood to make a success of the Party Conference. Diane leaned over and patted Elaine's hand.

'Fine: I understand entirely. But in that case why be so darned defensive about it? You wouldn't be a normal politician if you didn't want to be a Minister. And you shouldn't be left to stew. May I suggest you go out and show everyone this week exactly what they're missing if you are?'

Elaine's mood lifted. 'I'll put in a speaker's slip. Law and order debate maybe. Call for the death penalty for all crime, including insulting Prime Ministers. Especially previous PMs like Lady Thatcher. That'd go down well, wouldn't it?'

Three large Jaguar cars moved smoothly down the motorway towards the coast. In each sat a man for whom the Conference would have dramatic long-term results. Two were to love the same woman. Two had expectations, while the third, though beyond ambition, was the shrewdest and most worthy of all.

Roger Dickson settled himself into the back seat of his black bullet-proof XJ6. The low-slung vehicle weighed a ton; its solidity brought a sense of complete isolation from the outside world.

Half-heartedly he flicked over his papers. The briefings on the forthcoming European summit in Vienna were of great significance, yet for the moment their value lay more in the legitimacy they conferred on his use of both car and chauffeur. He could have taken the special train, but to read Cabinet documents in an open carriage was not allowed. If, however, urgent matters required his attention – and it was his own decision whether they could wait or not – then use of the government limousine was, naturally, essential.

Roger frowned slightly. There had been a time when such cynical considerations would never have occurred to him. As a junior banker on his way from cashier's desk to the boardroom, via marriage with the boss's daughter, he had eschewed contact with anything demeaning. As a government whip he had known many MPs channel money from the Fees Office into their own pockets – employing a wife as staff at £10,000 a year, for example, when the lady couldn't feed paper into a typewriter, or booking on a foreign trip a research assistant whose talents were solely in the bedroom. Such behaviour he deplored. Sometimes it had been his role to warn the more blatant perpetrators, but only on the practical grounds that they were in danger of being caught. Perhaps the demands of high office had blunted his sensitivities – necessarily, for a totally upright life within the rules would have been very uncomfortable. It wasn't as if ministerial jobs were well paid; had he stayed with Tarrants Bank, his income would have been at least twice that of a Cabinet Minister, possibly more. But was using the Jaguar – which privately he could hardly have afforded – so different? It amounted to misuse of public funds – well, almost. In other countries nobody would have turned a hair; only in Britain did it matter. He bade his conscience be still, and with an effort continued to read.

For him it would be a tremendously important Conference: his performance would be assessed for every nuance. If there were to be a leadership contest, would he throw in his hat? If he did, would he stand a chance against the more ideologically pure candidates? Would he go down well with the blue-rinsed brigade, those supporters whose long-suffering loyalty to the party guaranteed them a say of sorts in who should lead it? The question of who could inspire the average voter was seldom mentioned. Who might best lead the country was not a criterion which counted at all.

It would not be a long journey. Charming commuter villages slid past the smoked-glass windows, their window-boxes showy with pink and mauve autumn asters and trailing ivy, their smellier agricultural links long since sanitised away. Neighbourhood Watch boards vied with parish council notices and tidy litter bins. Roger saw a well-dressed woman out with her dog nudge the squatting animal into the gutter, and smiled. The Conference hotel would swallow him and his doubts soon enough. He abandoned the folder and lay back with his eyes closed.

The largest of the three cars was a flashy silver XJ12, its interior uphol-stered in cream leather. The travellers were a thickset olive-skinned man at the wheel, and his wife. The woman was handsome, dressed in a bril-liant yellow sari, her hair coiffed and oiled, face immaculately made-up. Chattering happily, she riffled through a pile of invitations on her lap.

'We have been invited to the "One Nation" party on Thursday night, to a South African Embassy reception, and to the Greater London Area reception tomorrow,' she enthused. 'Oh, Jayanti darling, do you think we will get to meet the Prime Minister? What would I say to him? I am so thrilled! Our first Party Conference! Now tell me – shall I wear my red sari tonight?'

Jayanti Bhadeshia knew that while his wife required an attentive audience she was not in the habit of listening to the responses. To satisfy her he grunted encouragement from time to time. Meanwhile he drove quietly, revelling in the six litres of power beneath his right foot. That he and his beautiful wife would make quite a stir in Brighton he had no doubt. The TV cameras would catch her swirl of silk, his flashing smile, as two obviously well-off Asians circulated among the white faces.

A plan was forming in his mind. If he genuinely wanted to become a notable figure in British life as opposed to a businessman known well only in his own community, then more time would have to be spent at events like this, where the couple's very uniqueness would attract attention. That would suit Pramila perfectly. It might never occur to her that they were being patronised, though with his greater experience Jayanti had no doubt that he would encounter prejudice and would feel it keenly when it came.

At last Pramila's prattle penetrated his consciousness. 'No, no,' he corrected her testily. 'I am not available on Thursday morning. You know that; I have accepted an invitation from Prima Cable Corporation for a business breakfast. At the Metropole Hotel. It is an important meeting and wives are not permitted. That morning if you are shy without me you should have breakfast in the room.'

'Could I go shopping, perhaps?' Pramila turned silkily towards her husband, so that, although he kept his eyes on the road, he was aware of her coquettish expression.

He suppressed a sigh. As she began to pout he knew he was beaten. If his wife exacted her price for being left to fend for herself it could be a costly breakfast.

In the third Jaguar George Horrocks listened with increasing dismay to the faint rattle behind the polished wood dashboard and cursed the time before Ford took over the ailing luxury car-maker. That would mean a full service and oil change after the Conference with a big bill to follow.

Maybe he could charge it to the company. After all, he had only agreed to attend in order to host the Prima breakfast, as its senior non-executive director. Party conferences were not his style usually but the chairman was in Hong Kong. The guest list was distinguished and would allow plenty of opportunity for lobbying – a couple of Ministers including, discreetly, the Industry Minister and the PPS to the Home Office, and the junior man at the Department of National Heritage. In London ever-vigilant civil servants guarded their charges like Victorian chaperons with precious virgins. The more sway a chap had, the harder it was usually to meet him. Other countries understood far better than the British the obligation to co-operate with businessmen. This was not corruption, as the Minister's staff would fear; this was legitimate lobbying, and George had no qualms about it.

The guest list contained several other intriguing or useful people – potential and actual investors, especially. He was not yet acquainted with Jayanti Bhadeshia but the name was increasingly quoted in the financial and gossip columns. Guessing that he might be a Conservative supporter, George had taken a chance in inviting him and had been gratified at the prompt response. He would make a point of seating Mr Bhadeshia next to a PPS or a Minister; then he'd watch, with detached amusement, to see which gentleman impressed the other more.

A couple of ladies had accepted. Dr Mary Archer – in fact, she was Lady Archer since her husband was a peer, but with justifiable pride in her own remarkable career the lady had a right to the label she preferred. She would grace any table. And another lady, Elspeth Howe, wife of the former Foreign Minister. If her husband had been soporific, the 'dead sheep' of legend, she was the opposite: headmistressy, kind and vigorous. He paused, then allowed his thoughts to rest on the last woman on the guest list, whose biography he knew, now, almost by heart.

In truth Elaine Stalker had nothing to do with Prima or tele-communications or the challenge of cabling every street in the nation to bring thirty-channel television into every home. She might have little to contribute to the discussion and was an unlikely investor. Yet when various MPs' names had been mooted it was the work of a moment to comment that there ought to be at least one woman MP at their table, and that Elaine Stalker was probably the most worthwhile. She had a reputation for asking intelligent questions. Male Ministers and their acolytes would be kept on their toes.

Most of all, George thought with anticipation, he simply wanted to see her.

'Much better here than at Blackpool, isn't it, Mrs Stalker?'

Elaine felt a sinking sensation at the ingratiating whine. The man was small and seedy-looking, his Fair Isle sweater dotted with shiny badges and congealed food. The shirt collar peeping over the top was mangled and the cuffs grubby.

Most people at Conference, particularly in years when party support nationally was a bit thin, were hard-bitten but genuine. Some, however, were groupies whose persistent attentions could be achingly depressing. Elaine lowered her coffee-cup into its saucer.

'Well, these facilities are much newer. And the atmosphere is better, you know, when we've just won an election.'

'Oh, yes,' the small man responded eagerly. His accent was nasal, Midlands. 'I should introduce myself. I'm Roy Twistleton. From Newcastle. Under Lyme, that is. I was on the council there . . . well, until a year or two ago.' His face fell, then brightened. 'But I'm going to stand again, although it won't be easy – we lost nearly every seat.'

He hesitated, before it came out in a breathless rush.

'And I've applied to go on the candidates' list. What I want to do, Mrs Stalker, is be an MP. Like you.'

Elaine suspected that ex-Councillor Twistleton read those books on self-improvement which recommend perpetual optimism. It might be a greater kindness to put him off.

'It's a hard life, Roy. Both before and after elections. Nursing a constituency can be tough, not to mention expensive – loads of travel and time off work. Have you talked it through with your family? And your employer?' She gestured vaguely at the appalling sweater. 'And then, you know, appearance matters. Have to dress smartly and that.'

Roy Twistleton looked crestfallen. His hand defensively twiddled a badge. 'I don't have an employer. I'm unemployed, to tell you the truth, since the factory closed, but I call myself a consultant. D'you think I'd have any chance?'

Elaine's heart softened. 'I'm sure you have, though in the end that's for other people to decide, Roy,' she offered gently. 'The voters, I mean. But you've been successful with them once and there's no reason why you can't do it again. It may take ages, but I hope we'll see you at Westminster in due course.'

As he grinned happily she moved away, to be halted at the door by the restraining hand of Betty Horrocks.

'I was about to rescue you. Who was that – anyone you know?'

'No, not at all. He wants to be an MP. I should have told him to try window-cleaning instead: it's easier and less precarious – and probably better paid.'

Betty chuckled. 'You've never served on a selection committee, have you, Elaine? You'd be amazed how many deadbeats turn up. If they can't make a success of life outside politics they think they're ideally suited to running the country. But from his delighted expression you were clearly nice to him and I'm glad. He might be successful somewhere, you never can tell.'

At this Betty took Elaine's arm and firmly propelled her in the direction of the main hall.

'If you plan to speak in the law and order debate, Elaine, you'd better get a move on; it's about to start. We'll be out there rooting for you. Go sock it to 'em.'

Inside the hall, at a nondescript table half hidden at the right-hand side of the podium, a shrewd-eyed woman was sorting speakers' slips. Rachel Dutch was organiser for the area covering Elaine's seat. She glanced up as Elaine approached.

'Hi! If you've come to ask whether you'll be called the answer is yes. About fourth, so be ready.'

'Are the others all hang 'em and flog 'em types?'

'Most of them, naturally. Conference debates aren't supposed to be taken seriously, Elaine, you know that. But the Home Secretary would be grateful for some intelligent support.'

There was no time to be nervous. In a moment her name was called and to polite applause she made her way to the rostrum. Like all other contributors she would be allocated only the same four minutes: enough for only a couple of punchy points.

A dozen cameras swivelled. As she began to speak their huge lenses peered into her face, framed by her blonde hair. To counter the all-enveloping mid-blue of the background she had chosen a navy suit with cream piping around the neckline – echoes of Margaret Thatcher in her heyday, perhaps, but that evocative image would do her no harm. The effect was cool, professional and elegant.

'Madam Chairman, ladies and gentlemen. I have listened with care and approval to the speeches so far, but have chosen to speak against the motion.'

Conference statements were so congratulatory about the government's successes both real and imaginary that less experienced delegates rushed to express their agreement. An 'against' slip simply increased her chances of being called. Once in place she could say what she liked. The tinny feedback of the loudspeakers startled her and she took a half-step back to bring the sound output more under her control.

'We have heard demands for more police officers, with which I agree strongly.' Applause rippled around the hall.

'As for arming the police, let me say this: it has long been our tradition that our police should be armed only when absolutely necessary. This is a unique tradition and the envy of the world. I don't think we should casually ignore that tradition and I hope Conference will agree.'

The repetition of 'tradition' enabled her to take a more liberal line and still receive applause. The Home Secretary was nodding thoughtfully. The notion of yet more weaponry on the streets made both anxious. A gun in the hands of even the most sober officer could turn him in a wild moment into a gangster. Innocent passers-by had been caught in crossfire. Such a step would not be easy to defend if matters got out of hand, but would be impossible to change back once the general move was made.

'But perhaps I can say this, as a mother as well as an MP. We go wrong too when we expect other people to sort out crime, or if we blame others for its causes. People today have blamed the teaching profession, or the church, or television, for the lack of moral strength in our nation. We should be looking closer to home. Indeed, to the home itself.'

Elaine raised her head and stabbed the air with a forefinger. Camera light bulbs flashed. The platform party leaned forward, eyes on the rising star.

'If our children do not know the distinction between right and wrong, that confusion starts – at home. If youngsters have a casual attitude to other people's property, that's an approach they may well have picked up – in their own living rooms. If skiving off school is normal practice, maybe they're copying a parent who slopes off from work. If bullying in the playground, pushing weaker kids around, has become the norm, maybe some parents haven't bothered to correct the first signs or, even when a teacher has tried to, have gone round to the school and *thumped the teacher.*'

Delegates were murmuring agreement but she stilled the applause. The 'one minute' warning light began to flash.

'So I have a different recipe. If, in fact, we want to improve our society, we have to start right at the basics, in the home, the family. We – you and me – have to set the highest standards, not only for our children but for ourselves. Surely we Tories understand that. We have to set an example. It's not enough to demand more police or more guns, or more prisons or probation or punishment – these are only useful *after* the event.

39

'Today's crime comes from yesterday's mistakes. If we want to do better tomorrow, we must start – right now. I beg to oppose the motion.'

The red light came on. Time was up, but she had finished bang on time. A roar of approval came from the body of the hall. Her hands shook as she gathered up her papers and returned to her seat.

Once there she sat watching the next speaker as flash-bulbs popped in her face. The pictures would look well the following day, showing her dignified and serious, exactly right for such a topic. Headlines would welcome her assertion of family values and link her urgings with the revived campaign for 'back to basics' for which the right wing yearned, but which had foundered on the blatant failure to espouse such values by too many members of the government.

An unfamiliar masculine voice sounded in her ear. It had a pleasant musical tone but was very deep.

'Well done, Mrs Stalker. You talked a lot of good sense about the police but they swallowed it. Quite an achievement.'

Elaine found herself looking into brown eyes a startling few inches from her own, set in a slightly craggy but handsome face. 'Thank you. It's a nerve-racking business, though.'

For a moment she imagined that the man might put his own hand protectively on hers, which still clutched the crumpled papers of her speech.

'We've met before. I'm George Horrocks. I believe you know my sister-in-law Betty Horrocks. I read out the results at your election count . . . do you remember?'

Here was an acquaintance she would happily renew. How great was the contrast between this slimly built man, his tie carefully chosen and knotted, a fresh white handkerchief peeping from his breast pocket, and sad, grubby Roy Twistleton. The next speaker was ranting vigorously about bringing back the birch. Behind a fierce woman hissed for silence. Elaine made ready to slip out.

'No, don't do that. Aren't you supposed to stay and listen to compliments from the Home Secretary? Anyway, we'll meet tomorrow. You're coming to the Prima breakfast. I'm your host.'

The breakfast had not surfaced in her thinking: the speech had been all. Suddenly it took on an interesting new aspect. It was a long time since a man had been that close, but the brief enforced intimacy seemed quite natural.

'I'll look forward to it, Mr Horrocks.'
'My name's George,' he whispered. Then he was gone.

'Oh, God, time to get up.'

Derek Harrison mouthed curses at the alarm clock and rolled over. A twinge of memory made him check whether there was another body in the bed and if so whose; but the young lady was already awake and a long, tanned arm was pushing yellow hair out of sleepy blue eyes. A firm freckled breast, its nipple rosy, peeped invitingly above the sheet.

Harrison composed his manner and kissed the warm young flesh. His tone became wheedling.

'I'm so sorry, darling, I didn't mean to wake you. Did you sleep well?'

'Uh-huh, sure. Well, I was knackered, Derek. You really know how to go for it, don't you? How many times was it – four? I lost count . . .'

She reached over and tried to caress his face, but Harrison knew that if he did not remove himself at once he would be late. He cast around in his mind for the girl's name but could only recall the Tory Reform Group party, ever a useful fount of nubile young women with independent ideas.

'You're super in the sack yourself, you know.'

He headed for the bathroom and switched on the shower. Its almost cold water made him gasp and dance. As he emerged, rubbing his hair dry with the thick hotel towel, the girl stretched languidly, pushed back the duvet and smiled slyly at him. She must have been about twenty, her skin peachy, her figure rounded, breasts and abdomen perfectly curved and firm. Her hand slipped down to the fuzz between her parted thighs. Their clothes lay in a tangled heap on the floor; to retrieve his own he would have to kneel near the toes wriggling over the side of the bed . . .

Some day, when she had landed a Conservative MP and adopted Jaeger suits and pearls, she would be tubby and formidable; but not yet. He stopped towelling and looked down at himself.

'Oh, damn,' he said. 'Oh, well.'

It was going to be a long day. The young waitress's feet hurt already. On duty at seven on a dismal morning for a measly £2.50 an hour – what a life. She pushed a lock of damp hair out of her eyes before ladling scrambled egg on to the heated plates alongside glistening slices of black pudding, bacon, extra-large sausages, tomato, mushrooms and fried bread.

'Sauté potatoes, madam?' she enquired.

Elaine had accepted only a sausage, egg and a slice of bacon. She noted the tired face and wondered how Karen was getting on. 'No, thanks. Enough cholesterol already.'

Beside her the tall spare man was even more disciplined and accepted only egg and tomato. George Horrocks shrugged self-deprecatingly at the waitress's disapproval. A few more like these two and the chef'd be out of a job. He turned to the lady. 'Where would you like to sit, Mrs Stalker?'

'Elaine, please. Where do you suggest?'

'Why don't you take the seat facing the door? I'll join you as soon as I've shepherded the rest.'

She watched with amusement as George Horrocks deftly placed his guests exactly where he wanted them. The Asian gentleman was introduced to the PPS to the Home Office on one side, while opposite Lady Howe could be heard engaging the Heritage Minister in her long campaign to appoint more women to public bodies. Not that it had worked with any of his predecessors either.

The Industry Minister counted himself lucky to be seated next to Dr Archer; soon the two were deep in conversation about solar energy. He judged it best to keep off the ravages of Lloyd's which had ruined two parliamentary colleagues. Fortunately they had had sufficient wisdom to stand down before the bankruptcy petitions were enforced. Bit like her husband in 1974, he recalled, and wondered if any of the current losers could write.

The waitress moved unobtrusively around the table offering seconds. At the Indian gentleman's place she hesitated. You could never tell from a person's appearance: he might be a Catholic like Hari Singh at college.

'Sausage, sir?'

Bhadeshia's first instinct was to demur but he had reckoned without Harrison's sadistic streak.

'Oh, go on,' Harrison urged him. 'They're very good – speciality of the hotel.'

The smell of the bacon made Bhadeshia feel nauseous but maybe a sausage would not be so bad. They were supposed to be mainly bread filler, anyway. He accepted and toyed with the obscenely shaped meat, then pretended it was a kebab, drowned it in ketchup and chewed quickly. It would not do to exhibit weakness in such a place.

'In my home I keep two cooks,' he informed Harrison as he wiped his mouth at last. 'One for western cooking and one for Indian. My wife's mother is still very strict.'

Harrison had not missed the Rolex watch, the heavy Cartier cufflinks, the tie-pin set with a single diamond. 'Must be tough, having all those servants,' he concurred. 'What did you say your name was? Jayanti? I'll call you Jay, if you don't mind. It's easier.'

Bhadeshia nodded but he had not quite finished boasting. 'We have five staff who live in. Two do the gardens – three acres. They are relatives from the poorer side of the family. It can be a problem getting work permits, you know.'

Harrison was not about to discuss the intricacies of British immigration law. It might be departmental business but the whole point of Conference was to make other contacts, outside the suffocating sphere of government.

'You a director of Prima, Jay?' Harrison enquired.

'No, not at the moment. But I am willing to make investments, particularly in forward-looking businesses like this. It is a good company. What about you, Minister? It is wonderful that despite your busy duties you can find an hour to attend such an occasion.'

Harrison accepted without demur the undeserved praise and promotion. 'We have to keep in touch. A private event like this can be very useful, though it is a pity that time is so limited.'

Bhadeshia pulled out a card. 'I would be honoured if you would come and have lunch with me in London. I am interested in receiving some advice of a . . . slightly personal nature. Nothing unpleasant, I assure you! But I want my businesses to expand, and I want recognition for my efforts.'

Harrison inserted the card into his wallet. 'I'll get my secretary to fix a date. I shall look forward to it.'

Elaine wondered when the more formal part of the proceedings might begin. Nobody fed anybody at Conference, ever, without at a suitable point gently tapping a glass with a fork, clearing the throat and politely requesting attention. American TV was more blatant – 'A few words from our sponsor!' – but the principle was identical.

'Your guests are making the most of this excellent spread, George. Thank you for inviting us.'

43

George Horrocks glanced at the clock. He still had a few minutes to spare.

'I hope you won't find the discussion too boring,' he began mildly.

'Why should I find it boring? Heavens, I hope you're not the sort of chap that assumes we ladies can't talk shop.' Her eyes mocked him, but with a steely edge. His heart sank.

'No – I'm sorry. Oh, darn it, Elaine, forgive me. I've spent so much time with businessmen – and I mean men: there are no ladies on our board – that I tend to slip back into small talk when there's a woman around.'

She relented. 'Look at it this way. If I were to say to you, "I hope you don't find all this politics boring", you'd feel patronised, wouldn't you? You'd ask yourself what kind of idiot said that, knowing that you'd come in the first place because you were curious about the subject. Same with me.'

He chose to misunderstand, slightly. 'But I find politics fascinating,' he answered. 'The way you handled your speech in that awful debate, for example . . . admirable. Now I'm no longer a Deputy Lord Lieutenant I can get involved, a little. But I haven't the foggiest idea where to begin.'

Not another who wants to be an MP, Elaine thought grimly. He had left it a bit late to start. Whatever maturity the job required had to be found in men under forty, for that was the preference of female-dominated selection committees. She indicated MPs around the table who talked with animation while eating steadily as was their wont. 'You're not thinking . . .?'

An opportunity to follow up this brief encounter suggested itself at once. 'I don't know what I'm thinking, Elaine, but a spot of advice wouldn't go amiss. How about meeting one evening – back in London? Or am I not allowed to ask an MP for a date?'

George was as startled at his own brazenness as she was. He bit his lip as she coloured, but did not retract. There was a sadness about her, a sudden slump of the shoulders, but it lasted barely an instant before she perked up and smiled at him.

'Oh, why not? We can talk about your ambitions, George, and you can explain to me whether in the wonderful world of satellites and cables the licence fee still has a future. And whether it's possible for women to be taken seriously, ever, in this dotty country of ours. You're on.'

*   *   *

Roger Dickson waited quietly, his wife at his side, behind the platform until it would be time to lead the Foreign Office team into the spotlights' glare. The podium seemed to have grown again. Its curved blue expanses spread out into the auditorium a few feet more each year, so that there were ever fewer rows of adulatory audience and ever more managed space to fill the television screens. In truth the event was no longer for staunch supporters from Tunbridge Wells or Trafford. Its main purpose, to which those retired majors were mere adjuncts, was a criticism-free opportunity for Ministers to shine; any pretence that it might be otherwise had long been abandoned.

At the signal enthusiastic applause broke out. Resolutely he climbed the steps and made a great show of introducing his team and their spouses.

Foreign affairs were different. By its nature fewer of the delegates had any knowledge of the subject matter, but to a man and woman they started from the viewpoint that, whatever was happening in the unknown terrain of 'abroad', British was best. To almost every remark Roger had added a patriotic rider; and, as expected, that produced unfailingly loud cheers.

The image was all. Behind him huge multi-screen monitors enlarged his face to twenty feet across. He held himself upright, head uplifted, the silvery streaks in his dark hair shining in the light like a halo. As he spoke he glanced half down at the tilted glass stands which reflected the text off a horizontal monitor and enabled him to speak without apparently reading from notes at all. 'Sincerity screens', they were called, introduced by Ronald Reagan and rapidly adopted world-wide. Roger hankered after his early days when he would speak with no aids at all; but that would never do here, not when a slip of the tongue could create an international crisis.

'We should be particularly proud of our Prime Minister's success in Europe,' he intoned loyally. The response was muted. Most of the audience would have preferred to pull Britain out of the European Union altogether.

'We have stood firm against the joint efforts of both France and Germany to dictate to us. We vetoed the appointment of the Franco-German choice as President of the Commission, and we were right to do so. That is what we mean by being at the heart of Europe. Yet what would our opponents do? *They would dismantle the veto entirely.*'

This bombast produced the expected roar of acquiescence. Roger pushed to the back of his mind the knowledge that Margaret Thatcher had also used the veto in 1985 against the first-choice appointment to the presidency of the Commission. The compromise candidate Jacques Delors came to symbolise all she hated about 'Europe'. In truth, there were no anti-federalists in the frame for Brussels's top job, but it was wiser to conceal that unpalatable fact from British Tories for a while yet.

Nor was he about to warn them that the larger the Union the less powerful was any single nation within it. One out of nine – the ratio when Britain joined – was not the same as one out of fifteen or twenty. Since the British were so bad at maths it would take them a while to work it out. Yet one alone was the worst of all.

Then, quite suddenly, it was over. As he resumed his seat, Roger saw with pleasure that the audience had risen to their feet and were cheering enthusiastically. The platform party, expressions ecstatic, were also on their feet, and were turning to him. A standing ovation was expected for a senior Minister, especially one whose elevation in the recent reshuffle had attracted such positive comment; but there was genuine warmth in this applause and it seemed to be going on for rather a long time. People were stamping their feet, chanting what sounded like 'Rog-er! Rog-er!' Up in the gallery a group started singing 'For he's a jolly good fellow'. He shrugged imperceptibly; he had not realised when he began the long process of writing it that the strongly patriotic tone of the speech would meet with such approval. Had he been more candid that might not have been the case.

With a modest, almost shy air he rose and acknowledged the noise. Enjoy the adulation while it lasts. In due course there would be a price to pay. He wondered, chilled, what it might be.

'What is it, dear? Can I pass you the marmalade? Or would you like more toast?'

The Prime Minister found himself looking into the anxious eyes of his spouse across the breakfast table in their private suite and realised that he must have been staring into space for several minutes. She was not yet dressed but was sitting in a feather-trimmed pink dressing gown pulled well up to the neck. He knew with absolute certainty that the feathered mules on her small pink feet matched the gown exactly.

With reluctance he dragged himself into the present, folded the *Daily Telegraph* neatly as was his wont and placed it by the side of his plate. Then he studiously wiped his knife on the remains of a slice of toast and when it was as clean as he could make it lay it straight on the plate, pointing at her. He put the toast in his mouth and chewed it thoughtfully. Then, lacking anything else to play with, he folded his hands in his lap.

'Something is the matter.' There was alarm in her voice. 'I haven't been married to you all these years without knowing it. You've been on another planet for the last few days. What is it? Is there anything I can do? Is it my fault?'

'No, of course not,' he answered testily. As if anything his wife might get up to would penetrate his world of high politics – except when she made her occasional forays into the public eye. Like that silly interview she'd given for the village newspaper, believing that her unflattering comments on members of his Cabinet would go no further than her local newsagent.

He wondered how he might break it to her and almost decided not to try. But she was, under all the frills, a worthy sort who had backed him steadily since his early days as a Young Conservative. He recalled her faithfully clutching scissors and umbrella in the rain as he shinned up lamp-posts to fix posters the year he was first elected as a councillor. She had abandoned her own career to make a home and had, virtually single-handed, brought up two fine children who had his good looks and her solemn self-protection. Her lack of depth was hardly her fault; that was how he had made her, how their life had forced her to be. There were moments when he understood exactly how Harold Wilson had felt about his wife. The popularity of these women with the general public was inexplicable.

He took a deep breath and began. 'How would you feel . . .'

Betts ran towards the only spare phone, elbowed the *Standard*'s stringer out of the way and trod hard on the foot of that stupid woman from *Today*. Bloody hell. Speeches over, he had been expecting to do no more than time the standing ovation – would it be seven minutes or eight? As long as Maggie's or (God forbid) longer? Tories must hold practice sessions at the bar of local Conservative clubs, timing each other and swapping tips.

Now this, totally out of the blue. Bang would go the whole weekend; he could kiss goodbye to a stroll by the sea with that smart little number from Channel 4. Both of them would be putting in a packet of overtime, but not with each other.

'Clear the front page.'

He'd always wanted to say that. The voice at the other end blustered but the *Globe*'s deputy editor was brusque. 'I'm dictating. Shut up and listen.' Betts could hear the chatter of Press Association tapes and calls to reporters. His voice was suddenly magnified at the other end as the phone was connected into the paper's public address system. At desks all over the *Globe* building heads were raised, pens poised, eyes alert.

'Today at the Conservative Party Conference the Prime Minister dropped the biggest bombshell of his career. As delegates prepared to deliver the traditional standing ovation – expected to last six or seven minutes as usual – a dramatic change came over the man who has led the nation for the last six years.

'In a shock departure from his standard text, in which he was to call for national renewal and a revival of Tory values in the wake of the election results, instead he stopped and appeared for a moment to have been taken ill. A wave of concern rippled around the conference hall. Men and women rose to their feet.

'Then he took out a large handkerchief. All concerned could then see that he was, in fact, weeping.

'As a hush fell, there came the sensational announcement. He would be standing down as Prime Minister, and would ask the Chief Whip to start the procedure for choosing his successor as soon as Parliament returns.

'He wanted, he said, to finish while still at the top. After all this time, he hoped to be allowed to lead a normal life with his wife and children. After winning two general elections against the odds, having seen Europe accepting his Euro-sceptical point of view, with the economy in good heart, inflation down, the deficit under control and the pound standing comfortably at just under two Deutschmarks, he felt that the time was ripe to make way for a younger man.

'Speculation is now rife . . .'

Chapter Four

Room 14 on the committee corridor was crammed to overflowing. Row upon row of dark-suited men jostled and chattered loudly like a flock of starlings. At the back of the panelled room and around the door, latecomers squeezed to get inside, their reflections distorted in the bulbous brass of the chandeliers. Above the Members' entrance a portrait of a stern-faced Cromwell glared while at the far end an exquisitely sad Charles I warned it would all end in tears.

Even the whips present could not conceal their eagerness. They could gain the most whatever the outcome. Soon several would be promoted to office, there to enjoy the modest appurtenances of power – the two-year-old ministerial Rover 416, the middle-aged lady chauffeur, the car phone paid from public funds and the overfilled red boxes, under the leadership of a new Prime Minister.

Sir Tom Reynolds, the chairman of the 1922 Committee, cleared his throat and basked in a delightful aura of self-importance. His long-hoped-for knighthood was secure. One or two worthy directorships had been recorded in the Register of Members' Interests. He would himself retire in due course to sincere plaudits from colleagues and constituents. Life was orderly, prosperous, fulfilling – and too dreadfully predictable for words.

A leadership contest, on the other hand, offered fabulous opportunities for intrigue and king-making. To date he had been wined and dined by all the potential candidates. None was present now, though in a few minutes, in an innovation he dearly hoped might become standard practice – thus inscribing his name for ever in the annals of the parliamentary party – they would be invited inside, one at a time, to deliver a personal message to the assembled troops. To handle a meeting of such charged emotions would require skills of the highest order: the chairman knew he was up to it.

'Ladies and gentlemen! Let's have a bit of quiet.'

A large glass ashtray was banged in sympathy by a nearby vice-chairman. Modern nonsense about 'no smoking' was not tolerated in party meetings: the pungent blue haze of several large coronas filled the air.

'Right! Now I'll explain the procedure to you, as many won't have been here last time. To be validly nominated a candidate must have just the two names, proposer and seconder. Nominations closed at noon today and I am glad to announce' – here he paused for effect and was gratified by shouts to continue, as if he were a popular music hall comedian – 'that we have three in the frame. There can be two ballots, possibly three. In the first, next Tuesday in this room, a candidate wins outright if he has an overall majority of those entitled to vote plus fifteen per cent. That means, since we have three hundred and forty-one Members, a total of two hundred and twenty-two. That's the magic number. Less than that, and we're into a second ballot the week after, in which the winner would be whoever gets an overall majority, which you'll have worked out as one hundred and seventy-one. If not, there could be a third ballot. That should be reasonably clear.'

He smiled down roguishly. 'And, of course, canvassing is perfectly legal!'

Members tittered dutifully: campaigning and placing wagers were part of the fun. Most would hedge their bets unless taste or experience favoured one name prominently over its rivals. A PPS or junior Minister would sit on the supporters' bench for his boss and expect his reward in due course, were his man successful. Some made their choice by a process of elimination, weighing up who was too right- or left-wing, too radical or traditional, too pro- or anti-Europe to tolerate. Others, particularly in marginal seats, had begun to take soundings from both party workers and the drinkers down the pub: what mattered most to them was the future leader's appeal to the ordinary voter, that bulk of the mass electorate who would settle whether their MP still had a job after the next election.

'Time to put them through their paces, I think. Alphabetical order.' The chairman nudged the nearest vice-chairman, who rose solemnly and headed for the door. Also time for a quick reminder.

'Now, remember, this is a *private* meeting. The press are a few yards away and they'll be panting for the least titbit. We maintain confidentiality – complete . . .'

The rest of his sentence was drowned in the well-orchestrated cheer as the first challenger entered the room. His head was thrown back, eyes protruding, face flushed, tie slightly crooked. He hitched up his trousers over a comfortable belly as he turned to face the assembly.

*   *   *

Down the corridor near the gents' toilet Jim Betts chewed on a Biro. You never knew when a Tory with a weak bladder might need to nip out and could be cornered among the urinals. Most would also be glad to relieve the tension. A few choice remarks and back inside: that wouldn't count, would it, as a leak?

Betts railed against the frustration of finding a fresh angle on the leadership contest. The broadsheets were full of serious statements from Portillo, Dickson and Clarke about 'maintaining the position of Britain', 'working to reduce the deficit' and 'making society work again'. Try as he might he could not clearly distinguish these sentiments either from each other or from the marginally more grammatical promises of the Labour leader. What was the country coming to, he wondered, when the two main parties' official pronouncements were so alike – especially when their private agendas, and their activists' passions, were so far apart?

It was a long way from his own early years, in Liverpool. You knew where you were, then: against the authorities of the day, whichever political colour they might be. Not that he had been remotely aware of politics as a boy, buried in the rough dark tenements near the Anglican Cathedral where names like 'Hope Street' served only as mockery. A strict hierarchy had operated, even at that level. You stuck to your own, but strangers from the other side of Prince's Park or Wavertree were fair game for an impromptu punch-up. Betts smiled grimly. He had been lucky, he supposed, that his first casual job on the *Liverpool Echo* had so attracted him. His erstwhile mates from the 'Pool had since been lost to sight, or if well known had acquired prison records. He had, in a sense, exchanged the violence of his youth for a particularly florid turn of phrase in a tabloid newspaper; and he loved every minute.

'Penny for 'em, Jim.'

The friendly face of a Labour Member hove into view. Keith Quin, MP for Manchester Canalside, so enjoyed politics that even the Tory leadership contest was a magnet.

'Who'd you prefer, then, Keith?'

Quin considered. 'Portillo'd make our job a lot easier,' he confided. 'That curling lip, the swagger – he may be bright but it's all a bit sinister, innit? Foreign, too, and a turncoat – his dad fought on our side in the Spanish Civil War. And he forgets – he may well be correct that there are far too many people living on benefits, but they all have votes.'

'Don't use them though, do they? You're lucky to get a turnout of sixty per cent in your constituency for a general election. Ain't democracy wonderful?'

Quin shrugged defensively. 'It's hard to think about voting when you've just lost your giro. Clarke would give us a lot of fun, and you always feel his heart is in the right place. Son of a miner, scholarship boy and that. But he's a bruiser: he'd cross the road to have a fight and that leaves a lot of bleedin' bodies. Not the best way to go about running the country.'

'So . . . Dickson?'

'Off the record, Jim?'

'Sure.' Quin's opinions didn't count for much anyway.

'He'd be good if they have the sense to choose him. It'd take a miracle to get us in next time, too.'

Ted Bampton switched on the table lamp. He motioned tiredly to the tall figure lounging on a sofa near the door, reading the *Tatler*.

'If that's all you can do, Derek, go and get us some McDonalds. I'm ravenous. There's one at the far end of Victoria Street. Make mine a Big Mac, double chips and a vanilla milkshake.'

Elaine stretched and rubbed a numb shoulder. 'That'll improve your figure no end, Ted. But I'm hungry too. I'll have a black coffee and a quarter-pounder, please.'

The basement flat was littered with papers, lists, folders, notebooks, files, wire trays, empty mugs and glasses, soft drinks and beer cans, overflowing ashtrays and waste-bins, newspapers, *Who's Who* and *Dod's* and *Vacher's* and back copies of the House magazine. The curtains were half drawn against the evening air as a computer screen blinked on Bampton's desk. A laser printer in the corner hummed. The clock showed five minutes to five.

With bad grace Harrison collected orders from the flat's several other weary occupants and sloped off.

Elaine put down her notepad and came to stand behind Bampton. She peered over his shoulder at the computer listing. 'Is our man going to win?'

Bampton impatiently pressed a button and the screen went blank. 'Damn. I'm still not used to this.' He motioned to the young man who had entered the room with a portable television set which he plugged into the wall. 'C'mon, Anthony, you're the expert. Answer Mrs Stalker's question.'

Elaine felt irritated that the Minister insisted on using such a distant title for her. The scruffy basement of Roger's house behind Great Peter Street, a stone's throw from the Palace of Westminster, was hardly a formal place. She knew the layout of the property better than she dared admit, after four years as the owner's lover. And she was not interested sexually in Bampton, or in Anthony York – both of whom seemed to have difficulty relating to her in a natural, unaffected way. Why couldn't they simply treat her as one of the boys?

Harrison was a different matter. Women, in his estimation, had one main function. As the woman present did not fill the bill he simply ignored her, even when regaling the assembled company with the intimate details of his previous night's conquest. Elaine found the man nauseating but the type fascinating: like the sight of a toad eating live butterflies, horrible but compulsive.

It had never occurred to her not to volunteer, even though it had meant the cancellation of two weekends' engagements. The moment after Conference broke up in such confusion she had contacted Roger's office to offer her help. Since then with a dozen others she had worked in a tireless frenzy. The two telephones and a mobile had been in constant use – the size of Roger's phone-bill did not bear thinking about. But she far preferred to be on the team – calling MPs' personal numbers, offering a chat with the candidate, parrying criticisms, hinting at dangers in the two opponents, offering what bribes and assurances were at her command and cajoling the unconvinced – to waiting at home as a mere observer.

The only difficult moments came when Roger himself was present, dressed unusually casually in a soft blue sweater and no tie. The bare flesh, so vulnerable at the neck, made her gasp inwardly and turn her head away. He was cordial but preoccupied and treated her no differently from anyone else: when he paused at the door one lunchtime on his way to persuade crusty old Sir Trevor, and thanked her, she knew he would make a point of doing the same to every single member of the team. She was nobody special. And that was how it should be.

Anthony York's tall form blocked the light. He tapped a few keys, then stood back. 'We'll know for certain in an hour's time. But on my count he's in there with a chance. I estimate we could take a hundred and fifty, maybe a few more. That'd mean we'd be well ahead and could win on the second ballot, if not the first.'

Anthony switched on the television and found Ceefax. Together the

three read the crisp text. The odds on Dickson had shortened consider-
ably since one of the other hopefuls had made ill-judged remarks about
high birth rates among lower-social-class women. However accurate,
such views were regarded as too harsh and quite inappropriate in a
potential leader of the nation. Elaine recalled a similar gaffe in 1974 by
Keith Joseph which had led to his withdrawal from the race to replace
Ted Heath; and the virtually unknown Margaret Thatcher had stepped
shyly forward.

There was just time to catch the early-evening news before heading
nervously for the Commons. Through St Stephen's entrance they would
step past banks of clicking cameras, up the stone stairs and ahead, then in
the lift to the committee room where the chairman of the '22 Committee
was to announce the result.

Of course Roger should be Prime Minister. He had all the right
qualities. Even if he lost this contest he might be able to try again in future.
Provided he did not disgrace himself – and repeated number-crunching
indicated a respectable total – his position in the leading triumvirate of
Ministers would be confirmed.

Nor, if he failed, did that mean automatic ignominy for his supporters.
His lieutenants' efforts would also be recognised: the retiring Prime
Minister had won accolades after his own victory by his prompt
incorporation into government of members of the defeated camps,
on the sensible grounds of party unity. Elaine hoped the same would
happen, at least for the hard-working Bampton and for Anthony, if not
for Harrison – or herself.

Police Officer Robin Bell took his place beside the desk in Upper Waiting
Hall, folded his burly arms and gazed with amused condescension at the
scrum developing a few yards away. After a quarter of a century in the
House he thought he'd seen everything. He turned to his partner, a
young woman officer.

'If their constituents could see them now . . .' A tactful man, Bell
left the rest unsaid.

The policewoman, from a younger generation, pulled a face. 'Best
leave 'em to it,' she murmured.

The corridor behind them was jammed with reporters waving
notebooks and pulling at sleeves. At the same moment nearly two
hundred MPs were trying to cram into Room 14, whose narrow doors
were blocked by bodies already inside. A television crew appeared – which

was not permitted – and despite protests started filming aggressively. The atmosphere began to turn ugly.

A particularly persistent journalist tripped, or was pushed – nobody ever knew – and suddenly there was pandemonium, with angry voices raised, fists flying, notebooks snatched; for a brief glorious moment battle raged, as furious Tories vented long-standing anger on the media for their intrusion into this, to them, entirely private event. There was no love lost between the two sides but, as the heaving mass threatened to crush weaker souls against the wall, Robin Bell waded in and separated red-faced Honourable Member Freddie Ferriman from the *Globe*'s deputy editor Jim Betts just as the former was about to land a punch on the latter.

'I shouldn't, sir, if I was you,' he calmly advised the panting Ferriman, who tugged down his disordered waistcoat and straightened his tie. The MP snorted an oath at his opponent, then turned and pushed his way through the crowd.

Betts pulled out a grubby handkerchief and secretly cursed his luck that the blow had never landed: a senior newspaperman rendered battered and bloody by an MP would have made a splendid story.

At the top of the stairs the chairman of the '22 and the Party Chairman halted in horror at the mêlée. After a quick consultation with the police it was decided that cowardice was the better part of valour. The two scuttled into Room 10 instead. The press were rapidly admitted and made to sit, like naughty schoolboys before a headmaster. After all, the dignitaries told each other, it was the press who really counted.

Back in the basement room Harrison absent-mindedly ate his chips and fiddled with the television remote control. Never one to waste energy, he avoided crowds, and had reckoned there would be trouble as the result was announced. What excited him was not so much the count – an outright winner first time was unlikely – but the reaction of those who came second and third, which would decide whether a second ballot would go ahead.

The cameras showed the oldest candidate at his desk in the Treasury, apparently nonchalant; but the familiar matey grin was belied by the darting of his eyes. He was in his mid fifties. This would probably be his last chance. The youngest of the three was pictured at home, his expression impassive and self-contained. The third was in a television studio, elbows on table, pursed mouth hidden by clasped hands, outwardly cool and joking with the crew, inwardly in turmoil.

What did it mean, to lead the country? For a brief moment Roger thought he must be mad. He had no sense of mission; no small voices in his head spoke to him of destiny. He had never planned this day. Yet somehow, perhaps from the first moment he had arrived at Westminster, his foot had been placed firmly on the bottom tread of an invisible escalator which now had brought him enticingly close to the top.

'Sit down!' roared the chairman of the '22. Betts muttered incantations against the chairman's mother and offspring. Every seat was taken. He subsided to the floor, pen poised.

'Right!' The chairman debated with himself whether to wipe his perspiring face first and decided against it. 'Are we ready? The count for the leadership contest, first ballot, is as follows . . .'

Down the corridor it dawned on three hundred MPs that they were being completely bypassed, and, what was worse, by the fellow they'd elected to put their interests first at all times. Jammed between Bampton and Ferriman (who had been widely congratulated at his contretemps with the hated press), Elaine joined in the widespread catcalling. In vain did the senior vice-chairman, who was equally annoyed, try to mollify Members' disgust.

Floor managers signalled. The candidates were hushed by sound recordists. Lights brightened, throats were cleared. Roger was conscious that his heart was thumping so powerfully that it must be visible through his shirt. He concentrated hard on the black spot at the centre of the camera's eye and made himself breathe slowly, in, out.

'I'll do it in alphabetical order. Clarke: forty-one.'

The figure in the Treasury bowed his head, then shrugged and smiled. At the back of Room 10 journalists yelled for the number to be repeated. The air of confusion increased.

'Dickson: one hundred and eighty.'

The Chairman roared it with a flourish like a darts referee in his local Conservative Club. Roger bit his lip. Better than predicted. Far better. Not enough to win on first ballot, but . . .

'Portillo: eighty. And that means there will be another ballot next week . . .'

Noise engulfed the room as reporters ran for the door; an intrepid few, ignoring the Commons' antiquated rules, pulled out mobile phones and started shouting into them. Into the rapidly clearing space in front of the dais the two chairmen stepped gingerly. Now it was time to face the Members.

'There shouldn't be another ballot.' The older beaten candidate leaned

56

forward in his chair. 'The party has clearly indicated its preference and I for one won't argue with that. I am prepared to concede right now.'

In the studio the TV producer gasped and kept the camera trained full on his target's face. An order was rapidly hissed down the wire to the stringer with the other loser. In view of what had just been said, was he also prepared to recognise the claims of a man who had won the support of over half the party?

The young pretender paused. The private struggle did not show, not in a single flicker. Behind him his wife's normally controlled face betrayed a mixture of anxiety and disappointment. There would be other chances. He had time on his side. To continue the fight would risk splitting the party; on the other hand, to give in gracefully would immediately make him heir apparent.

'Yes,' he said.

Harrison whooped and punched the air in delight. In Room 14 the assembly was made aware that the transition from one leader to the next had been completed. Some scowled and muttered but the main reaction was relief.

The interviewer turned to Roger Dickson and cordially shook hands. A new deference crept over his features.

'Well, Prime Minister . . .' he began.

Elaine heaved the cardboard box sideways along the hall and deposited it heavily on the floor. As she did so the bottom gave way. Out tumbled books, CDs, old letters, scruffy hairbrushes, spray bottles, a bedside light, assorted make-up, several unmatched socks, a radio, a teddy bear, an alarm clock in the shape of Donald Duck, two posters of the Cure and an ancient pair of trainers entangled with a skein of purple leggings.

'Thanks, Mum.' Karen, seated cross-legged on the bed, began to scrabble vaguely at the mess. She tuned the radio into the news for her mother. 'Where's my Dire Straits CD? I thought I put it in here.'

Hands on hips, Elaine looked around. Anthony York's house was a straightforward Victorian terrace of the kind which once attracted Pooterish assistant bank managers with harassed wives and numerous children, and which now offered a roomy home for couples on second marriages with combined offspring. The half-dozen staircases and lack of parking were a nuisance, but there was ample room for both partners to have their own space, the nanny her own quarters and the infants their own TVs. It was also perfect for a group of friends to share.

Outside the frontage was narrow and the garden non-existent, merely a few tired privet bushes and a dusty bay tree in a broken pot. Yet a handsome door with its original stained glass and art nouveau tile border hinted at a stylish interior, while the black-and-white chequered hallway and the airy conservatory at the back had won over its new owner at once. Battersea was almost walking distance from the Commons; the tip of Big Ben was visible from the end of the street. It would make an ideal base for aspiring MPs and the odd additional tenant, such as Ms Karen Stalker.

Karen had just fished two mugs out of another box and was heading for the kitchen. Elaine lounged against the wall and watched as her daughter made instant coffee, and noted with maternal affection how the girl carefully wiped up the small spills of brown powder and milk. She must be growing up.

'It's a splendid place. Your new friend Anthony seems to have both taste and the funds to indulge it. Do you get on all right?'

'Yes – well, he's a bit shy, isn't he? He must be over thirty but he's no idea how to talk to girls. Maybe he's the strong silent type. Rather attractive in a gloomy way so perhaps I'll have the chance to find out. Fred's OK, though – closer to my age, but a bit out of his depth. Could improve, probably. Lachlan is grand – he's the doctor, Anthony's cousin, and American. He works strange hours at the hospital, and of course Anthony and Fred are out all day and most evenings, so they don't get in my way.'

The radio was chattering excitedly about the first appointments by the new Prime Minister. Karen sensed that her mother's attention was on the broadcast. 'Will you be involved, Mum?'

'Doubt it. If I was, it wouldn't be today but tomorrow.'

'You mustn't spend the evening worrying about it. Would you like to come here for supper? I can't guarantee cordon bleu . . .'

The focus of mothering was shifting: pleased but patronised, Elaine shook her head. 'That's sweet of you, but no. Actually, I have a date.'

She knew it was a mistake the moment she said it. Karen whirled round, eyes alive. 'Great! Anyone I know?'

Elaine pursed her lips. 'No, fortunately. We're going to a club – Le Beaujolais in Litchfield Street. Next to the Ivy but friendlier, George says.'

'Ooh! George who? At least it's not that awful Roger Dickson. He may be Prime Minister but I could never understand what you saw in him. But I'm glad for you. After all, you're still . . . well, not bad for your age, Mum, are you? Anyway, I trust you to behave.'

Her mother raised an eyebrow. 'Chance would be a fine thing, to be frank. And now I'll leave you. Don't go making eyes at the boys. After all, at your age . . .'

She dodged a well-aimed dishcloth and the moment dissolved in laughter.

Yet as Elaine drove away she wondered quite what George had in mind for the evening, and afterwards. And whether she was still capable of responding.

Cameras clicked and whirled as each incumbent left Downing Street. For several, to be chased down the road by jostling photographers while trying to contain their joy and retain their dignity was an unnerving experience. The cavalcade resembled nothing so much as stolid grey Thames tugs pursued by hungry seagulls. Others, older hands, slid into waiting cars and informed their drivers, who of course knew already.

Up in the white drawing room where the interviews had taken place the atmosphere was still fraught. A crumpled piece of paper lay ignored in the corner of the room where it had been thrown. One or two MPs who had backed the wrong side had objected bitterly to being removed to make way for fresh faces. The new team was younger, leaner: a lot of old fat had been cut away. How right Gladstone had been, that the first requirement of a good Prime Minister was to be a good butcher.

Roger Dickson poured himself a stiff drink and motioned to his companions to do the same. His Private Secretary demurred politely; his job done, he gathered his papers and slipped out. At last Roger noticed how tense he had become, and with a heavy shrug relaxed the tight knots in his shoulders.

'Now, Peter. You wanted a word.'

Peter Aubrey hesitated, then took a seat on the elegant sofa and tucked his legs underneath. With a deliberate gesture he set his drink down on the polished walnut table. The old Prime Minister would have rushed across with a cardboard coaster to slip under the glass: no wonder he'd had a reputation for being naff.

'You asked me this morning to be your new Party Chairman and I have spent most of the day in Central Office. I thought it wise to bring you up to date at once with the state of affairs there. Particularly over money.'

He sensed immediately Dickson's famous knack, whoever was speaking to him, of giving that person his undivided attention.

'We have trouble. I'm not saying the old Chairman pulled the wool over anybody's eyes but he never was any good at maths.'

Dickson smiled. He had relished that sacking. 'He wasn't bad at promoting himself, and that was about it. We are still presumably in overdraft?'

Roger knew the answer to that one. The Party Chairman swallowed half his Scotch and grunted.

'Inevitably. Better than it has been: it stood at nineteen after the previous election and over sixteen halfway through the last Parliament. Millions of pounds, in case you need reminding. At that point, you will recall, our bankers decided they had to protect their own investors and took over the Smith Square lease. So we'd spent a fortune on the office only to lose the whole thing. Great accounting, that was.'

'What do you want me to do?' The question was put quietly. In this unrecorded conversation private arrangements could be proposed but denied absolutely later.

'We can't get the constituencies to raise more – they're stretched to the limit. Business is being very sticky. I think you're going to have to woo a few big donors. If I give you a small list of names, could we start off by inviting them here?'

Dickson grimaced. 'Will any of them be British?' he asked, an edge of sarcasm to his voice. There had been comments in the previous Parliament over donations from foreign businessmen, the fraudulent activities of at least one of whom had led to considerable embarrassment. Not that the money had been returned.

'One or two. Some of the others might like to be – or have a brother-in-law who'd give a bob or two for a British passport. The most obliging expect only a knighthood. Once upon a time they'd have coughed up simply to keep the other lot out, but not any more. Don't ask, Roger: you know the score. Nobody gives money to a political party without wanting something in return.'

'God, I loathe this sort of thing.' Dickson frowned. How speedily the pleasure of high office had become tarnished. He straightened. 'Right, Peter. Let me have a list and we'll arrange an event. Whatever you say.'

* * *

Joel Default broke open another pack of Gauloises and contemplated his next fishing trip. This time he and three cronies would take a boat out into the winter rigours of the North Sea and try for marlin and sea bass which, were he successful, would find themselves soon after on the menu at Le Beaujolais in a classic sauce with wine, cream, tarragon and a hint of lime. Keep it simple, especially if the fish itself was a little unusual. Too many restaurants composed the most fantastic rubbish, were fashionable for ten minutes (about long enough to be visited by Michael Winner) and then vanished. Thirty years in catering had confirmed Joel's natural prejudice for the cuisine of his youth. Survival in the competitive culinary world of London had taught him nothing was better than regular customers.

He patted a taut midriff. The French knew that it was not obligatory to eat a lot in order to eat well. His two establishments were comfortably situated in the heart of theatreland off Charing Cross Road. He was proud that taxi-drivers were not familiar with the name and would argue with customers that they wanted the better-known watering-hole next door. At street level the public façade was a wine-bar. But for those in the know – introduced by someone of whom Joel already approved – the real business was downstairs in the club, where he presided like a medieval monk in his cellar, with laconic Gabi the waiter as his perennial sidekick.

Elaine dipped her head and stepped gingerly down the stairs. The place was tiny – a single basement room with space for half a dozen tables. Its walls were covered in posters from France, ancient photographs of viticulture, framed cartoons and elaborately illuminated certificates from more wine syndicates than she could count.

'Ah, *chère madame*!' Joel was on his best behaviour. He kissed her hand, then deftly took her and George's coats. Elaine was immediately aware that sharp eyes summed her up, sweeping up and down quickly and lightly but without giving offence. Within a moment the two were seated. Elaine stared round in astonishment.

'It's exactly like a small family restaurant in rural France,' she whispered.

George glanced up from the menu. 'That's the idea. I hoped you'd like it. He's a character but the food is wonderful, and not expensive either.'

'Why is it a club?'

'So Joel can decide who comes, and when he wants to throw them out. If he likes you he'll sit down with a cognac and keep you talking half the night. His command of English is erratic but colourful, though he probably won't swear much while you're here.'

Elaine giggled and concentrated on the menu. *Magret de canard* seemed a safe bet, preceded by a thick fish soup. When it came to the wine George held a long discussion with the waiter and then chose, as he was expected to, the wine of the week, a light 1992 Saumur-Champigny.

She watched him quietly. He was conservatively dressed in a dark blue suit, blue-striped shirt and plain tie, but the effect was masculine and attractive. He must be some years older than herself but he moved easily, his body lithe and fit. Karen's remark returned and with it her pique at the assumption that older people are less interested in sex. Each generation assumes that the one before no longer indulges and that the one after does but shouldn't. To Elaine the thought of her eighteen-year-old daughter engaging in sexual activity filled her with anxiety. Like most parents she had no idea of her offspring's sexual history and probably would never know.

George raised his head and saw that he was the subject of careful scrutiny, not entirely covert, from his guest. Elaine coloured and pointedly contemplated the bright ruby of the wine. The closeness of this trim, spare man was oddly unsettling. She decided to take the initiative.

'Have you always been in business, George?'

'No, not at all. I was a career soldier with the Blues and Royals – a guardsman. I took my retirement only five years ago.'

That gave her a subject for conversation. 'I can just imagine you in a bearskin, chain stretched tightly across your chin, rigidly at attention down the Mall as the Queen went past.'

'It's a mounted regiment, Elaine.' There was a twinkle in his eye. The mistake was all too common. 'Thigh boots and cuirasses, a helmet with silk tassels. "Well mannered, well turned out in all circumstances, calm and collected – what one would expect of a Household Cavalryman", as my squadron was once described. Oh, yes, and "very pleased with ourselves". An accurate description, don't you think?' He postured a little to amuse his guest.

'I should think that applies to most MPs too, but with less reason. Sorry I got it wrong, but I know nothing about it.'

'There's a parliamentary connection: the Blues were raised in 1650 by a Colonel Crook, would you believe, as part of the first standing army in England. We were the original Ironsides in our dark blue coats. The colour was convenient when Lord Oxford took us over under the King, whom we've served faithfully ever since.'

'You say "we" as if you were there. Do you really feel the sense of history like that?'

'Certainly. Don't you look up at the stones of Westminster and feel a sense of communion, of continued, shared duty passing down through the centuries, with the MPs who've gone before? Of course you do. It's the same for us.' George was warming to his theme. 'But there's far more to it than ceremonial. Modern cavalry uses tanks and armoured personnel carriers. We've done our tour of duty in trouble spots – the Berlin Wall, Belfast, the Falklands, Cyprus. My first outing was in Malaya following the insurgency. Nee Soon Barracks in Singapore was not the most comfortable place to learn soldiering, I can tell you.'

He began to talk easily about places he had seen and men he had served alongside. Names famous in other contexts emerged – the young Earl Spencer, Diana's father, then Viscount Althorp, his face and once gangly figure so very like hers; and the extraordinary photo which had appeared in the *Sun* of the newly married Princess of Wales chatting happily and innocently from her carriage with her Travelling Escort commander, none other than the Lieutenant-Colonel Parker-Bowles, whose wife was the Prince's mistress.

Gradually Elaine glimpsed the enjoyment a man of action might gain from a military career. The duck arrived, juicy in its purple-berried sauce. The first bottle of wine was nearly empty. He was good company, and a bit of a surprise.

'What did you think of Northern Ireland?' she asked.

His face clouded. 'Bloody IRA. I did five tours in all and never relaxed once, not for a moment. It's partly the tension – in one four-month period we searched over thirty-three thousand vehicles at checkpoints and you just never know which one's going to blow up in your face. It's partly that you're stuck in barracks with the families far away; fraternising is dangerous, a quick way to get murdered. But mostly it was sheer frustration – knowing that in the end the only solution lies with the politicians. No soldier likes that.'

'Politicians don't like it either,' Elaine remarked drily. 'It's much easier when you win a war for us and settle the issue, as you did in the Falklands.'

George swirled the wine around in his glass. The bombast disappeared from his voice. 'The worst, you know, wasn't over there. It was the day in July '82 when we'd just come back from the South Atlantic, covered in glory, and were on parade in Hyde Park. A car bomb packed with high explosive and nails – well, you know about it. The strange thing was that

I was used to seeing dead men. But it was the horses that got to me: on the ground with bellies ripped open, their guts in a puddled mess all over the road, screaming in terror. One was standing stock-still with its front leg blown off, a shred of bone hanging. And there was a corporal with his arm buried up to the elbow in a horse's neck, covered in blood, trying to stop the flow. That was Sefton – his picture was in the papers. Do you know, his trooper had a nail right through his hand and was swaying, half conscious, but wouldn't let go of the reins. Christ.'

The evening had taken on a sombre tone. It was a relief to both when the cheeses appeared, with unknown names and sharp, over-the-edge tastes, and a second bottle.

'Sorry.' George had not expected to be contrite, but Elaine was looking troubled. She explained how close she herself had come to being an IRA victim, when Karen had accepted an apparently innocent gift from an IRA sleeper on the House of Commons staff. Presumably both could still be targets.

She continued, 'There are risks associated with our lives too. We know about them and we learn to live with it. For us there are additional problems, not so predictable, like the nutter who takes it into his head to have a go. The worry is that somewhere somebody may have decided that he wants to get me. People like that are attracted to Ministers especially, and to anyone well known.'

'So why do it? You could earn a good living at plenty of other things.'

She allowed an archness into her voice. 'For exactly the same reasons that you were a soldier. Because it's a job that must be done, fearlessly and honestly, one hopes; and while you're doing it it's utterly absorbing.'

He nodded. Joel brought coffee but left them tactfully alone. The evening was drawing to its natural close.

'That was a splendid meal, George. Would you be kind enough to see me home?'

Joel Default, marginally less steady than at the start of the evening, lit another cigarette and watched his old friend and customer Lieutenant-Colonel Horrocks climb the stairs behind his pretty lady guest. She had good legs and a shapely rump. It was a long time since *le patron* had seen this customer dine alone with a woman; mostly the colonel brought male business colleagues, whose company did not produce quite the same lively spring in his step. It was clear that the evening was not over yet.

*   *   *

Jim Betts sat in the litter-strewn pigsty which passed for his flat and chewed his moustache. On the bed lay the first editions, spread out, their inky pages making the grey sheets even grubbier. He should long ago have moved to a more salubrious location – as deputy editor of the nation's foremost tabloid, he could well afford it – but the effort of sorting the accumulated debris of years put him off. Inertia would ensure that he remained here for the rest of his days.

Dickson's face was everywhere. The changes he had wrought in the Cabinet were masterly. Naturally he had rewarded key supporters in his campaign for the leadership. Betts was not surprised to find Bampton elevated to the Cabinet, though probably he would have preferred less of a nannying job than the new 'Department of Health, Welfare and the Family': right mouthful that was. His sidekick and PPS, Derek Harrison, was tipped for a junior job the following day despite the gossip surrounding his private life. Betts chortled: the press would have a field day with Harrison's girlfriends. One of them would sing eventually. They always did.

He returned to the front page. It was not the small fry he was after when it came to illicit liaisons, though there was no doubt the more Ministers were exposed the merrier. With a wince of pain he recalled how near he had once come to confronting the new Prime Minister with evidence of his long-term affair with one of his own backbench MPs, the trim and delicious Mrs Elaine Stalker. Betts had been so close. It grieved him still that he had failed.

Yet it had to be possible to bring even a Prime Minister to heel; he was only a man, whose past inability to keep his trousers up would lead, some day, to his being found with them around his ankles. Whether the Stalker affair was still on or not, he would be revealed, sooner or later, as no better than any of the rest. But for the present Betts could not see how to do it.

The nation's interest in the peccadilloes of its politicians had not waned. You might think, Betts mused, that after a dozen revelations of mistresses and illegitimate children, resignation after resignation, the public would get bored and the incumbents learn to behave. Not a bit of it. At any rate it made for an entertaining life.

With an impatient gesture he swept the newspapers on to the floor, lay back fully clothed, and within minutes was sound asleep.

*   *   *

'Will you come in for coffee – or a Scotch, perhaps?'

It did not matter what she offered. If he was going to follow her further, up the stairs to the third-floor flat within division bell distance of Westminster, he would accept, and if necessary leave the coffee in its cup, untouched. Should this man be intrigued by her in any way, he would come, if only to satisfy his natural curiosity about her. And, perhaps, to signal his interest for future reference.

But a gentleman would demur. He would shake hands in the considerate way a gentleman would reserve for a lady, and he would smile wistfully, with a hint of self-denial. Then it would be appropriate for her to stand on tiptoe to cover the eight inches difference between them and kiss him lightly on the cheek. And that, regrettably, would be that.

She waited, hardly daring to breathe.

'Thank you, I'd love to.'

Suddenly she felt anxious. Her hand pushed back the thick blond hair and she bit her lip. Members of Parliament had to be so careful. But her fears on this score, as she unlocked the street door and stepped aside to let George enter, could not be real. This man, surely, would be the soul of discretion.

So what could be the source of her troubled feeling, as they climbed the stairs, chattering animatedly but softly so as not to disturb the neighbours? In the street outside a police siren wailed and faded, the ever-present warning of danger in the capital city. By the time she reached the flat, the smile on her face was forced and unhappy.

He began to move around the main room as she had anticipated he might, examining the bound copies of Hansard, the biographies of Macmillan and Thatcher and John Major, the well-thumbed diaries of Alan Clark, the unread Lawson. He picked up and glanced through several volumes as she pointed to the drinks cupboard and then busied herself in the kitchen with ground coffee and filters. When she returned he had poured two small malt whiskies exactly the way she liked them.

She forced herself to relax and sipped the drink. This man was now her guest.

'If you'd like to borrow any, feel free.'

He had seated himself on the sofa with a copy of the Longford biography of the Duke of Wellington, left over from her university days, in his hand. 'Thanks – I'd like to. The duke commanded us at Waterloo and said he'd never seen a finer regiment. The Royals captured the eagle of Napoleon's crack regiment; it's been our cap badge ever since.'

He caught her amused look. 'Sorry. I am, like all ex-servicemen, a bore on the subject. It's your turn to tell me more about yourself.'

She pondered. 'Have you ever sat in the gallery for Prime Minister's Questions? If not, you must come. I'll try and pick a day when there's a lively debate afterwards, but it's really pot luck. But didn't you tell me that you were interested in a political career yourself . . .?'

It was too late in the evening. George pulled a face. 'Another day, maybe,' he said. 'It's time to thank you for a delightful evening, Elaine, ask if we may do it again, and leave you. I expect you have a busy day tomorrow.'

Now she knew why she had hesitated as they entered the flat. After the years of easy intimacy with Roger, to start again with somebody else was daunting, even if her love for Dickson had entirely vanished – which it hadn't. A terrible ache rose in her for the man she had loved so dearly, who had so often come to this flat and made love to her in the bedroom behind, and who was not this man. It was a loss so complete that the void could not easily be filled, and certainly not by a stranger.

They rose formally but her voice was shaky.

'Sorry, George. I'm not very good at this. I'm not exactly a gay divorcée, I'm afraid – I don't make a habit of going around with lots of men.'

God, he was tall. Close to, she was conscious of his brown eyes, not the same as Roger's, the face longer and lined, with more prominent cheekbones. And he wore aftershave, musky but not unpleasant. She could never begin to imagine that this was her ex-lover, and the reminder was exquisitely painful.

'It might help you to be aware, Elaine, that my sister-in-law Betty, who cares very much about you, has told me about much of what has happened to you. So I do understand. I am not pushing for anything you don't want to give, believe me.'

The gentleness unnerved her, as if he were talking to a young subaltern away from home for the first time. Her eyes misted with tears as she stumbled slightly, not meaning to lean against him. With a firm movement he took her into his arms, her head on his shoulder, and soothed her, talking quietly to her, his hand smoothing her hair in a gesture of infinite tenderness.

After a moment she pulled away.

'Sorry – oh, heavens, we seem to have spent the whole evening apologising to each other. And that's not how it's been, has it? But I think you'd better go, really. Borrow the book, do, please. I'll be in touch about PM Questions. I'm fine, honestly – a bit too much wine, perhaps.'

'Or maybe you're not used to enjoying yourself?' Persistence was obviously his trademark but the judgement was shrewd. 'If I were to ask you out again, Elaine, please would you come – to the theatre, or an exhibition, or whatever you would enjoy?'

She considered, then nodded, head still down, but was not surprised when he did not kiss her. At the top of the stairs she watched as he started to descend, book in hand, then realised with a rush of shame how poor her manners had been. She leaned over the banister.

'George!'

He turned, his face inscrutable. 'Yes?'

'Thank you. And yes, please, I'd love to see you again.'

Elaine closed the door and slowly put herself to bed. Her sleep was uneasy, punctuated by dreams. At three she awoke with a headache and lay for a long while, tossing. Eventually she fell into a heavy doze, and thus slept through the alarm.

The phone was ringing. It must have been ringing for ages. Cursing, she sat up in bed and picked up the receiver.

'Mrs Stalker? Ah, at last. Ten Downing Street here . . .'

Chapter Five

'Who's pinched all the Frosties?'

Fred, still in the ample Marks and Spencer pyjamas his doting mother had given him as a going-away present, his hair tousled and chin unshaven, peered inside the empty packet and shook it, as if hunger alone would generate a further supply.

'Nobody pinched 'em, Fred. You're the only one who eats those. But nobody told me, either, when I went to Sainsbury's yesterday, that we were out.'

Lachlan's American drawl softened his remonstration. He was casually dressed in dark trousers, white shirt and tweed jacket, ready for a day with patients. He pushed his grapefruit husk away and turned to a bowl of All Bran and skimmed milk.

'I can't eat that tasteless muck.' Fred slouched to the breadbin. 'Oh, good, you remembered to buy some fresh bread. Can we have white next time, though? I'll make do with toast. Anybody else want some?'

'Thank you, yes.'

At Karen's voice Fred whirled round, consternation on his face. He clutched at his sagging pyjama bottoms as Lachlan chuckled. The tall girl, wearing a long red sweater and black leggings, walked into the kitchen and stopped uncertainly.

Lachlan looked at him critically. 'If you don't want a female to see you in a state of undress, why don't you get up a few minutes earlier and come down to breakfast like an MP instead of an overgrown schoolboy?' The American was only a year or so older than Fred, but he had already assumed a fatherly air.

Karen deftly removed the toast from the toaster and spread it with butter and Bovril. Fred, chastened, slid on to a chair and hunched gloomily over the table.

'What we need is some order,' the girl suggested. 'I'll put a list on the kitchen wall, and whenever anything's nearly gone write it down. Whoever goes next to the supermarket should take it with him. Or her.'

The house in Battersea had established itself at once as a haven of equality, though making it function smoothly as a going concern was proving more difficult. A rota had quickly been set up for household chores and had as quickly failed, so Anthony had wisely decided to avoid disputes by obtaining the services of a cleaning lady. Mrs Perkins had arrived with recommendations (including one from Lord Boswood) as thorough, competent, honest and discreet. Twice a week she would come and cluck her way through the mess like a mother hen. The occupants learned to keep out of her way, for she had a sharp tongue and, with the exception of Anthony, whom she treated with due deference, would not spare her remarks. Fred's bedroom had been a particular target.

'I'd go a little further than that.' Lachlan saw his opportunity. 'We should be respectful of the fact that this is a mixed household. Everyone should get dressed before appearing in public. Standards matter – we're not slobs. Are we, Fred?'

'The best way', Karen interjected gravely, 'might be to think of your constituents, Fred. How would they react if they saw you now? Would they admire you – come to you for advice? Or would they' – she considered the blue and maroon stripes, as Fred began to colour – 'well, would they laugh? I mean, those are *curious* pyjamas . . .'

That did it. With a strangled cry, and followed by the hoots of his fellow tenants, Fred dropped his toast and fled.

Martin Chadwick, forty-four years old, slim and soberly attired, glanced around the conference room of the new Department of Health, Welfare and the Family to which he had recently been appointed. Delicately he adjusted notepads and Biros at the top table and checked the water carafes. The press conference was scheduled for ten, with a photocall outside the building, despite the chilly autumn weather, at half past. Thirty minutes would be quite enough – too much, in Chadwick's opinion.

He fingered the flowered tie which was his hallmark and sole permitted eccentricity. All over Whitehall senior civil servants were adjusting to their new masters and urging them on a largely indifferent press. It was not like a change of government, he reflected – not that he had ever experienced such an event as a senior official; the recent election had prolonged an extraordinarily extended period of one-party administration, such that, like many of his contemporaries, he had only briefly served under any other.

Press conferences were really the responsibility of Daniel Wilson, the department's press officer, a former journalist, hard-bitten and (it was reputed) hard-drinking, who bustled in leading the hacks. Cameras and lights had been installed earlier; their bored operators untangled cables and checked monitors, relieved that something was happening at last.

It was increasingly obvious that the event would start late. Chadwick wrinkled his nose in distaste. The faint whiff of alcohol which had accompanied the press officer was not in his imagination. There was little he could do except disapprove, for Wilson and his cronies in other departments were not answerable to the Head of the Civil Service but to the chief press officer – another ex-journalist – who served the Prime Minister himself.

As the room filled, Chadwick slid out and picked up a nearby phone. In a moment three figures clutching red folders were at his side, one short, portly and shining with pride, the second lanky, arrogant and drumming his fingers, the third, a blonde woman in a pink two-piece which would photograph well, though she was pale and nervous.

Chadwick had never wanted to be a politician, preferring both the anonymity of the Civil Service and its continuity. No fickle electors would decide his fate. Over twenty years' public service had reinforced his prejudice. The rewards included far better pay than any Cabinet Minister's; his salary scale's *minimum* started several thousand pounds above Bampton's and was more than twice as much as that of ordinary Members of Parliament, with the possibility of yet higher scales to come. Next year he'd make more than the Prime Minister, like all his senior civil and military colleagues. His retirement date would be largely his own choice, certainly before his sixtieth birthday, with a suitable honour and a quietly lucrative career in the City to follow. Not many MPs could expect such a smooth upward progression. Few would ever wield half as much power. And the deal included no public scrutiny whatsoever, and thus no pain.

Even his private life was effortlessly sweet. His wife, a classicist like himself whom he had met at Oxford, was settled in the country where she ran the local WI and Meals on Wheels and chaired the parish council. Her only occasional moan concerned the proposed bypass which would come within half a mile of their home. She seldom came to London unless for the opera, which left her husband in his Westminster *pied-à-terre* free to indulge whenever time permitted. Not that his pursuit of suitable young men had been entirely without danger.

Chadwick swallowed as he remembered his relief that the HIV test had come through negative. It had not been necessary to enlighten his wife. He had been scrupulously careful since.

'Morning, gentlemen,' Bampton started. The woman journalist sitting a few feet away waited for the greeting to be extended, then frowned. 'Welcome to our new department. Sorry about its over-long title, but the Prime Minister, when he appointed me, said he wanted to emphasise the role of the family as the cornerstone of a strong society. I share his view on that.'

For form's sake Bampton delivered the few sentences which appeared on the press release. Questions began. Most concerned changes in emphasis or direction with the new team in place and were dealt with easily, mainly by Bampton. Then a hand went up.

'Secretary of State, is it true that you disagreed with the Prime Minister about this job? Didn't you tell him you'd rather be in an industrial department?'

Chadwick cursed the Prime Minister's press officer for a rascal and a fool. That information would have been slipped out over a few drinks in the Red Lion opposite Downing Street.

'Load of rubbish, that.' Bampton batted away the challenge comfortably. 'We've a big job on here – second largest budget in government after Social Security. Bigger than Education, bigger than Defence. And much bigger than Trade and Industry, especially after all those cuts. With which I totally agree, of course,' he added hastily. 'Next question?'

Jim Betts put up his hand. 'I've one for Mrs Stalker.'

The room shifted; attention turned to Elaine, who had so far been attentive but silent. The hazel eyes were luminous; her hair shone in the television lights. The slight tremble of her hand was barely noticeable. A whirr indicated that cameras were rolling once more.

'How does it feel being the only new woman appointed by the Prime Minister in the reshuffle?'

The ministerial folder in front of her was filled with skimpily grasped bull points on policy, yet Bampton had fielded all the relevant queries. The reference to Roger made her tense. Two spots of red appeared on her cheeks. She glanced sidelong at the Secretary of State, but his attention had promptly wandered; he was doodling on the pad. She was on her own.

'It is a great honour to have been appointed. There are several women in the Cabinet, of course. I am sure the PM has more in mind for future appointments: we have plenty of capable candidates, women *and* men, on the back benches.'

A lame response. She should have produced a quip, something witty and sparkling. As he had asked her to serve, Roger had declared that he wanted a bit of colour in his administration. The Private Secretary seated quietly on the other side of the white drawing room at Number Ten had smiled encouragingly. It had hurt that there had been no opportunity for a private word, none at all.

Betts hadn't finished. 'And I'd also like to know, Mrs Stalker, how you feel about being a "Minister for the Family" when you're divorced? I mean, won't that make it difficult to pronounce to the nation about the virtues of marriage and family life if you haven't got one – or had it and, you know, lost it?'

The hack's face was contorted in an unpleasant sneer. Elaine froze. Next to her came a suppressed snigger. The woman writer was looking furious. The issue could have as readily and with more point been put to Derek Harrison, who had never married. She started to reply, only to find Bampton cutting in brusquely.

'I'm sure Mrs Stalker, like all the Ministers in my department, will be promoting the ideal of stable family life, whatever her personal experiences. Now, gentlemen, shall we go outside and you can get your pictures?'

He had only been trying to help, Elaine told herself as they arranged themselves so that the new brass nameplate was visible. A cold wind blew round her ankles and wet leaves scurried in and out of shot. Bampton was not known for his tact, but at least he might have allowed her the chance to respond herself.

Elaine was not the only person put out. To Chadwick's fury the photo-session outside deteriorated rapidly as chilled photographers demanded changes in the line-up. Only when the most junior Minister had been persuaded to stand in the middle and was flanked by her colleagues – as if both men were merely adjuncts and she the centrepiece – were they content.

Such a reordering of the hierarchy would not do, Chadwick murmured to himself. Neither man would accept it; Mrs Stalker should have had both more sense and more modesty. He began to revise his expectations of a quiet year.

Lachlan pushed back the pile of files thoughtfully and checked his notes. As an American he always felt he was given certain privileges; the chance to go through patient records before ward rounds was one example. In fact he was simply more assiduous than his fellows. The English male students would be shambolic that morning after the Rugby Club dinner. No wonder doctors had a far higher rate of cirrhosis of the liver than the population at large, if that was how they carried on at medical school. The two women students were impatient to move on to study post-puerperal psychosis, while the Asian boys' interest was perfunctory, for there was no money in psychiatry, at least not in Europe. Lachlan chided himself: racial prejudice had no place in his character. But even the most able of the Asians, Amit Bhadeshia, was so darned lazy. Spoiled daft by doting parents, probably.

The session to come intrigued him. Several patients were up for review under the Mental Health Act. Born into a nation where mentally ill criminals regularly faced the electric chair or a lethal injection after years on death row, Lachlan was impressed by the compassionate efforts of Europeans to distinguish the potentially treatable from the sane but culpable. Yet it was a risky matter.

And it implied effective care for the mentally disordered. More, it involved a blurring of the division between people who had committed a crime and were, in the quaint phrase, 'detained at Her Majesty's pleasure', and those who had not, even though their diagnosis might be much the same. For Lachlan the question was not what a patient had done, however violent: the issue was what the poor bastard might do in future, and at what point he could be judged no longer a hazard to the public or, in the case of depressives, to himself. Only then could an individual be released, at best to a competent psychiatric nurse in the community, and to the shrugs and ignorance of society.

Lachlan started: a quiet stooped figure had entered the study room and was gazing down at him. He jumped up, upsetting the folder in his lap. Papers scattered as he cursed. The new arrival, the senior professor in psychiatry, bent down to help.

'Sorry I startled you, Lachlan. I must get out of this habit of prowling around like one of our more psychotic clients.'

The young doctor grinned up sheepishly at his tutor. 'Well, Mr Dunn's file is now in a mess – I'll sort it out. He's up for release soon, isn't he?'

The professor grimaced. 'He was acquitted of that wounding in Leicester, but I can't say I'm entirely convinced. That man is altogether too plausible for my taste. Yet the law says we've no right to keep him unless he's sectioned – since the acquittal he's a free man. If he wants to leave, we can't stop him.'

Lachlan flipped papers back into place and pondered. 'He is a bit of a puzzle, I must say. The reports from St Kitts are detailed and worth reading: he seems to have good empathy there. And he responds well to medication and therapy.'

'Gets his confidence back, more like. You'll have to come to my postgraduate class on release policy. It's secretly subtitled "These we have failed" – should turn your hair a bit.'

'It can't be that bad, surely. I mean, isn't the whole point of research to ensure we know what we're doing when we sign discharge papers?'

Lachlan's earnestness made his tutor smile. 'You mean, is forensic psychiatry an art or a science? The latter every time, naturally. But in a case like Dunn's it's all guesswork when you come down to it. Still, there's one consolation.'

'And that is?'

The older man paused, but Lachlan was waiting respectfully.

'That case in the European Court recently. Highly relevant, though our professional bodies were hostile. It ruled that the Home Secretary, not medics, has the last word on the release of convicted murderers. That's intended to keep the bad guys inside, of course, but it works both ways.'

The young American shook his head, puzzled. His professor clapped him cheerily on the back and moved him towards the door.

'Don't you see? If anything goes wrong, we point our finger firmly at the politicians. After all, whoever heard of a doctor getting the blame?'

It was dark and miserable by the time Karen pushed open the front gate. Sodden leaves on the path made it slippery; feeling virtuous, the girl fetched a brush and piled the mess into a plastic bag to be left by the bins for collection. Then she shook raindrops off her jacket and hung it in the hall.

House-sharing was not quite as she had expected, not least because the other inhabitants were new acquaintances. Older men, really: Karen was a bit hazy about their ages and hadn't liked to ask for fear of exposing her own youth. Most of her college friends were in halls of residence where they moaned bitterly about the outrageous expense and persistent thefts, or in digs with rapacious landlords or bad drains or damp. She was fortunate to have the smallest bedroom in this house with such a relatively civilised bunch.

With the television over the fridge switched on she made hot chocolate and listened to the early-evening news. It would be sometime before anyone else came home, but she hoped there might be an opportunity to eat with a companion. There were chops in the fridge and potatoes to bake in the microwave. Somebody had bought avocado pears which would have to be eaten soon or they would go black – those could do for starters. Followed by cheese, the runny smelly kind Anthony liked. No one would starve.

Which of the other tenants might she prefer to come home first? Which – if only one were to be here for supper – might she choose?

Karen had had only two boyfriends – if you could call them that – one had turned out to be a murderer and the other, Jim Betts the tabloid journalist, had asked her out only to winkle out information about her mother. Years ago now. They'd had a lot to drink and later, at the flat, he'd got . . . very nasty. The memory was still vivid and horrible. For a moment she held her head in her hands. Jim Betts was an animal. If the chance ever came, she, Karen Stalker, would punish him, though goodness knew how.

But then London was full of dangers. These dark nights the walk home from the Tube gave her the shivers. Karen was well aware that her naturally swinging walk, and her pretty face, would turn heads, and saw no reason to hide herself. But that had implications. She ought to learn self-defence – karate or something similar. Maybe the local sports centre would have a class. She resolved to find out.

Yet she was not anti-sex – on the contrary, once she allowed herself to think more calmly about it. She wriggled on her seat and wondered how she would react if a charming and good-looking man put a proposition to her. If he put his hand on her body and whispered in her ear, would she recoil and scream blue murder?

There was one way to find out. A small experiment. Cautiously she moved her own hand over her breast and felt her nipple harden. Then she ran her palm gently but firmly up the side of her cheek like a caress. The effect was soothing but made her tingle. She paused before playing her fingers up the inside of her thigh – even done lightly it made her catch her breath. She sat back, pleased. Everything appeared to be in working order. Maybe it was simply a question of the right chap; and that, surely, was only a matter of time.

Or maybe, if she found somebody she liked, she ought to take the lead:

the best, kindest man might be terribly shy. Anthony, most certainly; even Fred and Lachlan. She could imagine each of them confronting a girl they liked yet being hesitant. If the moment came, she would not waver – she'd make the most of it.

Like a dog she shook herself, then realised that the temperature must have fallen outside and the kitchen was cold. Snow was forecast. She rose and adjusted the heating thermostat and settled down again at the table, trying to retrace her thoughts. Before the spectre of Betts had entered her mind, she had been about to start on a much more entertaining track – what was it? Ah yes, which of the three men with whom she shared the house might she like to come home and share her supper? And maybe eventually more than a meal?

Most girls would envy her such flatmates. All graduates, working and earning, all with superb prospects. No unpleasant habits – at least, nothing serious, especially if Fred could become slightly better organised. Anthony, she realised, must be wealthy – he never mentioned a mortgage on the house – and Lachlan too; it cost a fortune to go through medical school in the USA. Fred was a different matter – he often said that his parliamentary salary at just over £33,000 was the most money he'd ever earned and felt like riches. Remarks like that made the other two exchange amused glances which the good-natured Fred didn't seem to mind.

Fred, then? Would she like him to be the first home, to sit with her across this table, and maybe touch knees under it? It was hard to see him like that. Although he was probably four years older than she was, his lack of familiarity with London, his continual surprise at being there at all and his general inexperience of life made him seem awkward and adolescent. Some girls like to mother their boyfriends but her preference would be for a man to look up to. Fred was a pal, and she could foresee herself becoming very fond of him, but as a potential lover he was not in the frame.

What about Lachlan? She pictured the slim American at the door, shaking the night from his coat and unwinding his scarf. His hair would be wet; would she jump up and fetch a towel, or would that be too obvious? In a house like this good manners were essential: they had to respect each other, as Lachlan had asserted that morning. It might be better to have a hot mug of tea or soup ready instead. She rose, filled the kettle and plugged it in. That would be neutral – appropriate for anybody.

Lachlan was a dear, and nice-looking. He treated her with courtesy, but in the end he was only in the UK for a short while and was buried in his studies. He shared with his cousin an essential seriousness about life which to Karen was attractive but strange. Not wildly academic herself, she had never known the thrill of pitting her wits in an intellectual battle and winning. If a book bored her, she put it down. If it was a set book, she would struggle and complain bitterly. Neither Lachlan nor Anthony, she knew instinctively, would be satisfied with that. Fred would have understood completely.

That left Anthony. He was the eldest and, as she had said to her mother, did not seem at all sure of himself when it came to girls. He was unmarried and did not appear to have a girlfriend. Not that he was gay – at least, there was no evidence; he was manly enough. A curious contrast was emerging between his apparent shyness and the complete confidence on display when it came to his job. Anthony was full of gruff comments in the morning as he read *The Times* or picked up nuggets from radio or TV news. More than once he'd been collected early from the house by a BBC car. His tenants, pretending nonchalance, would listen for his contribution, and hug themselves with pride when he did well, and congratulate him later in the day. The whole household was wrapped up in Anthony's career, even Fred, who had never been approached by the BBC and received calls only from the *Milton and Hambridge Gazette*.

Suppose she could get Anthony to unbend a little? It was hard to believe that he'd *never* had a sexual relationship – he must have, surely. Perhaps he'd had an unhappy love affair and was still upset. A fresh young girl like herself could coax him out of his unhappiness. As the child of an MP she understood the pressures of his job all too well. In fact they had a lot in common. And as the landlord – the boss, the authority – he ought to have first refusal.

Have to play it carefully, though. He might easily be scared off. He'd need a companion for the Blue Ball or constituency events: she'd be willing. It had been such ages since she'd dressed up for any lad, and Anthony was a *man*. He had a fine body and looked splendid in a tuxedo. Maybe he'd buy her a ball dress in blue silk, or a necklace, or both . . .

The back door clattered open. Gusts of freezing air blasted into the kitchen. Karen started, a guilty expression on her face, as if her thoughts might be instantly readable.

'God! It's foul out there. Evening, Karen!'

She jumped up. 'You need a coffee. I'll put the kettle on.'

'Great girl. Thanks.'

The door opened wider and two more figures entered. Karen started to laugh. The three men had arrived home together.

'Right, now let's have the review of the week. Chadwick, what's on the agenda?'

Ted Bampton was enjoying himself. When you thought about it, one government department was much the same as any other. He had been wrong, he realised, to jib at this mongrel conglomerate of a ministry and he should never have opened his mouth to the Prime Minister in protest. That tiff had rapidly become part of Whitehall legend and he would always regret it. Funny how there was no such thing any more as a private conversation.

If it came to prestige, there was plenty to be had in the DHWF – he was already thinking in the jargon. He had reason to be grateful. Under different circumstances he might have entered the Cabinet as the most lowly of its twenty-three members; but the sheer size of his new empire guaranteed his position at number eighteen. And if he handled the job well that'd bring a leap to a more significant department next time. He sighed inwardly. Even in his wildest dreams, the role of Chancellor of the Exchequer did not come to the likes of Ted Bampton and privately he doubted if he was capable of its complexities. Better to make a success of the task in hand.

The wife had been thrilled and the girls had danced a jig around him and flung their arms around his neck. The constituency association had decided to throw a party. Local newspapers had carried many versions of Bampton's ruddy visage, at the count and in the department, proudly displaying a Secretary of State's gold-encrusted red box. It was, he reflected, probably the right job at this stage in his career: high profile, but needing a calm, mature hand. A pity, therefore, that he hadn't had more say in the choosing of his team.

Harrison, for example. A good chap, but . . . flaky, was that the word? And put straight to number two despite his record. Bampton and his wife had discussed Derek in the peace of their marital bed, where he often expressed concern, knowing no words said there would ever go any further. She distrusted the man but acknowledged his charm and slickness with the media. Bampton rehearsed the phrases he might have to use, about a Minister's private life being nothing whatever to do with his ability at his job. He hoped Harrison would have the wit to practise discretion.

And Mrs Stalker. Goodness knows why she'd been promoted. Never even been a PPS: knew nothing of the inner workings of government. Yet there had to be a woman, he supposed, otherwise militant feminists would cause an outcry. It was all wrong, this positive discrimination. Choosing on the basis of sex – colour was even worse – kept good blokes out of the frame. The old Prime Minister had got it right when he declared he always promoted on the basis of merit alone. To the dollies that was a deliberate insult and had made them livid; to Bampton it was no more than the truth.

Back to work. Martin Chadwick was leading the team through the parliamentary agenda.

'And the second reading of the Matrimonial Causes Amendment Bill will be on Thursday. It's Lord Chancellor's business, so the Home Secretary will open the debate, and we're invited to close it. I thought Mrs Stalker – '

'Oh, we can hardly allow a debate that's been opened by a Cabinet Minister to be closed by a junior,' Derek objected. 'It ought to be you, Ted, surely? We'll all be in support of course.'

Bampton would not otherwise be involved in the bill and would not expect to serve on its standing committee. The winding-up speech of an important debate so early in the session would require a trough of hard work for which he was not about to volunteer. 'Not needed, I think, on this one. But how about you, Derek? Minister of State's about the right level.'

Harrison tried to sound hesitant but he had got what he wanted. 'If you're sure, Secretary of State . . .'

'That's settled. Mrs Stalker can attend during the day and take notes for you. Now, is there any other business?'

'Only to remind all Ministers to read the document you will find in your boxes tonight on the financial position of the department following the Budget.' Chadwick had a copy in front of him, marked 'secret': only civil servants had seen it as yet, after bitter feuds with their counterparts at the Treasury. 'Inevitably money is tight. There will have to be some difficult decisions before the year is out, I'm afraid. Ministers might like to start briefing affected Members – at least, those minded to be friendly – in the next few weeks.'

'By difficult decisions you mean hospital closures, I take it?' Bampton wished Chadwick would say exactly what he meant. To make the point he exaggerated his own Yorkshire bluntness. The sentence emerged as aggressive, almost hostile.

Chadwick recoiled fastidiously. 'There may have to be some, yes, Secretary of State. You'll find a possible list as an appendix. These decisions are entirely for Ministers to make.'

'Do they know – those on this list? I mean, have any hints been dropped?'

The civil servant feigned horror. 'Hints? No, certainly not. Apart from anything else, not all those listed will close – they're only suggestions at this stage. But I'm afraid we won't get by without . . . ah . . . a few.'

Bampton sighed. 'Derek, take a good look at this, and put some ideas on my desk by Monday. Ask the special adviser to help you; I need a political view on all this, not' – he glared at the imperturbable Chadwick – 'not just a Whitehall *fait accompli*. And now, gentlemen, it's nearly lunchtime. I suggest we head off out of this air-conditioned hive towards some proper food at Pizza Hut. Anybody hungry?'

Papers were cleared away and the session broke up. Elaine was subdued. Apart from sitting for hours on the front bench during the forthcoming debate – which would involve her reading up the subject in its entirety, in case interventions were required – only one item of work had fallen to her, the response to a late-night adjournment debate initiated by veteran MP Frederick Ferriman. He was known to be in the pay of a large pharmaceutical company, a matter duly (indeed proudly) recorded in the Register of Members' Interests, and wanted to complain about the lack of research on some esoteric disorder. As yet no treatment existed. But, if the department gave way and coughed up, a marketable product might be found. Then Freddie's share options would make him a rich man. Not that that had anything to do with his interest in the topic, of course.

The discussion left her ill at ease. It was not merely Bampton's continued, grating use of 'gentlemen' when there were several women in the room – that was trivial. Somehow she had been sidelined, though she could not see how. Did it happen like this in all ministerial teams? Nor, as the little group trotted down Victoria Street towards the fast-food restaurant, could she begin to figure out what she might do about it.

One more humiliation awaited her. As the three Ministers and the special adviser, now a jolly quartet, argued about football over pepperoni pizzas in the stuffy but friendly restaurant, a gaggle of middle-aged women, pushing each other in timidity, plucked up courage and approached, autograph books in hand.

Bampton and Harrison spotted them coming, exchanged resigned glances, wiped their mouths, put down their forks and waited expectantly. Elaine, who had taken little part in the conversation, was still eating, though the food was too greasy for her taste. A touch on her arm brought her out of her reverie.

'Mrs Stalker – it is Mrs Stalker, isn't it? We're down from Lancashire for the day. Sorry to bother you, but could we have your autograph please?'

It was impossible to brush them off, even had she wanted to: the whole clientele was watching in curiosity, whispering. Quickly Elaine complied, then gestured loyally at her companions.

'You ought to ask Mr Bampton and Mr Harrison here as well. They are much more important than I am.'

The women looked uncertain and scanned the proffered faces. 'No, it's all right,' the leader demurred. 'Thank you, Mrs Stalker. We see you on the telly. Congratulations on ... you know, being a Minister and that. And good luck.'

The rest of the table sat silent, though Harrison seemed to be mouthing something at the women's retreating backs.

Bampton turned to Elaine. 'You'll have to teach the rest of us how you do it. Carry on like that, and they'll be saying *I'm* the junior Minister in *your* department.'

He stood and hitched up his trousers, laughing at his own witticism. Elaine, her face burning, turned away. She had no idea how to reply.

Prime Minister's Question Time was over. A nervous Roger had persisted, reminding himself constantly that his side had won the election, against the odds, so there was no need to be defensive.

A Ten-Minute Rule Bill intervened, with a Labour Member demanding a commission on the Health Service. No response was required and no vote would follow: even as the man boomed away most Members were heading out. Roger could recall as a child a hernia operation which required ten days' stay in hospital, a dismal business he wished never to repeat. These days it was all done with staples and the patient could return home within hours. Of course the unions didn't like it; but neither did the ostlers, Roger was wont to remark, when the steam locomotive wiped out the stagecoach. Change always brought casualties.

He should spend twenty minutes in the Members' Tea Room and make himself available to the troops. Some would take the opportunity to lobby him and immediately afterwards rush to a phone to press-release the conversation. Others, more helpful, would regard it as their duty to cheer him up or warn him of hazards to come. It was the politician's way of pressing the flesh with other politicians, an essential part of keeping himself ahead. And he enjoyed the indulgence of the Tea Room's traditional toasted muffins.

The debate on the Matrimonial Bill was about to start; Roger had left, slipping out a fraction late, and become entangled in moving Ministers and whips while the Home Secretary and the Health and Welfare team took their places. As he stepped aside he was pushed up against first Harrison, then the junior Minister. And there, for a brief, bitter-sweet moment, he smelled again her scent, looked once more into those candid hazel eyes.

'Are you answering the debate?' Roger asked, quickly. 'If so, I'll try and get back for it.'

She was glancing back, sliding to take her seat, anxious not to be late or attract attention. How quickly MPs who have sought the limelight adopt the dull camouflage of ministerial life, Roger realised sadly. He hoped Elaine would not lose her sparkle or be disappointed at the job he had given her. He'd wanted to send her to the whips' office to boost the number of women but the Chief Whip had whistled at the ceiling and asked if he was serious. No more had been said.

'No – not my turn tonight,' she responded. She seemed downcast, on edge. The answer troubled him, yet he had no choice but to nod sympathetically and leave her to it.

Anthony was restless. It was eight-thirty. The closing speeches would be called within the hour. The chap on his feet was a Tory – which meant there had to be another Opposition Member first. His stomach rumbled discreetly. In the four hours since he had taken his place he'd had nothing to eat but a surreptitiously nibbled KitKat.

As usual at supper-time the Chamber was virtually empty. A solitary hack sat up in the press gallery next to the Hansard recorder, both of them struggling to stay alert. The public gallery held a motley collection of bewildered tourists plus four men and two women sitting solemnly together, whom he took to be representatives of bodies connected with the debate. The other seats upstairs were empty.

At last his fellow Tory, a former Minister long forgotten, sat down.

Dutifully Anthony uttered a 'Hear, hear', and mouthed 'Well done', though he had hardly noticed what the chap had said.

The bill made him uncomfortable, and he would say so, though there was no question, as a loyal right-wing government supporter, of his voting against or abstaining. Ambition alone would keep him on the straight and narrow for a long while. Yet the purpose of this legislation – to make divorce easier – was ill advised, if the government meant what it said about shoring up the institution of marriage. Anthony wondered if it would be a frequent occurrence that his conscience and his desire to stay well in with the whips would come into conflict, and decided not to explore the question too closely.

Everything else was going fine. The house had been a bargain, in excellent condition, bought from a retired colleague embarrassed by yet another call from Lloyd's. His tenants – companions – were likeable and easy to get on with, though he wished Fred were more clued up. It was even a good idea to have that young woman, Karen, Mrs Stalker's daughter. She added something – made it more of a home, perhaps. It had certainly been delightful to find the kitchen warm and a meal on offer on his return the other evening. He ought to repay her a little, perhaps with supper one evening in the Strangers' Dining Room.

She was so young. Did girls become womanly by instinct? Did men automatically become protective? How were marriages made? His mind was clouded on the matter. There had been girlfriends, but nobody special. One or two had made advances, but his reserve had intervened: he had never felt drawn and drifted away as soon as they became querulous. A protective shell, hard and opaque, shielded his body whenever one tried to get close. Not that he recoiled: touch with another human being was not unpleasant. But if it implied commitment he was at a loss how to respond.

Maybe the dreams had something to do with it. If only they would stop, he would be all right. It was so strange – the only person in those dreams was himself but he couldn't understand what was happening. There hadn't been any for some time. Maybe now he was a success they would leave him in peace.

Suddenly he became aware that the elderly Member opposite was on her peroration and he was likely to be called next. Quickly he checked that his papers were neatly arranged, the documents he wished to quote on the seat by his side.

'Mr Anthony York!'

The Deputy Speaker settled back in the chair to listen. Anthony rose, cleared his throat, and launched into the third parliamentary speech of his career – the one, he hoped, which would make his name.

Members nodded as he explained his concerns; without knowing it, he was echoing the worries even of Ministers. The legislation did not match either their theories or their preferences.

'I should like to see a return to older values,' Anthony urged. He let his voice rise a little. 'I really don't care if that sounds priggish or old fashioned. We should frown, as a matter of policy, on casual or irresponsible behaviour. My Honourable and Right Honourable friends will aver with due caution that the personal morality of individuals is nothing to do with Ministers, but surely that is nonsense.'

The clock showed he had been speaking eight minutes – almost enough. 'We create moral codes by the laws we pass in this House, and we set a moral tone by our attitude to modern manners. I wish to put on record that I for one disapprove of many aspects of today's society. If by this bill we make it easier to walk away from responsibility then I say to Ministers that they can count on my support only as long as they can reassure me, and others of like mind, that amendments will be introduced to meet our anxieties.'

He looked around calmly, aware of judgements being made on him. The Minister stared stonily ahead, his back to Anthony.

'We should be in the business of raising personal and moral standards, not lowering them, and, most particularly, not accepting that they have been lowered irreversibly. We are the arbiters in this House of what is right, and not, Mr Deputy Speaker, mere followers of fashion.'

He had expressed himself more forcibly than he had intended; as he resumed his place, a murmur of approval ran round the benches on both sides. An unusual number had come in to listen and clearly they liked what they heard.

There was a tap on his shoulder. It was the former Minister who had spoken before him, whose own days of glory were long passed.

'Nicely done, lad. You'll get plenty of Brownie points for that. One little problem you'll have to watch, though.'

Anthony craned around and looked enquiringly into the rheumy eyes.

'Just remember this. If you're going to take your stand on "Back to Basics" and all that, you'll have to be like Caesar's wife. If not – if you're only human like the rest of us – bear in mind the eleventh commandment. D'you know what it is?'

Anthony waited politely.

'Don't get caught.'

Chapter Six

The wintry sun filtered through leafless branches. In the darker corners, street lamps began to glow amber. Indoors on the refurbished top floor of the Department of Health, Welfare and the Family, modern neon emitted an inadequate light, not helped by the cigar smoke wreathing lazily in the low-ceilinged room.

Ted Bampton, as Secretary of State, was entitled to the grandest office in the building, but on his first day had prowled around until he found what he dubbed his 'eyrie' under the roof. He had a point. It was quieter and cosier; security advisers were happy because it was also further from street entrances. Not that anyone had yet tried to barge in and shoot a Cabinet Minister, but it was better to be wise before the event.

The three Ministers sat in armchairs close to the coal-effect gas fire. On the hearth rug were scattered the morning's newspapers, and a fresh tray of coffee had been brought. No one else intruded: even the special adviser had been asked to leave. In silence Bampton puffed thoughtfully on his Havana. It made Elaine's eyes sting uncomfortably. The department had long since adopted a 'no smoking' policy but this was his territory. There was nothing she could do but put up with it.

As Derek Harrison returned from closing the door, his expression one of studied innocence, Bampton's look darkened.

'It's really you I want a word with, Derek, but what I have to say applies to you both. I've been checking through our weekly diaries. Now mine shows, hour by hour, what I'm up to and who with. Yours, Derek, has a few gaps – too many for my liking.'

Harrison was motionless. He had an inkling of what was coming.

'Look at this here. For both Monday and Wednesday: "Lunch – private engagement". I've no objection to you dining with your pals, even in the working week, but your office tells me that Monday was at the Savoy and you weren't back till three-thirty. So may I ask what was so important that two appointments had to be delayed because

87

you were late and a third postponed till next month? And it's not the first time.'

Harrison wriggled. 'It was . . . a friend . . . that's all.'

'As it happens, Martin Chadwick was also at the Savoy that lunchtime with the chief executive of the Pharmaceutical Society. He tells me you had a table in a favoured place in the window and were eating with a coloured gentleman. Would this be a constituent – or a business acquaintance?'

'He's not coloured, he's Asian. And a very good supporter of the party. In fact he was asking me how he could help – wants to make some big donations.'

Bampton sniffed. 'Does he indeed? Then the person who should've been feeding him is the Party Treasurer, not you. You know the rules about business links for Ministers, don't you? Margaret used to have a fit if there was any impropriety, and Major made 'em even stricter. You can't get entangled with anything that could compromise you, or the department, in any way. So, whoever he is, get somebody else to look after him – and no more, d'you hear?'

Harrison kept his eyes to the floor. Open defiance would be a mistake; least said, perhaps.

'And what about Wednesday – yesterday? Who was that?'

Silence.

'It was at L'Amico in Horseferry Road, and Richard Littlejohn, wasn't it? Don't try and deny it. What the blazes were you doing stuffing yourself with that freak? He's the worst kind of journalist from our point of view. You can't pretend *he's* a friend of the party.'

Derek opened his mouth to respond but Bampton thrust the morning's edition of a tabloid newspaper on to his lap.

'Full of gossip and bile, it is, against the government. With the sole exception of you, Derek, whom he praises as "the only original mind in the whole stupid bunch". Congratulations. Who paid for the meal – him or you?'

A protest was in order. 'We've been told to improve our news management and that's all I was trying to do, Ted.' Harrison's defensive words were belied by his aggressive posture. 'I was at school with him. I'm sure he can be trusted.'

Bampton grunted. 'Oh, yeah. As far as you can throw him. From here onwards, if you're meeting press of any kind, say who. Then we'll know the source of some of these stories, won't we? You too, Elaine. Be very careful. Now, Derek, there's one more matter about your official diary, which I must say has more holes than a piece of Swiss cheese. What's this item here, two afternoons this week, for "research"? What kind of research might that be?'

Chadwick had asked Derek the same question when the driver had dropped a hint, and he'd been told to mind his own business. The official had retired with pursed lips and a prim expression. The same rebuff would certainly not do for Bampton.

Derek pulled a face, then engaged his boss's eye and indicated, man to man, that Elaine was listening. But Bampton was not playing that game.

'I'm waiting, Derek. Whatever you have to say, it'll go no further than this room. What, and with whom, is this "research", and how does it help the government or the party?'

Harrison capitulated. 'It doesn't. It's my girlfriend. She works evenings – she's an actress. So I can only get to see her in the daytime.'

Bampton glowered. The answer was no more than he had suspected. 'You'll get set up one of these days, Derek. Some pretty little tart'll lie in wait and you'll be up to no good the whole afternoon, banging away dressed to kill in a purple football shirt or her frilly knickers, while somebody's busy taping the conversation or taking pictures. Look what happened to David Mellor and *his* actress: neither of them knew the place was wired. Nothing much in our world happens by accident. You're being a big fool and it's got to stop.'

The two junior Ministers sat silent. Elaine could think of nothing to say: while in wholehearted agreement with Bampton she could nevertheless sense Harrison's humiliation and resentment. She wondered who would be made to suffer.

Bampton decided to draw the reproof to its close. He leaned over and wagged a stubby finger under Derek's nose.

'Whatever you're up to, do it in your own private time, not the department's. And don't go using official cars, for God's sake. If you haven't enough work to do, Derek, we can always find some more. How about the next session of the Cabinet Sub-Committee on Women's Issues instead of Elaine? It's at eleven next Wednesday. Followed by coffee and sandwiches.'

'But I'd have to cancel . . .' Harrison stopped. The following week's diaries had not yet been circulated.

'Exactly. Crab paste with the formidable Miss Widdicombe should cool your ardour. And stick to Young Conservatives from now on.'

* * *

'I am anxious for you, my darling. That's all.'

Pramila Bhadeshia pulled her sari closer and scuttled out of the way of an overladen baggage trolley pushed by a hefty American. Above her the incomprehensible echo of announcements mingled with clatter and loud voices and snatches of muzak. She could see nowhere free to sit. Behind her a hand brushed against her leg, but it was only an enormous young Viking stretched out over several seats snoring loudly. There was litter everywhere, a tattered tide which engulfed the feeble efforts of the only cleaner visible, another diminutive Asian woman in a green uniform. Construction of the new terminal at Heathrow was causing chaos, with both local and international flights crammed into Terminal One. What a dreadful impression it gave of Britain, Pramila thought sadly, then turned again to her husband.

'I wish I was coming with you, though I am not happy with this proposed visit. The new President makes promises, but who can tell if he's any better than the last one?'

'They say he's a good Muslim,' Jayanti muttered vaguely as he rummaged in his coat pocket for tickets and passport. 'That should make a difference.'

'So was Idi Amin. At least he claimed to be. It didn't stop him throwing us all out, Muslims, Hindus or no.'

'You are not to worry yourself. President Mangaluso has indicated that he is deeply interested in my proposition to revive our old operations there. You saw what he said in his letter: that the lessons have been learned, and the Africans now understand that it is necessary to work with people with international business acumen.'

'It is dangerous. I am frightened for you. I would feel much happier if you were heading for home in India, not some hell-hole in East Africa.'

His flight was called. Jayanti checked the departures board anxiously for his gate, and made to kiss his wife on the cheek. Crossly she moved her head sideways and he missed. In retaliation he allowed himself a moment of exasperation.

'Home, you say. *This* is home, as I keep telling you. We have no other loyalties now. Do you know my name was passed on to the President by the British Board of Trade? So, you realise, my success here is noticed at the highest level. I will come back with many contracts, you will see. And I promise you I will be careful.'

Pramila bent her head, chastened. Winter holidays were never an easy

time, what with Amit wanting to take Varun out on New Year's Eve with his
college friends and get him drunk, the girls Priya and Sabita demanding
permission to go to parties alone with European boys, and her mother
wailing and covering her head every time Jesus was mentioned on the
television set. Devout Hinduism was all very well but combined with
tremulous old age would try the patience of a saint.

'You will bring me a present?' It was their way of ending a tiff.

'Of course. Now will you let me kiss you and go? I'll phone, and I'll
be back in a fortnight.'

Elaine cradled the phone handset on her shoulder and reached for her
diary. 'What are your plans, Karen? You planning to be in Warmingshire
for the Christmas holidays at all?'

'Oh, yes, Mum. But I've promised Dad I'd go and spend Christmas
with him and Linda and the baby – it'll be the only time all year that
I've seen them. Hope you don't mind? And for New Year's Eve – well,
I thought it might be fun to go to Trafalgar Square, and Fred wants
to go – first year in London for us both – so that leaves the week in
between. Can I come then?'

It was on the tip of Elaine's tongue to reply tartly that her home
was not a convenience motel, but she feared making her daughter feel
unwelcome. Karen's itinerary would leave her mother alone for three
out of the four weeks of the recess.

The girl must have sensed her mother's disappointment. 'What about
you, Mum?'

Good question. 'Apart from sending out three hundred Christmas
cards? Well, carol singing on Christmas Eve at the local hospital for a
start. We parade around in nurses' cloaks and carry lanterns, just like
Florence Nightingale. I enjoy that: most patients have gone home, and
the staff make a point of booking in anybody who's got no family. So
we have a merry time. On Christmas Day I may return to help serve
the turkey – the consultant surgeons carve and have the patients in
stitches. If you see what I mean.'

'But don't you get asked to lots of Christmas dinners? Last year you
complained you'd eaten enough turkey to make you cluck.'

'Yes, but that's before Christmas – and sometimes afterwards, well
into January. Christmas Day proper is a different matter. Most families
are a bit reluctant to invite outsiders.'

'Do you want me to cancel Dad?' Karen was clearly reluctant to be
forced to choose between her parents.

'Of course not. Give him – them – my best wishes.'

'You should have booked a holiday away. Or had lots of friends in for a party. That's the best way.'

Elaine laughed ruefully. 'I'm on call most of the recess. As for a party, I'd have had to think about it a month ago, to send invitations out. Good idea, though, for next year.' She did not add that holding on to friends outside the political world was almost as difficult as maintaining a family life. There was no point in burdening her daughter. More cheerfully, she added: 'New Year's Eve is fine – George Horrocks is having people in for drinks and I'm invited to that.'

Karen giggled. 'Take some mistletoe with you and make sure you get a kiss, for luck.'

'What are you trying to do to your mother, miss?'

'Oh, you can look after yourself, Mum. Remember, I've not met this George yet – saw him briefly on the telly at the count, but that's all.'

'I'm sure his intentions are entirely honourable.'

'Hope not, for your sake, Mum. See you soon. 'Bye.'

Elaine was not the only person uncomfortably aware that her responsibilities now limited her options to an unexpected degree. Similar considerations ran through the mind of Anthony York as his train sped west into the setting sun.

The Times lay open but unread. In the window as countryside flashed past he could see the faint double reflection of his own face: regular features, fair hair that turned lighter in summer, broad brow, eyes set wide apart. The Victorians might have found him handsome but today's preferences were for a more pliant, less stern set to the mouth. A slight frown mark, present since early youth, was deepening between the grey eyes. Weight marginally more than on his arrival at Westminster six months ago, but that was no surprise. And he had nowhere really to go other than to his parents' country house near Cheltenham: the only place he had ever called home.

It had been, as far as Anthony could tell, a happy, uneventful childhood. True, his parents were old to bear children, having fallen in love, as they put it, in their dotage – though surely only at about the age he was now. To him and his elder sister they had often seemed so wrapped up in each other that he and Harriet had been left much to their own devices. That had suited both children, for the old house and its rambling gardens were a lovely paradise. In long vacations when the sun always shone he would take books from the library and a bottle of pop and be found hours later, half hidden by buttercups, dozing over Ridley's life of Palmerston or Theodore White on Kennedy, and dreaming of his future.

Harriet had gone on to marry well and produce infants of her own in Hertfordshire. The two siblings retained the closest affection for one another, but in truth most of Anthony's favourite memories were of moments of solitude. It might have helped had there been a brother, or boy cousins or other boys nearby, though he doubted he would have been entirely at ease in a gang of any kind. Instead he could picture in his mind's eye the grave child and youth he was then, content with his own company.

That tendency to solitude had made it harder in adult years to establish a social life. There had been some talk of a skiing holiday, but when he had phoned a few old pals from Christ Church everybody had made excuses – except one who declared himself a committed admirer of Tony Blair and threatened jocularly to spend the entire vacation putting Anthony right. He tried his old address book for people he had known in the bank but with as little success. He had forgotten how many were now married or in firm partnerships. Some had started to produce offspring they were required to show off to proud grandparents, 'particularly at Christmas'. Two couples, together for years, had already split up. One girl alone like himself was much too eager to accept; another old acquaintance, a man, was more than pleased to go abroad, preferably at Anthony's expense, in order to escape the depredations of the Child Support Agency.

Anthony was surprised. The perspective created by his erstwhile friends troubled him. Clearly, by contrast, his own needs had not moved on much in the last ten years. Perhaps it was time to take matters in hand, and think seriously about finding a girlfriend and settling down.

He pushed to one side the chilly muddle of the British Rail pre-wrapped sandwich. She would have to be suitable, certainly: a Member of Parliament needed a wife, and that wife must possess certain qualities. However much in love he might fall, Anthony knew he would assess the object of his desire against a subconscious checklist. Not that he had ever been in love – except for a crush on a prefect at school, which had ended with rough embraces in a study with the door locked. He could still recall his puzzled shock when the young man had taken off his shirt and invited him closer. The events of that evening had gone violently against both his principles and his instincts and the love had vanished on the spot, leaving him bereft and miserable. That sort of thing, clandestine or otherwise, was absolutely not for him.

So marry he could, and would. But what should she be like, his choice? If he could determine that with any clarity, the search could start.

Appearance first, though common sense dictated that that mattered the least. He could not readily see himself with a girl with top-model looks. Any element of competition was unwelcome. And probably she'd have to be British. An English rose, then.

What about her dress style? Any woman willing to adopt the role of an MP's wife would need to be natural in the style expected. Suits were not *de rigueur* as for women MPs, but skirts shouldn't be too short nor sweaters too tight. Not over-modish, either. What was fine for Battersea, where sophistication was sported like a badge, was definitely not OK for constituents at Newbury or family events in Cheltenham. Her clothes should have British labels. Quality fabric in clear but not bold colours. Beige, mostly, with real pearls. Jaeger or Alexon.

With a start he realised this image suggested a woman his own age or even older. Ah, that woul not do. A woman in her thirties and never married would have her own career which she might be reluctant to abandon. Anthony had no intention of playing second fiddle to anybody or anything else.

That his wife might have an interest to pursue, preferably unpaid and uncontroversial, was just about acceptable, but it would be better if the future Mrs York did not work at all. She would have to engage herself in the constituency: that would mean a constant round of fundraising events, lunches, church and charity and garden fêtes. Some she would have to organise and at many she would have to deputise for him. Career girls on several times his parliamentary salary would hardly find the prospect attractive.

Another worry with a woman his own age occurred to him. She might be a divorcée; she might have another man's children. Anthony brooded. It was too much these days to expect a bride to be a virgin on her wedding night, but nevertheless the thought of his future spouse having cavorted with any other man filled him with distaste. If she'd had a bad time he would be sympathetic and protective, but he could not feel happy with the idea that every time their names appeared in gossip columns, as was inevitable, her previous liaison would be trotted out. As for pre-existing children, with the best will in the world he could not see himself as a stepfather. In his generation (and for many

MPs) complicated parenthood was becoming the norm. For himself it was firmly to be avoided.

So a young girl it would have to be. One unspoiled, but sufficiently cultured to be a partner, kind enough to become a genuine support and helpmeet, and docile enough to put him first, always.

His face in the window gazed sternly back at him. How very selfish he was. Wasn't this cogitation similar to the cold calculations of Prince Charles when he picked out Diana? That hadn't worked out at all. Ah, answered Anthony, but I have no Camilla, no great love whom I should have married when I had the chance. In fact I don't love anybody, and never have, so that's not a difficulty.

As for coldness, here Anthony struggled. Of course he was looking for warm emotional ties. But given the horrors of parliamentary spousehood it would be madness, indeed cruelty, to persuade the wrong woman to marry him. Not to mention the damage a public disaster could do to his career and prospects.

It might be worth discussing the matter with his father, though Anthony suspected that, at least in the docility stakes, his mother did not qualify. Their partnership had lasted nearly forty years. Maybe it would be more fun to be challenged by a livelier character: Anthony reckoned that his identikit wife, should he locate her with the attributes so far ticked off in his head, might be a little dull. Better that, though, than a spirit so bright it would be broken by the demands of the job.

The train began to slow as it approached the station. He rose and pulled down his coat and bag. His mind felt marginally clearer. Yet one matter he had resolutely excluded from his musings, for he had no idea how to approach it.

Marriage meant sex, whichever way you looked at it. Anthony took a deep breath and confronted his ignorance. What would she be like? What would she expect? Did all today's young women demand sexual athletes? Would he be able to satisfy her, or would a partnership made in heaven and entirely perfect for his political and personal needs founder in bed?

The train had ground to a halt. He was glad there was no more time to think about it. It was hardly a matter, he concluded grimly, he could discuss with anyone else.

Once back at her new house in the heart of Epping Forest Pramila Bhadeshia parked her BMW, walked quickly once round the garden and spoke sharply to the Irish head gardener about work left undone. With a toss of the head she decided not to leave him a Christmas box. But as she returned up the gravel drive she reflected that despite her current anxieties about her husband's safety she had a great deal to be thankful for.

Not many husbands would have so readily agreed to buy this mansion. Indeed he had taken some persuasion and had complained vociferously about the size of the mortgage. But she had had no choice. Hendon had become drab and common. It was difficult to park at Brent Cross shopping centre, which was terribly downmarket. Essex was far smarter. At Lakeside she could indulge herself to her heart's content.

And it had to be admitted that the house, with its grand rooms and chandeliers and gold-trimmed ceilings, was *gorgeous*. All her friends said so. The children had been stunned into silence, and even her mother had at last stopped muttering about how much wiser Pramila would have been to marry Nazmudin, who had been so charming and wealthy.

For a kindly fate had determined that Jayanti had turned out reliable and good-natured as well as hugely successful. He was, in addition, willing to let her dabble in the business, which enabled her to keep an eye on him. Not that she had ever seen him as a philanderer: it was not in Jayanti's nature. But she suspected that, left entirely to his own devices, her husband might have been full of great business ideas never costed or followed up. Faced with opposition he might have given way a little too easily – many men did. Nothing was more cut-throat than the commercial retail world now dominated by the Bhadeshias and other Asians, so much more hard-working than the lower-class Englishmen whom they had replaced. But that left no room for weakness. How fortunate that it needed only one sharp glance from Pramila and a tilt of her head to strengthen her husband's resolve.

The result was an entirely happy partnership which suited them both. Jayanti took great pride in making the money and receiving the credit due, and Pramila as proudly spent it. Her domestic role meant she kept the family on an even keel and insisted on the maintenance of the highest standards, both British and Indian. All that was still lacking was the recognition, the national labelling of her husband as a success and as the very model of a modern British Asian. That grated; he deserved some reward, especially now she had hers.

The clash of pans and raised voices from the kitchen indicated that her mother and sister were fighting once more with the cook. It might be better to skirt well clear of their territory. That evening she would have to be effusive in her praise of each morsel for fear of upsetting either relative. The cook didn't matter.

The in-tray in her small office would keep her busy for an hour or two. It might be wise to flick through the mail, Jayanti's included, in case anything was urgent.

She hesitated at the item marked 'Confidential' and turned it over cautiously. It was a long white envelope in fine-quality paper. On the back was a crest. Short-sighted, she peered for a moment, then with a reluctant sigh perched her spectacles on her nose and looked closer.

A red crest in an oval circle. A horse – no, a unicorn and a lion. Crowned. Small, neat lettering. With a gasp she let the envelope drop as if it had burned her fingers. 'Prime Minister', it said. *A letter from the Prime Minister!*

This was too important to await her husband's return, and too precious to be entrusted to the vagaries of the post. He would understand. She would have to open it.

With trembling fingers she reached for the letter-opener with the crystal handle she had given to her husband on their tenth anniversary. Pulse racing, she slid the knife blade under the lip of the envelope and squealed in delight as it opened without a tear. Everything, including the envelope, would be kept for posterity.

A moment later the kitchen door crashed open and Pramila stood swaying on the threshold, clutching a piece of paper in her hand and yelling as if all the devils had got her. The three women inside stopped scratching at each other and stood stock-still in astonishment. A large pan of soup hissed unconcerned, then started to boil over. Everyone ignored it. Even the cook, tiny, illiterate and cunning, was mesmerised by the sight of her mistress, usually so glacial, in a state of terminal madness.

At last Pramila made them understand. 'Jayanti! He has an invitation – from the Prime Minister! He's to go to lunch there, next month. Downing Street! Oh, my goodness. He will have to get a new suit – I must ring his tailor. And shirts – where's the phone book? And shoes – and I will buy him a tie-pin, a diamond, bigger than the one he has now. It says he is invited "in recognition of his donations to charities and his standing in the community". My goodness: my Jayanti! Oh, I must sit down . . .'

But she did not sit, and instead danced round the steamy kitchen, hugged everyone in sight, ran outside and told the gardener and gave him £25 and the rest of December off, scurried over to neighbours and boasted to them, accepted several unaccustomed drinks and at last had to be rescued by her mother, apologetic and tiddly, still holding the letter to her bosom as if it were her very life.

She had run out of excuses. Boxing Day might be a bank holiday but the paperwork had to be done: the post office would call in the morning. Elaine carried the ministerial boxes into her study, fetched a bottle of wine and a glass and set to work.

'I should be most grateful if, before PS leaves, she could glance through Professor Sims's preliminary report and agree that it can be published during the recess.' The note was initialled 'MRPC' – that would be Martin Chadwick – and gave his telephone extension number.

Not that Chadwick would be around during the holidays. Somewhere Nordic was his destination, to make contact with opposite numbers in Helsinki and Stockholm, so that he could return to demonstrate his knowledge of the health systems of Britain's new European Union partners. No doubt he would try the skiing and smorgasbord at the same time.

Nor was there any question who was to do the work meantime. 'PS' meant herself – the Parliamentary Under-Secretary. The common shortening to 'PS' made her feel an unnecessary and forlorn postscript. Quite deliberately she had ignored Chadwick's demand and stuffed the script into her bag to be dealt with after Christmas, and not before.

At least she could study the thing properly and tranquilly at home. She poured herself a drink and settled with the box – black for a PS, not red – on the sofa.

Professor Sims's analysis of the pattern of homicides in England and Wales committed by mentally ill people was important stuff. Given that 'mental health' had appeared unbidden by her name in the list of ministerial responsibilities, she should read it thoroughly.

Half an hour and half a bottle of wine later, Elaine was deeply worried. The short report needed more than publication – it needed action, but it was not at all clear what she should do.

The inquiry had been set up following a murder, unprovoked and apparently unmotivated, on the platform at a London Underground station. The perpetrator had had a long history of violence and mental instability. In a second case a care worker in a hostel had been stabbed to death while trying to persuade a discharged patient to accept his medication. Surely, given their known histories, an efficient system should have kept both men out of harm's way.

The laconic prose tried to reassure. Of over 235,000 admissions annually to in-patient psychiatric units in England and Wales under 17,000 – about 7 per cent – were formally detained under one of the relevant sections of the Mental Health Act 1983. By far the majority of those admitted were voluntary patients, willing to receive whatever care would relieve their misery. Still, 17,000 compulsorily 'sectioned', as the jargon had it, for their own good and the public safety was a huge number of madmen. And women.

In any one year there were 600–700 cases of homicide, Elaine read. Most murderers were sane; barely 100 of those responsible were, on average, subsequently admitted to psychiatric care. Of those, many had a breakdown as a concomitant to or even consequence of the murder, especially of a loved one. Some should have been spotted and helped earlier, but had fallen through the net – the deranged mother who killed her baby after giving birth was a good example. Most killings were of family or close acquaintances. The murders which most terrified the public – of a complete stranger by a deranged lunatic on the loose, the sort which had given rise to Sims's commission – were extremely rare, only one or two a year.

'And I will have to answer for the next couple, no doubt,' Elaine mused. It filled her with foreboding.

It was not clear, however, from the report whether she was to be reassured or further bothered by the fact that of the group of mentally ill murderers checked out by the inquirers two-thirds appeared to have had no contact with psychiatric services before their crime, while in some cases papers were lost or doctors refused to co-operate. Everyone seemed to know what happened to the convicted killers *afterwards*; but what about beforehand, when something might have been done?

Of the hundred murderers in the original sample, there were only twenty-two people, fifteen men and seven women, whose case histories could be analysed in any detail. Two had been completely discharged as better, and had still gone on to kill. One had been an in-patient and killed a hospital worker. The rest had been judged safe enough to go home. This, despite the fact that previous violence appeared on the records for *most* of them.

Whatever the intention of the NHS staff, there was clearly a gap between desirable management and what actually took place. Two people's names got lost in the system when they changed addresses. It was also discovered that five patients had not been taking their medication and eight others had failed to keep appointments, thus avoiding treatment. That was more than half – and nearly two in three of those judged well enough to go home.

Rapidly Elaine performed some mental arithmetic. If two in three mentally ill murderers were not receiving treatment before the crime, and two-thirds of those who were supposed to were avoiding it, then it wasn't a question of a couple of inexplicable fatal mistakes a year. Instead most of the hundred deaths might have been avoidable. Nearly two murders *a week* were caused by men (and a few women) who were mad, known to be dangerous and untreated. And out there, unrestricted.

There was a huge difference between one or two unpredictable random murders a year, which had been her first reading of the document, and two a week. Slowly she poured another glass and sipped the wine. It was her responsibility now.

Elaine could easily imagine the howls of rage from Liberty and similar groups if she proposed legislation to restrict patients' rights, and doubted in her heart of hearts whether it would work. The most effective answer saddened her: it was to lock such people up more often and more securely, where treatment was compulsory, and throw away the key.

There was hardly an over-supply of suitable places, either. The closures paper had mentioned the large mental hospital, St Kitts, which although ten miles away served her constituency. The old county asylum was an unloved and neglected monstrosity. But did unloved mean unwanted? What would happen to those who relied on it? Would their fragile health collapse? Had the whole closure programme, which in three decades had seen over 100,000 NHS hospital beds for the mentally ill vanish, gone much too far?

No one would campaign much against the closure. This was not St Bartholomew's in the heart of London with 900 years of history behind it – and even that effort had failed. The land was worth more for housing. The council would pitch to get half an acre for old people's bungalows. If she resisted as a local MP – it wasn't even in her patch – everyone would think she was playing politics. Indeed, it suddenly struck her, it would be her own signature on the closure order.

She turned back to the report, blonde hair falling across her face in the light of the reading lamp. With drug therapy mad people could be practically normal. How would she feel, normal, knowing she was deprived of her freedom for years, maybe for ever? No wonder they would do anything, including lying to social workers and slamming the door in the doctor's face, to stay clear of authority.

The evening was drawing in: it was time to close the curtains and turn on the main light. She rose and gazed out moodily at the dark garden. Then with a sigh she reached up and pulled the curtain cord.

Something was out there. It moved in the blackness – a shape: an eye caught the yellow of the light. She jumped and cried out in fear, then the thing was gone.

For a moment she stood stock-still, heart pounding, then backed away from the window. It was just the effect of reading that stupid report. The security light had not turned on, so it couldn't have been anything substantial – a cat, maybe. To steady herself she drained the remainder of her glass.

Her manner a little forced, she laughed at herself. But before she settled down for the night she checked, as usual, that her doors and windows were shut tight and curtains drawn.

Only a cat, of course. What else could it be?

He shouldn't be out. It was a terrible night to be out, raining hard, the sleet lashing his young face and stinging his eyes. A wild night, with murderous clouds scudding fitfully across a weak moon. Particularly stupid to be abroad on an evening like this with only a bicycle, and with a flat tyre too.

The bike was heavy and mud-laden, its handles slippery. His hands were so frozen he could barely grip the sodden rubber. He bent against the wind as the bike pedals banged awkwardly against his bare shins, and pushed on.

The fact that he was late, that everybody would be wondering where he had got to, added to his anguish. His mother would be worried, would fuss and cry; her reactions were always embarrassing. His father would be stony-faced and say nothing. He could not reveal to them or anyone that the battle up the deserted lane made him frightened and desperate to get home. They would label him a coward, a sissy. He bit back a sob.

The lane seemed to go on for ever. Hedges dripped on both sides and menaced in unfamiliar shapes. A huge tree shook its skinny branches as he rounded a bend. He stopped, wiped the rain from his eyes and peered into the gloom. He had to go forward. The alternative was to stay in the sopping pathway all night.

A cloud scudded across the moon. Suddenly it was very dark. His teeth began to chatter and he felt himself shrinking, physically becoming smaller.

The wet had trickled down the back of his neck and his shoes were saturated. The dribble of water underfoot which made the surface so treacherous was now a rivulet, fast-running and black. He urged the bicycle along until the force of the water against him made it impossible to go further. Then he realised that it had become a small stream with steep sides; if he were to progress he had to lift the bike up on to the bank among the tangled tree roots, a machine bigger than himself, upwards. Or abandon it. He stopped, frantic, and at last let tears join the rain as it slicked down his cheeks.

A voice: a man's voice, up ahead. An offer of help. He peered into the gloom, hardly daring to hope. The wind whipped his thin body and stole his warmth for itself. A tall black figure was coming towards him. It opened its arms in an embrace. He stood, panting and crying, rooted to the spot.

Then he saw . . . that it had no face . . .

'Anthony! Anthony – for heaven's sake, wake up.'

With a loud cry he opened his eyes. Mrs York stood over him in her dressing gown, her white hair in an untidy halo, her face creased in anxiety. With a sigh she sat down on the edge of the bed, and gently touched her son's face.

Chapter Seven

'Leave your wallet at home, Fred. There'll be plenty of pickpockets in Trafalgar Square trying to bring in something else besides the New Year.'

Karen wrapped a long blue college scarf several times around her neck. A large blue beret was pulled down over her hair. She checked her body-belt for money and keys and pulled a purple sweater down over it, hitched up black leggings and finished off the ensemble with an overlarge denim jacket, fleecy-lined. The effect was odd, as of an aubergine on legs. She caught sight of herself in the mirror and giggled.

'No wonder my mum sniffs at the way I dress. But you have to be ready for anything on a night like this. These may be old clothes but they're *reliable*.'

Fred buttoned his navy overcoat, pulled on leather gloves and felt somewhat out of place. Then a new-found confidence made him shrug. If he was to be observed by television cameras he intended to be seen as a dignified scion of Westminster, albeit out enjoying the celebrations. Karen and Lachlan's strictures had struck home. In the winter sales he had spent what seemed to his old self an incredible sum of money, over £700, on two new suits and this coat. As he took Karen's place in front of the mirror he refused to be fazed. He was, he would admit, rather pleased with his appearance.

'You won't be ashamed to be out with me, then?' Fred was fishing. For Christmas he had been given Sue Townsend's latest edition of Adrian Mole's diaries. To be truthful it was the nagging recognition of traces of the awful Mole in himself as much as the remarks of his fellow tenants which had driven him at last to Moss Bros.

'Come on. Stop admiring yourself, Fred. Though I must say, you look splendid. I could almost fancy you.' So saying, Karen pulled Fred out of the door.

She did not notice the blush which suffused the young man's cheeks nor the pensive silence in which he accompanied her down the street.

*　　*　　*

103

It was a hell of a party. The penthouse apartment was packed to overflowing. The neighbours were either present or out of town or there'd have been complaints about the noise, and police raids. That would never do. MPs and peers, especially the younger and more vigorous, needed protection from prying eyes as well as fine food, fair company and plenty to drink. All of which Lady Sommers certainly knew how to provide.

The old woman, it was rumoured, had been a high-class hooker in her time. After a dazzling and lucrative career she had retired into marriage, first with a scion of the Churchill family, then with an arms dealer who had conveniently died a year later, then with one of the premier earls of England. The latter's untimely demise had left her enormously well-off, able to indulge her taste not only in the erotic art which adorned the walls of the flat but in the artists also. Yet her preference remained for the more imaginative inhabitants of the foothills of politics, though she had no objection to an occasional bishop or film producer as well.

Harrison could not decide which to do next – grab another glass of champagne from the tray sweeping past in the waiter's gloved hands, seize another smoked salmon and caviar canapé from the silver platter by his right elbow or slide his fingers over the back of the lissom girl perched on the red silk sofa on which he currently lounged. What was her name – Marie? Theresa? Something inappropriately holy, anyway, given the way she'd nudged him all evening.

The girl leaned back against him, laughed and passed him a joint.

'C'mon! Don't be a stick-in-the-mud. This is the finest stuff, I tell you. My brother grows it under glass at his farm. Best Dutch, he calls it. The locals think it's tobacco. Well, it is, sort of.'

She twisted around and peered at him. 'It'd make you great in bed, Derek,' she whispered appealingly.

Harrison preferred to keep off proscribed drugs. It might be a respectable libertarian point of view to urge their legalisation, and most young people had a casual attitude to their use, but his older voters would disagree. Instead he drank deep of the excellent champagne – a 1975 Dom Pérignon – then moved his hand firmly on to the coltish thigh. The warmth of the skin, the firmness of tone, made him much more interested. She kicked off her shoes and wriggled her toes at him invitingly.

His hand slid beyond the stocking tops and up into the darkness beyond. He was not in the least surprised to find that the girl was not wearing panties. Probably none of the girls did, least of all his plump hostess, who would expect her pick of the guests, male and female, before the night was out.

'No problems on that score,' he murmured, and circled an exploratory fingertip. The girl threw her head back and mewed like a cat. Obligingly she opened her legs a little wider. He leaned over and kissed her roughly on her open mouth, pushing his tongue down deep, his fingers busy.

The party was getting wilder. Freddie Ferriman was jigging furiously on the tiny open square of carpet, jacket off and tie askew, beer belly swaying up and down, his face puce with effort and pleasure. His dancing partner was a girl ten inches taller who was in the early stages of discarding her blouse to whoops of encouragement from Freddie. Nearby their hostess paused to watch, her tiny eyes glittering. Not that the girl had breasts of sufficient bulk to make the display worthwhile, Harrison judged, though the nipples had turned hard already. Lazily he wondered where his fellow MP's wife had been packed off to this evening, then smiled with anticipation as Marie's more ample flesh began to escape from the loosely ribboned sweater heaving beneath him. She wasn't wearing a bra either.

Carefully he put down his glass. Pushing a second finger inside the girl he continued his rhythmic pressure as she gurgled throatily at him. With a flick of his free hand he untied the nearest ribbon and began to suck the nipple which emerged.

The girl slid back on the sofa. One leg was stretched out, her skirt rucked up to her hips; she raised the other leg and rested her foot on Harrison's shoulder. He bent over her, his mouth on her breasts and neck. With one hand she pulled his head back and kissed him again energetically. From the reefer she took another quick puff. Then she reached down and affectionately squeezed him between his legs.

'Nice. Oh, let's stay here and do it. Give 'em all an eyeful. Better in public, isn't it?'

The white panelling of the parlour gleamed cosily in the chandelier's light. Beyond its yellow curtains a thousand acres waited patiently for winter to end. Down the avenue beech trees soughed; the rose garden nearby lay bare and silent. A grandfather clock ticked softly. From the Great Hall came the sound of discreet merriment.

Gravely the Prime Minister poured a glass of ten-year-old Veuve

Clicquot from the Chequers cellars for his wife, filled his own and clinked the two.

'We'll have to join the staff soon to see the New Year in, but let's have a few moments together. What shall we toast?'

Caroline Dickson looked around at the elegant room with its vases of flowers and side tables crammed with cards. A small tree, still glossy and with its needles intact, stood in a corner, its baubles twinkling in the soft light; the big tree, a gift from Scandinavia, stood twenty feet tall in the Hall. She smoothed her silk dress and self-consciously touched the diamond necklace borrowed from the safe. Rumour had it Mrs Thatcher had grieved openly when the previous Prime Minister's wife had been seen with it, but this was hardly public, and Roger owed nothing to the baroness.

'I'm not sure, Roger. I certainly didn't expect to be seeing the New Year in here. Did you?'

He put the glass down and joined her, slipping his arm around her waist. 'I must say you've coped beautifully and I'm proud of you. I am sorry it was such a shock, but I had to move quickly. Funnily enough it feels quite natural now. I can understand why Prime Ministers get so attached to the job.'

'You've had a honeymoon so far. It is lovely, having almost fifty per cent approval in the polls. You're a long way ahead.'

'Don't take them too seriously. Blair did and look what happened to him. John Major used to tell a story about comparing notes in the late 1980s with Brian Mulroney, the Canadian Prime Minister, who told him nobody in Britain had any concept of what unpopularity meant. In their polls he'd hardly ever seen his percentage climb above the level of inflation.'

'Oh, dear,' Caroline chuckled. 'What happened to him – Mulroney, I mean?'

'Him? Got chucked out by his party, but it did them no good. The subsequent election was a complete wipe-out – left with only two seats. Vanished into the blue yonder.' Roger bent to sip the champagne, then remembered that no toast had been proposed.

He hugged his wife and kissed her brown hair. A faint memory of another woman, blonde, smaller, brighter, surfaced but was pushed away into the furthest recesses of his mind.

'We've such a lot to be thankful for. Let's just toast each other, and pray for another good year.'

*　　*　　*

'You're a man of hidden talents, George,' commented Betty Horrocks appreciatively. Around her came cries of astonishment and a ripple of applause.

George Horrocks, white chef's cap at a rakish angle with a sprig of holly pinned to it, arranged a handful of fresh herbs around the magnificent roast Suffolk ham, almost 15 lb in weight, cured by his friend Nigel Jerry in Peasenhall in a mixture of stout, spices and molasses which was now deposited carefully as the centrepiece of the buffet. George's tasks, modest by comparison, had included soaking and then cooking it for nearly five hours. An hour before his guests had arrived its mahogany-coloured skin was removed, the fat scored, patted with mustard and honey and demerara sugar and criss-crossed by cloves before it was finished off in the oven. Beside the ham stood a traditional game pie with chunks of venison and hare lying in juices rich with port, brandy and thyme, its crust golden and barely cool. A huge platter nearby held an Italian risotto with three kinds of mushrooms, while the two vegetarians present cooed happily over the prettiest dish, roasted red peppers stuffed with fennel oozing pepper berries, coriander seeds and hot olive oil. The bread basket was piled high with crisp rolls baked a moment earlier, their aroma redolent of home and hearth and gastronomic pleasures to come. Still hidden were the puddings.

With a flourish George raised the carving knife and sharpener and deftly began to strop. 'Plates over there, cutlery on the tray, baked potatoes behind you, plus caramelised baby onions, red cabbage, parsnips, salads if you prefer – everything's ready. Now, who's first – Elaine?'

'You should have warned me he could cook, Betty,' Elaine commented several minutes later as with piled-up plates and full glasses the women settled in the living room.

'He's a man of many parts, is George.' Betty peered thoughtfully at her brother-in-law, who was obviously in his element as he ladled food on to plate after plate.

'I know,' Elaine remarked, then wished she hadn't. Betty was grinning broadly at her. She touched Betty's arm. 'Don't go match-making, please. You would embarrass us both. He's a sweetie, but I think I'd rather have him simply as a friend.'

Elaine omitted to mention the afternoon at an exhibition in the Mall Galleries sponsored by George's firm followed by a lively and crowded tea at the Ritz, or the chaste evening at David Mamet's play *Oleanna* where after arguing amicably right through the interval, he taking the woman's side, she the man's, they had parted with a laugh and quick peck on the cheek outside. If this was companionship, so far it had been all she might have asked; if courtship, its leisurely pace was well judged and undemanding. Those few hours in his company had, however, begun to imprint the image of George's face on her mind. Without effort she could summon up his quizzical smile, as if he were always thinking private thoughts which might be shared if only trust could be firmly established. Roger was still powerfully in her thoughts. To picture anyone else felt disloyal and uncomfortable. Yet also present, unexpectedly and increasingly, was George; and if one relationship was going nowhere, where might the other lead?

Betty pouted. 'You could do a lot worse. How many men do you know that can take care of themselves, and are content doing so, are complete gentlemen – and can cook like a dream, too? I tell you, I wish I was fifteen years younger: I'd be batting my eyelashes at George right now, so I would.'

Her companion hid her interest as she forked strips of ham and home-made salad into her mouth. She hadn't eaten so well in the entire holiday. 'So why isn't a man like that married? What went wrong?'

Betty hesitated. 'That's for George to tell, if he's a mind to. But', she added hastily, 'there's nothing unpleasant to hide, nor anything shameful, I assure you.'

As unobtrusively as she could, Elaine observed their host, who had moved on and was offering sorbet made from mulled wine, or champagne jellies and syllabub with brandy and a truffle torte laced with rum, or a vast apple pie. Some guests guiltily asked for a little of each and George obliged. An enormous Stilton, its knobbly skin swathed in a red-checked cloth, also demanded his attention as he scooped out portions with an antique silver spoon.

What a contrast he made with her former husband, whose infrequent forays into the kitchen produced nothing more elaborate than a sandwich, and who seldom rummaged in a cupboard other than for jaffa cakes and ready-salted crisps. His new wife Linda would almost certainly be a more enthusiastic housewife than Elaine had been, and in that sense at least would make him a suitable partner. Karen too could live quite happily on junk food and chips, though the girl had recently shown interest in a proper diet. Maybe lodging in a house surrounded by men was having an effect. What, Elaine wondered, would Karen make of George, a genuinely masculine man who yet clearly knew his way around a cookery book?

A bottle of 1982 Louise Pommery champagne appeared ready to refill her glass. Looking up she was startled to see her host's angular face bent solicitously over her. She waved the drink away politely. 'I've had too much already. I have to drive.'

Was there a flicker in that eye? It was hard to tell. Betty speedily excused herself and headed with her plate towards the still-laden table.

George looked down gravely at Elaine and tried briefly to assess his own emerging feelings. He liked the elegance and stylish simplicity of her blue silk evening suit, and the fact that she forced no one to gaze at acres of flesh. Neither tonight nor on their outings would she flirt with him, and he found that appealing. Yet in this festive environment she seemed much less the efficient Tory MP, the rising star, the lady Minister to whom everyone deferred, and he liked her better. The jewellery was discreet but pretty; her hair was swept up revealing the fine bones of her face. She really was a most attractive woman. He wondered how she'd spent Christmas. Suddenly it seemed especially important that Elaine should relax here, in the comfortable home he had created for himself, and be happy.

'You can always stay a bit later,' he responded easily. 'Anyway, it is New Year. You surely can't welcome it in with orange juice . . .'

All over the country, as midnight approached, families and friends switched on television sets and stood, glasses in hand, to cheer the somewhat artificial jollity of Hogmanay. Kilt-swirling Scotsmen alternated on the screen with the antics of 100,000 young revellers in Trafalgar Square. In the square itself the noise rose to a crescendo as snatches of music blared over loudspeakers, with the songs taken up roughly by the heaving crowds. In one corner a lively conga led by two frantic African drummers snaked its way in and out of the bollards. Lights around the base of Nelson's Column advertised the last trains of the night. Mounted police waited nearby, their expressions studiously friendly but mouths were close to walkie-talkies and eyes wary for drug peddlers and thieves. Few arrests would take place in the busy cockpit of the square itself, except of those whose over-exuberance became dangerous; instead criminals would be followed by officers in plain clothes up St Martin's Lane, then challenged near a hidden police van, out of harm's way and far from the public eye.

Karen grabbed the tail of the conga as it passed her and screamed to Fred to follow. Keeping up and still communicating was difficult. 'I think . . .' puff '. . . it's a shame . . . Whoah! That's my foot . . . that the fountains are turned off. And boarded over . . . it'd have been wild to have a midnight paddle, wouldn't it?'

It was impossible for Fred to respond other than with a yell of agreement; hugely excited, he tried to concentrate on the rhythm of the bongos as he kicked his legs first in one direction, then in the other. A big West Indian girl behind him, her hands clutching quantities of his new worsted coat, seemed to have the right idea. A feeling of abandon suffused every nerve of his body and he realised he was singing loudly. For a moment he lost his grasp, lurched forward and regained it only by digging his gloved thumbs firmly into the waistband of Karen's belt. From there on he clung to the girl for dear life, swaying his hips and yodelling tunelessly but with much energy.

The line lurched and broke on the edge of the paved area. Several people fell, laughing wildly. Somebody screamed. Fred found himself losing his foothold and tumbled on top of Karen as the big black girl crashed into him from behind, her soft bosom squashing him. With a struggle he twisted away and for a brief moment his cheek was next to Karen's, his mouth close to hers. In an instant police were on the spot hauling people upright. Some years earlier one such collapse had got out of hand and two women had died in the crush. No one would take any chances on a repetition.

Elaine, George, Betty and the other guests smiled at the giddy predicament of the young people on the ground, until faces swam into focus. 'Karen!' Elaine cried out anxiously, and: 'There's Fred Laidlaw too.' George put a reassuring arm round her shoulder. 'They're all right – everybody's getting up. They're having a ball. Don't worry about them.'

The picture switched to Big Ben as the minute hand swept jerkily up to 11.59 p.m. In the square, movement slowed. The swaying crowd linked arms and started to sing 'Auld Lang Syne' in something approaching unison, though few knew the words. Fred awkwardly crossed his arms in front of his body then quickly took his gloves off and stuffed them in his pocket so that he could hold Karen's hand properly, skin to skin. He could not remember when he had had so much fun in one night.

Elsewhere Lady Sommers's party came to its high point as, having taken their cue from Harrison and Marie's display and bets from other party-goers, two couples in a state of near-nakedness bounced sweatily in the middle of an expensive Persian rug. In a drunken circle around them the revellers screamed encouragement and counted loudly as the exposed buttocks heaved up and down in time to their chant: 'Ten! Nine! Eight! . . .'

Roger and Caroline, George, Betty, Elaine and a million others more decorously raised their glasses as midnight struck.

The copulating couples on the rug reached climax exactly at twelve, eyes popping with the effort, arms outsplayed like winning cyclists, to hoots and jeers and champagne thrown over their flushed and straining flesh.

As the song ended, Fred flung his arms around Karen and planted a firm kiss on her cheek. When she did not resist he took a deep breath and tried again, more deliberately, on the mouth this time, as if he had never kissed a girl before.

'Happy New Year!'

Once midnight passed the guests began to drift away quite quickly, for many of George's friends, particularly from the regiment, lived some distance away. He was bid goodbye by several women guests with two kisses on the cheek in the French fashion that was rapidly becoming common practice, even in rural England. The men, mostly as tall as he was, shook hands and slapped him in a comradely way on the back. The television was turned off and glasses collected. Betty Horrocks supervised the cutting up of the remaining cheese, leaving some for George and tucking a substantial piece into her handbag. Elaine helped clear plates and cover the remainder of the pies with clingfilm. The emptiness of Christmas had vanished: she felt elated and not at all tired. In the centre of the littered table the ham still stood proudly, the bare bone gleaming like pearl. She picked up a remaining pink morsel and nibbled.

'That was some feast, George. Marvellous. How did you do it?'

'Delighted to have you all. The secret's alcohol – in almost everything, did you notice? They'll go home a lot cheerier than they arrived. That bone'll go in the big fridge, please; I may be able to use it for soup, if I still have the energy.'

He did not ask if she was content to help, but appeared simply to assume it. Betty reappeared in her coat, her bag bulging, hugged them both quickly and left. Elaine's eye was on him; many people seemed to like him – loved him, indeed. He gestured quickly to her at the table. 'Don't worry about that lot – my cleaner will be in tomorrow afternoon.'

The house was emptying; he went to the door, called goodbye, warned

111

of the bend in the path, waited several minutes, switched off the outside light and returned inside. Suddenly the place went very quiet. As he disappeared decorously into the downstairs cloakroom he called out to her, seemingly casual.

'If you're not in a hurry, Elaine, would you please fill my glass? I've hardly had a sip all night. You too.'

She found a fresh bottle of champagne at the back of the fridge. With a struggle she managed to get it open and realised her hands were trembling. Its bubbles made her nose wrinkle in wistful pleasure. What, she wondered, should I be thinking? What doing? Making my excuses and departing, of course. I am the last person left. Yet I feel at ease, and *I don't want to go.* My home is cold and empty. It has known precious little love or even affection for a long time. On my mantelpiece sits a Christmas card from my former lover, the Prime Minister, and his wife, showing them on the stairs at Number Ten, personally signed perhaps, but serving only to remind me that there is no man in my life now, and hasn't been for a long time.

The two glasses fizzed gently on the kitchen table as she gazed out of the window at the darkness and the retreating tail lights. She heard George come back into the kitchen, but pretended to be distracted and did not turn.

He stood behind her and reached for the wine with his right hand, lifted it to his lips and watched her face in profile. She picked up her own drink and smiled at him, banishing far-away thoughts and lost dreams. He smelled faintly of food and fresh soap. He was very close. She waited.

Then, as if a decision had been made, George Horrocks put down his glass on the table, removed Elaine's from her hand and placed it alongside, took her firmly but gently in his arms and kissed her.

Thank goodness the buses and Tube ran late. The party seemed to be continuing as thousands of young people poured away from the city centre and headed down the stairs into the Underground. That would take them to Waterloo and thence home. Fred and Karen had to link arms, indeed cling to each other, if they were not to be swept apart.

The excitement and singing continued the whole way, though as journey's end neared and weariness took over the two slumped together, hands still tightly clasped, like small children. Karen let her head rest on Fred's shoulder and her beret slipped sideways. Her dark silky hair brushed his face and he smelled shampoo, clean and sweet, and such youth and vitality and beauty it made him catch his breath. He became all at once very nervous.

Was he supposed to say 'I love you'? He wasn't entirely sure that he did love her, though to have announced, even in a hoarse whisper, how he really felt – that he *fancied* her, and had done so right through the evening, ever since that first throwaway remark in front of the mirror – seemed gross and impossible.

Fred had been so overtaken by his new life and the business of setting up in London that thoughts of girls had barely crossed his mind. The strange Commons hours, which required him as an unpaired newcomer to be present for nearly every late-evening vote, had not left much time for a social life or an awareness of its lack. The exhilaration of politics filled his brain to the exclusion of all else. The dearth had caused him no grief. Indeed he had hardly noticed. Until now.

Karen was leaning on him, humming happily. He was going numb. He pushed her upright, then shook away the pins and needles from his fingers before putting his arm protectively around her shoulders.

The tube train arrived with a lurch at their station. Sleepily they got out and mounted the stairs, murmuring 'Goo' night' and 'Happy New Year' to other travellers.

As they approached the house Fred began to walk more slowly. He realised that his heart was thumping with more than the exertion of the short distance from the station; for he was running out of reasons why he should not take Karen to bed.

The house was empty: Anthony was with his parents and Lachlan had returned briefly to the States. What had always inhibited him to date had been fear of being caught, or heard, or interrupted. Of course he knew what to do, and indeed had done it. He recalled with a twinge of embarrassment quick fumbles in a borrowed car after a college disco; once in the sand dunes on a summer holiday he had managed to go the whole way several times, but the gritty sand got into every crevice and had left his privates sore for days, an experience he had not been tempted to repeat. Never once had he found himself entirely alone with a highly presentable young woman, with comfortable beds at his disposal and all the time in the world. He began to panic.

No such worries troubled Karen as she found the key and turned it in the lock. Instead she reflected hazily what a wonderful evening it had been; and so much better for a proper companion, who had looked after her so well. Perhaps she ought to revise her opinion of Fred. There was more to him than she had realised – he was much more adult than she had believed. He was taller than she was, which was a joy, and he didn't mind that she wasn't dressed up. In fact throughout the long hours he had been quite the best escort a girl could have had.

She took off her coat and hung it up. 'I'm bushed,' she announced sleepily. 'Night, Fred. See you in the morning.'

His jaw dropped in surprise. Did she not want . . . expect . . . ?

'Karen,' he protested. 'Don't go yet. I wondered . . . I mean, would you like to . . .?'

She was looking at him, puzzled. 'Umm?'

He couldn't just say it, could he? Out loud? He could see the shape of her breasts under that sweater. The thought brought the blood rushing to his head and he could sense himself stirring. It was now or never.

'It's New Year. Special. We're alone. We've been out and I – I kissed you, and it was very . . . *nice*, Karen.'

She giggled. She was beginning to get an inkling of what might be on his mind. How sweet he was, standing there, stuttering. Well, why not? It was a special night, and he was a decent bloke. She might even be able to teach him a thing or two, and it had to be admitted that being a nun was a bore. If she were to bring this barren patch to an end she could do worse than here and now. Maybe this was the best way to make a real friend out of Fred. Correction: maybe this was the way to make a *man* out of him. The best man in the house was still Anthony, but he wasn't around, and he need never know.

'Sure. Pleasure,' she said, and pulled off her sweater, shaking her hair loose and smiling at him. Then with an easy, almost impatient gesture, she reached behind and unhooked her bra. Fred was trembling. He stood rooted to the spot before the half-naked girl, still in his overcoat.

'Come on, then.'

She took a step towards him and slid her hands up his chest, then down over his shoulders, and pulled him out of the coat – the precious new coat, which slid unheeded to the floor. Light from a street lamp gleamed over her skin and showed the outline of full breasts and brown nipples. She began to unfasten the buttons of his shirt as his arms hung helplessly at his side.

In a moment his shirt and a Damart vest had joined his coat on the floor. Karen's eyes danced as she ran her fingers over him, lightly. Goose-flesh rose on his arms. He was conscious of his lack of manly hair and the chill on his bare back.

'What you're supposed to do, Fred, is this.' She took his hands calmly in her own and placed them on her breasts, then helped him massage them, palm to curve, round and round, rubbing the pert nipples with his thumbs. He gasped, then looked down at her in amazement.

'Oh, Karen, you're so lovely!' was all he could manage, before she leaned up against him, arms around his neck, put her mouth to his, and enquiringly put her tongue inside.

They stood together and she writhed obligingly for several moments, thinking how much more palatable Fred was than she had imagined, and what a good idea this was of his. Her healthy young body would enjoy itself thoroughly tonight, and she would ensure that Fred, too, would sleep content. As long, of course, as nothing came of it.

'Mmm,' she murmured. 'You're not bad yourself. Got any condoms?'

'What?'

'Condoms. You know, Fred. Don' wanna get pregnant, do I? Or catch anything.'

'Er, no. Haven't you?'

She disengaged and stared at him. 'No – you're the first boy I've kissed in ages. That's why it's so ... "nice", as you put it. But d'you mean to say you were expecting me to do it without? That's not on, Fred.'

He blinked at her helplessly. 'I could go and get some from an all-night chemist, if you like,' he offered weakly. The question had simply not occurred to him. 'Or maybe Anthony or Lachlan ...'

'Yeah,' she shrugged regretfully and reached for the sweater. 'Well, I'm tired, anyway, Fred. I'm going to bed. If you find any, just knock on the door.'

And with that she trudged sleepily up the stairs, the sweater trailing behind her, leaving Fred to watch her retreating body in utter anguish.

Elsewhere her mother was having more luck.

The kitchen was still cosy from the cooking and full of homely, satisfying smells. In a corner a big dishwasher steamed and whirred. A long line of dark green empty bottles testified to the thoroughness and generosity of George's hospitality. The rest of the house still had lights blazing, but it seemed almost to be slumbering.

For the moment she relished simply being held close; he was so much taller that he could rest his chin on her hair, and did so, softly stroking her head, as on the first occasion when they had embraced. A clock chimed the half-hour.

115

'"Had we but world enough, and time . . ."' he murmured. She had forgotten that George the soldier was accustomed to take the lead – and to get what he wanted. He leaned back and smiled at her, the request clear in his face.

She knew the piece. '"Time's winged chariot hurrying near"?' The smile played around his eyes but he did not answer. She tried again.

'That poem is called "To His Coy Mistress". He's telling her not to mess him about. To get on with it – or, at least, let him get on with it. Is that the message, George?'

She wanted him to respond, but still he would not, teasing her, requiring her to match his growing need, to make the journey at his side, willingly. She touched his face, tracing the fine lines across his brow, down the bridge of the strong nose, and so to his lips. He kissed her fingertips, one by one.

'If I sleep with you now, George, will we still be friends? I want nothing more. But I won't accept anything less.'

He nodded quietly, but there was an amused flicker in his eyes. Thus it was agreed, without further words, for George himself wanted no more. For the time being at least.

'Only there is one thing,' he cautioned as they climbed the broad staircase arm in arm. 'I call it "making love". Old fashioned, maybe. Will that suit?'

Gracefully he led her into his bedroom and removed from the bed a coat which had been left behind. He unbuttoned her jacket and kissed her neck and shoulders, all in a steady, controlled way; his hands were strong and cool and it was a delight to let him caress her as and where he wished. His lovemaking when it came was strong but measured and sure, as if he knew himself very well, and considerate of her. It was not until later, after they had rested a little, that she moved suddenly and flung hungry arms around his naked body: then a fire seemed let loose in him and he took her again with great driving power, until they were truly together, calling to each other in the night, two lonely people whose capacity for love had never faltered.

Love. There was no other word. Once long ago with Roger she had pulled away from her lover, sweating and panting, and had thrilled him with rough sexual words that had made him laugh. Her husband used to say 'I love you', but in a perfunctory fashion, and was as likely to pat her rump and mutter, 'I needed that', before sloping off to the bathroom to clean up. But George said little: only at the moment of climax he called her name and laughed out loud, as if he had forgotten the joy of

116

a woman's loving body, moving under him in rhythmic sympathy with his own.

He cradled her head on his shoulder and pulled the bedclothes over her.

'Warm enough?'

She nodded.

'Then sleep.'

Chapter Eight

Jayanti Bhadeshia tucked the ticket into his breast pocket, grasped the leather briefcase more firmly and headed for the departure lounge of Kampala airport. The flight home would give him time to think.

Last time he had left this airport it was 1972. Barely nineteen but already a man, he had shepherded sisters and his mother through those doors into the packed and terrified crowd. He had tried ineffectually to protect them from the prods of Amin's Nubian guards, glassy-eyed brutes who ransacked the luggage and tore gold bangles from the women's arms. When towards the end of a seven-hour delay he had visited the toilet, he had been confronted by a huge African, military tags gleaming on sweaty chest, armed with a wicked leer and a machine-gun. On the slippery floor were tufts of bloody hair and a couple of teeth. Without a word Jayanti had handed over his wallet and signet ring. The acrid smell of blood and urine and terror had never left him.

He squared his shoulders. Those days were far behind him. So was the misery which followed, their arrival in freezing England able to speak only Gujarati and Bantu. He had learned 'Please', 'Thank you' and 'No' very quickly. Life in this sunnier part of the world had been good to them in the earlier years: he could feel almost nostalgic. East Africa may have had a turbulent history, but its rolling hills were beautiful to his eyes compared to desiccated urban England. It was good news that the new western-educated leaders were committed to peaceful progress and prosperity for their people. Or so they said.

The audience at the presidential palace had been followed by the ceremonial signing of papers which now nestled in his briefcase. It was widely if grudgingly agreed, President Mangaluso had intoned gravely, that capitalism could benefit everyone only if it were run properly by men whose first objective was commerce, not politics.

'On the other hand,' Mangaluso had gazed at him intently. 'I am not keen to give favourable treatment to huge multinationals and let them have their own way. The turnover of some corporations is larger than our entire gross national product. I prefer to encourage a genuinely local response to our needs. I want experienced people sympathetic to us – like yourself – to promote new enterprise. We particularly lack modern shops and distribution. That is why I thought of you.'

How smooth they are, these politicians, Jayanti reflected, and how similar the world over. There's not a flicker on that bland face. A month ago he'd never heard of me, and here he's talking as if he chose me personally.

'I am at your service, Excellency. Exactly how can I help?'

The President sipped a chilled pineapple juice. Above them a fan turned languidly. Outside beggars drowsed in the shade as the tarmac sizzled. Jayanti, he explained, would be a free agent.

'You can develop how and where you like. Of course it will take several years, but we seek expansion from you. You can import what you need in sophisticated goods, but you will find many of your ordinary supplies right here, though naturally our traders will need guidance to produce goods of higher quality. They will learn from you. Isn't that how Marks and Spencer operates? Why shouldn't it happen in my country too?'

In his mind's eye, and increasingly in Jayanti's, a magnificent new emporium, Bhadeshia's, rose brick by brick to grace the city centre, with smaller versions in provincial towns. Its local suppliers would grow fat with it. And from success in one country the spread throughout East Africa was guaranteed: a wonderfully bright future beckoned.

'On your head would be heaped great honour, of course,' the President remarked, watching Bhadeshia's face carefully. 'If your shops do become the Marks and Spencer of East Africa then you will be our Lord Sainsbury and Lord Sieff rolled into one, will you not? Maybe that is what you should be. I have met your Prime Minister. I would put words in the right ear for you.'

Jayanti pricked up his own ears. It was one thing to be recommended for the honours list by friends and relatives; to be endorsed by the President of another country in fair standing with the Foreign Office might push his chances up quite a notch.

The President had risen and shaken hands. 'As you know, we cannot offer you any funds for this project. Nor does it qualify for direct aid. But I feel sure banks in the City of London will be interested. And there will be no strings attached by us.'

The conversation had concluded on an amicable note. Money, however, was precisely the problem which engaged Jayanti's attention as he settled back into the plush aeroplane seat. He would have to

119

acquire land not only for the shops, but for depots, warehouses, garages – an entire infrastructure. Staff who could barely read would have to be trained in using computers. The President's virtual insistence on rapid growth was risky, since it entailed areas up-country where barter was commoner than cash. Then there was the question of who expected bribes, and how much, and for how long.

It hadn't come at an easy time. The loan for Pramila's house had been larger than expected, mainly because she had unaccountably been driven to buy a property favoured by several wealthy purchasers whose intervention had bid up the price. His personal guarantee for half the value had been given only with great hesitation. The position he had confidently presented to the mortgagee was not quite accurate. For example, those useful funds once deposited at BCCI had long since been written off in his mind but not in his books. There was the constant conundrum of playing down profits for the Inland Revenue while upping them for the bank – the machinations were beginning to confuse even their beneficiary. Meanwhile the family in India were also insistent in their pleas for money. He could not see his way to refusing any of them.

It was all very well, this assumption that because he had the trappings of great wealth there must be bedrock. The core business was founded on dozens of small local shops. On the whole they catered for the lowest-income families: anyone with a car headed straight for a supermarket. So prices were low and margins tight. A little dishonesty on the part of his managers could push him into big losses. Insurance was a nightmare, break-ins frequent. However much his worth on paper, the fragility of the figures was a source of great anxiety.

And now East Africa. The whole operation would cost a packet. Every penny he owned, and more.

'God help us! They've gone and done it.'

Ted Bampton threw back the bedcovers, turned up the radio and hurriedly slid his podgy feet into his slippers.

'What's that, dear?' his wife called out soothingly from the bathroom. Jean Bampton, plump, motherly and long reconciled to middle age, did not pretend to understand the political world, though her judgements, when expressed privately to her husband, were shrewd and reliable. She did, however, recognise the outraged alarm in her husband's voice.

Quickly she pulled an ancient towelling robe across her bosom and poked her head into the bedroom. The smell of English Lavender talc wafted in with her. 'Does that mean you'll want the bathroom right away before I'm finished?'

'Hush!' Bampton listened intently, then rose and headed for the door, taking the radio with him. As he quickly showered, shaved and brushed his teeth, Jean could hear him exclaim 'Bloody 'ell' and 'They can't have' to his image in the mirror. By the time he was at breakfast and rapidly putting away sausage, fried egg, bacon and tomato with a large cup of tea – she would not let him use a mug at table – his face was red and his expression very angry indeed.

He glowered up at her. 'Did you catch that? The bloody Germans have gone and done it.'

'Done what, dear?' Jean kept her voice neutral. The driver, hastily summoned, would arrive with the official Rover in ten minutes.

'Set up the single currency, that's what.' Bampton took too large a gulp of tea and spluttered. 'Created a currency union out of the blue. Treasury said it couldn't be done. Shows what they know! As from midnight all their paper currencies are legal tender in the countries concerned – that's Germany, Austria, Sweden, Benelux, Denmark – and of course the French are in: Chirac wouldn't let the Germans get away with anything. Next week new notes start circulating. So two hundred million people on the Continent will be using the same money. Blimey.'

Jean murmured diplomatically, 'Is it bad news? What does it mean for us?'

Bampton shrugged. 'Depends on your viewpoint. The sceptics'll be cock-a-hoop because it puts clear water between the Europeans – correction, *other* Europeans, as our new leader wants us to call 'em – and us. The speculators will lose out – that's fine by me. Euro-fanatics will see it as progress of sorts. But it means the others have gone ahead, as they always said they would. It'll save continental businesses a lot of hassle, and cash, and make them more competitive. And we're not in it.'

'Should we be?'

Her husband pulled a face. His businessman's instincts were not to be denied. On the other hand, there was no need to take a stance until the Cabinet's line was agreed. 'Um. At the least we should've been consulted. That's what makes me mad. But it's our own fault. The signs were obvious and we took no notice.'

The doorbell rang. Ted picked up his two red boxes and pecked his wife on the cheek.

'Can it be put right – can we join in, or is it too late?'

Bampton considered. Jean had a helpful habit of asking deceptively simple questions. Many similar queries would be put to him in the coming months, from constituents, in television interviews. He should have his answers ready.

'Oh, I've no doubt we could if they wanted us, though among that lot we'd be the poorest. Makes you think. D'you know the only places in Europe with a lower income per head than us are Ireland, Greece and Portugal? There's some doubt as to whether Spain hasn't overtaken us already. When I was a kid we were the richest – hard to believe now.'

He opened the front door and with a curt nod handed the boxes to his driver. But Jean was not going to let him leave her in suspense. She, too, would face enquiries, in the post office, at the ladies' branch meeting.

'So that's it? Is there no way?' she prompted.

'Only if we have a positive vote in Parliament to say we go in, and that, frankly, is unlikely. How do you convince that bunch of flag-waving dummies in the House that banknotes designed in Frankfurt are the best thing since sliced bread?'

Roger Dickson pushed a lock of hair away from his face with an irritated gesture. He tucked the phone between shoulder and jaw so that he could make notes.

'Peter, I have a Cabinet meeting in half an hour. We're faced with a serious crisis about the new currency union in Europe. Can't this wait?'

Peter Aubrey, the Party Chairman, was unruffled. 'You also have a donors' lunch, remember? It can't be cancelled. You have another crisis there. Our old supporters have fallen away with a vengeance. British Airways used to give us forty thousand pounds a year and now not a penny. Allied Lyons's annual contribution was a hundred thousand under Margaret, also nothing. United Biscuits've backed out too. Do I make myself clear?'

'It seems ironic, then, that we're accused of being in the pocket of big business,' Roger remarked ruefully. 'What have we done to upset the biscuit boys?'

'They claim they're international operators now and since so much of their activity is regulated from Brussels there's no point in contributing to any national political party. It doesn't help that the next general election is a long way off. Meanwhile our expenses mount. So be nice to your guests.'

'Life'd be a lot easier if we had public money,' Roger mused. 'That's quite normal in other, perfectly civilised countries. I can't see why it would be regarded as so corrupt.'

Aubrey snorted. 'Make us soft, that's why. If we didn't have to tout for donations we'd never listen to our donors. And that means, Roger – please – everyone coming today expects something in return. We will have to deliver. Got it?'

'You must look your best. The *blue* tie. Otherwise comments will be made.'

The slight rise in Pramila's voice meant she would brook no argument. Regretfully Bhadeshia returned the red-spotted tie to the drawer and took the proffered replacement.

'I am told that in many parts of the country blue is not the Conservative colour. In Lincolnshire it is red.'

If he hoped by his greater knowledge to silence his wife he was mistaken. She sighed. 'All I know is that when I wear a red sari, even though it is the most fashionable colour, the Tory ladies sniff.'

But Pramila had more than his accoutrements in mind. As Jayanti sat and began to pull on his shoes, she wandered restlessly around the room.

'Jayanti . . .' she hesitated. Then, 'You know my cousin Rajiv. He came for our wedding on a temporary visa and stayed.'

Jayanti looked up and frowned. 'He is being deported? Well, he's had a good run. Our political friends have done their best. He will have to go back to India – there is no more we can do.'

'You could mention it to the Prime Minister when you see him today.'

Jayanti exploded. 'I'll do no such thing. Mr Dickson will think I am just another stupid Asian trying to protect illegal immigrants. I cannot have my name associated with such actions. No.'

Pramila shook her head. 'The laws here are so strict. He has married . . . has a family . . . three lovely daughters. Nobody thinks about that. How are they to find husbands without a father – without dowries?'

'You mean they are not going back?' Jayanti was genuinely surprised. 'Still, British born and educated, the girls will have no trouble. More like they'll fall in love and want to choose their own partners. They'll take no notice of the family. Today's young people are all the same.'

His wife pulled a face. 'They say they are British. Brummies, they call themselves. They have no wish to live in the heat and flies of Calcutta. So Rajiv returns without them.'

'I am sad for him,' her husband answered soberly. None of his new-found friends, as they pontificated about repatriation, ever considered the results. 'But you are telling me this for a purpose. Do you want them to come and live with us, is that it?'

'How well you understand me, Jayanti! You are such a clever man.' Her husband grunted and waited. Pramila continued, 'No, they will live with his sister in Leeds. But everybody is looking to you. Rajiv's wife phoned me yesterday and she is desperate. So please, if you get a chance, do tell the Prime Minister. I have written it down and you just hand him the letter.'

Jayanti frowned but took the letter and put it in his jacket pocket.

'And there is one more thing. Rajiv's business in Slough – car hire and leasing. Very sound, his wife tells me. It has brought them a good income. For their sakes she wants you to take it over and run it for them. You can pay her a regular amount and take the rest. Please will you do it – Jayanti, darling – for me?'

As the vehicle pulled away from the kerb the taxi-driver glanced in his mirror at his dark-suited passenger.

'We can't get into Downing Street now they've put them big iron gates up, but I'll drop you nearby in Whitehall. That do?'

Bhadeshia tweaked his tie nervously. The slight drizzle meant he might get wet. The driver tried an old ploy.

'Going to a meeting there, are you? Don't I know you from somewhere?'

Bhadeshia smiled broadly. 'Oh, I don't know,' he demurred. 'Perhaps you read the financial pages of the newspapers. My picture has been in them recently. But I am only a humble Gujarati shopkeeper.'

The cabbie examined him with faint curiosity. One Paki looked much like another. 'Why – what have you done?'

Jayanti had toyed with the idea of keeping his East African project quiet for fear of competitors, but Pramila had pointed out that if he intended to raise serious money on the Stock Exchange or by a private share placement the whole operation would have to be talked up vigorously to foster demand. In addition his name had been put forward, not for the first time, for the coveted 'Asian Businessman of the Year' award. The result was a sudden flurry of publicity. The timing was perfect.

'I have merely worked hard to make a living. That is all.'

The cabbie stopped, reached out behind and opened the door with a practised flourish. 'Well, I hope you have a good lunch, mate. I hear the food's terrible.' He took the proffered five-pound note for a £3.60 fare and was not the least surprised when his passenger told him to keep the change.

Jayanti turned at a familiar voice.

'Ah, Jay old man. Good to see you.'

It was wonderful, Jayanti had to admit, to be hailed by name in the political heartland of the nation, and more so by a rising star instantly recognisable to passers-by. Derek Harrison's smooth looks and slick way with words underpinned a growing reputation. In a smart overcoat against the winter chill he was crossing Whitehall from the cream and red brick building of the Department of Health, Welfare and the Family. He came up to Bhadeshia and shook his hand warmly.

At the heavy gate separating Downing Street from the public, burly police officers inspected Derek's ID and Jayanti's invitation card and then waved them through.

'You going to the reception? Me too.'

'I,' Jayanti announced proudly, 'am invited to stay for lunch with the Prime Minister.'

Derek grinned. 'The reception's for donors of over a thousand pounds and the lunch for over ten thousand, or so I hear. Your connections must be doing well. Any tips?'

It was only a short walk up the drive but both were early. A crowd of fidgety pressmen largely ignored them; their quarry, as they stood damply waiting, was the Prime Minister, who would comment after the emergency Cabinet session. A casual observer might have noted the two men chatting earnestly by the black door until another couple of guests caught them up.

'I think that's marvellous.' Harrison patted Jayanti on the back as they stepped inside. 'I don't have a lot to spare, but I'll tell everybody to buy. You're a good chap, Jay.'

Cabinet was running late. The pillared room with its red leather chairs and folders marked 'First Lord of the Treasury' was stuffy.

The arguments were heated, but no clear consensus on action had emerged.

'If we give in and join,' the Secretary of State for Defence was saying, 'we abandon all idea of sovereignty. You can't have a single currency between a dozen nations alongside an independent economic policy. They're mutually incompatible.'

'That's right,' whined the Secretary of State for Social Security. 'We lose flexibility. We lose the right to decide our own future. I am totally against.'

The Prime Minister wanted no one left out. He indicated Ted Bampton. 'The problem', growled Bampton, 'is that the only adjustment we've ever made to sterling is downwards. Our precious right to decide has only ever taken us one way. Given a choice between forcing British industry to be competitive and debasing the currency we've always chosen the latter. Where's the sovereignty in that?'

'I agree,' came firmly from the diminutive Secretary of State for Education. She was the sole person present capable of negotiating with her European counterparts in fluent French and German, so had been put into virtually the only Cabinet job where such skills were not required.

'We have to be realistic.' The Chancellor of the Exchequer loved a fight, but this one held ghastly dangers: the party could easily split on it. 'Look ahead ten years. Suppose we don't join. Then there'll be three world currencies – the dollar, the yen and the Euromark or whatever it gets called. Where would sterling be then? I'll tell you: nowhere. And neither would we.'

'Nonsense! We could be the Singapore of Europe.' That, airily, from the Secretary of State for Wales. Bampton raised an eyebrow. He couldn't quite see Aberystwyth competing with the Chinese and Malays.

'The Queen won't like it,' came gloomily from the far end of the table, but no one was sure who had uttered this profundity.

'Oh, she'd still have her head on the banknotes. That's not the sovereignty we'd be losing. Anyway, it's nothing to do with Her Majesty. If we can't afford the royal yacht we certainly can't afford to put nostalgia ahead of the country's future.' The new, young Secretary of State for Health was a fully signed-up member of the pro-European tendency.

Dickson glanced at the clock and tapped his glass with a pen for silence. 'The debates in Parliament will guide us on how people feel. Both Houses, the week after next. If the answer's yes, we're into a referendum.'

There was a stir at that. Bampton put the question in every mind. 'Supposing the Commons' answer is no?'

Dickson's eyes roved coolly around the table, asserting his authority. The moment had come to make his own views clear.

'Then it'll be like Maastricht. We will have another debate, and another vote. Until we get a "yes", reluctant or otherwise.'

The tiled hall was crowded and buzzing. A large metal coat-rack laden with garments obscured the marble fireplace where dignitaries posed for pictures with the Prime Minister. Umbrellas dripped in a plastic bin. The smell of winter was in the air.

A tubby woman assisted Bhadeshia out of his coat and nodded towards the corridor. 'Along there and up the stairs. Cabinet will be over soon, then the PM has to spend a few minutes outside with the press, but you're to have a drink meanwhile. Lunch is at one-fifteen, prompt.'

He was surrounded by faces he recognised and others whose assured manner suggested he ought to. Mostly male, mostly white, though several non-European faces shone like his own with ill-concealed delight. There was a jostle on the main staircase as guests including Jayanti revealed their unfamiliarity with Number 10 by examining the portraits of Prime Ministers on the walls. At the first step Dickson's new portrait in subdued colours made him look dignified, authoritative, severe: a suitable conduit for the trust of the nation, especially in such uncertain times. John Major and Margaret Thatcher followed, then others in strict historical order, as if early incumbents had been elevated to a distant politicians' paradise.

The doors of the white drawing room were thrown open, leading into two further salons. Silk sofas, ornate mirrors, Old Master paintings with elaborate frames, carved mantelpieces, red and white striped drapes, brilliant chandeliers, everywhere alive with a hubbub of people: Jayanti gaped and tried to take it in.

One August at Pramila's insistence they had gone as anonymous tourists round Buckingham Palace. The royal rooms had been much larger, the ceilings high and mighty; but although the Queen's residence was impressive it showed neither taste nor elegance. He had felt oppressed by the grandeur and Victorian heaviness of its furnishings. By contrast Number 10, a century older, had been designed for gracious living.

Pramila had to see this; and then he checked himself, for if that happened a flurry of furious redecorating would ensue in Essex. As it was she had splurged £2,000 on souvenirs of the palace including a white and gold tea service of the utmost vulgarity. She would probably phone the Prime Minister's wife and demand details of damasks and velours. On second thoughts, therefore, he would play it down a bit when he went home. That would be safer – and cheaper.

A waiter was at his elbow with a tray of drinks. Jayanti chose the orange juice. He needed his wits about him.

For twenty minutes he circulated cautiously around the noisy throng. He recognised Elaine Stalker but she was too far away to reach. He spotted near her that military chap, the chairman of Prima, who had given him breakfast at the Party Conference. The Prime Minister's father-in-law, Lord Tarrant, the distinguished banker, was talking gravely to a cluster of nodding acolytes. Everybody seemed to know everybody else.

Derek Harrison was still at his side and had made several introductions for him, usually as 'Jay Bangeshia' or some such variation. That there was a distinction between Bangladeshis and Gujaratis was clearly beyond Harrison's comprehension. Once or twice Jayanti had attempted a correction, then he caught the flash of annoyance on Derek's face and desisted. Yet it occurred to Jayanti to stick close to Harrison, and the two formed a shifting focus of attention, the tall, charming Minister and the small, intense Asian, so unusual in such a gathering.

The main topic of conversation, inevitably, was the currency crisis. The Stock Exchange had closed. All foreign exchange dealings were suspended, but these were no more than precautions. Not that anyone present thought it odd that the reception for party donors should go ahead willy-nilly. Cancellation would have been unthinkable.

Jayanti found himself quizzed politely about his activities and background. Rumours of his deal with President Mangaluso had reached the City: intelligent queries were murmured in his ear. Soon he had run out of business cards and had a pocket full of other people's. Such contacts would be invaluable. But most usefully he was rapidly garnering the style, vocabulary and body language of men whose support of the party was generous, loyal and automatic, though not uncritical and never unconditional. He was exhilarated.

These gentlemen, with their directorships, their clubs and lodges and networks, had their hands on the real reins of power. Many were or had been officers in local Conservative Associations; some were the party's national officers, chairman of this, treasurer of that. Several were ex-MPs or MEPs. They expected their reward, and got it. The place was peppered with knighthoods and CBEs. Many held posts in the public service, health trusts and the like, with honoraria at around £20,000 a year for a two-day week. The Nolan Committee mightn't like it, but who else would do the job?

Jayanti watched and listened. His chest swelled with pride. He was one of them. Or shortly would be.

There remained the problem of the letter about cousin Rajiv's deportation which was burning a hole in his pocket. Sympathetic and responsible as he felt, to present publicly such a missive in a gathering like this, with or without an explanation, was clearly out of the question. Yet he dare not go home without having done his duty.

The waiter nearby had successfully offloaded all the drinks on his tray except one fruit juice. Harrison's back was turned. Jayanti took the remaining glass and placed the letter on the tray, avoiding the damp patches. He spoke quickly.

'It is for the Prime Minister's office. Will you ensure it gets into the right hands?'

The man nodded, face inscrutable. As he turned away Jayanti wondered whether he should have offered a tip. He sighed: it was so difficult to know what to do.

'Here – he's coming.' Harrison touched his sleeve. All eyes turned to the main door and the way parted. With a broad smile as he entered and shaking hands, Roger Dickson led members of the Cabinet into the room, their erstwhile glum expressions rearranged for public consumption.

George Horrocks sipped a large gin and tonic and watched Elaine's face surreptitiously as the Prime Minister moved in their direction. She had herself well under control, but her eyes were on Dickson's face and two spots of colour suffused her cheeks. George was beginning to understand. That she still wore her heart on her sleeve for Dickson was evident only to those in the know, of whom George suspected there were very few – Betty and himself, probably nobody else. Could she have imagined, years ago, when the affair started (and George was hazy as to details, for Elaine refused point-blank to discuss the matter), that the day would dawn when her lover would be the nation's leader? And that such knowledge would be so dramatic, so dangerous? She could wreck the government with one bitter word. Yet here she was, a significant member of it, and cool as a cucumber, or nearly.

To his surprise George felt an emotion akin to pity. What an impossible situation for her. It must hurt dreadfully to know she could not take the man in her arms again, could never gossip about him, nor seek help or advice to alleviate the pain. For George, now that he was himself on intimate terms with the lady, had no doubt it had been a true love match, on one side if not on the other. Elaine was not capable of a casual liaison. Whatever her motivation – and he could well believe that ambition had played its part – she must have been deeply attached to the Prime Minister. And still was.

Then the Prime Minister turned smoothly away and headed in a different direction. George watched again as Elaine's head dipped and for a brief moment her eyes were sad. He gripped his chunky glass tightly in both hands. He felt protective, but the underlying sensation was excitement. A woman like that was a great prize. He must ensure he did not force the pace with her; but, if she was available to be won, then he would win her.

It was time. Shooed gently by junior Ministers, for no civil servants could attend such an occasion, guests began to drift down the stairs and away. Elaine explained that she must return to a working lunch back at the department. She smiled at George in a preoccupied way, and bade him goodbye with regret.

Fred gazed at his bank statement in the deepest gloom. The days when overdrafts were printed in red might be long past, but the repeated 'O/D' symbols next to every figure in the right-hand column were unmistakable.

He added up the numbers once more. His Commons salary came to just over £1,500 per month after all stoppages. Petrol money hovered around £500 monthly but that entailed driving backwards and forwards to his constituency more frequently than he liked. The train journey was much more convenient but brought in no spare income whatever. The contribution to his rented second home in the patch, with every twist he could make, did not make him much profit. His outgoings regularly grabbed more than was coming in and the overdraft had exceeded his monthly salary. It had to be admitted that the bank were right to drop hints.

What could he do? Fred put his head in his hands. He had no marketable talents in the outside world as far as he knew – he had been so young to enter the House and had had no time to develop a career beyond politics. He had no savings to speak of, indeed no assets at all. So it would have to revolve around his current status and importance.

If only somebody outside would offer him a job. Nothing excessive, just a few hundred pounds a month. Surely an MP was worth *something*. It would have to be declared, of course. He would be entirely open about it. And he would work honestly with whoever was paying him, offer sensible advice and information about any parliamentary activity which might affect their future – generally justify their investment, in fact.

Might they expect more than mere advice, though? Fred bit his lip. A one-way exercise might produce no more than a few quid. Would they want him to go further, to make speeches in the House on their behalf? It was permitted, indeed common practice. 'I have to declare an interest as parliamentary adviser to the Towns and Gardens Ironmongery Association. This interest is duly recorded in the Register.' Then he would use the pages they had prepared and press the Minister in the direction they wanted.

It would make life easier in one way, and not simply financially. Instead of hours of research in the Commons Library, not really understanding the tables and charts, a ready-made argument would be thrust into his hands. He would sound much better informed and up-to-date. Over a period of time he could develop expertise in some esoteric subjects which would secure his worth. It might even be fun, along with the occasional dinner in a decent restaurant he could never afford himself. And if he lost his seat – not beyond the bounds of possibility – a place on the board of an associated company might assuage the grief.

No wonder so many colleagues followed this path. It was so damn obvious. More than a hundred of them, according to Lord Nolan's calculations, were advisers of one sort or another: around a third of everyone on the government benches not actually disqualified by being in government. On the other side it was done differently but with the same result: the trade unions put money into local party coffers and expected the sponsored Member to declare it proudly, then speak and vote their way. If he or she did not, there could be trouble.

Maybe it would be more than occasional speeches. Would they tell him to volunteer to serve on a bill, and put down amendments to their benefit? Would he be expected to conceal the fact by using somebody else's name? Or allow his own to be used in the same fashion, dog eat dog? Many ways existed to get round the rules. Fred shook his head dolefully. It was virtually impossible blatantly and openly to put down written questions to the Minister which reflected a financial interest – the press would be on to him like a shot. Oral questions were easier, if only because the spur of the moment could be pleaded.

Yet the whole finicky operation felt more like a minefield than a bed of roses.

Fred had found it hard to believe at first that the number of backbench MPs who like himself gained nothing extra whatever from their parliamentary employment was so small. As he ran his finger once more over the bank statement he could see how naïve he had been. Even without a family to support he could not survive this way: either more money was needed, or he would have to cut his lifestyle back severely.

He squared his shoulders. It was a precious thing to be elected; his constituents expected him to use his judgement freely and without favour. When he spoke out, they would want to feel he did so because he cared, not because somebody had paid him for it. He'd rather be a poor fool than a bought man. That was an expensive proposition but at least it meant he could live with his conscience.

But it would be wise not to trumpet the fact around Westminster. Everyone else down the corridor would think he was mad or stupid, or both.

Back in Number 10 those invited to remain were singled out with practised tact by uniformed staff, like steers lassoed by ranging cowboys, and whisked into the neighbouring dining room.

It was smaller, more intimate, with warm wood panelling, another superb chandelier and a long narrow table. Wineglasses sparkled and silver shone. The plastic roses which had been the table decoration under the previous Prime Minister had been rapidly replaced by fresh chrysanthemums, narcissi and snowdrops sent daily by Bedfordshire growers. The air was filled with the welcome smell of roast lamb and rosemary.

Jayanti found himself seated almost opposite the Prime Minister with the Party Chairman and Lord Tarrant within earshot. Alert to every nuance, he found himself deferred to and treated with elaborate courtesy. His aversion to meat forgotten, like a hungry hamster he nibbled, sipped, nodded, demurred, concurred enthusiastically with what was said to him and generally enjoyed himself hugely.

Dickson cursed silently that he had not managed to read and memorise the personal details of everyone present, though some were old friends and sponsors, including the shipping magnate from Hong Kong and a slightly mysterious South Korean who was good for a quarter of a million.

The Labour Party had reportedly turned down a cool £5 million from a Bangladeshi on the grounds that he had nothing to do with Britain and merely wished to be associated with the winning side. Perhaps had the offer been accepted they would have *been* the winning side at the last election. Such scruples were a luxury Roger could not afford.

Despite the sterling crisis the job in hand demanded his complete concentration. Peter Aubrey had not needed to remind him. The chap opposite – he checked his seating plan discreetly . . . Bhadeshia – had been a donor for some time, but his name had recently come to the fore as his contributions had increased dramatically. Roger wondered gloomily what exactly Bhadeshia hoped for in return. The man's eagerness to please and the fawning way he agreed with Peter suggested it was not a safe seat in Parliament or help with the Customs and Excise.

Perhaps Mr Bhadeshia wanted to be loved. Respected, certainly: Roger had no qualms about that. Having started life in a family with no shares, no cars, no home ownership and no opportunity, the Prime Minister had a healthy respect for anyone who had built financial success from nothing. He was familiar with the Bhadeshia history and after a well-placed question was soon better informed about his guest's burgeoning commercial prospects. He chuckled quietly to himself. If the future was as rosy as Bhadeshia painted it he'd have no trouble being loved. Wealth always attracted admiration as well as jealousy, but with luck would be followed not long after, normally, by recognition and adulation.

And honour. Maybe an appearance in the honours list would please Mr Bhadeshia and keep his money rolling in? Needs must, and it was the easiest response, entirely within his control. It was hard to tell with these people. Dickson fixed Jayanti's face firmly in his mind, and turned with a suppressed sigh to his neighbour.

The rain had stopped but a cold wind blew down Whitehall, skittering leaves, flapping trouser legs, wriggling unwelcome inside thin jackets. The press had vanished. A few tourists consulted sodden maps and shivered. George Horrocks hesitated, then buttoned up his overcoat and turned left.

As he entered Trafalgar Square he bought a copy of the *Evening Standard*. Its huge headline – 'ECU CRISIS' – told too little; the story explored only the political implications, the blow to British sensitivities, the government's fury that the French and Germans appeared to have stitched everything up. Patriotism galore but little of substance, George rapidly decided. Realism was too much to expect.

He turned to the pink sheets of city coverage. Alarm bells rang there loud and clear. A company such as Prima, operating across frontiers and keen to grow, would have to decide quickly whether to calculate in sterling, dollars or this new international currency. Accountants and financial advisers, he had no doubt, had cancelled their lunchtime engagements and were working feverishly on it. Maybe he should have done the same?

Yet to have been in Downing Street at such a juncture, to have caught that flicker of worry on the PM's face, to have heard the hints about Cabinet splits and uncertainties had been worth any quantity of virtuous sandwiches. Moreover, the contacts, in business terms, had been superb – such as Lord Tarrant, who had confirmed an invitation to George to join the board of his bank. That would be a tremendous step up. George was not bothered about the additional £25,000 that would bring him but anticipated learning a great deal about international finance. In return he planned to encourage his new friends to take more interest in the fast-moving cable industry. At the moment their complacent ignorance left the Americans with all the juicy options.

Then there was Bhadeshia, who had promised a prospectus on this new share issue for his overseas activities. Now that South Africa's politics had settled down and Rwanda and Sudan and Ethiopia had run out of citizens to slaughter, an uneasy calm had descended over much of Africa. The result was an inviting water-hole into which smart operators were dipping their snouts. That scheme, handled well, could be a tremendous goer.

George squinted up at the sky: the rain would hold off a while yet. One other countenance had pleased him mightily. It had been good to see Elaine, and firmly to insist that she came for dinner at his house on Saturday. She was not the easiest lady to court.

Chapter Nine

In an unguarded moment Mr Bulstrode would confess that he enjoyed his rota at the MP's surgery. Now that his days as the local bank manager were over his position as Fred's chairman had revived his air of natural authority. Saturday mornings would find him, clipboard in hand, scurrying around inside the draughty village hall, ticking off names and ordering this person or that to sit and wait. Supplicants and complainants alike would be treated with a mixture of suspicion and disdain. Mr Bulstrode would then usher them into the inner room and the great elected presence, where all problems would be resolved.

At least, that was the idea, he reflected grimly as Mrs Hepworth's shrill voice penetrated the thin partition. This was her third appointment with the new MP. The young lad was making heavy weather of it. The previous Member, wily Sir Nigel, had eventually given instructions that the list was to be full when she phoned. Bulstrode glanced up. New arrivals were becoming restless. He rose, coughed discreetly and tapped on the door.

Fred's agitated face appeared. 'What is it?'

'Your next lot's here, and the ones after that too. If you don't shift the old biddy soon you'll lose more votes than you're gaining.'

'She has a lot of worries,' Fred protested. 'Her two sons are in prison, and there's what she calls the Social, and her granddaughter's been suspended from school . . .'

'Aye, I'll bet.' The Hepworths were well known. Bulstrode tried to peer inside but Fred hung on to the handle. As he closed the door once more he caught Bulstrode's parting shot – 'Has she told you yet about her six Rottweilers?'

Fred returned to the small desk. He sat and pressed his fingertips together in what he hoped was a mature pose. Mrs Hepworth, large, shapeless and not very clean, was still gabbling angrily. He had the uneasy sense that he had missed an important piece of the story. She paused for breath: it was now or never.

'Er ... yes. But what I'm not clear about, Mrs Hepworth, is what exactly you feel I could do?'

The woman glared at him. 'Do? I don't suppose there's anything you can *do*, Mr Laidlaw. Nobody's ever been able to *do* much for me, not since my husband died.'

Fred blanched at the possibility that he was about to hear the late Mr Hepworth's grievances as well. He rose hastily.

'Well, then, Mrs Hepworth. I hope you've found our discussion useful. Do contact me again.' And he propelled her out, still whining.

It was to be another hour before an exhausted Fred staggered into Milton Conservative Club and leaned heavily on the bar. Stolid faces indicated that he was to buy the next round. Wearily he obliged, then with relief downed half his pint. He began to flip through his notes.

'If I'd realised ...' he started, then stopped. Everyone in the club, Bulstrode and the steward included, believed MPs were overpaid and underworked. There was no sympathy to be had.

He tried again. 'I wish there was a course on how to be an effective MP,' he said. 'Look at this lot – three people bothered about pensions or social security, one's got gypsies in his garden, two would like the taxman hung up by his toenails, and thirteen people brought a petition against that new planning development. And everybody thinks I have a magic wand.'

'Ah, that planning application,' murmured Bulstrode. 'I meant to have a word with you about that.'

'Don't worry, I've got that one clear,' Fred assured him. 'I'll oppose it strongly, I told them.'

'I hope you won't,' was the ominous reply. 'The developer's my brother-in-law. So go easy, will you?'

The problem, Fred had to admit as he drove away, was not so much his ignorance or inexperience but the expectations of his electorate. That worked two ways.

Partly it was politicians' own fault. Elections were fought and won over who made the most plausible promises. Were the contests conducted on a more realistic level then voters might demand less afterwards and probably end up much more satisfied. But there was a fat chance of that ever happening.

Meanwhile it was widely believed that MPs had greater authority than a court of last resort; that they were omnipotent. Thus if a visit to the

MP produced nothing effective it was the MP's fault. It had not taken Fred long to recognise that in fact he had no power to compel anyone to do anything; throwing his weight around was mostly a waste of time. The best he could manage was to pass on queries, suitably articulated on House of Commons notepaper, to those who did so jealously guard the right to decide. He was no more than a jumped-up postbox. The realisation had left him feeling distinctly deflated.

Fred sighed. The frustrating first year as a constituency Member had flattened his enthusiasm in more ways than one. He had slowly learned not to give his own opinion too readily. His honesty had got him into difficulties and he would have to hold his tongue more. Obfuscation was the name of the game. No wonder the profession was so despised.

It was beginning to rain. He switched on the windscreen wipers and wished he hadn't had that second half; in due course he would have to stop and add a further delay to his journey back to London. At least the rest of the weekend was free. He let his mind roam ahead, and wondered if anybody would be in the Battersea house and available for a comradely evening.

He swallowed hard. Suppose it was Karen? How would she react, if he suggested going out together? True, she did not seem to harbour any grudges about the New Year's Eve débâcle; she had not mentioned it once. But Fred was deeply conscious of his loss of face with her that night. The memory made him cringe with embarrassment – if only he had thought ahead he might by now have been her regular boyfriend. Instead he had seen her glance more than once across the breakfast table at Anthony and smile happily if the look was returned.

Fred wasn't jealous so much as laid low by his own naïvety and incompetence. Yet the image of Karen minus her sweater under the hall light on New Year's Eve, lovely warm glowing Karen, ready to press up against him and to lead him upstairs – even as he drove, the picture made his head swim and his manhood respond.

He would try again with her; he must. He had visited a chemist and provided himself with the necessary requisites. The woman at the checkout had not even looked up when he had made his purchase. Pride, and his increasing need to share his doubts and fears about his strange life, demanded a real friend, preferably a bed friend. Someone to have fun with, who might understand and offer a murmur of support on the pillow in the deepest recesses of the night. Surely it wasn't too much to ask?

A huge artic surged past and drenched the windscreen in spray. Fred slowed and began to look for a service station. Let the silly bastard in that lorry take risks in this weather; he, Fred Laidlaw, had too much to live for. Next time the chance came, he would be ready.

The columns did not add up. Jayanti Bhadeshia bit his lower lip and tried for the fourth time. That something was wrong he was sure: the group had thirty shops in North London with much the same turnover; twenty-eight of them seemed to be performing satisfactorily, yet in these two in King's Cross there had been a sharp drop.

It could mean only one thing: he was being robbed.

What a bloody nuisance, on top of everything else. Those lost deposits at the Bank of Credit and Commerce International would have been so handy, especially since the bulk had never been accounted for to the Inland Revenue. That several of the known thieves had been jailed was hardly consolation. If Pramila knew how their fortune had been so drastically depleted by that unfortunate collapse, she would have been shocked and hysterical for days.

Nor had he kept her fully informed about the potential losses of Rajiv's car hire company. Rajiv had returned weeping to India; the Prime Minister's office had sent a baldly worded letter of regret that nothing could be done to bring him back. But the firm's finances had turned out to be a disaster. In accepting his family duties Jayanti had found himself the principal underwriter of a small insurance operation on the side. The books there were a complete fantasy. Claimants were queuing up but instalments had ground to a halt. Meanwhile a steady stream of guaranteed payments went to Rajiv's grieving family, leaving Jayanti ever further in the red. He fretted that he could not tell Pramila and seek her advice: to do so would seem like a reproach.

And interest rates were about to rise once more. He cursed again. That was fine if you were in funds, awful if you were a net borrower; and try as he might it began to appear that his liabilities threatened to exceed his easily realisable assets. That was not a comfortable position. In fact it was not a happy situation at all.

He had worked so hard and been so successful that the effects of other people's incompetence and criminality were that much harder to bear. Yet his fortunes were still to be made: the biggest project of all was at last under way. Beneath the ledgers and dockets on his untidy desk nestled the glossy prospectus of the East African project with the artist's impression of Bhadeshia's Emporium in downtown Kampala.

Work had commenced and stage payments were due. With luck it would be a gold-mine.

Jayanti found himself sweating despite the cool of the evening. A sense of panic touched his heart but he pushed it roughly away. His whole career had depended on his calmness under pressure; his family's prosperity and status in the world were his responsibility and he would not let them down.

He squared his shoulders. How could he fail? He, who had so recently dined with the Prime Minister, who knew Ministers and lords by name, who was a friend of presidents and a respected adviser to governments? The idea was unthinkable.

On the contrary: his political contacts were yielding fruit. Wasn't he in demand tonight at a Conservative businessmen's dinner at Lord Tarrant's private house in Lord North Street? He must take a few prospectuses with him. In a minute he would have to change into evening dress. Financially he might be skating on thin ice, but plenty of willing hands were extended to bring him safely to solid ground. White hands, establishment names: people who for the party's sake could not let him sink.

Such distinguished personages would not, however, approve if he ignored a straightforward matter of theft, probably by his own employees. Pramila too would expect him to tackle the matter head on. He looked out of the window. It was late afternoon and raining. He could deal with it on his way in to Westminster.

In a small flat in North London Jim Betts tapped laboriously at his laptop and cursed. Weaned on shorthand and grubby notepads he was still not at ease with the hissing luminosity of the small screen. Sometimes one of his fingers hit a wrong key and the screen would go dark. When he managed to recover his position the last eight or ten sentences, so carefully crafted, would have vanished. That never happened in the days of pen and paper.

He had had no choice but to master the damn thing. The *Globe* was a modern operator and the gadget had a modem: all he needed to do was plug it into a phone socket and press the right combination of buttons; then the text would magically transfer to some other idiot's screen, without any of the clutter – or reassuring certainty – of hard copy.

He reached across the table and swore again. No cigarettes. That made the task in hand not merely difficult but impossible. He pressed 'save', satisfied himself that the machine was on standby, collected his jacket and headed for the nearest tobacconist.

As he pushed open the shop door it was apparent that some kind of row was in train. He liked this shop; it was unpretentious and friendly. It had had a succession of managers, mostly, like the current incumbent, blokes in reduced circumstances, Irish or ex-pugilists.

'Look, Mr Patel, you gotta understand.' The young shopkeeper pulled lazily at his pony-tail as he tried to explain.

'My name is not Patel, it is Bhadeshia. I have told you that before.' Jayanti, his bow-tie askew, dress shirt rumpled, was seething. The shop was dirty and it was evident from dates on the crisp boxes that proper stock rotation was being ignored. The manager was supposed to get a cut of profits, but he was expected to make the profits first, and not by playing games with the health inspectors.

Betts waited, enjoying the scene. It did him good to see a dressed-up Asian twerp being put in his place.

Jayanti glanced over his shoulder. 'You had better serve this customer. Then you can tell me where the gross is going.'

Pony-tail knew Betts's preference and wordlessly reached for a couple of packets. A five-pound note changed hands; coins tinkled on the glass counter. Betts moved away into a corner, unwrapped his purchase and examined a rack of girlie magazines.

'This is a heavy area, Mr Patel,' Pony-tail hissed. 'We get geezers coming in I gotta look after, see? Or they'll drive a van into that plate-glass window and nick the lot. One big bust here, and you'll be red-lined. So see it as a kind of insurance.'

Jayanti winced. He had trouble enough persuading respectable insurers to accept his shops as risks. The advent of less reliable versions was most unwelcome.

He should call the police – set up an undercover operation. Recruit a tough nephew, one versed in the martial arts, to replace this artful dodger and ensure the capture of whichever small-time gang was running the protection racket. He looked into Pony-tail's face: the young man returned a stare of such insolence that Jayanti recoiled in disgust.

'And what you should remember is that a businessman is only interested in a business as long as it contributes, not if it sucks money away from more valuable projects,' he warned. Take too much, he was saying, and I'll close the place.

As Jayanti pulled his cashmere overcoat closer around him and pulled open the door to the street, Betts half turned towards Pony-tail and caught his eye. 'Trouble, these Pakis, aren't they?' he remarked casually.

The manager glanced at Jayanti's retreating back, waited till the door clanged shut, shrugged, and tossed Betts over a couple of free packets.

'Minister? I have your draft diary for next week. If you'd kindly glance through it . . .?'

Elaine finished wiping off the television make-up. 'The worst thing about breakfast TV is having to rise at six o'clock and be bright and cheery when the world at large feels like death warmed up, but it does impress the electors,' she commented. 'The best is having a complete make-over at a time when I can't see straight. But today they overdid it.'

Fiona Murray waited quietly. She had expected a promotion after two years in charge of a Minister's office at the same junior level and felt put out, to her own discomfort, at having a woman boss instead. The senior ranks of the Civil Service were still predominantly male: status and praise for an ambitious woman official such as herself would be earned by coping well with a male master, the more difficult and macho the better. To be bag-carrier to another woman was like wearing vanishing cream.

Elaine flicked through the pink pages, consulted her pocket diary and exclaimed in anger and despair, 'But I said I couldn't do the Frost show! It's a Sunday, which means I lose my only part-day off; and it's in London, so not worth going home again. And it ought to be the Secretary of State doing it – a long prime-time interview, on all aspects of policy — '

'I think he feels the same way as you do about his Sundays, Minister,' Fiona remarked delicately.

Elaine chewed her lip. 'And I thought I asked for a pre-meeting before next week's nurses' conference – or am I to go straight in without a moment's reflection on what I'm to say?'

'There's not really any time. Your diary's rather full. But officials will brief you the day before, if you wish.'

'That'll give me no time to change anything. I'll be making your speech, not mine.' It couldn't be helped: as a newcomer Elaine was keenly aware of her lack of expertise to argue with staffers for whom detailed policy was meat and drink. Yet she was troubled that without a considerable effort she would become merely their mouthpiece. Perhaps that was the intention. 'Will there be questions after? Better keep them to a minimum.'

'It might help, Minister, if you did feel able to spend the occasional weekend in London. There are still many engagements here that you turn down. And although Mr Harrison has a London seat he is not always . . . ah . . . available for duty.'

I am not standing in for that lazy bugger any longer, reflected Elaine grimly. *I am certainly not going to let down my constituents in order to cover for him.* She wondered whether to voice her mutiny aloud, glanced at Fiona's composed face with its disciplined superiority and thought better of it.

'I think I'm going to minute the Secretary of State,' Elaine decided at last. 'My diary's crackers; by the time I'm driven back to my flat on Thursday nights I've done sixty solid hours, not counting the boxes, with another couple of fifteen-hour days on Friday and Saturday, and you're planning to bag Sundays too. I'll ask his permission to cut down a bit.'

Fiona maintained her diplomatic silence. Elaine sensed her disapproval and threw the papers down with a weary gesture.

'Don't you see? It's not on. I'll crack up, or lose my cool in public. Or get fed up. Worst of all, I'll start making mistakes. Nobody wants that, do they?'

The *Globe* was not one of the great movers and shakers, it had to be admitted. It drifted along in modest profit, aiming for readership gaps between the *Daily Mail, Daily Mirror* and the *Sun,* for those customers too simple-minded for the first, too right-wing for the second and two fastidious for the third. The *Globe* was keen on the environment and global warming and natural foods; in favour of a united Ireland by referendum and a disunited Europe by the same means. Articles abounded on staving off middle age, value for money in second-hand cars and home decoration. Not for the *Globe* exposed breasts and buttocks; their female readers would take offence.

Nevertheless the newspaper prided itself on sensing the pulse of the nation. More than once a campaign derided by rivals had taken off, resulting in increased circulation and delighted advertising agencies. The pressure was on its staff to come up with original ideas. That included Nick Thwaite, news editor, in the chair at the morning editorial conference, and Jim Betts, investigative reporter *extraordinaire* and Thwaite's deputy.

Suggestions of varied degrees of dottiness and gravity had been considered, sifted, rejected. The plague of newts in East Anglia had been overdone. The wilder sexual behaviour of MPs was old hat: either they'd been caught out or had learned to cover their tracks more effectively. Lady Bienvenida Buck was only of future interest if she *married* Max Clifford. Even 'My son's father is a priest' stories were ten a penny, though such peccadilloes went down well in the Irish edition. Betts reached for a cigarette; thoughtfully he examined the packet, then interrupted with a chortle.

'I've got it: we ought to look at Asians in Britain,' he announced. 'Bloody successful, lots of them. I read somewhere that they own ninety-five per cent of all the independent shops within the M25 area. Now they're moving on, multi-millionaires, coining it. And they want their share.'

Thwaite frowned; Betts cast a sidelong glance at his boss.

'Oh, we'd dress it up, sure. Talk about their contribution to British life and so on. Praise them to the skies. Tell 'em we think it's about time their efforts were recognised, that sort of thing, so we'd get plenty of interviews, photos in their houses. That'd tell us a thing or two about lifestyles. Open a few eyes.'

He leaned forward and jabbed a finger in the air. 'Corner shops, for instance. Young children work there. Late-night groceries. Cash and carries. Textile companies – bet we'll find a few sweatshops, no fire regulations, the odd illegal immigrant. Plenty of material for a hard-hitting newspaper. And we don't have to use it all at once, of course.'

'You're an unpleasant bastard at times, Jim,' Thwaite parried mildly.

Betts was not to be deterred; his voice took on a self-righteous tone. 'They come to this country but do they keep to the rules? Pay their taxes and National Insurance like the law says? What about all those relatives they employ – are they legit? How many jobs are they taking away from the rest of us? Lots of questions there.'

'How would you avoid a whiff of racism, Jim? We have guidelines about that and the owner doesn't like it.'

Betts offered a cigarette. Thwaite hesitated, then accepted.

'Not sure we'd want to, would we?'

She wished he wouldn't. Even the officials exchanged glances as Bampton lit his second cigar of the morning. If challenged, which nobody would dare do here, he would boast that he had given up cigarettes long ago. Nor was there much doubt, at least outwardly, about his rude health and energy. What a man did in private was of course his own business. But his puffing away so aggressively in the weekly departmental meeting attended by all Health Ministers, the whip, the special adviser, officials and PPSs including the new chap York was defiance of a high order.

A sudden twinge of dislike surfaced, but she pushed it away. She had no choice but to work with Bampton under whatever conditions he imposed. The issue she needed to raise with him was nothing to do with his actions but her own.

Elaine waited until the meeting had drawn to its close, then placed herself squarely in front of her boss.

'Could I have a moment, Ted?'

Bampton turned impatiently to his junior Minister. She had spoken softly but her hand rested on his arm.

'I've got a briefing in a minute for tomorrow's debate. You know we lost another vote in the Lords last night, drat 'em. It'll have to be quick.'

Elaine pushed away the reflection that it would have cost nothing had her boss's reaction been more kindly or courteous. Of the three Ministers at DHWF only Harrison knew how to be utterly charming. It was a talent Bampton professed to despise. Given Harrison's example, he had some justification.

She hesitated till the room was otherwise empty. He looked at his watch.

'Go on. What's the problem?'

'Well – there are two things, Ted. I put a note in your box over the weekend about diaries – did you see it?'

Bampton was shuffling through papers and did not look up. It was impossible to tell whether he had seen the note and ignored it, or had failed to read it. Bampton was not noted for his assiduity.

She ploughed on. 'First, I am getting overwhelmed by invitations: to open new hospital units, to speak at conferences, do TV, attend charity events linked with our department. All are accompanied by advice that everyone will be terribly upset if I refuse, but the result is that I'm clocking on fiendishly long weeks and my constituency is suffering.'

Not to speak of my personal life, she did not add. While she adhered willingly to Bampton's instruction about no outside activity during the week she did resent having virtually no free time. She and George Horrocks, with much manipulation of diaries, had managed to see each other just twice in the weeks since Christmas; and while Karen kept in touch by phone, usually when funds were low, mother and daughter had not been together at all, despite living barely a mile apart. If she didn't make a stand she would be working every waking hour. That could not be right.

Bampton sucked his teeth. 'You said two things,' he grunted.

'The point is, Ted, that I wondered whether it would be all right to start saying no – even if there's a fuss. And some of these events are more appropriate for a senior Minister – Derek, or yourself. They only ask for me because it'll attract loads of publicity if I go. But . . .'

She stopped, aware of her own tactlessness in hinting that her presence was preferred to her boss's. Except that it was so, and beyond her control, and becoming hateful.

'Just tell 'em to sod off, Elaine.'

She swallowed. She was perfectly capable of doing that but, whereas a Secretary of State could withstand accusations of being high-handed and arrogant, her career was still too precarious. A male Minister might face less relentless scrutiny: fewer journalists would be waiting to catch him out. Men were not tall poppies as women Ministers were. It was tough at times being a woman. Maybe that was also the root of the second problem.

'The other thing is, Ted . . . this is hard to put, but when you're handing around the projects during a departmental meeting, as we've just had, well, I don't seem to get very much. We have three Ministers here, not two. I am a hard worker. Maybe if I had more to do within the department, or the Commons, I'd have more reason to refuse a visit to Little Puddlecombe or wherever. Even the officials recognise that our job here comes first.'

Bampton looked at her as if she were mad. 'You've just been telling me you've got too much on your plate, you can't cope, and now you say I don't give you enough? I wish you'd make your mind up, Elaine. Anyway, I'm busy, even if you're not. If you want a move, speak to the Chief Whip. Other than that, talk to your diary secretary. It's your job to sort her out, not mine.'

With that he swept up his papers and walked out.

'I do hope I haven't kept you waiting.'

It occurred to Anthony, even as he shook hands with his father and kissed his mother on the cheek, that there ought to be a language of greater intimacy to use to one's parents. He hoped his smile was welcoming.

'Not at all. Anyway it was so interesting to sit here.' As his mother moved he caught her favourite fragrance, faint and old fashioned, the same she had used for years. At school there had been no women other than distant chambermaids and the housemaster's wife, who smelled of soap and clean linen. Karen, when she bothered, sported a distinctive sexy perfume, while Fred had been trying out different kinds of aftershave recently, to the mocking comments of his fellow bathroom users. His father smelled of his pipe.

'I suppose congratulations are in order? You'll have to explain to us what exactly a PPS is, and what you'll be doing.'

Mr York was pleased at what was undoubtedly his son's promotion, but it would be a lot easier if the title were more obvious.

Anthony demurred: 'It means I'm a general gofer, that's all, in the new Department of Health, Welfare and the Family. An extra pair of hands, though I don't get to do much in public except hover. You'll probably see my back on TV when my Minister's being pursued by the press.'

It was nice to know his parents noticed the details of his life. Anthony, however, was aware that his elevation served mainly to swell the ranks of the obedient. His veiled threat to withhold his vote so early in his career must have had a lot to do with his being drawn quickly into the spider's web. From here onwards his role, in a small way, would include persuading other potential rebels that the government's agenda was both worthy and workable.

For a moment the Yorks stood, not touching, heads uplifted, and absorbed the magnificence of Central Lobby. Then Anthony took his mother's arm and propelled both parents gently down the corridor into the Lower Waiting Hall, past the bust of a preoccupied Disraeli and a cheerful policeman on what was effectively points duty. They turned right under the Gothic arch and entered the Strangers' Dining Room.

A high-ceilinged but small room, walls oak-panelled to waist height, then covered with lurid Pugin wallpaper, it had an intimidating air. Each chair sported the portcullis stamped in gold on the green leather. Square tables too small for the plates, cutlery, ashtrays, flower vases, cruets, menus and other paraphernalia were crowded a little too close. On the long wall hung *The Other Painting*, by Andrew Festing, paid for in 1986 by 156 cross Honourable Members omitted from the official picture painted by June Mendoza, which also hung in the room at the far end. Given the crisp figures captured by Festing relaxing in the Library and bars, so different from the watery Mendoza, Anthony knew who had obtained the better bargain for posterity.

'This is the main dining room for our guests in the Commons,' he explained. 'The Members' Dining Room is next door and we get exactly the same food. There's a very smart à la carte restaurant, the Churchill Room, but strictly speaking that's in the House of Lords. And a café downstairs which is a bit sausage-and-mashy, or one of the private dining rooms where you wouldn't see anybody. I thought you'd prefer this.'

'It's splendid, Anthony.'

His mother was trying not to stare at nearby tables in an effort to spot famous faces. Anthony took pity. 'In the corner, the bald man is Sir Bowen Wells – a delightful chap, and one of the better whips. That's Paddy Ashdown just behind you, back from the Balkans once again. The lady opposite's Mo Mowlam, Labour front-bench spokesperson on something or other: she's a capable woman, but when she started wearing designer suits her party workers complained, so she's back to Islington grunge, as you can see.'

This was the Commons style into which Anthony had slipped without complaint; almost automatically, he would find something positive to say about a fellow party member and an equally disparaging remark, deserved or not, about an opponent. The protective, identifying garment of party colour already enveloped him.

Heads bent to examine the menu. Mrs York, mindful of her struggle in Harvey Nichols with a size 14 skirt, chose grilled sole, while her husband, after a day's ferrying her around London, plumped for lamb cutlets. To avoid any hint of criticism of their taste, as he had done all his life, Anthony followed his father. A dilemma over wine was avoided by a glass of house white for his mother and a bottle of Mouton-Cadet for the men. He wished fleetingly that his family could be more adventurous.

The wine and starters arrived quickly; the waiter left them to it. The running three-line whip which had confined many Members to the House made it a busy evening. 'I need a clear head because I have to go and see my Minister at ten,' Anthony remarked as he poured himself half a glass.

'Goodness!' Mrs York exclaimed. 'Isn't that a bit late? You're not in any trouble, Anthony, are you?'

'Of course not. That is normal practice here. In fact it'll be about twenty past ten, after the last vote. We have a breakfast meeting at eight with the pharmaceutical industry tomorrow morning and he wants to brief me – it's Derek Harrison.'

Anthony was to discover that Derek would often use the late hours to conduct ministerial business. For the rest of the day, and on lighter-whipped nights, he continued to find better uses for his time.

The fish arrived; his mother examined it with her fork, removed the feather of fennel and began to eat delicately, wary of bones. His father struggled for a while with the over-cooked lamb chops, then gave up and concentrated on his potatoes. The old man's routine had been disrupted. A night at a hotel was another obscure hurdle to be negotiated; it would be another day, after an hour or two back in the office and then blessedly *home*, before his equanimity would be restored.

Watching his father's gloomy expression while still trying desperately to charm both parents, Anthony silently regretted the invitation.

Mr York wiped his mouth with the napkin, folded it on the table, finished his wine and sat up. His long bony face, mouth set in a thin, disciplined line, told of Nonconformist antecedents embroiled with the work ethic, of a half-forgotten Protestantism too rigid and stilted for comfort, long since intertwined with a preference for strong leadership, quiet patriotism and public morality. He cleared his throat.

'Your mother and I would like you to know how proud we are of you, Anthony. You and your sister. You particularly have never let us down. We have set the highest standards for our children, as you know. Our hopes have been amply fulfilled.'

Anthony gruffly muttered his thanks, but the bleak formality of the remarks chilled him. Did all families speak to each other like that? Across the room conversation was more animated and natural; laughter came in bursts from the table behind him. The Battersea house was full of humour, teasing, genuine affection. By contrast, how seldom he talked to the two strangers who were his guests. He would as little think of confiding in them as in the waiter.

His mother would be shocked and frightened to know that the dreams had returned not only on the one occasion at Christmas but more frequently since. He had never mentioned them to his father, though he suspected his mother might have done so. There was no point in discussing the issue: he was not going through that psychiatrist business ever again. Nobody would broach the subject if he didn't, and especially not in this glittering place, where the objective was to celebrate an only son's dazzling success.

Had his parents ever said 'I love you' each to the other? He must suppose so; that was a romantic generation, brought up on *Brief Encounter*, Bogart and Bacall. Yet he could not recall a moment when either had ever uttered the words to him, nor to his sister, and he had never put the question. Come to that, he had never spoken to another human being of love, ever.

Anthony folded his napkin exactly the same way as his father and called for the bill. He wondered if that stiff little speech meant he was at last worthy of their love, or whatever they might call it.

'Home, Sheila, please – and if I fall asleep and start to snore, kindly ignore me.'

The plump driver in the blue uniform nodded into her rear-view mirror. Mrs Stalker looked washed out. It must have been a tough week.

'Got anything nice planned for the weekend?' Sheila did not add 'Minister'. Elaine did not stand on ceremony.

The blue Rover car, polished and valeted, would always be at the kerbside for the first appointment in the morning and last thing at night. The drivers of the government car service saw and heard everything, far more than the whips. The unsung heroes of Whitehall who worked longer hours than anyone else, they saw their masters under the most extreme pressure, in tears after a row, or late for *Panorama* or a three-line vote, and in the most relaxed circumstances – splayed out, ties and flies unbuttoned, floating groggily home, incapable of putting two civil or coherent words together, let alone driving.

Elaine had asked for a woman driver on principle, knowing that the men got the plum jobs and most of the overtime. In the months since she had become a Minister she had cautiously begun to make friends with the down-to-earth Sheila, whose industry and good humour she admired.

'Not too bad. I have an advice bureau, then a careers fair at the local college and a flower festival at church, but after that I'm free. And I'm invited out to dinner.'

Something about the blush on her employer's cheeks, the dimpled smile, gave Sheila the clue. 'Nice, is he?'

'Lord, Sheila, is it that obvious? How do you know it isn't my local Rotary?'

Both laughed, a shared conspiracy of women past the first bloom of youth but not yet ready to settle for middle age.

'You married, Sheila?'

'Sort of. About thirty years since our wedding day. My old man's had a stroke. Lost his speech, and needs constant looking after. So he went back to live with his mum.'

The tragedy in the tale made Elaine catch her breath. 'Was that your choice?' she asked gently. The older woman shrugged but her expression in the mirror was sad. 'If I'd stayed home, given up my job, we'd have been penniless, and I'd probably have done away with him sooner or later, or myself. This way, at least he's well cared for.'

'But not much home life for you, after long days ferrying me around whatever the weather.'

Sheila's eyes twinkled. 'Look at it this way. If I had my old man the way he used to be, all warm and waiting for me, I wouldn't have taken this job, now would I?'

The miles slid past as night fell; Elaine kicked off her shoes and stretched her legs out on the back seat, her coat loosely covering her knees. Garish yellow motorway lights flashed rhythmically overhead until the urban areas fell behind and darkness enfolded them. The quiet movement, the soft purr of the engine created a cocoon of sanctuary and trust. Elaine stirred.

'Don't you miss the sex, Sheila?'

The grey-haired driver pondered. Male Ministers and drivers shared confidences – often they saw more of each other than of their spouses. Her Minister looked wistful.

'You can answer that for yourself, at a guess. You're on your own, aren't you? Don't you miss it? Don't we all?'

Damn cookery books. Damn Delia Smith. Damn female bookshop assistants who goggled when a male customer asked for culinary guidance. All he had wanted was a few fresh ideas: the best the shelves had been able to offer was a collection of dinner party recipes from the *Australian Women's Weekly* under the excruciating title *Time for Romance*.

The Aussies' idea of romance, George had decided crossly, was not quite right. The suggested gazpacho with avocado in crouton baskets was all very well, but the thick chunks of bread had to be deep-fried, with no guarantee that the cold soup wouldn't seep through and make a sticky puddle. Nor did he feel that chicken, even dressed up with mushroom and thyme sauce, was in the least romantic – whichever way you looked at it, it was still chicken. He guessed Elaine would see quite enough of that.

In the end he had settled on something clean and sweet and simple: butterfly lamb, marinaded overnight in olive oil and lemon juice with ten crushed cloves of garlic and fresh rosemary and Dijon mustard – the boned joint would take only twenty minutes in the oven. Polenta triangles were fun and easy to do and the green salad, with those small firm apricots from South Africa he'd found in Sainsbury's, would make a colourful contrast to the meat.

The pudding was crucial. How might he tempt a woman known to be careful with her figure, but not have to disappear to the kitchen to cook just as he wanted to pour her another glass of wine and edge the conversation towards intimacy? Then he found it and set to with a will.

As he measured and poured, beat and rolled, and wrinkled his nose at the evocative aroma of coffee and chocolate, George hummed cheerfully. He smiled at his own absorption. It gave him the greatest enjoyment to prepare this meal for a beautiful woman, as an elaborate prelude to bed, if he handled matters well. The fact that in a traditional world the lady would be the cook and he the guest had not escaped him. It was a long time, he reflected, since he had so looked forward to sharing the outcome of his labours and imagination. A gift, a bonding, a pleasure.

He had wrestled also with the choice of starter. Delia had won, though the wild mushroom and walnut soup took some finding, tucked away in her 'Vegetarian Christmas' section. Why should the vegetarians get the best recipes? Again he could make it ahead of time and thus spend the evening not over the stove but mostly at the table, with Elaine. All he would need to do apart from reheating it was to add a few slices of fresh open-cap mushroom and a quick stir of cream, dry sherry and lemon juice. Perfect.

The table was laid; on second thoughts, George removed the silver candlestick and replaced the pink bud roses with white narcissi from the garden, whose fragrance filled the room. The roses could go upstairs. It would not do to be too elaborate – Elaine probably had enough of smart dinners, especially as she so often had to sing for her supper.

He examined himself in the mirror. The jacket was best left over a chair. The dark slacks, plain shirt and simple tie were exactly right. George would not have admitted to a shred of vanity but, as he twisted about, his appearance passed muster with him.

He checked the clock; he walked into the kitchen, stirred the soup once more, ensured the oven was hot, basted the glistening lamb, rearranged the bread rolls, fiddled with the salad. She

151

was not late, not yet. But he wanted her to come: he was on his marks.

She was worth it. Had she been an ordinary woman he would not have been so intrigued by her. For a moment, cautiously, he allowed himself the unaccustomed danger of examining how he felt about her. Some of her appeal was obvious. She was fun to be with, and endlessly interesting; her conversation brought the newspaper headlines alive. That was partly who she was, of course. The slant of insider information she offered, the 'true story', could hold him on the edge of his seat, so that tea at the Ritz or a brief encounter at an official reception, which would not lead to more personal contact there and then, were joys which left him longing for the next time.

So was he in love with her? George pulled out a chair and sat down, elbows on the table, hands folded under his chin. For his generation love meant marriage, but George equated marriage with misunderstanding and lost hopes and misery, all to be avoided. His parents had split up when he was young. His mother, embittered, had lavished her love on her dogs and garden, and sent away to school a lonely boy for whom she was a distant shadow. His own marriage seemed to have followed a similar pattern. When Margaret announced she was leaving him for someone else there had been little ill-feeling, if only because hardly any emotion had been invested from the start by either party. Margaret had not been a friend as his male acquaintances were. Once her sexual interest, frustrated by his frequent absences, was drawn elsewhere, no reason compelled them to stay together. Still, it left him with an unalloyed sense of regret and of failure. He suspected that Mrs Stalker, relatively recently divorced, would understand entirely.

The doorbell. My God, he'd forgotten to put the wine in the fridge – he jumped up, and the chair went crashing over. He bent to retrieve it and banged his head on the table corner. He leapt to the door as Elaine raised her hand again to the bellpush.

The two stood on the doorstep, mouths open: 'Oh! I thought maybe – '

'Sorry! I was just – '

Elaine laughed and pointed. 'You've got a bump coming on your forehead. You all right?'

Ruefully George rubbed it. 'Ouch! So I have. You've caught me at sixes and sevens. Now don't stand there, come in, come in.'

She entered and slipped off her coat, noting the glance of approbation he gave her blue silk dress which clung and swirled and hinted at the body underneath. Her blonde hair shone and was set off by big pearl earrings. As she handed over the bottle of Vouvray she had brought she gazed around appreciatively.

'Smells wonderful. I hope you haven't gone to a lot of trouble.'

'Of course I have. You'd have been offended if I'd offered a simple cheese sandwich. I could have taken you out but I figured you wouldn't mind my efforts. I hope you enjoy them.'

I wish, thought Elaine fleetingly, as she allowed George to fuss over her, I wish my husband had done this just once in the fifteen years we were together. It was above all the knowledge that Mike had resented her career, and expected no more (and no less) of her than cooked dinners on demand in a whistle-clean house that had caused the marriage to disintegrate.

Soon the two were seated and tucking in. Tiredness was forgotten as wine was poured and food served; the sink filled up steadily. The soup was a great success and required a detailed explanation. Then, as she ate the last of the succulent lamb, Elaine paused and laughed out loud.

'You're a marvel. I can't tell you how good that was.'

He watched her shrewdly. 'You certainly look more relaxed than when you arrived. "Peaky" is the word I'd use.'

She picked at the remains of a lettuce leaf and shrugged.

'Ministerial life not quite what you expected?'

'That about sums it up. Can I bore you for a minute while I think aloud, George?'

'Go ahead.'

'Well ...' she paused, considering. 'There is definitely a downside to it. Everybody thinks politics is such a fabulous life. They don't see the frustrations, which aren't what you might think. For example people ask about the pressure but that doesn't bother me. To be totally honest, stress suits me fine and I'd never get a thing done without it. Nor do I mind now being in the public eye. It distressed me to begin with but you get used to it, get hardened. And that's part of my worry – I *am* getting hard. Those aspects of my public image I don't like are becoming truer every minute.'

'I don't see it like that – you're a thoroughly nice woman underneath, Elaine.'

She grimaced. 'Thanks, but that's precisely the point. *You* know me in private; others don't. I don't want to be what my image has become, but I've lost control of it. If you'd said that to the world

153

at large, no one would have believed you; indeed, it's essential to be seen as tough and thick-skinned, for the moment the press reckon a Minister's vulnerable they're in for the kill. Only the good guys bleed, didn't you know that?'

George removed their plates and refilled her glass. 'What I know is that nobody ever resigns these days. If Ministers won't take the blame for what happens in their departments, how can they preach responsibility to the rest of us?'

Elaine pondered. 'I don't think that's quite fair. So many hands are tied. Ministers are no longer in charge, though we're loath to admit it. There's Brussels on the one side and quangos on the other – agencies headed up by anonymous men who earn a lot more than I do. Decisions are taken by others but the government is held to account. My task tends to be to carry the can when things go wrong. No wonder some MPs don't want the job.'

George put down his glass and leaned over the table to take her hand. Absent-mindedly she let him stroke it, and continued in a low voice.

'In theory I'm rewarded with the excitement of an inside view – and it is exciting – but that implies a favoured-observer role, which wouldn't be enough for me. If I behave, promotion might come – I do accept that I have a lot to learn yet. What is also supposed to materialise is the chance to influence policy. Unfortunately that doesn't appear to be happening.' Sombrely she recounted to George her run-in with Bampton.

'What about the other chap – Harrison? He seems a good sort.'

'You think so? Well, he's not terribly helpful. I dropped hints to his office that some of the invitations being channelled my way were more appropriate for him. He had a fit and stormed around saying he wasn't taking my leftovers.'

She looked up and to his consternation George saw that her eyes were filled with tears. 'I feel I'm losing control – of how other people see me, of how I spend my time, of how to make a worthwhile impact. Whatever I suggest is pooh-poohed by Derek or Ted. I'm too weary to fight back, and don't know how. I've never before felt so professionally isolated or undermined. The only bit of policy I'm exclusively in charge of is mental illness, and that's because no one else wants it! I am starting to doubt my own judgement – that's never happened before, and it scares me.'

Her face was so doleful that any thought of levity was banished from George's mind. He rose and moved to her side of the table, raised her to her feet and folded her into his arms. For a long moment he held her, as he had on New Year's Eve, and stroked her hair. His own heart was beating fast: he lifted her face, wiped away the hot little tears with his thumbs and kissed her softly until the spasm passed.

'We haven't had dessert yet!' Elaine protested, laughing. 'I bet you've made something wonderful. What is it?'

'That's better,' George murmured approvingly. Then, as he released her: 'It's my version of tiramisu – Italian trifle with marsala – with two sauces, chocolate and vanilla.'

Elaine followed him into the kitchen and watched as he placed the sliced cake, plates, small white jugs of sauce, spoons and the rest of the wine on a tray.

'Enough of the formalities,' he said. 'Time to eat somewhere more comfortable.'

She raised an eyebrow. 'Upstairs?'

'Certainly. Up you go.'

'Yes, sergeant-major!'

'I was a colonel, and don't you forget it.'

And there he spooned her pudding as she sat, then leaned back on the bed; the alcoholic sweetness lingered on her tongue, and was shared with him, and she ran her finger over her lips and asked for more. In answer he put the dishes to one side, reached up and removed her earrings. Deftly he unbuttoned her dress down the front, slipped a hand inside, found her breast and caressed it. Then she pulled the dress up over her head and unfastened her bra as he allowed himself to touch and linger, and feed her a little more.

'I think it would be wonderful if you would take the rest of those pretty undergarments off, and roll over on to your front,' George ordered.

Elaine, amused and relaxed, obliged. Quick rustling sounds behind her suggested that he was no longer clothed either, but there would be plenty of time to see. She stretched out, her head pillowed on her folded arms, and closed her eyes.

Then he began. Starting at her neck his strong hands proceeded to massage the tired muscles, kneading and pressing, shifting knots and stiffness, over her shoulders, touching the sides of her breasts with his fingers, lightly, down on each side of the slim waist and firm hips, caressing and rolling, as she began to move with the rhythm. As his hands came to the cleft of her buttocks and then to her thighs she moaned and raised her hips to him.

'That's marvellous, George. Don't stop.'

'Not yet. We need some massage cream,' he told her and reached across for a half-full jug. 'This may be a bit cold. Don't wriggle or you'll make a mess.'

She felt the trickle of chocolate cream between her shoulder blades, and opened one startled eye to see a naked George, a wide grin on his face and clearly ready for her, dribble the dark stream right down her spine, making her gasp. With the edge of his thumbs, which had wiped away her tears a few moments before, he drew circles on her skin. Then he parted her legs and knelt between them, leaned over her back and gently, thoroughly, starting once more at the nape of her neck, licked it all off.

Only this time, when he reached the base of her spine, his fingers continued and slipped inside her, while his other hand slid around under her waist and lifted her up; and so he entered her from behind, deeply, and she arched her back and they drew together, flesh to flesh, warm and sticky and sweet and loving. She whimpered: she felt full, engorged. He grasped her haunches tight and pulled her into him to make her rear up, and seized her breasts, so that he could nuzzle her neck as a lion does his lioness. Then he became more urgent and she went down and grabbed a pillow and balanced on all fours to brace herself against his strength, shuddering as he drove home. She felt him thrust far inside her, again and again, until at last a great cry came from him. For a moment he held her, both gulping for breath. Then he slackened, not leaving her, but let her down inch by inch until she lay prone. Still panting he covered her entirely, from head to foot, with his own warm body.

She shifted: he was surprisingly heavy for such a trim man.

'If you don't move soon, George, I'll suffocate,' she whispered. 'What a way to dine! Did you have this in mind when you stirred that chocolate sauce?'

'Not guilty,' sighed George regretfully, as he eased himself out and stretched comfortably at her side. The room was heated; she would not get cold. In any case, he had merely paused, not finished for the night.

She rolled on to her back and spoke with mock sternness. 'Chocolate stains, you know. I hope you got it all off.'

'No problem: I didn't miss a drop,' he teased. For a moment they lay quietly and drank the remaining wine, contented in their closeness. Then he bent and kissed each nipple and traced a finger over the flush which suffused the smooth skin over her breastbone. 'You are lovely, Elaine. I don't know what to say to you, often, and I can't compete with your tales of the great, the good and the infamous, but this is one place where you will always be welcome.'

She giggled, but was pleased. How neatly George judged her mood. Had he started to pledge his undying love she would have felt uncomfortable; but what seemed to be on offer, at least for the moment, was an appealing blend of companionship and romance.

Both pudding and chocolate were gone. He leaned across her for the second jug with the vanilla sauce, and smiled happily down at her.

Chapter Ten

Roger Dickson paused in front of his wife's long mirror, adjusted it to his greater height and surveyed himself critically.

Over six foot tall, moderate build, broad shoulders; strong features, fine brow, deep-set brown eyes. The silver streaks through the once dark hair no longer troubled him, for a Prime Minister should not look too young or unmarked by experience, a handicap poor Tony Blair had discovered the hard way. Instead, greater maturity allied with self-discipline and long hours had brought Dickson not a crumpled visage and a thickened waistline but a firmness to the mouth and a cool economy of expression which had not been there before.

He turned away, satisfied. The man in the mirror looked authoritative, trustworthy, competent and calm. The image doctors had done well with their advice to wear navy-blue suits with simple pale-coloured shirts and understated ties. For the sake of the cameras he had shed a stone, slowly, to avoid attention and silly questions about diets. In his pocket nestled a mini-electric razor to keep down that insidious growth of beard which once had plagued him. Everything was under control.

He was always on show, *always*. There was never a relaxed moment: he could never rub his face absent-mindedly, scratch his cheek, hitch his trousers or blow his nose without checking first that there wasn't a camera pointed at him. Out of grim necessity he had developed virtually a sixth sense – he could tell where hidden watchers might lurk, as if some invisible antennae were ever vigilant.

Dickson sighed, picked up his jacket and put it on, adjusted his tie and patted the clean handkerchief in his breast pocket. He took the small lift downstairs, walked along the corridor, turned right, bid a gruff 'Good morning' to the two blue-uniformed attendants and pushed his way through the baize-covered doors which connected his home with the Chief Whip's official residence at Number 12 Downing Street.

He was greeted quietly by the two Chief Whips and the Party Chairman. The four men, all with grim expressions, exchanged brief remarks and sat down. Dickson poured himself a coffee from the Thermos flask in the centre of the table. Before him he placed a small notebook and a silver propelling pencil. 'I'm listening. Bad news first.'

James St John Gordon, tenth Earl of Hamilton, ran his fingers through faded red hair, pursed his aristocratic lips and grimaced. 'We have effectively lost control of the Lords, Prime Minister,' he began. 'When you asked me to take on the job as Lords Chief Whip, you felt an hereditary title might appeal more to their lordships than a life peerage, since our majority is so dependent on the ... ah ... traditional element. Unfortunately it isn't making a scrap of difference. We've lost twenty-two votes this session, with more to come.'

He rubbed his eyes. 'The old boys are willing to attend for the day, but most are elderly and toddle off by eight – we can't keep them. We certainly can't persuade any to get out of bed at two in the morning when there's an ambush, as there was last night. Add to that, our few supporters among the life peers are often busy and can't come in at all, whereas Opposition and cross-bench peers seem to have a bee in their bonnets over just about everything and are fearsome attenders.'

'The problem which has emerged recently', the Commons Chief Whip concurred, 'is that the rebellions are led by our own side, and very capable they are too. Ex-Cabinet Ministers in the Lords are no longer content to troop through the right lobbies. Too many are seeking revenge. Look at the industrial training cuts. The campaign's co-ordinated by the former President of the Board of Trade, Lord Heseltine, now nutty as a fruit-cake, but with eyes agleam at the prospect of outsmarting those Ministers you appointed to replace him.'

Lord Hamilton nodded gloomily. 'You'd think the chaps would show some loyalty, but they get the bit between their teeth and they're off. It doesn't matter how much damage is done. They just laugh and tell us to draft better legislation.'

Roger wondered silently how that might be done, given that there was seldom enough time, with Conference demanding populist policies and tax cuts above any other consideration.

'The point, Roger, is that we need about twenty fresh true-blue supporters in the Lords, people who'll turn up on command and vote for us no matter what. Preferably under sixty and in sound health. Loyalists who will toe the line.' The Commons Chief Whip was worried. 'Otherwise we may have to abandon half our bills – at this rate we'll be proroguing Parliament at Christmas instead of October and the next State Opening won't be till Easter.'

That was an exaggeration, but the dilemma was genuine. The Upper House had power only to delay, but its ability to be awkward was legendary. Roger frowned and pinched the skin at the bridge of his nose.

'So do you have a list of such paragons?' he asked, an edge to his voice. 'Men and women so fascinated by politics that they'd adore the appointment, sufficiently distinguished that such honours appear deserved, and docile enough to oblige from the minute they arrive?'

'I don't think we have much choice, Roger.' Party Chairman Peter Aubrey had been silent but now responded testily. 'And yes, I do have a list. You've met quite a few of them.'

Roger grimaced. 'Donors?'

'Donors. So what? At least they'll know which side their bread is buttered. And so will we.'

Roger examined the list with a murmur of distaste, then flung it on the table and brooded, hunched, seeking an alternative. None came.

'I appreciate what you are trying to do, but we have to be so damn careful, Peter. Asil Nadir gave us four hundred thousand and it did us no good, nor him either. And what do we know of some of these names? Look at that chap who offered the Labour Party five million – Moosa bin Shamsa. Claimed to be a writer and thinker in Bangladesh but it turned out he ran a manpower agency and had been beaten up by people he'd promised to arrange jobs for. A con-man, in other words. You sure about the bona fides of everyone here?'

'Look,' Aubrey explained patiently. 'We've had them screened, as far as possible. They come with recommendations from local party chairmen, Ministers, MPs . . .'

Roger held up a hand. 'Don't put me off even more.' He tried one final time. 'James, you need your votes. Peter, you need your money. But if I were to say I loathe the whole business of linking the two and do not wish to proceed the three of you'd think I was losing my marbles, wouldn't you?'

The Chief Whip, who considered Dickson a mite too soft to be an effective leader and coveted the job for himself, smiled.

'Well, Prime Minister, I couldn't have put it better myself.'

'Dad.'

'Um?'

'*Dad.*'

Jayanti Bhadeshia looked up impatiently from the jumble of papers on his desk. 'What is it? I have to check this VAT return. It is overdue again because my fool of an accountant is so lazy.'

Before him the young man pouted but did not budge. Bhadeshia put down his pen with a sigh and switched off the calculator, but in truth he was not averse to the interruption.

He examined his younger son with barely concealed pride. Varun was the handsomest of his four children, the one who physically most resembled his mother. Amit, the eldest, was more serious and engrossed in his medical studies at St Thomas's; the girls – Priya and his adored youngest, Sabita – had heads full only of boys and pop music which, he supposed, made them normal young women. But Varun, solid, charming and equable, had shown the greatest interest in a future in commerce and thus had increasingly attracted his father's approbation.

Bhadeshia's voice softened and he relaxed. 'So, my son. Come and sit here. What can I do for you?'

'The other way round, Dad. I want to help you,' the boy responded with a new solemnity of manner. 'I've heard you talk to Mum about the East African scheme and all your plans. I'm eighteen now and old enough: I don't intend to go to university. Do you want me to go out there to oversee the project?'

'My goodness! But you are too young for that. And I have managers who are very good.' It was not, however, such a stupid idea, Jayanti reflected to himself. At least his son was someone he could trust.

'Oh, go on, Dad. I have to start somewhere.' The eagerness made his father smile indulgently.

'You should start by managing a shop.'

The boy pulled a face and pointed out with some asperity that he had frequently been placed in sole charge of shops at various times since he was fourteen years old. As he spoke his father watched him carefully and became thoughtful.

'There is something you could do,' Jayanti remarked at last. After shuffling files he found what he needed and showed it to his son. 'This is a schedule of my bank loans. As you can see most are secured on assets including the shares of our main company. If the value of the shares rises we can borrow more.'

Varun nodded. He could see what was coming. 'You want me to buy some shares, Dad, is that it? And get a few more people to do so too? My cousins, for a start. We've got plenty of contacts in the community. Small placements, some new shares, some from the market, nothing to attract attention. Shouldn't be too difficult for a sound business like ours.'

At that his father began to talk eloquently of turnover and profit margins while the young man listened intently, asked brief questions and made a few notes. Then Varun grinned.

'There's only one problem, Dad. I haven't any money. Come to that, neither have most of my friends – at least, not the sort of numbers which would make much impact on the share price.'

Jayanti pulled out the company's cheque-book. 'That's easy,' he answered as he wrote. 'It's all going back into the firm, one way or another. Anyhow, it's the bank's money, not mine.' He handed over three cheques and the boy whistled.

His father shrugged. 'So? You'll use it well. Don't cash them all at once – be discreet. Just one more thing: don't tell your mother. She's never happy about what we owe, and I doubt if she'd feel comfortable with your little operation. So mum's the word, yes?'

At the threshold of Elaine's office her Private Secretary Fiona Murray paused. Behind her Anthony York stopped also. The Minister appeared not to have noticed their arrival.

Fiona glanced around. Some Ministers made no impact whatever on their rooms, apart from the obligatory family photo. Others showed off shamelessly. Kenneth Baker had filled one wall with his remarkable collection of political cartoons, many featuring himself. David Mellor as Heritage Minister installed an elegant glass-topped coffee table, the better to display large illustrated books, including the latest publication of whichever great personage was about to pay him a visit so that he could get it signed.

Mrs Stalker's room showed evidence of a lively if unorthodox personality. Most items were gifts. A stuffed-carrot doll came from a healthy eating campaign in Stroud. An enormous blue hippopotamus named Michael was a gift from Scottish Young Conservatives. An ugly vase from the Finnish Minister for the Family was filled with flowers, paid for by Elaine, as was the fruit piled up in a matching bowl on the table.

'Are you ready for us, Minister?'

Elaine looked up. 'Is Mr Chadwick ready?'

'He's in the office now, Minister, and other officials are on call if you need them. And Mr York is here too.'

'Fine. Come on in.'

The following day was set for First Order Questions, when the Department of Health, Welfare and the Family would be on duty at 2.30 p.m. sharp. The questions had been placed on the Commons order paper a fortnight before, some of the more helpful ones having been planted via friendly backbenchers by Anthony, though naturally everyone would vigorously deny it. Nor was it technically illegal to put down questions of value only to commercial interests. A fuller reply would have been available to an enquiry by letter; but that would have diminished the mystique of the Commons, not to speak of a seriously deleterious effect on the income of the Honourable Members involved.

The public scrutiny, on a four-weekly rota, lasted forty-five minutes, and, since Prime Minister's Questions followed, it was televised to the nation and, via CNN, around the world. As a result Elaine had received religious literature on the iniquities of teenage sex from Tucson, Arizona, a video proposing the legalisation of drugs from Hawaii and two proposals of marriage from the Philippines, complete with photographs of the ugliest men she had ever seen.

The preparation of responses was routine, but Elaine, still feeling insecure, feared the unscripted supplementary which might trip her up. She opted to do her homework the day before.

With Fiona, Anthony and Chadwick she ploughed through the order paper. At the right-hand side of each question were scribbled the initials of Bampton, Harrison or herself. Only one of Elaine's was likely to be reached before time ran out, an anodyne query about a new clinic in Southampton. She sat back listless: all this work, apparently for nothing. She understood suddenly those Ministers who don't bother to prepare for dispatch box appearances, then recalled with a shiver the many occasions when such complacency had been caught out.

She forced herself to concentrate. 'Satisfy my curiosity,' she said. 'Who decides which questions are allocated to which Minister? For example, Mr Bampton has the one on community care, but it's my brief.'

Chadwick raised an eyebrow and considered. 'Ah, *we* do, at least as a preliminary. But that's Question One and the Secretary of State likes to get into his stride. So he's taken it, though he'll expect you to be up to date on the matter.'

'I see. In case he changes his mind at the last minute. So you want me primed to say things like' – she flicked through to the suggested reply – '"We recently issued guidance on the discharge of patients from psychiatric hospitals. Patients should not be discharged until it is safe to discharge them." Not exactly a reassuring or fresh approach – or deathless prose, is it?'

Chadwick answered huffily, 'But it is the *line to take*, Minister. Should you wish to change it, we have to consult the officials. That takes time.' He pointed delicately with a Waterman pen. 'There's always the "proposed new discharge registers" and our "plans to introduce the power of supervised discharge" to mention.'

She made a note. 'When will that be?'

'Ah . . . when the parliamentary timetable allows.'

Elaine felt increasingly angry. 'That's a useful formula, isn't it? It implies that it's the Opposition's fault if we can't make progress.'

Chadwick shrugged. 'I'm not sure a civil servant should comment on that, Minister.'

'And yet . . .' She leaned back and stared at the ceiling, then at Chadwick directly.

Across the table Anthony York sat looking faintly anxious. It would do her PPS no harm to observe how real Ministers and real civil servants dealt with each other; the day would come when he too might face the same brick wall. She continued.

'The suggested answers are full of party-political remarks, aren't they? Swipes at the unions, criticisms of local councils controlled by our opponents, repeated references to 1979, the winter of discontent and the last years of Labour rule. It gives the impression we're not keen on responding in a straightforward manner but only on points-scoring against the other side.'

'That is how Ministers have preferred to deal with First Order Questions,' Fiona interposed smoothly. She and Chadwick exchanged glances.

'Well, it makes me feel distinctly uncomfortable,' Elaine answered crossly, 'and I'm fed up being fobbed off. For example, is it really true that the NHS now spends over one hundred million pounds *a day*, that we're treating ten million patients a year in our hospitals, and that resources have increased since 1979 by over sixty-four per cent in real terms?'

Chadwick didn't bother to check. He knew both slogans and statistics off by heart.

'Yes, Minister.'

Elaine glared at him.

'Then explain to me – why the hell do we still have waiting lists?'

Chadwick opened his mouth, then shut it again. Two spots of pink had appeared on Elaine's cheeks. He wondered with a suppressed sigh quite where all the frustration came from; and, with misgivings, where it might lead.

This is definitely not my cup of tea, Jim Betts decided. But it had been his scheme; and the job was infinitely preferable to doorstepping Number 10 in the rain or listening to some Minister at a press conference drone on about his latest achievement.

The maid took his damp raincoat. He smoothed down his hair and composed his features into an expression of expert interest.

His hostess as she appeared was a bit of a surprise. She was short, with a good if matronly figure: early forties, at a guess, though with the unlined face, clear eyes, sleek black hair and red marriage spot on her brow she looked a little younger. The features were delicate, the smile showed even, small white teeth. She was dressed in buttercup silk, a sari which along with all that gold jewellery must have cost a mint. She was thus a handsome, elegant woman, if a mite florid for his taste.

'Good morning. Mrs Bhadeshia?' He had practised in the car to get it right. 'Name's Betts. How do you do?'

'Good morning. Please, Mr Betts, come with me.'

Pramila was horribly nervous. She pulled at her sari and wondered if she had overdone it for a gloomy English morning. On the other hand her luck had obviously turned. She could hardly believe it: a national newspaper, the *Globe*, wanted to write a major feature about her home. Something different, an exotic mixture of east and west, traditional and modern, they'd said. Time a prominent Asian family was highlighted, but it would be done with taste and modesty. Pramila had frowned slightly at the later point.

The article was to be spread over two pages. Her own participation, in several outfits, was required, for was she not becoming one of the country's best-known hostesses? The voice on the phone proposed a photo-spread like those in *Hello!* magazine. Indeed, it was highly likely that, once the *Globe*'s piece (which would be an exclusive) had appeared *Hello!* would call wanting their own version. That settled it: any restraints in Pramila's mind had vanished.

First, hospitality. Pramila led her guest into the conservatory. She had expected somebody more prepossessing, but it was her task to impress him, not vice versa. She prayed the maid would serve the coffee without a spill and that her mother would remain firmly out of sight.

'It is a delight to welcome you here,' she said brightly.

Betts placed his notebook on the glass-topped coffee table and gazed round. The airy room was crammed with cane furniture and white Clarence House fabrics. He doubted that children ever played in the room, though the family could afford an army of cleaners. Carefully he sipped from a Royal Doulton cup and hoped his shoes had not dirtied the pale cream carpet.

Before he could respond, the doorbell rang. Pramila sprang up, hands fluttering. 'The photographer! Already!'

Within a few moments, as Pramila posed with cup and silver coffee-pot in hand, then draped herself on the reproduction chaise-longue in another room and lingered by the velvet curtains and the Directoire mirror in the hall, it was clear that she at least was in her element. The photographer was a grey-haired man with big hands which exchanged cameras and lenses deftly as if they were old friends. Betts followed unobtrusively, faintly attracted by the swish of silk against brown skin, and scribbled whenever a particularly useful remark fell from the lady's lips.

'Yes, I chose everything myself – with help from Harrods, of course,' she told him in answer to a question. 'I subscribe to the *Architectural Digest* – do you know it? It is full of such good ideas. This room, for example, is taken from the fashion designer Marc Bohan's lovely home in France. I adore the contrast between red velvet and the leopard-skin fabric, don't you?'

The photographer made supportive noises. His taste was for simple Habitat, when he could afford it.

It was the turn of a white satin evening dress, its bodice encrusted with beads, with two huge pendant earrings to match. The glorious shimmering whiteness of it, tight at her waist, made Pramila's bosom swell with pride. With a deep breath she paused as instructed on the bottom step of the curving staircase, one hand on the gilded banister, the other sweeping her skirts behind her. Head held high she smiled radiantly as if about to greet guests.

That she should be the model for other women! Dressed thus, she was beautiful, a Soraya, a Shakira Caine; seen as such not only by her husband but soon by the nation. Her eyes fell on the scruffy journalist, who was licking his lips as he watched. 'Great, Mrs B,' he murmured in a nasal accent she could not place. Surely he was not the *Globe*'s society reporter? Embarrassed, she glanced away, until the photographer complained and coaxed her back.

'Right! Got enough down here. Upstairs all tidy?' The photographer handed Betts his light-meter, reflector and spare film. Pramila began to lead them up.

On the landing panic suddenly assailed her. Was it acceptable to admit two men to her marital bedroom – and that its secrets should be revealed? Indeed, should she even enter it with these men without a chaperon? The photographer was already inside fixing up his lights. It was not too late to fetch her mother.

Mother would not allow it. But the room had been newly decorated. The four poster was oak, a Tudor reproduction. The whole theme was English country style by Dorma Vymura: flowers everywhere – linen, carpet, rugs, wallpaper, ceiling, dado, hangings, cushions, complemented by overfull peonies in an elaborate vase and rose-scented pomanders. Jayanti didn't like it, but then he never claimed to have taste.

'Need you in a nightie for this one,' the photographer suggested. His manner was quick and professional. 'Got anything really glamorous?'

Pramila blushed, hesitated, closed the door and headed for a wardrobe. Her favourite feather-trimmed Dior négligée and wrap were perfect, she knew. Then she stopped. It was one thing to have her décor displayed for the world to admire. Her own person was a different matter. She returned slowly to the room, still in the white evening dress, eyes downcast.

'No, I cannot do that. To be in night garments on a bed – no.'

'Paula Yates does it all the time, Mrs B,' the journalist wheedled.

'She may do. I can't. I am a married woman, a respectable person.'

The photographer beckoned Betts into a corner. A whispered discussion ensued. The photographer shrugged. Then the two returned to Pramila, who was beginning to bite her lip and look upset.

'It's all right, Mrs B, you pose in whatever you like,' said Betts soothingly. 'You got some lovely clothes. How about a cocktail dress – a short, western-style one? Then you can show us your furnishings in 'ere. That do?'

Honour satisfied, in a few moments she emerged from the dressing room in a royal-blue velvet shift and high-heeled shoes, to the contented nods of the photographer. Betts appraised her frankly and grinned, then stared out of the window. Shyly, she allowed herself to be positioned close to the flounces and frills of the bed.

Flash! Her head was beginning to spin. 'A big smile, now,' the photographer asked. 'Lean back . . . a little more – that's it. Arch your back. Point your toes – yes, we'd like to see your ... feet. *Very* nice.' He had managed to stop himself saying 'legs'.

Suddenly it was over. Betts had said little but had taken lots of notes. He appeared to have forgotten her full name completely. As the cameraman packed up, Pramila retreated and dressed hurriedly in slacks and a sweater; redoing the sari would have taken ages. The two men refused lunch and seemed anxious to get on their way.

'Do you have any idea when the item will appear?'

Betts shook his head. 'Not decided yet,' he answered truthfully. 'Depends how the photos come out, Mrs B. We'd still like some pictures of your husband in his office as a contrast. Did you manage to persuade him yet?'

Pramila sighed. 'I will, don't worry.'

She stood in the doorway and waved them off. It had been a success, hadn't it? Everything had been in place, immaculate, opulent, impressive; her clothes and figure were superb and would excite envy. So why, as she watched the *Globe*'s representatives drive away, did she have such a dreadful sense of foreboding?

'Position four!'

'*Hai! Hai!*' As they lunged and leapt, Karen and her fellow pugilists expelled their breath in the regulation manner, so that the entire hall seemed filled with manic piston-driven steam-engines. The effect was splendidly menacing. The narrow eyes of their teacher, a muscular Korean whose two stripes on jacket and trousers indicated his rank, darted from one white-jacketed group to another.

'Ouch!' For a moment Karen had lost concentration and moved too close to her sparring partner. The tip of the other girl's toe glanced against her head and knocked her sideways. She flopped to the floor, more surprised than hurt.

'Position five!'

Rubbing her ear ruefully, Karen jumped to her feet. With a twitch she set her jacket straight, hitched up her trousers, pulled tight the tie around her waist and began the new exercise. She was nowhere near gaining even a single stripe, not when such an easy point could be scored against her; but she was not about to admit defeat. An hour of Tai-kwondo twice a week had firmed all her muscles and made her lithe and supple. Although her signature was appended to the declaration required by both the governing body of the discipline and the sports centre promising never to use these newly acquired skills in anger, it was also a comfort to know that in an emergency she could look after herself.

All too soon the session was over. The participants, mostly youths and men but with a sprinkling of girls, scrambled to their feet and stood row by row, panting and red-faced. On command arms were raised to the heavens, fingers and thumbs forming an O. Their activity was but a service to the gods. Then bare heels came together, hands to the sides, and a short bow was offered to the master, whose grunt and bobbed head indicated approval.

An hour later, showered and changed, Karen bounced happily into the kitchen of the Battersea house, her carrier bag of dirty laundry under her arm, and headed for the washing machine. She felt tired and a bit sore but exhilarated. In other parts of the house her fellow residents were immediately aware of her arrival as the door banged and the machine began to churn.

Anthony was seated upstairs at his desk, trying to gain familiarity with every dot and comma of the bull points for First Order Questions. He had reminded Fred and other supporters to be on duty, on time, the next afternoon. Conscience demanded that he read through the material once more and commit as much as possible to memory.

He could hear Karen singing a pop song; he smiled and allowed himself to be distracted. How much more cheerful she made the place. How much better to have a girl in the house than men only, which would have produced a much duller atmosphere. But one could have too much of a good thing. *Two* girls would have been too many; together they'd have felt an obligation to organise everything, each vying with the other. Karen seemed content as the sole female. And because of her mother she knew the ropes politically, better, in some respects, than he and Fred did. Pretty to look at, too, and kept herself well, so that it was a repeated pleasure to find her seated opposite at the breakfast table and innocently pouring him a coffee. His skin tickled at the thought of her boyish short haircut, her cotton T-shirt and the bare neck it revealed.

He would go down soon and make a pleasant remark to her, something personal, simply to indicate how glad he was that she lived there. The gratifying notion flitted around his mind. He wondered with a slight tremor if at last this was that spark of sexual attraction which had eluded him, so far, his entire life.

Lachlan had seen Karen stride up the garden path from his room at the front of the house. He liked her, and was delighted at the positive effect she had had on both Fred and Anthony, both of whom brightened up whenever she was about. With her natural warmth and charm, and that hint of earthiness in her character, she had made him revise his opinions of the British. He had been dismayed during his first weeks in Britain when he stayed at his aunt and uncle's home. His cousin had seemed a cold fish, whose ideas of entertainment had run only to the local pub (full of cigarette smoke), the nearest rugby club (full of jocks) and the bar of the House of Commons (full of politicians, all of whom commented with varying degrees of rudeness on his accent).

But a household with three blokes and a single girl had a glaring drawback. Lachlan would willingly have formed a foursome with his cousin and a couple of female medical students or nurses, had there been any co-operation from Anthony. It occurred to him that an alternative course of action might suit: he, Lachlan, should simply find one young lady, then suggest that the numbers be made up by Anthony and Karen herself. Or perhaps two spare women – Lachlan did not doubt his persuasive ability – if Fred couldn't find his own.

Meanwhile there loomed exams and a research paper to submit. The love interest, such as it was, would have to wait; but he would mention the matter to Anthony, for future reference.

Karen's step on the stair had a dramatic effect on the building's fourth occupant. In his room at the top Fred had been trying to finish reading a biography of Harold Macmillan, his hero. It wasn't fashionable to admire the former Prime Minister, he of the patrician airs and long, mournful face. The author seemed far more engrossed in the amorous adventures of Lady Dorothy, his wife, and Robert Boothby MP, supposedly her great love. Fred could see the point of the revelations – if Macmillan had been cuckolded his whole life, and knew it, it was all the more admirable that his frustrations had been sublimated into a remarkable political career.

Fred pulled a face. He did not wish to believe that only those unlucky in love would have the drive to succeed; anyway, he was of the firm view (based on little experience) that a man's private life should be regarded as having no effect on his performance of official duties – provided, of course, that the chap did not lie. The public might snigger at adultery and raise eyebrows at misalliance, but only faced with downright hypocrisy did they get truly angry. At least, he hoped so.

At the sound of Karen, now only a few feet from him, moving in her own bedroom, perhaps taking off her day clothes and preparing for bed, Fred felt his heart leap. Agitated, he shifted around the items

170

on his desk, turned the blotter over, tore off scribbled pages from the jotter pad and fiddled with the miniature engraved carriage clock, a gift from Mr Bulstrode after the election. Two cherubs on either side of the clock-face taunted him. Their baby nakedness, the curves of arms and thighs as he fingered them, made him almost frantic.

What kind of man was he? What was he frightened of? Surely not another rejection. He would know the phrases to use and would be more persistent, not let her wriggle away. His time as a Member of Parliament had taught him tricks of fluency and manner which had eluded him before. He heard her go downstairs again and the tumble-drier start. Other feet creaked on the stairs. Then, muffled by distance, he heard Karen and Anthony exchange a few words, and her sunny laughter as she climbed back to her room.

The clock ticked on. Fred heard doors open; Anthony and Lachlan were heading into the lounge, presumably to watch the late news on TV. A high degree of privacy was *de rigueur* in the house. Nobody entered a bedroom without knocking and waiting until invited to enter. That meant that if he could get into Karen's presence while the others were occupied elsewhere he might have a few moments alone with her. And start afresh the complicated process of getting her into his confidence, and into his bed.

It was completely dark outside. Fred rose and drew his curtains. Heart pounding, he approached his own door, reached for the handle, jumped back as if burnt, returned to the mat in front of the mantelpiece and tested his appearance in the mirror. It would not do. Hurriedly he combed his hair, considered and then rejected a splash of cologne on his cheeks, patted his inside pocket where certain supplies nestled encouragingly and checked that all visible zips and buttons were fastened. He took a deep breath to calm himself. Then he opened the door, tiptoed out into the upper hallway and to Karen's room, and tapped softly.

Karen, still savouring the friendly remarks uttered by Anthony, was plucking her eyebrows in front of her dressing-table mirror. At 10.30 p.m. she did not expect visitors. With a flutter of excitement she replaced the tweezers and wondered whether she had given Anthony the impression she was ready and waiting for him. If so, what would she do?

Ask him in, of course. It was about time – perfect timing, in fact. With no worries, either. Since that daft episode with Fred, Karen had laid in her own supply of condoms. The knock came again, more insistently. Quickly she made sure that the little foil packets were in the bedside drawer, pulled the bedclothes smooth and plumped up the pillows. Damn the old shirt and jeans – there was no time to improve her own appearance, or change. She sauntered over and opened the door.

'Hullo, Karen.'

'Oh! It's you – I thought . . .'

'Can I come in?' Fred prayed that he sounded more sure of himself than he felt. The startled expression on the girl's face was distinctly off-putting.

Karen shrugged. He stepped inside and she shut the door. If Fred wanted to start talking secrets, it was best his privacy be guaranteed. That was only a courtesy.

He looked around. The room smelled enticingly of Karen, her perfume, her shampoo, her talc. A fluffy toy cat and a pair of blue pyjamas lay on the pillow, though with a man, he anticipated with a thumping heart, she would lie unclothed. Posters of sultry pop stars adorned one wall but more innocent symbols, photos of school and college, cuttings from newspapers and magazines of hats and boots and fashion pictures filled the main space. Fred turned, then deliberately sat down on the bed.

'Come and sit here,' he said, patting the coverlet beside him. His voice, pleading, was not entirely under his control.

Karen considered. She was not about to order Fred out of her room. After all, just a few months earlier she'd been willing to go a lot further – and it was only his incompetence that had stopped them. He was a friend, and in a good-humoured way she was fond of him. 'Sure,' she said, and complied.

Fred swallowed hard. This was proving unexpectedly easy – going almost too fast. But that was her style, wasn't it? On New Year's Eve she'd given him no time to think as she flung off her sweater. He gazed at her, brooding. Should she decide on a repeat she would not find him inadequate. With a jerky movement he reached across and took her hand.

'If . . . we . . . that is . . .'

He gulped and started again, twisting to face the girl directly.

'Look, Karen, I'm not very good at this. We've hardly touched since – well, you know. And I have felt such a fool. So the first thing is, I'm sorry I messed it up so badly.'

Karen made no attempt to withdraw her hand but instead stroked Fred's arm in a thoughtful, gentle gesture. 'That's OK,' she murmured, and wondered what was coming next.

The image of ghastly Mrs Hepworth at the advice bureau unaccountably came to Fred. That cow had no trouble putting two words together, or forty. He gritted his teeth and concentrated.

'And the second thing is . . .' Then he blurted out: 'D'you think we could try again?'

Without waiting for an answer he leaned across and kissed her, full on the mouth, first lips only, then deeper, as hard and passionately as he could.

The kiss lasted several minutes until both had to break off to come up for breath. Karen, choking slightly, dimpled at him.

'Well! You seem to have a much better idea now, Fred,' she remarked, intending it as a compliment. The look on his face told her, however, that he had hoped for a more lustful declaration.

He squared his shoulders. 'I hope so. Made a fool of myself last time. And I don't intend to miss a chance like that again, I can tell you. I've thought of nothing else since.' He could feel her breath on his cheek. Her lips, so full and moist, were twitching but he could not tell whether she was delighted or astonished or about to laugh at him. Urgently he crashed on: 'So how about it? I'm not so terrible, am I? And I fancy you like crazy, Karen. I think you're terrific. Honestly.'

'Darling Fred!' Karen said softly. She moved her free hand slowly across his face from brow to chin. The caress made something turn over inside him and his body became aroused. He looked down a little sheepishly, then lunged towards her. He had to touch her breasts – he *had* to.

'No, Fred.' Karen grasped both Fred's hands firmly together and placed them on her knee. 'I am very fond of you. If there was nobody else around, I'd say yes – in fact I'd tear the clothes off you right now.' Fred groaned and she shushed him, glancing at the door. 'But there is somebody else.'

'Lucky beggar, that's all I can say,' growled Fred, his spirits sinking. Now he knew she was unavailable he wanted her more than ever. 'Anybody I know?'

'Mmm, yes, actually,' Karen said. She shifted imperceptibly away from him and sat upright once more, though she kept hold of Fred's hands for fear of their wandering. 'Anthony. Oh, he hasn't done anything yet, but I can tell. He just told me how pleased he is that I'm in his house. In his shy way that means a lot. He's older than you, Fred: more my type, I suppose.'

'I see,' Fred muttered. That Anthony might be a rival had not occurred

173

to him. He was deflated, yet puzzled. If this were true, then he'd have expected Anthony to pass some joshing remark when Karen was absent, the sort one man utters to another to stake out desired territory. He searched Karen's face but her sincerity was evident; the shining eyes, the half-smile, were not for him.

He was not ready to give up.

'I've never thought of him . . . like that. He never talks about women, ever. In fact he never talks about sex, even when you're not around. Doesn't seem interested.'

'So what?' Karen was indignant, but uncomfortable. In a few words Fred had encapsulated the unspoken problem. Then she relented. 'I think he's simply a bit timid with women and I can help with that. Or maybe he's had a bad experience in the past – he's over thirty so he can't be a complete virgin, can he?'

Fred regained possession of one of his hands and scratched his head. How boyish, Karen thought.

'Could be. Some blokes aren't interested because they're made that way. If he's one, you're wasting your time – even you. Or you could make yourself very unhappy, and I'd hate to see that. Some like poor Stephen Milligan have to do weird things to get them going – women's clothes, ligatures. If that's his scene, Karen, run a mile, please. And others . . . well, has it occurred to you that he might be gay?'

'Anthony?' That was an extraordinary suggestion. There were gay men at college. The entrance hall was covered in adverts for the annual Gay Pride march through the streets of London. But they were different; they looked and dressed distinctively, and had a code of their own. They wore earrings in strange places; some shaved their heads and were noisy and aggressive. None of them wore a suit and claimed to be a Member of Parliament. She frowned as she tried to get her mind around the picture, then brightened.

'I honestly don't think so. Let me tell you why. He's made speeches about homosexuality and said he was against it, isn't that right? I've seen his name in the Pink Paper the Gay Club hands out at college as somebody who tends to vote against equal rights. He wouldn't do that if he was one, would he?'

'Oh, Karen. He might.' Fred pondered. 'Some of those who most virulently denounce gays may well be that way inclined. Puts the dogs off the scent, see. But, I agree with you, Anthony's not the sort to do that. If he disapproves, that's genuine. There's still one other possibility.'

Relaxed, almost sleepy, Karen leaned into Fred's body. His heart was calmer. It came to him that there might yet be hope, if his assessment of their landlord was anywhere near correct. More like a brother than a lover, he put his arm around Karen and gave her a squeeze. From downstairs came the closing music of *Newsnight*. He would have to return to his own room soon.

'The worst thing, Karen, would be this: suppose he is gay, and doesn't know it?'

The two young people sat silent. Without another word, Fred rose, bent down to kiss her gently on the cheek, and left.

Karen slept well, her body weary, her mind and conscience untroubled. At some point deep in the night she awoke. Something had penetrated her fuddled brain and, stretching lazily, slipping in and out of sleep, she tried to identify it.

A strange soft noise came from downstairs. It sounded like a child, or a small animal perhaps, a whimper, faint and intermittent. Karen listened for a few moments – perhaps she ought to investigate? But once again all was quiet: the dark warm house and its inhabitants slumbered.

Maybe it was her imagination, she concluded, as sleep reclaimed her. And in the morning, though she remembered waking, she had entirely forgotten the cause.

Chapter Eleven

'Was this entirely wise?'

Jayanti Bhadeshia held the copy of the *Globe* at arm's length and twisted it this way and that. Behind him Pramila tried to compose her anxious face. If he did not absolutely adore the article then it must have been, as she had feared all along, a terrible mistake. That her friends had been telephoning the whole morning, their voices creaking with envy, was no consolation. They would say the most effusive things on the phone, then titter behind her back. Only her husband would be both tactful and accurate.

'The house looks wonderful. Interior decorators have asked me who did it,' she ventured.

'Maybe you should set up a new business,' he answered drily. 'It would have helped had we paid all the bills. But that is not my main worry. The pictures. They make you look . . . not as you are to me. What have they done?'

He bent closer and examined the pose in the cocktail dress. His calmness was beginning to unnerve his wife completely. At last he put down the paper, stood upright and turned to her.

'So, does your mother approve of you showing your legs to all and sundry?' he asked, but his voice was gentle.

That did it. Pramila burst into tears.

'I am sorry! I did it for you. They said they wanted to demonstrate how a successful Asian family lives – for you . . .'

He pulled her close to comfort her. 'Ah, my silly lady. You see their secret intention: they make us out such greedy fools and we are not – or no more than anyone else. Don't cry, my dearest, mother of my children. I understand what you tried to do and I am proud of you.'

He fished out a handkerchief and gave it to her. For several moments she wept, then slowly subsided. Over her shoulder he could still see the display and shut his eyes. He had enough on his plate

176

without this. Those images, he feared, would return time and again to haunt them.

'*How* much?'

Elaine, cheque-book in hand, recoiled in horror. Behind her somebody giggled. At her side Karen looked crestfallen.

'Two hundred and twelve pounds, fifty pence, Mrs Stalker.' The Marks and Spencer assistant commiserated. 'Young people are expensive these days, aren't they?'

'But we've only bought a couple of bras and a few pairs of knickers . . .'

'Actually you've had twelve bras between you at ten pounds each, plus matching panties at a fiver, and a few other items besides. Do you want to put anything back?'

It wasn't fair to blame her daughter; most was for herself, the hidden cost of running two homes. But Karen had added to the burden with her sudden desire for lace-trimmed silky undergarments. Hence the shopping trip.

The queue of customers behind shifted, torn between compassion, impatience and curiosity. What was this celebrity doing here, taking up so much time? Why wasn't the famous Mrs Stalker at her desk? And as for the outlay – wasn't she extraordinarily well off these days, now she was a Minister?

Elaine paid up with a rueful shrug and led Karen swiftly past the sweater counter and away. Out in Oxford Street she hesitated, then turned left for Selfridges. In a few moments the two were installed in the second-floor café surrounded by green foliage and bamboo for a modest lunch.

'Crumbs. I hadn't realised it'd be so much, Mum. I'm sorry.' Karen made her eyes round and soulful.

Her mother chuckled. 'Not your fault. Perhaps if more of Her Majesty's Ministers did their own shopping instead of leaving it to their spouses we'd guess where the "feel good" factor went.'

'They're mostly blokes, that's why.' Karen wondered if she dare ask for a cake, a strawberry-packed tart with piped cream, the sort she could never normally afford.

Elaine grimaced. 'Not all, but I know what you mean. Chirac's put twelve women in his government. We've barely that number in the whole parliamentary party.'

It was enjoyable, talking. Karen sipped her tea. 'But you get judged the same, now. There's no distinction, is there?'

'Of course there is. Just look at us. The occasional male Minister or MP seen shopping with his family wins good marks. For a woman it's the opposite – she's sloping off, incapable of isolating her career from her other obligations. Makes me grind my teeth.'

Karen was only partially sympathetic. Like most of her generation she took it for granted that her sex would be no barrier. Her mother had eaten only one slice of Welsh rarebit, so the girl, still hungry, reached over and helped herself. Elaine, musing, barely noticed.

'I know I bang on about it, but there are days when a woman's place seems to be not in the home, or kitchen, or the House of Commons, but in the wrong, whatever she tries.'

Karen glanced pointedly towards the counter. The remark of a college lecturer on the issue seemed apposite. 'We used to seek equality of opportunity; but what we're really after is equality of outcome. That'd need positive discrimination. Then other people lose out, like good men. Tricky, isn't it?'

'True. As the Labour Party could vouch, with its battles over all-women selection.' She eyed her daughter. 'Now then, my lass, you're supposed to cheer your mother up, not make me feel worse. You still peckish? Would you like a cake?'

Karen jumped up with alacrity. A few moments later she returned from the counter with her plate piled high, seated herself and tucked in. After a few moments she licked her fingers in contentment and eyed her mother. 'Mum,' she said quietly.

The tone of her voice made Elaine look intently at her.

'Mum, did you get an invitation to baby Jonathan's christening?'

Elaine assented but added nothing. She had been nonplussed to receive a friendly letter from Mike and his second wife Linda, whose new baby was the cause of the event.

'It was my idea they should ask you. After all he is my half-brother, and his dad is my dad. You shouldn't be on bad terms. Please will you go?'

'We aren't on bad terms. We aren't on any terms, good or bad.' Elaine pondered. 'I don't think it would be wise for me to attend such a public occasion. Linda's family will be there and everyone would get very embarrassed.'

Karen was downcast. Elaine squeezed her fingers. 'I can see what you're trying to do and I approve. Would you be happy if I went to their home to see the baby a few days before? I can take a gift and say I've another engagement on the day of the ceremony. Then honour would be satisfied all round.'

The girl nodded contentedly and returned to her cake. Elaine watched her covertly for a moment. How precious her daughter had become to her. But she was not an only child. There had been another once, long ago: a son, Jake, born after Karen, who had suffered from a congenital defect, an enzyme deficiency which meant he had arrived apparently normal but had slowly and terrifyingly deteriorated before their eyes. It was the way the family had been treated, the downcast eyes and muttered excuses, which had first pushed Elaine into the political world. Maybe Karen, barely four when her brother died, retained some half-forgotten memory which fostered her interest in the new baby; or maybe, growing young woman that she was, she was beginning to think of motherhood herself in due course. Elaine smiled at her daughter and wondered.

A woman in a red coat walked past their table with a tray, hesitated, turned around and stopped.

'Why, it's Mrs Stalker! What are you doing here?'

The tray carried a meal of cheese on toast and pot of tea identical to their own. Elaine realised suddenly that she was tired and that her feet hurt. The bleep had been silent too long: she would have to get back. An ordinary mother might have swept her daughter off to a matinée at a cinema or theatre. She gestured at the food.

'Much the same as you, I guess.' She smiled weakly.

'Well, yes,' the woman answered doubtfully. 'I saw you in Marks and Spencer and I must say I was surprised. Don't you get preferential treatment – you know, having the place opened before other customers? And I bet you get discounts, too.' She nudged Elaine's arm and waited expectantly to be told the truth.

Once Elaine might have made a wisecrack or a sharp response, but there was no future in being as rude as her interlocutor. 'I don't have the nerve to ask, frankly, though some do. And I doubt if my daughter would get up so early.'

'This your daughter? I thought it must be a policewoman, in plain clothes. Don't you get protection? Pleased to meet you.' The woman nodded uncertainly at Karen as if she didn't believe a word.

A small crowd had gathered, whispering. Hastily Elaine collected coats and carrier bags. With as much dignity as they could muster the two moved out into the street.

Karen noted her mother's stony face, took her arm protectively and steered her firmly towards Our Price. 'The British are mad, Mum,' she whispered. 'Anyway, although I'm very proud of you it looks a dismal job. I shouldn't mind if you weren't a Minister at all. People seem to want to eat you alive.'

'Ah! George. *So* good to catch you.'

George hesitated, took the phone from his ear and cudgelled his brain. Though the accent was distinctive he couldn't put a name to its owner.

'George Horrocks here. May I ask who's speaking?'

'My dear George! It's your friend Jayanti – Jay Bhadeshia. We last met . . . let me see . . . at the reception at Number Ten in January. Now do you remember?'

The voice was squeaky, though with what emotion George could not tell – excitement, or anxiety perhaps. He kept his own tone non-committal.

'Of course I do. And you were on my Prima guest list at conference, too.' He wondered what the man wanted, but recalled writing his own home number on several business cards which he'd handed out quite casually. There was no point in being irritated if what amounted to an invitation to intimacy was then taken up, as this chap clearly proposed to do.

'I wanted a quick word with you, George.' The voice took on a wheedling tone. 'You're a non-executive director of Tarrants Bank, aren't you?' Without waiting for an answer Jayanti hurried on. 'With Lord Tarrant – the father of the Prime Minister's beautiful wife – he was there, at Number Ten that day too . . .'

'Indeed he was. How can I help you?' George had figured out what might be coming and was unsure whether he liked it or not.

The Tarrant board meeting the following day was to consider Bhadeshia's preliminary application for funds. For the next few moments Jayanti outlined the details of his great project, its splendid prospects in the new Africa, the assurances received from the President and its potential cash flow. As the voice enthused about the new buildings, the well-trained workforce, the excellence of the facilities and the desirability of helping a newly democratic state to achieve its full potential, against his better judgement George felt a twinge of admiration.

This man was prepared to have a vision and take tremendous risks to bring it to fruition. Were he successful he would become a household name to millions, almost a messiah bringing affordable consumer goods to people long starved of the most basic necessities. A worthy objective, not to be dismissed lightly.

The problem, as George could see it, was that Bhadeshia's estimates were full of holes. How much? He couldn't say for sure. When would the shops be open? Next year, the first one, some time. How exactly would he recruit and train staff? Oh, that would not be difficult. Was he sure he would get import licences, for example for the computerised cash tills and stock system? What about overseas managers – would they be granted work permits? Was he sure he could repatriate profits? On those points Jayanti was indignantly definite. His close friend the President had promised every assistance. Except money, thought George.

If it worked, with low costs and rapid expansion the profits would roll in. But it was a gamble and no pay-off was likely for some years. That brought into question whether any British banks, so accustomed to short-term gains, would be content to invest. And if not respectable backers, then who?

On the other hand Bhadeshia's track record to date, in so far as he had been able to ascertain it before the Prima breakfast, seemed solidly based and credible. The retail activities in England must do well: that would be ready money, all cash. The same family names turned up as directors elsewhere. He had heard that the Bhadeshias had diversified into car leasing, which could indicate HP and merchant bank finance somewhere in the background, and probably insurance links. The community of which Bhadeshia was an important and respected member was shrewd, hard-working, entrepreneurial and tough. His British colleagues could learn a great deal from their skill and energy. If anyone could pull off this enterprise in East Africa, then the person on the other end of the phone had a better chance than most.

'Right, I've got that. Thank you. It sounds like a marvellous scheme and you are to be congratulated on your drive and imagination.'

'Imagination? No, this is not a dream.' Jayanti tried to control the tremor in his voice. As ever, under pressure, his accent became stronger and he spoke too fast. 'This is *reality*. All it needs is the financial input. Some is already lined up. I know you will take an excellent decision tomorrow with Lord Tarrant and the other distinguished gentlemen. I spoke to him about it when I was invited to dinner at his house. He knows me very well. Soon I will be able to thank you. Maybe we will have lunch together?'

Jayanti stopped, panting. He knew he should extract a firm positive commitment from George but, as with Lord Tarrant and the other British businessmen with whom he came into increasing contact, he did not know how. With his own people his standing itself was security, his word his bond. His loyalty to his family and his willingness to employ and help them above others was regarded as a strength; to his local English bank manager it was a weakness which suggested nepotism rather than objectivity. Every attempt to cross from one culture to another met with disdain and rebuff, but in his frustration he could only bluster, and thus sounded less rather than more convincing.

George sighed. No wonder nothing had been forthcoming from Bhadeshia into Prima: the man had other fish to fry. That was understandable, but George was not reassured that this might be the start of a close friendship.

'Certainly. Perhaps your secretary would contact mine at Prima tomorrow afternoon? Good luck, and thanks for calling.'

The Daimler slipped away from the bustle of Brussels airport and headed the short distance to the grandest of the UK's three embassies.

'The trouble with Europe', Harrison asserted lazily, 'is that the Commission is obsessed with petty restrictions. Far too many rules, which are then ignored by other countries. We, of course, behave impeccably. That's why we lose out.'

'I think we overdo it at times,' Anthony murmured.

'Really?' Derek stared at him. Anthony flushed. In the front seat next to the driver, Chadwick half turned and gave the PPS a wink of encouragement. At least the new chap had some original views, unlike his boss.

Earnestly, spreading his hands, Anthony continued, 'We go mad in Britain. Often, quite unreasonably.' He went on to give several examples.

The noise from Chadwick might have been a chortle, had that not been impossible from the normally humourless Deputy Secretary. Derek slapped Anthony's thigh.

'The secret, old boy, is to blame Brussels whatever happens. People at home know so little about what goes on and it's so sparsely reported that we can agree to whatever we want out here, then scream blue murder that it was imposed on us. Don't you go interfering, there's a good man.'

'You see,' Chadwick continued the lesson smoothly, 'we'll agree this health directive today. In return we'll get concessions. Our rights to border controls and quarantine, for instance.'

'But why should we want that?' Anthony was exasperated. His

182

father, whose business transcended international boundaries, had forceful objections to paperwork at customs posts. 'Other countries are nowhere near as paranoid about rabies. Why not?'

'Because they vaccinate everything in sight. Pets, dogs, cats, the lot. And put down dosed bait in the forests for foxes. At public expense. So they have hardly any cases.' Chadwick waved an airy hand, as if the idea in Britain were unthinkable.

'Wouldn't it be better if we did the same? Look at the millions who cross the Channel every year. Maybe we have no rabies simply because our neighbours haven't either. Nothing to do with quarantine. It seems so darned old fashioned to me.'

There was a stunned silence in the car. Anthony's statement amounted to heresy.

Chadwick concealed a smile behind his hand. 'Ah, but you see,' he intoned, 'if we took your position and followed the practice of our partner countries, we would lose something terribly precious.'

Anthony was puzzled. 'What's that?'

'The right to be different – even wrong. It's called sovereignty. You wouldn't want to challenge that, would you?'

'Now then, gentlemen. Proposition four (c)?'

Fourteen voices murmured in unison. 'Agreed.'

'Four (d)?'

'Agreed.'

'Thank you so much.' Lord Tarrant looked around, satisfied. The board was behaving itself beautifully today. It helped that that fool Ferriman was missing, on a fact-finding tour to the Seychelles, or so he claimed. The proof that all was above reproach was that he'd taken his researcher with him. And Bob Horton was elsewhere, sorting out the latest rail strike. Funny how nothing had ever happened till he was appointed to run Railtrack – frightfully bad luck, really. Might be time for a quick sherry before lunch.

Behind him and on both sides dark portraits of his predecessors stared down like grim ghosts, men with side whiskers or luxuriant beards, gimlet eyes and solemn jowls. The encrusted gilding of the frames and the soft but well-placed spotlights enhanced their claim to the highest integrity allied with perfect financial wisdom. After lunch Lord Tarrant would be sitting for his own, an experience he secretly found delightful.

He turned a page. 'Proposition five needs more thorough consideration, I fear. We are being asked to be the lead investor in a new development in East Africa, in . . .' He named the country as he removed his spectacles and placed them neatly on the page, the better to impress on those present the need to think deeply.

'Not the lead investor – Barclays have agreed to take on that role, though they've only offered two million to start.' This came from Atkins, smooth as ever, the youngest chief cashier the bank had ever appointed, whose economics PhD from Cambridge gave him a dismaying intellectual edge.

The correction appeared to irritate the noble visage. Atkins hastened to restore harmony. 'We're asked to put up around three million. But you're right, chairman. Our support will make the difference. With two banks in, the proposers won't have any trouble raising the rest.'

'What is it they want to build?' The newly ennobled Baroness Gorman put her own spectacles on her nose and searched through the papers. Tarrant suppressed a sigh. Why hadn't she bothered to read the stuff more carefully; it had cost enough to courier to her country house in Essex?

'Shops.'

'Shops?' The baroness brightened. That sounded an excellent idea: Thatcherism and the consumer society brought to the natives. Indeed, if the shops at home were good enough, perhaps the natives might be persuaded to stay put and not keep nagging to come to Britain.

'Yes – but they don't exist yet. And the country is still in a mess after a civil war, a revolution and a coup in the space of seven years.' The chairman could feel himself making up his mind. 'Does anybody here know this Bhadeshia chap?'

George Horrocks intervened. 'I know him through Prima. He was runner-up in the Asian Businessman of the Year. Started twenty-odd years ago with nothing and has built up a substantial empire of retail outlets. Diversified recently into textiles and engineering, though that side faltered a bit during the recession. Big contributor to the Conservative Party, chairman. In fact you met him, though it may have slipped your mind, at a function last January at Number Ten.'

'Aha!' The Prime Minister's father-in-law perked up. 'Sounds a good sort, then?' Tarrant wondered vaguely if the fellow could have been at that tedious Treasurer's dinner at his home. With forty unknown names provided by Central Office it had been difficult to cultivate more than a few.

George assented. 'Thoroughly nice chap. But I have serious doubts about this venture. Not because of Bhadeshia, but because the location is so dodgy.'

The baroness looked unhappy. Other directors darted surreptitious glances at the ornate clock behind the chairman's head. An aroma of roast beef was seeping into the boardroom from the nearby kitchen and the clatter of plates could be heard.

'Shall I move that proposition five be put back, until further information is available?' suggested Atkins helpfully.

'George, you happy with that?' the chairman enquired. One wouldn't want to come between a board member and his friends.

George was silent. Bhadeshia was counting on him. The banks were under heavy criticism, much of it justified, for not co-operating with adventurous new businesses; but his duties as a director must be placed ahead of any faint loyalty to Bhadeshia. He raised his head and nodded.

'Excellent. Then I declare the meeting closed.'

It was not a question of how he was seen and assessed by other people. Anthony York knew, as he examined himself in the bedroom mirror, adjusted the white tie and straightened the tails, that for him there was one judge and jury – himself.

His mind roamed over the day's events and kept returning to the spat in the car. He had not intended to be so forthright, but the official stance had seemed puerile. Yet that was the position Harrison had faithfully taken later in the day and the 'victory' was duly won and trumpeted. Anthony's duty required him from here onwards to give full, if not fulsome, support.

Would there be any diminution of his principles if he simply kept them to himself? That was a different question entirely. It might make life easier. It would not require conformity to anybody else's ideals, or lack of them. On the other hand, as Edmund Burke had gravely declared, all that was required for evil to triumph was that good men do nothing. Surely that also implied that all that was needed for foolishness to predominate was that wiser counsels stayed mute. Not to air objections left them stillborn; an argument not expressed was not an argument.

Margaret Thatcher and Keith Joseph and Alfred Sherman had never kept quiet – they shouted from the rooftops their beliefs in privatisation, home ownership, trade union reform, personal responsibility and free trade and carried a whole generation of voters with them, including

185

Anthony himself. Half the new nations of Europe had copied them, replacing the dead hand of communism with the blunt certainties of Thatcherism even as that creed was discarded in its homeland. He wondered if Mrs Thatcher had been warned to keep her crazy nostrums to herself. At the start the answer must have been, often. Yet she took no notice.

Mr Major, on the other hand, had never challenged anybody's complacency. His name, indeed, had become synonymous with caution. Whereas ministerial office under the blessed Margaret could only have been the experience of a lifetime, service under her successor, especially in a lowly post, would have been a dreadful anticlimax. It was not hard for *his* successor to be a far stronger personality. Yet somehow, without anyone being able to put a finger on *why* and *how*, John Major had stayed at the top far longer than most Prime Ministers.

It was a great conundrum. Maybe he, Anthony, should simply observe and absorb, at any rate while he was in such a junior job. If – when – he was promoted, once he had built a coterie of like-minded people and learned how to deal with the press, that was the moment to move ahead with original announcements. Then he could stick his neck out. Not now.

The manservant gave a discreet knock at the door. It was time to go down for dinner.

He squared his shoulders. It was settled. In his personal behaviour, both outward and private, he would incorporate the high standards of honour, decency, straight-dealing and decorum laid down for him by his parents. The York name would gain further respect through his tenure of it. In his open statements and politics, meanwhile, he would be discretion itself. There would be no repeat of that morning's outburst.

As Anthony reached the top stair, the door to Chadwick's room opened. The civil servant, freshly shaved and bathed, was dressed similarly to Anthony but with a gold-filigree decoration as Commander of the Bath at his throat. Courteously Anthony waited, but could not hide a raised eyebrow at Chadwick's red necktie.

'Oh, this?' Chadwick chuckled self-deprecatingly. 'The award is virtually routine once one gets to certain levels. As for the slight unorthodoxy of dress: we have to conform so very much, but we are allowed one small quirk. To keep us sane, you might say. My neckwear is my sole flamboyancy.'

'It's splendid, Mr Chadwick.' Anthony wondered if he should try

186

something similar – red-spotted handkerchiefs perhaps – as a reflection of his new-found self-control.

'My dear chap – the name's Martin. At least while there aren't too many junior clericals around.'

An arm was placed briefly around the younger man's shoulders and the two men's eyes met with the ancient conspiracy of the educated upper-class English male.

Anthony laughed and relaxed. 'Then you must call me Anthony, please. You can't really call me anything else – not Minister, anyway.'

'Not yet, Anthony. But keep your mind as sharp as it was this morning and it won't be long.'

The Ambassador, Sir Clifford Mawby, was tall, spare, cultured, affable and sharp as a needle. A superb example of the British career diplomat, he had previously served in the Paris embassy. There, his originality and style were immediately apparent for he had contrived to arrive via the Channel tunnel which was still under construction at the time, and thus became the first representative of the English monarch to travel to another state over dry land for 400 years, since the days of the first Elizabeth when the last one had ridden north to Scotland.

As he waited in the hall the Ambassador reflected grimly that ministerial delegations could be a trial. They expected to stay in the residence, which was extra work for all concerned, though Douglas Hurd, to do him credit, had frequently opted for a hotel – but then he'd been in the Foreign Office game long before he entered Parliament. Official visitors often failed to realise this was a *home* and that they were *guests* – even if everything was provided with public money, or perhaps especially so. They shouldn't expect a hairdrier, a kettle and a well-stocked mini-bar in every room. They shouldn't arrive minus basic items like deodorant or toothpaste and expect them to be supplied for free. Some insisted on bringing British equipment such as radio alarms and caused a great nuisance over plug adaptors, which then disappeared home in their luggage. Nor should embassy staff be treated as room service – one's house guests were supposed to rise at a reasonable hour in the morning and, as consolation for their intrusion, make sparkling conversation at breakfast. Most of all, since the evening's banquet was laid on in their honour, it was appreciated if they could *turn up on time*.

The Minister of State appeared at last, his face flushed, white tie slightly askew. Sir Clifford glided forward, mouth twitching, eyes hard.

He had heard of Mr Harrison's habits. It had been a mistake, as Ernesto the head steward had warned, not to move that young chambermaid temporarily to other duties.

The reception salon was full of chattering figures on their third drink. The doors were thrown open and with some relief guests began to move to the table, murmuring with appreciation at its crystal, silver and porcelain. A huge central arrangement of fresh flowers filled the room with the heady aroma of lilies.

Harrison would have preferred a night on the town. Not exactly a rave, Brussels, but one or two nightclubs had lively reputations. Didn't anyone realise what a nuisance it was to carry on working after a busy day, this time dressed like the chorus line in some off-form Folies Bergère? Mawby was all right, and his wife, reputedly French, was attractive enough. But the NATO chaps were ghastly and the steely-eyed commanding officer of the Rapid Reaction Force at Rheindalen, who happened to be in town, far worse. The locals, fat Belgian dignitaries whose titles he had not ascertained, told bad jokes in laborious English. Female numbers were a bit low and were augmented by embassy staff with neither a witty word to say nor a worthwhile bosom among them. Then there was the dismal Head of Chancery groaning on about the cost of this place. Awful. Harrison sighed at his misfortune, reached for the Muscadet, stuck an exploratory fork into the salmon mousse and recalled with relish the dimpled maid upstairs.

As he feared, Harrison was seated by the Ambassador. His discomfort was not shared by Anthony York, who was more at home with the formality. The most junior visitor present, he found himself at the far end of the table between an earnest young woman diplomat on her first posting and the wife of one of the generals. The main course turned out to be British lamb, shipped live from Derbyshire hillsides to a Belgian abattoir and cooked beautifully in the continental style, slightly bloody. As the mint sauce appeared the general's wife's face paled. She whispered to him that she was a vegetarian.

On the other side of the army wife Martin Chadwick quickly showed his skill. Anthony watched as Chadwick called over a waiter and had the lamb deftly replaced by an omelette. In a few moments the lady had been charmed back to life with graceful stories and much platonic flattery. Anthony cautiously tried a similar technique on the young woman staffer and was amused as she began to gossip a trifle too freely about backstairs goings-on at the European Commission.

Martin, Anthony reckoned, would be about ten or twelve years older than himself. About the same height, but thinner, his body lean, dark hair immaculate, long face settling into lines on the forehead and around the eye sockets that would intensify with age. The two men's antecedents were close – public school, Oxbridge, classics and history degrees, nothing zealous like maths or science, though Anthony guessed that Martin was much the cleverer. He seemed so practised in these social graces, particularly with the women. His manner was so agreeable, so inviting of confidences, that as a towering *bombe Alaska* wobbled over their shoulders the older woman was laughing merrily.

The next logical thought in Anthony's head should have been a thorough examination of the way Chadwick handled these ladies. Instead he found his attention drawn steadily to Chadwick himself.

The cheeseboard was served, British style, after the dessert, to the bewilderment of the foreigners. Anthony helped the young woman to a sliver of Brie and applauded with Martin as she commented with asperity that the British were becoming more European by the minute without realising it: the evidence, she revealed, was that they now knew how to pronounce 'quiche' and 'Camembert'.

Anthony's thoughts returned to Martin. What kind of man was he away from the office? Married – that much he knew. 'My wife' littered his conversation, together with appropriate references to children, gardens and Sittingbourne. But he was obviously not a ladies' man, not like that oaf Harrison, whose offensive descriptions of the females present would doubtless be his main topic of conversation on the return journey. Would Martin be called handsome, Anthony considered. There was no gentleness or sweetness in the man's expression, but the intelligent eyes and faintly cynical twist to the mouth moderated the inscrutability which was clearly the impression he preferred to give. Anthony wondered if Martin were conscious of the examination, and caught him glancing over the table towards himself just for an instant, then turning quickly away.

A silver fork tinkled delicately against crystal. Mawby cleared his throat and rose solemnly to his feet.

'Minister, ladies and gentlemen: I give you – the Queen.'

Chairs were scraped back, glasses raised. 'Her Majesty the Queen.' The generals, as serving officers, harrumphed a little and added the military salutation, 'God bless her!'

Mawby stayed upright, lifted a condemnatory eyebrow as Harrison too quickly tried to resume his seat, and continued.

'And, since we have present both Monsieur Fratermann from the

Belgian Ministry of Health and the Burgomaster – we are deeply honoured, gentlemen – I ask you also to drink to the health of – King Albert and Queen Paola.'

Harrison could not be bothered to get his tongue around that lot and contented himself with 'The King and Queen!', loudly.

Sandalwood boxes of cigars and cigarettes appeared with liqueurs in tiny glasses and brandy in balloons, while a fine port in an old decanter was passed around. Anthony declined the tobacco but accepted a Courvoisier. His attention wandered as rotund persons made ponderous speeches of thanks. The perfume of the lilies seemed to intensify. He was not required to perform; that was the Minister's role. Fortunately Harrison was fine at that sort of thing and once on his feet carried it off without incident.

At ten-thirty on the dot Lady Mawby rose and apologised daintily to the senior figures on either side, who naturally were obliged to rise also. Sir Clifford sprang up; white-gloved waiters reached to move chairs. The Belgians and the generals found themselves eased away from the table and shrugged with disappointment. Coats and wraps were reclaimed. Derek Harrison made his excuses and bolted upstairs.

Anthony, Chadwick and the Ambassador drifted towards the drawing room. Another hour of comradely discourse followed until the house guests regretfully abandoned their drained glasses and bade their host goodnight.

'Not a bad life, that,' Anthony remarked as he climbed the ornate stairs at Chadwick's side. The wine, brandy and excellent food had filled him with bonhomie. He felt more at ease than for ages. As they turned a corner and passed a small vase of lilies on a window-sill the pollen brushed off against his jacket, leaving an orange stain. Even that did not break his mood. Flicking at it ineffectually, he continued: 'I have never envied you your job, Martin, but if I wasn't an MP then Her Britannic Majesty's overseas service might well have attracted me.'

'Heavens, no,' the civil servant teased gently. 'All those cocktail parties, buttering up bores? And night after night entertaining the likes of us? Surely not.'

He stood on the top stair, a hand resting on Anthony's arm, his worldly face creased into a pleasant smile. He seemed to hesitate. Then: 'May I come in for a minute?'

Anthony was puzzled; it was late. But perhaps there was something

Martin wanted to say, at the tail end of a successful day. 'Of course.' He held open the door, and stood to one side.

Once in his own room it was natural to remove the tailcoat and brush it, then to hang it up and undo his over-tight tie. He breathed more deeply and felt a little drunk. Martin seemed in no hurry as he examined the oil painting over the fireplace and the pile of leather-bound books on a round rosewood table.

'You have a point, though,' Martin remarked. 'These chaps know how to live.'

Anthony reached behind the door for his towelling dressing gown. Perhaps if he laid it out rather ostentatiously on the bed Martin would get the hint and come to the point. As he turned back, however, Martin was suddenly before him, very close.

Their eyes were at the same level. Martin's were deep-set, with dark lashes, long for a man, and crinkly lines at the outer edges. Their colour in the dim light was indeterminate, but gazing into them, in a manner which he normally avoided as far too direct, Anthony felt himself being drawn in, as if to a secret, private world. It was so strange: the unwavering iris became a path down which he felt himself glide, without fear, without resistance. Then he seemed to round a corner and found himself on the edge of a deep pool which lapped lazily at his feet, as if he were a swimmer uncertain whether to plunge in but aware that something remarkable, and precious, might be hidden just below the surface.

It must be the alcohol, surely? Startled, Anthony found his gaze held and a hand once more on his shirtsleeve. Through the fabric he could feel the other man's skin, the tension of the fingers. Normally he would have let himself shrink from such an intimate contact with another human being; but not at all with Martin, a man whom he knew well, and admired, and trusted. The hand tightened and the eyes widened, as if to assure him that the water was warm and welcoming. Anthony sensed that the pool was not empty, that he would not be alone, but with amiable spirits who would soothe away every pain. The faint smell of lilies lingered in the room, the smell of death, of decay. A promise was being made, or offered. His head buzzed and he shook it slowly from side to side.

The other man's voice was soft, caressing. 'You are a fine young man, Anthony, but you never seem happy.'

The whisper seemed to come from far away. Anthony's mouth went dry and he could feel his heart begin to pound.

'Why aren't you happy? Are you missing something? Maybe I can help you . . .'

He could not breathe. He could not drop his eyes from Martin, whose own breath, with its masculine allure of brandy and good living he could almost taste in his own mouth.

The pulses in Anthony's head gathered pace and throbbed. The hand moved up his arm, over his shoulder, the fingers played on his throat as if seeking the most sensitive place, as he stood stock-still, not daring to move. Flesh to flesh, above the collar, the fingertips were light, reassuring. Martin's lips, slightly parted, seemed fuller as he smiled, and the tip of his tongue slowly laid a silver film of moisture on them. Martin wanted . . .

Martin – no, *he* wanted . . . Martin to . . . kiss him . . .

'No!' Roughly he knocked the man away, but with the door behind him he could not budge. 'I . . . what are you thinking of, for Christ's sake?'

'I am thinking that you may need help to get to know yourself better, Anthony, and that when that happens you'll be a lot happier.' The mouth, enunciating the words so distinctly, was only a few inches away. All he had to do was –

'No! No!'

With both hands he shoved, but the body before him was surprisingly resilient. A sneer, ironic, complicit, played over the other man's features. Chadwick was mocking him, as if he had recognised some secret emotion, some flicker of unrealised desire. The horror and ecstasy of the moment made Anthony shake violently – that anyone should have come so close, should have gained an unguarded glimpse into his soul . . .

Anthony raised his fist and shut his eyes. Panic and fury brought a surge of unexpected strength. He aimed somewhere in the general region of Chadwick's chin, more to create space for his own escape than with intent to cause injury. There was a crunch, an anguished cry from his own lips and a grunt from Chadwick, who fell backwards against a chair, which tumbled over in its turn. Anthony forced himself to look: the man was sprawled on the carpet, his decoration ripped from his neck, legs splayed out, all dignity vanished.

Panting hard, breath rasping in his throat, Anthony backed away.

Gingerly, warily, Chadwick climbed to his feet and rubbed blood from his mouth.

Without a word he picked up his gold-filigree pendant, stumbled towards the door, checked both ways along the corridor, and slipped out.

Chapter Twelve

'And tell me, Mrs Stalker, are you interested in astrology?' The young woman paused, Biro in hand, and smiled encouragingly. To play for time Elaine took an apple from the dish on her desk and bit into it.

She could not recall when or why she had agreed an interview for 'Your Week in the Stars', except that the piece would appear in the revamped *Radio Times*, purchased by one and a half million households. Of course politicians should communicate widely, that was essential. In her casual acceptance of the magazine's bid, one among many, she had, however, forgotten that the content of the communication mattered too. Now she was stuck.

'I tend to think', she said between mouthfuls of apple, 'that astrology's a throwback to an era when people believed in the sun, moon and planets as deities which decided our fate. The moon does affect us – the tides, for example – but that's no reason to worship it. So do I think the stars have any influence on us? The honest answer is no.'

The reporter was too dim, or too unconcerned, to put the obvious query of why, in that case, Mrs Stalker had agreed to be quizzed on the subject. She ploughed on: 'Your star sign is Libra, isn't it? Did you realise your planet is Venus? Do you think the fact that she's the goddess of love is significant?'

Elaine pulled a face. 'Yes, I did know that. Venus always struck me as a dozy lady – a bit excessive. Not me at all.'

'Couldn't keep her hands off the blokes, eh?'

Elaine gave her a frosty look and did not reply. The girl tried again.

'Librans tend to be balanced – that's the symbol, of course. On the other hand, as a Libran would say' – she giggled at her own perspicacity – 'they sometimes have trouble taking decisions. Does that apply to you?'

'No. I tend to know what I want to do. The problem usually is how to go about it.'

The journalist persisted. 'Really? Not the wavering or hesitant sort at all?'

What a daft question, Elaine thought to herself. Here I am, a government Minister at the age of forty, and the girl wants to know if I spend my days in a dither. She shrugged and threw the apple core in a bin. 'I've been lucky in my life, so far. Most of what I've set out to do has been successful. A lot of other people have been involved so I can't take that much credit for my achievements.'

The girl scribbled laboriously. Her subject spoke too rapidly for her underdeveloped shorthand. She glanced down at her notes. 'Would you say, then, that you're a bit dogmatic at times?'

Elaine smiled. 'Well – obviously *I* wouldn't say that, but no doubt other people would. They may well be right.'

'What would *you* say, then?'

'Oh, that I'm perfectly reasonable, naturally. Go on.'

'Librans tend to be tactful. Would that apply to you, Mrs Stalker?'

Oh dear, thought Elaine. How do I respond? What am I being now if not the soul of tact when I don't feel it at all? 'I do try. I prefer to deal with people honestly wherever possible. For example, I tell my constituents they may not always like what I have to say to them – about the necessity for a new road, perhaps, or that an unattractive factory will bring much-needed jobs – but I'll always speak the truth. That way they know where I stand, and that's how I'd like to be seen.'

'Right,' muttered her inquisitor uncertainly. Her prepared notes appeared to include a long list of enquiries on the same theme, permitting little deviation. Nor was she in the least tempted by her interviewee's attempts at more serious replies. Elaine, intrigued, concluded that while there was no evidence of malice – a pleasant change – neither was there much of intelligence either.

'With Libra being the Balance, it's often said Librans can't make up their minds, which makes them followers rather than leaders. Would you say that applies to you?'

Elaine was beginning to feel irritated. 'No, I wouldn't. I'm not easily led at all. In fact, the opposite – I prefer to work out what needs doing and try to give some leadership until it's done. That's part of the job of a Minister, even an MP in his or her own patch. We don't have much power – that's a myth; but we do have influence, and can exercise that through leadership.'

She waited, wondering if the youngster would rise to the bait of a genuine discussion of power, ambition and politics, which might enliven the ten minutes remaining. The revisionist thought that a young *man* might have leapt at the chance was firmly brushed aside.

'And, finally, I have to ask you about your speeches. Do you write them yourself?'

'I try, but when we speak on government policy obviously we stick to the line. Then we have to use precise phrases and tone to reinforce that line, and ensure we don't make policy on the hoof. Is that what you mean?'

The girl gazed back at her. 'Well, not exactly. My editor got me to read some of your speeches, and you never seem to quote anyone. When I did debates at school, we were told to start by looking up key words in the dictionary and quoting the definition, and then to try the dictionary of quotations. But you don't seem to do that.'

So that's a liberal education, Elaine reflected drily.

'To tell you the truth, I hardly ever quote other people in my speeches – it's too mannered a style, and you rarely find precisely what you want. Better to spend that time figuring out how to put your point across crisply in your own words. You'll end up with other people quoting you – and they do.'

The girl wrote down Elaine's remarks, then closed her notebook with a gulp of relief. Elaine pressed the silent bell beneath her desk. The door opened and Fiona waited to show the journalist out. The next visitors, a delegation from Derbyshire sent to complain on behalf of the left-wing council, were already rising to their feet in the ante-room.

'I suppose', Derek Harrison joked as his eye swept down the glossy menu, 'I ought to declare this lunch in the Register of Members' Interests.'

The Connaught Hotel waiter hovered respectfully, hands clasped over his order book. Jayanti looked alarmed. 'Surely not. This is a trivial amount. Aren't you permitted to have lunch with a friend?'

Harrison reached for the champagne. The Dom Pérignon 1990 may be, as he recalled Oz Clarke writing, the 'fiendishly expensive number in the funny bottle not worth the fat wad of folding ones the makers demand', but it was wonderful stuff in the middle of a busy day; and the price was none of his business.

'You have to understand, my dear Jay,' he continued easily, 'that since the Nolan Committee reported we're supposed to record every scrap of friendship and favour we receive. Absolute rot, of course. Angela

Rumbold once made the point by declaring each diary and calendar which came her way at Christmas. Then there was the lady Member who declared a gift of black stockings and was never allowed to forget it. Personally, I think Enoch Powell was correct back in the seventies when he denounced the whole idea of the Register as a mistake.'

It did not occur to him that an Asian might not treat the opinions of Mr Powell with the same respect. Bhadeshia glanced around unhappily. His manner became more confidential and he drew his chair in closer to the table, despite the fact that in the lofty room, with its deep carpets and muted chandeliers, nearly twenty feet separated them from other diners.

'It's very difficult for you,' Jayanti sympathised. 'I have a lot of money but no influence. You, on the other hand ...' He spread his hands expressively and allowed the inference to float unspoken in the air, that for Derek it might be vice versa. 'Ministers in this country are so badly paid. It is a disgrace. Why, the salary that Gladstone drew a hundred years ago, in modern money, would be worth around half a million pounds a year. Yet our Prime Minister – the top man – earns less than many people he has appointed to the highest ranks in public service.'

'We're all in favour of more money.' Harrison grinned. 'But even if you paid us a king's ransom there'd still be a few – not me, naturally – who'd be keen to make a bit on the side. Margaret Thatcher was firmly of the opinion that we ought to be involved in outside activities – that it was good for us – so only part-time remuneration for a part-time job was justified. Anyway, how on earth would we convince the public to double or treble our salaries in the present climate? My constituents don't reckon I'm worth the pittance I do get, and given the endless sleaze in the press I don't blame them.'

He called over the waiter. 'I'll have a steak tartare. How about you, Jay?'

Bhadeshia had long abandoned his adherence to vegetarianism, which had never been strong. The thought of raw meat was another matter. Yet he was here to make a good impression. He hesitated, then concurred. Derek smiled. His choice had been deliberate.

As they broke bread rolls and began their gravadlax starters, Derek sat back. 'Nice piece about your house in the paper. Do you a lot of good, that will. Everybody likes to be associated with success.'

Bhadeshia perked up. 'You think so?

'Sure. And your wife has a smashing figure – lovely legs.'

Jayanti bent his head silently over his plate.

Derek leaned across the table. 'You're a good chap. You'd like to get on in the party, wouldn't you?'

Bhadeshia's eyes rounded. He paused, a morsel on his fork. 'You have some advice for me?'

'Well – only a minor matter. It's your name. Bit tricky for us to get our tongues round. Say it for me.'

'Jayanti Bhadeshia.'

'Yes – see what I mean? You should shorten it. Jay's better. And how about Bhadesh? Jay Bhadesh is easier for us. Like Nirj Deva the MP: his full name has lots of syllables.'

I will not be offended, Jayanti told himself as he struggled to find a reply. But I wonder how he'd feel if I suggested he call himself Dirk Hass, to make it simpler for me?

'Thank you, I will think about it.'

A gleaming trolley was rolled to his side and the white-jacketed waiter, brow furrowed in concentration, began to mix the steak. It was a pleasure, he told them, to serve the Minister and his distinguished guest. For a while the corruption scandals of the nineties had emptied the dining room as public faces deserted it for more private addresses. Fortunately the fuss had died down, though not before a total of fourteen Ministers and hangers-on had been obliged to retire. Not that in the end, the waiter murmured, these minor spats did the finer venues any long-term harm; for within months of resignation most of the chaps had found alternative, more lucrative employment and were back, complete with expense accounts and new clients.

Derek still had a bee in his bonnet. 'That just shows you,' he said. 'The problem with the Register is that nobody will tell the truth. If, for the sake of argument, I were to take a significant bribe of some kind, I wouldn't announce it, would I? So whatever it says in the big green book is almost certainly irrelevant to its purpose. Instead people use it to boast – about the range of overseas visits they've made, or how many directorships, as evidence of their worth. It's a bit of a game – that's how any MP with sense treats it.'

Jayanti peered gingerly into the pile of seasoned raw steak and wondered if it would be against etiquette to pick out the onion pieces and eat them alone. He must abandon that inbred instinct of politeness which obliged him to choose the same dish as his companions. The potatoes were delicious but were now soaking up blood and turning purple. He suppressed a shudder.

198

Derek leaned forward and prodded Jayanti's meal approvingly with his knife. 'Go on, old man. It's very good – the dish of kings, you know.'

He fixed Jayanti with a broad smile. Enough of pussy-footing around. 'So what can I do for you today, my dear fellow?'

It was a simple matter to do a quick detour. Easy enough, as he exited from King's Cross station, to turn his back on the taxi rank, head eastwards past the scruffy Thameslink entrance a few hundred yards down Pentonville Road and keep going. At night the area was busy with prostitutes and kerb crawlers, but in the gloomy light of day its desolation was compounded by drifting litter and graffiti half obliterated by torn posters for failed pop singles and marches for political causes long since abandoned.

Outside the newsagent's window he hesitated. Nothing on display suited his purpose, but that was hardly a surprise. He had no idea what to ask for: the names of the magazines he needed were a mystery, though he'd know them at once when he saw them.

What would the shopkeeper think? The name over the door, J. P. Bhadeshia, licensed to sell tobacco, was not English. Suppose it were a small dark Indian lady – her big eyes reproachful, sitting in an old sari behind the till – who would handle the material with studious disdain? In that case, he couldn't do it; couldn't give that sort of stuff to a woman, and a respectable one at that.

He peered inside, conscious that he must look odd, a tall man in an expensive overcoat carrying a black leather briefcase marked 'EIIR'. The only figure he could see behind the counter was a scruffy young white man with a pony-tail. That was more like it. Anthony took a deep breath and pushed open the door.

If it were done when 'tis done, then 'twere well it were done *quickly*. He hesitated for a moment to get his bearings, then walked rapidly into the depths of the shop.

The manager was engrossed in a much-thumbed catalogue and nodded only cursorily at Anthony. The fourth that day, guilt writ large on their flushed faces. All heading for the porn shelves, way up high at the back, as if hidden; but the well-heeled bloke who was stretching up and flicking through what he'd found there might as well have shouted his intentions from the rooftops.

The pony-tail twitched. He was lucky, he supposed, to get as much sex as he wanted instead of missing out and merely reading about it. His girlfriend had once earned her keep on these streets and was into the tricks – whips, leather, bondage, plus some exciting variations. She liked to keep her skills honed, she said, just in case he ever let her down.

The customer was taking his time. The manager made a quick bet with himself: girls or boys? If he was after children, paedo stuff, or animals or what-have-you, he'd not find that on the open shelves. Nor in the locked cupboard under the counter, not since the visit the week before by plain-clothes men from the local cop shop who'd removed most of his stock. Another expense, that was, keeping them sweet.

Anthony stood, uncertain. The female breasts and buttocks on the front cover of *Eros* moved him not at all, but it seemed wisest to take the copy, along with *Men Only*. At home, alone, he might find them more arousing. But he could not stop his eyes wandering to the other part of the shelf where the flaunted pectorals and thighs were of a different gender. *Hunk* and *Prowl* were new to him, *Gay Times* held no interest, but *Vulcan* and *Steam* shrieked at him to buy. Hurriedly he gathered a collection and returned to the counter.

Face to face. 'I'd like these, please.' A twenty-pound note was handed over. Pony-tail made a show of checking prices but offered no change. As the magazines were thrust casually into a flimsy plastic bag Anthony raised his eyes long enough to register that the man's teeth were stained and foul. He picked up the bag, shoved it clumsily into his briefcase and was gone.

'How're you getting on, Jim?'

It could not be said that Nick Thwaite liked his deputy, but it was an essential part of his duties at the *Globe* to keep his team sweet. Not that he trusted Betts further than he could throw him. Given the whisker of a chance the nasty little Scouser would shove him aside and step into his shoes without a qualm. All was fair in love, war, business and newspaper offices. Yet there was something so unswervingly cynical and amoral about his subordinate as to make even Thwaite squirm. Sell his own grandmother, he would; and that's what made him indispensable.

'Got enough to start on a few of our overseas friends and their links with the party in power,' Betts informed him. He pulled down a couple of red folders from a shelf. 'More than I expected. Did you like the piece about what's new in Essex?'

'You were a bit gentle with them, I thought.'

'Oh, sure. But the file on Essex man, or at least that one, is coming

200

together nicely. Those pictures will be very handy.' He pointed to a list. 'I've been pursuing political links. Bhodesh, or whatever he calls himself, is a big contributor to the Tories. Quite a few others hedge their bets by supporting both sides. One guy's donated twenty-five thousand pounds each to two think-tanks, for each of the main parties. Must have it to burn.'

Thwaite grunted appreciatively. 'Hang on to that stuff. We're interested in the government side at the moment; not that the other lot aren't equally dodgy, but since they don't have their hands on the reins of power yet they've nothing much to be corrupt *with*. And Blair's lot are such a ghastly boring bunch.'

Betts concurred. 'Correct. Could be the downbeat lifestyle. A socialist diet of beansprouts and grated carrots won't do much for a man's libido, or oblige him to search for a few readies to pay the bills. The Tories, now, they have standards to maintain.'

'I'm old enough to remember Labour under Wilson and it was exactly the same.' Thwaite corrected him. Neither had a shred of sympathy for politicians of any colour: unless a local candidate was particularly attractive neither bothered to vote.

'They claim it's our fault, too, that's what makes me laugh,' Betts agreed. 'Blame the press. As if we tell lies, when what *we* do is merely report what goes on. Don't they realise we don't need to make it up?'

'If everybody behaved according to the rules they'd have nowt to fear from top investigative journalists like yourself, Jim.' Thwaite slapped his deputy on the back.

'Right. Nobody's hounded by the press unless he sets himself up as a victim in the first place.'

'Though if all we ever got in public life was prudes and sea-green incorruptibles we'd have governments composed entirely of John Selwyn Gummers and Oppositions full of Dennis Skinners,' Thwaite mused. 'Never get a thing done, and in the long run far less entertaining. The lack of contamination by real life'd mean they'd end up knowing bugger all. D'you know Skinner's never had a passport, never been abroad, yet he's full of loud opinions about foreign parts, mostly hostile.'

Betts wagged a finger. 'We don't need to make the argument for them. Plenty of smarmy so-and-sos are already on the box pontificating about how much worse it'd be if MPs had no outside interests, how it would make the place even more insular and peculiar. Which reminds me' – he hunted for a notebook – 'talking of the peculiar, I meant to start the rounds of the latest PPS appointments. You never know.'

'Catch 'em while the pants are still down, is that it? Surely this new PM is more careful?'

Betts found a packet of cigarettes and snorted. 'Don't you believe it. He's virtuous, they're not. In fact they're getting worse. It may be our fault, as you say. The question is, has the press scrutiny which has so illuminated British politics recently driven the brighter sparks away, in which case we're all losers? Or are the press simply less respectful to authority, less obsequious – which you and I'd see as a good thing – so we refuse to stay mum when a juicy bit of tittle-tattle pops up?'

Thwaite was laughing out loud, but he glanced thoughtfully at his reporter. The man was not stupid: his faults lay elsewhere. 'The trouble is, Jim, that you couldn't give a fuck either way, could you?'

Pramila tapped urgently on the door, waited anxiously and then opened it a few inches. Immediately she was enveloped in thick steam, which billowed across the tiled floor from the bath and threatened to escape down the stairs. Her husband did not like to be disturbed, but the fact was she had no choice. With the white mobile phone clutched tightly to her bosom she tiptoed inside and closed the door.

The wail of soulful but rhythmic bangla music floated from a radio placed on the floor by the bath. Jayanti was warbling along with the music and waving a backbrush to keep time. Only his dark head was visible, the sleek wet hair decorated with the bubbles which enveloped the rest of his body.

The lunch with Harrison had given him plenty of food for thought. The dinner to come, the political committee of the Carlton Club, black tie with all the trimmings, would offer a further chance to imitate the manner and style of a Harrison, so carefully observed, and to put some of the man's suggestions into practice.

In his heart Jayanti Bhadeshia knew he could never be accepted as an English gentleman. The establishment existed, was alive and well, and would keep him at arm's length. But he was sure he could get closer, enough to move easily in the inner circles and to ignore the occasional snub.

His common sense and integrity told him, in any case, that it was foolish to be resentful at the sneers or exclusion. The type of person who did not wish him to sit at his table was not worthy of consideration. The best course of action was to ignore such people. Whether the origin of such snobbery was anti-immigrant prejudice or a misguided sense of their own importance or both, if those who challenged it were successful then the old guard would eventually wither away. Look what had happened at the turn of the century as the British aristocracy, after first deriding Americans as rough and ignorant colonials, ended up marrying them for their money. Thus was their entry to society secured. It hadn't happened yet with Asians – the only hereditary Asian peer, Baron Sinha, had never taken his seat and remained in Calcutta – but it must, sooner or later. Naturally the gatekeepers would be choosy. The elevated ranks could best be strengthened by the ennoblement of those who were already top-notch. Such as himself. Then there could be no further argument: as a citizen honoured by the Queen, he could not be gainsaid.

In response to the Minister's blunt question, Jayanti had decided on the spur of the moment to be equally forthright. That was not his way normally. In his circle haggling was a refined and elegant exercise. It offended his sensibilities to be too explicit. He had been brought up to perform the formalities first, before negotiation; he harboured the belief, buttressed by years of experience, that a deal struck too easily probably would not hold when things went wrong.

Harrison, of course, knew about the East Africa project, but had professed gratifying surprise at progress made to date. Within a few moments he had expressed a desire to acquire shares, if that could be arranged. A nominee shareholder trust might be set up, he hinted, in a tax haven away from prying eyes; since no money would change hands it did not have to be declared.

That was an unusual version of a private share placement. On the whole Jayanti preferred to be paid for his shareholdings, but there was no doubt that Derek was highly persuasive as well as extremely useful when he chose. Promises of funds had materialised from contacts whom Derek claimed to have cultivated, people whose names were bandied around on the back pages of the *Financial Times* but whom Jayanti had never met. Their *Who's Who* entries indicated the barest links with politics. Yet Derek knew them, and their potential – or said he did.

Jayanti pondered the remark attributed to parliamentary lobbyist Ian Greer that 'you need to rent an MP like you rent a London taxi', and dismissed it as too crude. A long-term relationship was safer. It was much harder to rent a Minister and had to be done with finesse. But it was not impossible.

Should he, Jayanti, feel guilty? That was ridiculous. Only the British were so horrified by backhanders, which in most parts of the world were standard practice. Indeed, making money on the side had been expected of men in public office throughout most of British history, if only people were honest enough to admit it. Business demanded the greasing of palms. It helped the smooth running of commerce, from Singapore to Peru. The British were the odd ones out. Those outbreaks of breast-beating which occasionally infected their media were a complete mystery, and in his private view rather immature and silly.

Then there was the enquiry, murmured over a delightful but highly alcoholic *zabaglione* and brandy, whether Derek's host secretly harboured any other ambitions or needs. A long sigh and silence followed as Jayanti toyed with his coffee spoon. But Derek had proved to be very helpful, so far. Nor had it seemed crazy, talking confidentially to one parliamentarian, to confess that he wished to become another – not in the Commons, subject to the hassle of elections and public scrutiny, but in the Lords.

'My wife has royal blood, you know,' Jayanti explained. This was no time to air the doubts he usually felt over his wife's antecedents. 'At home we are a well-known family. She points out that businessmen like myself are seriously under-represented in the Second Chamber, despite the fact that we are numerous and respected in this country. We are proud of Lady Flather, the first Asian lady peer, but Shreela is not a businesswoman and she is married to an English lawyer. As for Lord Desai – he's Labour, for a start, and is a professor of economics. A teacher merely – with a mad eye and straggly hair. He may resemble Albert Einstein, but he does not represent *me*.'

Derek had nodded, waiting. Both had ignored life peer Lord Chitnis, a Liberal Democrat. Jayanti needed no encouragement to continue. He lowered his voice. 'You must not let the idea get abroad, my dear Harrison, that the party is happy to take our money but will not recognise us. You are not racist and neither is the Prime Minister. Nor the Home Secretary. "We will have no racialism in this party" – I heard Mr Howard say so at the Party Conference. The time has come to show you mean it.'

The Connaught's bill had been stratospheric but worth it, for Harrison had shaken hands warmly and promised to see what he could do on all counts. Now Jayanti wondered how safe it might be to approach a few other cronies, especially at that holy of holies, the Carlton Club. Then it dawned on him that that was exactly where to do it.

The music changed and he let his own voice soar in harmony. An agitated face appeared out of the steam above his head.

'Jayanti! Will you stop making that terrible racket? There is a telephone call for you. Very urgent . . . must speak to you before you go to the dinner tonight.'

His wife's hand thrust the mobile phone towards him. He reached out to switch off the radio, then put the earpiece to his ear and blew foam from his mouth.

'Hello! Jayanti Bhadeshia here. Who's that?'

The accent at the other end was smoothly urbane. 'Mr Bhadeshia? So glad I've caught you. Number Ten here, private office. You are going to the political committee dinner, aren't you?'

'Yes – yes.' Jayanti sat up, as if the caller had entered the bathroom in person.

'Excellent. You will find yourself seated next to Peter Aubrey. The Party Chairman, you know? A charming gentleman. He will have one or two things to discuss with you, quite informally, and we will understand if you say no.'

'Wait . . .' Jayanti could not grasp what his caller might be hinting at. He switched the phone into his other hand and began to feel around on the floor for a towel. Soap was getting into his eye and he was finding it hard to concentrate.

'Are you still there, Mr Bhadeshia? Ah, yes. Now you will want to listen carefully. And of course we have not had this conversation . . .'

A few moments later Jayanti, moving as if in a dream, pulled out the plug and rose to his feet still covered in foam, the phone held limply in his hand. He switched it off, slowly pushed down the aerial and looked at it in wonder. He gazed around the bathroom, fixing in his mind for ever its streaming walls, the piles of thick white towels on the heated rail, the damp green ferns draped gracefully over the shelves, the brass and gilt and mirrors and tiles, all chosen by Pramila with more concern for design than comfort. Yet for the rest of his life it would be a very special and unforgettable picture.

As he slipped a white bathrobe over his shoulders and opened the door, Jayanti was grinning broadly.

It had been a long day: an early night was most welcome. The Chief Whip reached the last page of his novel with a contented grunt, polished off the whisky and replaced his glass on the bedside table. Beside him his wife snored gently.

What a very good story it was. The tattered orange Penguin edition had been rescued from the second-hand bookstall. Maurice Edelman's

The Minister was an elegant piece published in 1961 when most of the current crop of MPs were in their cradles. How times had changed: all the politicians were male, while the women sported petalled hats and had lives empty of activity or purpose except to cause trouble to the men.

He contemplated contentedly the pile on his bedside table. Long ago he had realised that if he did not read a little for pleasure before retiring his sleep would be disturbed by the unsettled issues of the day. Fiction was a different matter: he could muse on the characters' fate, but in the end close the volume and leave them to it.

The next on his list was Tim Renton's *Dangerous Edge*, a tale of intrigue written by a former holder of his office, though probably – at least in that post – one of the least competent of modern times, who had lasted only a year under Margaret Thatcher. Too nice for it, if truth be told.

No wonder Chief Whips tended to be central characters in many political novels – Michael Dobbs's, for example – though both Dobbs and Jeffrey Archer tended to over-glamorise Westminster. The reality was far more prosaic and grubby. And it was going too far to make Dobbs's hero Urquhart a double – or was it treble? – murderer, though there were moments when, faced with a particularly obstreperous Member, similar fantasies flitted through his own brain. The Chief smiled tiredly at the thought, and wondered if he might ever be the model for a future work.

He would save the Critchley for later. Dear Julian, once voted the Commons' favourite journalist by MPs fed up with being harried by the press. The reviews of his autobiography, *A Bag of Boiled Sweets* ('the most entertaining set of political memoirs to have been published in years'), had betrayed bewilderment over the hidden charm and undying attraction of such a career. TV's Jeremy Paxman had pondered the compulsion that drove patently normal (and nice – and honest) men like Critchley to devote their lives to politics, especially when the opportunity to influence events was so limited.

The Chief stared at the ceiling: he knew the answer to that one. Because when chaps set out to enter the political arena they don't know they'll be so wasted. Only after a long stretch in Parliament with its multiple frustrations did those with a flicker of intelligence wonder why on earth they had chosen that path. By then, most likely, they were too far along it to do anything else. Or too lazy: it was an easy life, and brought in its wake an office in central London, free telephones, first-class travel, staff, subsidised canteens and elevated status. Westminster was still the best gentlemen's club in London.

Many queued to enter, few fought to leave. No wonder: politics was a tender trap which remained endlessly fascinating to the entangled, offering a drip feed of inside knowledge and an excellent view of the great events. The magic remained. The green benches could take an ordinary decent chap like Critchley, who might have achieved precious little in the outside world, and transform him from a mere observer into a participant and – oh joy, just once or twice in a lifetime – into a prime mover.

The Chief Whip's wife stirred, muttered, opened a single reproachful eye and rolled over. Obediently her husband turned out the light and pulled up the bedclothes. He lay back, arms under his head, and wondered whether the day might ever come when his political career took a wrong turning and he ended up writing novels. Not if he could help it.

There it was again – a whimper, like a child in distress, but with something more animal about it, less human. A faint intermittent cry which floated up the stairwell and hovered in the air. Nothing for several minutes, then it would start again, neither louder nor softer. The bedroom door didn't close properly and had swung open an inch or two during the night. Now she could hear it clearly.

With some reluctance Karen slipped her feet out of the warm bed, hitched up her pyjamas and padded to the door.

All was still; yet it was not her imagination and this wasn't the first time. Was it a stray dog or cat perhaps? More likely a fox, one of which was often to be seen, cheekily handsome, at the corner under the street lamp when she came home late. The screech of mating foxes in the park had kept several households up half the night. But that wasn't it.

She stood uncertainly on the top stair, head cocked, shivering slightly and strained to hear. There – it came again, and closer. Below her, definitely. Slowly she started down, keeping as quiet as she could, listening intently. Her heart beat faster with each step.

It wasn't a ghost. The noise was too substantial and anyway the idea was preposterous. And, while it did not seem normal, nor did it suggest danger. Whoever or whatever was crying was in pain – or desperately unhappy.

At breakfast she'd tell Anthony. It would be his job to approach whoever was responsible and have peace restored. To be awoken repeatedly at night was not funny, especially with a mock exam the next week. Anthony was the best and most sympathetic of landlords, though he had looked peaky lately; working too hard, no doubt, in the same office as her mother, where the burden never seemed to let up.

He wouldn't think she was foolish. In fact, it was likely that as they discussed their lives here in such close proximity the chance might arise to pursue her aim of persuading Anthony to see her in a more romantic light. She needed him to focus his attention on her, though his mind seemed often half engaged elsewhere; maybe he did find her attractive, and simply didn't know where to start. In that case it would be up to her. If that involved a degree of boldness on her part, she would not flinch.

But first this strange, sad weeping. Nobody else in the house, apparently, was disturbed by it. She came down two short flights of stairs and found herself on the landing underneath. A narrow darkened corridor turned left towards the main bedroom and the *en suite* bathroom which Anthony had installed. It gave the big double room a lot of privacy, aided by the fact that there were no occupied areas above.

She stopped outside Anthony's door. What on earth . . .? Surely that wasn't him. A grown man didn't cry like that – that was a terrified child. Her heart turned over with pity. What a dreadful sound, the worse for its intermittence, as if the weeper became exhausted in between his desolate sobs.

Tentatively Karen turned the handle and pushed open the door. It took a moment for her eyes to become accustomed to the gloom, but she could make out Anthony's suit neatly hung up, a clean shirt ready for work and an untidy pile of magazines on the rug. On the far side of the double bed, its covers tossed and tumbled, the figure of her landlord strained and shuddered, fists raised and crossed as if warding someone off: yet there was nobody else in the room.

She tiptoed across. Anthony's eyes were screwed shut. His head twisted from side to side and a low moan came from between clenched teeth. Tears streamed down his face and his breaths came in great gasps.

'Anthony! Anthony – for heaven's sake, wake up.'

'What – wha . . .' It emerged as a wail of pain. Anthony heaved himself over on his side, away from her. Eyes still closed, he rubbed at his mouth frantically as if trying to remove a horrible taste, coughed, and groaned.

'Anthony, come on. You shouldn't just go back to sleep. Were you dreaming? It sounds like you were having a nightmare.'

He forced his eyes to open, then to focus. The room was still dark. Karen turned the bedside light on. She was sitting anxiously on the edge of the bed, her pink pyjamas loose and chaste about her, her young face furrowed in concern. The clock on the bedside table told them both it was past three o'clock.

She wrapped her arms around herself. 'Heavens, it's cold in here. I've got goose bumps. Shove over a bit and let me in. Then we can talk if you like. At least till you've calmed down.'

He did not move. He looked away from her, his expression still fearful. Mutely she reached for his hand and stroked it gently as if caressing a frightened pet, but he seemed too numb and shocked to respond. At last Karen's ministrations began to take effect. He sighed and relaxed a little, and turned to her sheepishly, his voice throaty.

'Thanks for waking me up. You're right – it was a nightmare, one I get . . . from time to time. Pretty horrible, to tell you the truth.'

The look she returned to him was full of compassion. In the lamplight his dark hair was matted across the sweaty brow. The rest of his face was in shadow. Cautiously she raised her hand and brushed back a strand of his hair. It was a gesture of simple friendship; it could be, if he wished, something more.

Anthony was not responding but nor had he stopped her. She shrugged, then lifted up the duvet and slipped under it, keeping her icy feet well away from his body. She could feel him tense beside her, though his breathing was more regular now.

It was up to her, then. She wriggled down the bed until her head rested on the pillow next to his. He lay on his back, staring upwards, as if the subject of his fears had not vanished but only retreated towards the ceiling. She reached again for his hand and clasped it; his fingers twitched briefly, then grasped hers in turn, but more like an infant with its mother than a lover.

'Would you like me to stay with you a little while?' she asked softly. The closeness of the man was having its effect on her own body, as she had suspected it might; her pulse had begun beating more strongly. Anthony did not reply. The incongruity as well as the sexual impropriety – or opportunity – of their position suddenly reasserted itself, and Karen stifled a giggle.

'What is it? What's so comical?' Anthony turned his face to hers. He was only a few inches away. It would be the easiest thing in the world for them to kiss.

'I was thinking of poor Fred upstairs,' Karen whispered. 'If he could see us now. He's been trying to get me into bed for months; I think he's in love with me. But honestly I'm not sure he's my type.' She felt emboldened by Anthony's silence. 'I think *you* are. And maybe if you have worries I can help. At least, I can listen.'

She was conscious that Anthony was now looking at her, and could not avoid the impression that there was more puzzlement than yearning on his face. It dawned on her that perhaps he did not know quite what to do next; it wasn't every night that a man woke to find a pretty girl in his bed. Maybe the transition from nightmare to fantasy had been too swift. Or maybe the whole episode was a mistake she would come to regret, witness to her own ineptitude and immaturity.

Karen kept her eyes fixed on Anthony's face. Apart from their hands their bodies had not touched, though she could sense his warmth. She disentangled her fingers from his grasp and slid her hand up and over his hip. He wore ordinary striped pyjamas, quite conventional, which felt cosy and inviting to her touch. She shifted her body closer to his, then found the slit in the front of the pyjama trousers, and slid her fingers inside.

The pubic hair was stiff and curly, not like the fine hair on his head. Her mouth was dry and she wondered what he would like her to do, if anything. If he preferred to talk, that was fine: after all, she'd also had a miserable patch long ago and was familiar with that terrible conviction of being quite alone and misunderstood. She waited.

He did not push her away. Her fingers slid a few inches further, and rested at last on his flaccid penis.

It was wet. The trouser fabric too was damp and slimy. Karen swallowed hard, then made her voice mild. 'I thought you had a *bad* dream, Anthony. Seems to have been more than that.'

He put his own hand over hers as if in explanation. 'I have this . . . difficulty . . . from time to time,' he muttered hoarsely. 'Comes from not having a girlfriend, I suppose. I'm sorry.'

Whatever had happened to Anthony was clearly not part of his conscious apparatus. She let her hand rest loosely under his: to pull it away would have shown disapproval. 'It's not important, not really. You shouldn't brood about it. No point in being upset – you've every reason to be on top of the world. Everybody speaks so highly of you, Anthony. And I like you very much – I'd like to be a close friend, at least . . .'

Then her essentially generous nature took over, mixed, she had to admit, with a whisker of impatience. Why was it that forward men were generally not worth knowing while the sweet ones had to have it all done for them? She leaned over and kissed him on the mouth, lightly but repeatedly, while starting to rub, backwards and forwards, on the limp organ. With some satisfaction she felt it begin to stiffen.

'No!'

A cry came from Anthony's lips. He flung back the bedclothes and stood upright, pushing himself back into his pyjama trousers with shaky hands. Karen sat up, aghast.

'I can't, Karen. Not with . . . it's not you, you're fine. It's just . . . I can't explain. And certainly not now. We both have work in the morning. I'm going to the bathroom. When I get back, I'd be glad if you were gone.'

Mutely Karen nodded. At the door Anthony turned. The misery on his face was similar to the dreadful stricken look as he had wept in his sleep half an hour earlier.

'You won't . . . tell anyone, will you?'

She shook her head, but stayed modestly covered up in the bed until he had disappeared. Then she rose sadly and silently, found her slippers and tiptoed out.

Chapter Thirteen

Karen flicked over the pages of the *Radio Times* and turned as usual to the horoscope. Holding court in the centre of the kitchen, surrounded by men rushing to eat their breakfast against a background of the *Today* programme, she peeled a banana and read bits out loud.

'Fred – you're Pisces, aren't you? It says here: "By now it should have dawned on you that there is no way you can accomplish all your ambitions in the time scale you have set yourself." Cheerful, that.'

'And correct, probably.' Fred lunged for the marmalade. In his haste his arm trailed over his plate and a blob of butter stuck to his shirtsleeve. 'Damn. It'll take even longer if I have to go and change.'

Karen was sympathetic but made no offer to take care of the shirt for him; it would not have occurred to her or the others present that it was anybody's job to look after Fred's laundry but his own. She half turned.

'And Lachlan – Taurus? "Beware of going over the top or overstating your case, even though you may have every reason to be angry or disillusioned." That's exactly the opposite of you. A more measured or balanced soul I could hardly imagine.' She grinned at him good-naturedly. He gave an affectionate nod.

Before she could reach her own prediction her eye was caught by a cartoon which looked familiar. It was her mother, with a short paragraph in quotes. She read it and frowned, then exclaimed as she threw the paper down.

'It makes me so mad,' she declared, 'the way they trivialise Mum. I bet she didn't say those things – or if she did it's all been taken out of context.'

Fred reached over, picked up the paper and read out: '"I know Libra's controlled by Venus but she seems to me a rather dozy lady, a bit excessive. By contrast I've never had trouble making decisions. I tend to know what I want and how to go about it; I've been lucky in that I've usually achieved what I set out to do. Other people would

212

say I'm dogmatic but I think I'm perfectly reasonable. I'm not known for my tact but you know where you stand with me. I'm not easily led at all. I rarely quote other people in my speeches – I let other people quote me. And they do.'''

Anthony surfaced from behind *The Times*. 'It was probably written without even asking your mother. I should ignore it. However, Karen, I feel left out. What does it say for a Virgo?'

Karen traced a finger across the page and her spirits sank, but she was not quick enough to manufacture something more suitable. For a brief moment she wondered if the predictor had a genuine talent. She kept her voice light.

'For you, Mr York, it says, "Although you maintain such a cool exterior, deep down you are certainly more emotional than you care to admit. The time has come to let the mask slip, show others how you really feel, and reject once and for all the foolish notion that to ask for assistance is in some way a sign of weakness."'

Both Fred and Lachlan were engrossed in toast, radio, post. She bit her lip. He did not meet her eye but his hand on the coffee-cup trembled and he put it down quickly.

The damage was done. She grabbed her jacket and bags. 'Right! I'm off,' she announced, pulled open the door and fled.

With the greatest care Pramila moved plates, cups, butter and preserves out of harm's way and spread open on the table the copy of the *London Gazette* which had arrived in the post. Her mother peered around her right elbow; the kitchen was unaccustomedly calm as her sister Lakshmi waddled into the breakfast room, respect and envy mingled in equal parts in her expression.

'So you will be Lady Bhadeshia?' The old lady spoke in a hushed tone but her voice was anxious. 'This is not a joke?'

Pramila wanted to scream it from the housetop, but the imminence of the title and its extraordinary responsibility weighed heavy on her. 'Yes, this is real,' she whispered. Then her natural exuberance reasserted itself. 'I will have to have new notepaper printed. Blue, with gold lettering. No: plain cream, heavy vellum, with dark blue lettering. And robes with ermine for Jayanti. Do we buy them, or have them made, or what?'

Her mother looked worried. 'It will cost a great deal of money. You will have to put up a fine show.' She laid a hand on her daughter's arm. 'Tell me – was it very expensive?'

Pramila brushed her off impatiently. 'Don't talk like that, Ma. Don't even think it. Your son-in-law is being honoured because of his charity work, and his efforts for the Conservative Party over many years – look!' She pointed at the framed photograph of her husband at the 1990 Blue Ball alongside a smiling Lady Thatcher. Her heart missed a beat as she pictured her husband seated right beside the baroness on the red leather benches of their Lordships' House.

More immediate concerns preoccupied her. 'And it says here we will have entitlement to a coat of arms. My goodness – do I put that on my notepaper or not?'

'A coat of arms!' Lakshmi was so startled she reached for a chair and sat down heavily. The large white envelope with its royal crest served as a fan. 'My God! Soon you will be too proud to stay in the same house as us, your own flesh and blood. You will walk around with your nose in the air and be mighty important. What will become then of your old mother and your poor unmarried sister? Are we to be turned out?' And she put her teatowel to her eyes and began to wail.

Debrett's Etiquette and Modern Manners had been Pramila's bedside reading for a week since Bhadeshia had returned from a private visit to 12 Downing Street. The many hints dropped to her for more than a year had turned out to be well founded. But that posed the most monumental problem for her. Jayanti had threatened divorce if she breathed a word. As she had been sworn to secrecy with oaths and threats, she had decided that the only way to keep the momentous news to herself was to take to her bed as if ill.

These had been the hardest days of her life, having to pretend an infectious illness, with even her closest relatives barred from her room. The curtains had stayed drawn and the telephone went unanswered. In this state she had striven, and prayed, and kept silent.

At last it was a secret no more. She could not use the title officially, of course, until Jayanti had been invested into the House of Lords, which might take months. Yet from the instant of the honour's gazetting, and the arrival in the same post of the official notification from the palace, the book insisted that she behave like an English lady – and that meant putting a stop to her sister's caterwauling.

Pramila rose gracefully, head held high, and kissed first her mother then her sister, and hugged Lakshmi, cooing at her, until the latter's shoulders ceased to heave. A new order was clearly already in place.

Shows of mutual affection between the females in the Bhadeshia household, where there was much jostling for position, were normally restricted to noisy embraces when someone else was in the vicinity, or moments of particular emotion such as a romantic film on TV. Lakshmi, the precious envelope still clasped to her bosom, collapsed into an astonished but wary heap.

'You will stay with me and Jayanti, and you will come to the ceremony and sit in the gallery of the House of Lords,' Pramila announced regally. 'Both of you will have a new outfit. Yes, Ma, you too. You cannot stay home on such a special day.'

'Will they give you a coat of arms, or can you choose your own?' Lakshmi's eyes were enormous.

Pramila knew the answer to that one. 'We discuss it with the Garter King-of-Arms and tell him what we would like included.' The possibilities began to entertain her. 'I think maybe . . . something to do with commerce – scales, perhaps, and a roll of cloth, since we have been in textiles, or a bag of rice to represent our lives in the grocery trade.'

'Nothing from our origins?' The old lady was instantly suspicious. 'Remember the sages tell us that if we forget where we come from we can never feel at home anywhere else.'

Pramila pondered. 'A gazelle, maybe, for East Africa,' she conceded, 'and a rose for Gujerat. Or do you want a holy symbol? The flaming sun of the Lord Krishna – that would bring us luck.'

The design committee, brows knitted, considered the suggestion reverently and nodded gravely in unison.

'No good crying about it, Deirdre. It's over.'

Derek Harrison strode back to his desk in impatience. The girl hovered limply by the door, her weeping increasingly noisy, the file she had used as a pretext for entry upside-down in her hands.

What had he seen in her? Under his lashes he subjected her to a cursory examination. Nice figure, certainly. She had a pleasing habit of wearing thin cotton dresses with puff sleeves and low-cut bodices which showed off her breasts tantalisingly. Pity the face was so ordinary. He had not meant the affair to last long; it was a bit risky, a liaison with a higher executive officer in the heart of the department, especially one who confessed to not being a Tory. You never knew who you could trust.

Her sobs were likely to attract attention if he could not shut her up. With a grim sigh he walked over and stood before her, his hands on her arms. For a moment he felt the warm flesh tingle beneath his palms and a whisker of desire stirred in him. Then he remembered her big feet in their sandals and her irritating efforts to talk politics to him.

'Look, Deirdre. You knew it couldn't last. You're a lovely person. You should find some nice bloke from the print section and marry him and have loads of kids. Forget me.'

The girl sagged as if to fall into his embrace but he held her rigidly away. An anxious thought occurred to him.

'You're not . . . pregnant, are you? You did say you were on the pill . . .'

'No, don't worry.' There was a sudden tinge of malevolence in her tone. With the back of her hand she wiped her eyes and tossed her head. 'You're pure shit, Derek Harrison, you know that? After all you said about love . . . I believed it, every word. Well, I hope you're pleased with yourself. You've wrecked my life.'

Derek resisted the sarcastic rejoinder that her life couldn't have been up to much if a brief fling could so easily have damaged it. He was becoming bored. With as much gentleness as he felt the occasion needed he turned the girl around and propelled her to the door. He was not prepared for the bitterness in her voice as she left.

'And if the chance comes, I warn you, I'll do my best to wreck yours.'

Time to make a start, Jim Betts told himself, on the series of articles about Asians in Britain. A few general remarks first. He entered his password, pressed the key for 'TEXT' and began.

When Idi Amin announced in August 1972 that all non-Ugandan citizens must leave the country within 90 days, some 72,000 Asians left, scattering to Britain, Canada, India and Australia.

The *Globe* is interested in what has happened to these people since. How have they fared? Where are they now? And have they put our British hospitality to good use, or only into their own pockets? Over the next few weeks, in a hard-hitting series of articles, we intend to bring you the facts, and let you decide.

216

Not too bad. Betts lit a cigarette and scrolled through the piece. He like the way it assumed right from the second paragraph that something underhand was going on. That set the tone nicely.

For the next half-hour he tapped energetically. Each article would profile a different selection of families or individuals to create human interest. Photographs taken in sumptuous homes and offices had not been difficult to obtain: vanity was much the same whatever the background. These men and women of substance would be held up as examples both of success and of the un-English methods adopted to obtain it: characters like Nazmudin Virani, who was estimated to have lost £100 million in the collapse of the BCCI after playing a vital role in hoodwinking its auditors. Once he had rubbed shoulders with Prime Ministers and royalty; more recently he had spent a year or so in Sevenoaks Prison as an unwilling guest of Her Majesty.

The idea, however, was not to pin the tail on one donkey but to set a whole herd by the ears. The *Sunday Times* had tried to subvert not one but ten MPs over the 'cash for questions' lark and captured two, thus making it appear as if the whole place were awash with greed – which, on the whole, in Betts's view, it was. Thus the pattern of reportage in which he was about to indulge was likely to produce a more accurate picture than targeting a single luckless individual like Virani alone.

One name, however, leapt out from his most recent researches: Jayanti Bhadeshia. He was not only easy meat but tremendously good value. His wife had posed for some memorable pictures surrounded by evidence of her excessive wealth and atrocious taste. And here he was, about to step from obscurity into the limelight as one of the nation's newest ennobled legislators.

His emergence on to such a public platform could only be cause for rejoicing in the *Globe* office. All being well, Bhadeshia'd make some priceless boobs in debate; and he, Betts, could guarantee those utterances would get every scrap of the publicity they deserved. Even if the remarks were anodyne, Betts had sufficient confidence in his own ability to make something sinister, or foolish, out of them. The man was a sitting duck and in a week or two would know it.

But what if the bloke didn't say a word – or, like Lord Young of Graffham, a former Secretary of State for Trade and Industry, attended only four times out of nearly 200 sitting days in a year? So much the better. Then his absences would be a perfectly good if slightly weaker story, and attention would divert more to the foolishness of the government which appointed him. Both would be ripe for ridicule.

217

For the moment the question was where, with the mass of information now at his fingertips, the attack should start. Betts pondered, then reflected that the less familiar world of Bhadeshia's East African antics might do nicely. His contacts had turned up a juicy episode of which he suspected even his victim was unaware. He opened a new file for a fresh article, typed in opening sentences which reminded his readers of the scene set so far, and continued.

A cynic might point to what happened in Uganda after the so-called refugees left. The African states lost badly from their departure. The Asians' expulsion was popular but the locals who took over their businesses did not have the necessary knowledge or skills.

Now the wealthiest Asians are returning. Governments such as that of President Mangaluso have issued fresh title deeds to the owners of properties confiscated over two decades ago. All the returners have to do is evict the current occupants, who overnight have the status of unprotected squatters.

Numerous cases have been reported of Asians being threatened and attacked while trying to reclaim 'their' property. Not only a home is lost but the livelihood too. No official compensation is available. The result for the losers is homelessness and destitution.

There is, however, the strange tale of Mr Jayanti Bhadeshia, British citizen, whose name appeared unexpectedly this week in the list of new government peers.

He seems to have had no difficulty evicting two families, including twelve children, from the six-bedroomed mansion he once owned in Kampala. Perhaps the presence of armed police and dog handlers had something to do with it. Yet never at any time have Mr Bhadeshia or his associates been near a court.

But then it is rumoured that he has friends in high places – as high as you can go – both in East Africa, and closer to home in Whitehall.

On second thoughts Betts altered 'six' to 'ten', and then to 'eleven'. Nobody knew how big the house was, though his contact, who had been more than happy to fly up from Jo'burg for a day or two's scouting around, had produced splendid snaps of its former inhabitants ranged miserably on the roadside surrounded by pots and bundles. At least, Betts had to hand pictures of a bunch of scruffy Africans with too many children outside a large white house. That'd do.

Bhadeshia had not yet been approached to check the story, but that was a minor detail. It was his house: the actions had been taken in his name, of that Betts was certain. Bhadeshia's expostulations would make a petulant addition to the next article in which his name would appear. Should the beggar dare to sue, the *Globe* would be covered in court provided that the response – an opportunity for further revelations – had been given due prominence. Just to be safe, Betts added:

> We offered the gentleman concerned a chance to respond to these allegations but so far no explanation has been forthcoming. So come on, Mr Bhadeshia – what exactly have you been up to?

The journalist smiled to himself. These activities in East Africa were a mere sideline, a diversion and an introduction to a fresh national villain. Betts's thoughts returned to the preposterous new Lord Bhadeshia and the fun to be had in making a fool of him. The question was wide open as to why and how this name had appeared on the honours list at all.

That was the issue which really intrigued Betts and, through him, his readers. How did some people get to be on the list of the great and good, find their names put forward for honours, receive invitations to Buckingham Palace garden parties and the like, when the bulk of the population, however hard-working and worthy, were excluded? He chewed his moustache. It could not possibly be an entirely honest system: the very term 'patronage' told its own story. That meant money and, with it, the old tale of who you know. How much, exactly, had it cost? And who benefited from the exchange of largesse? For it was unthinkable that an obscure Asian shopkeeper, and one as insignificant and undistinguished as Bhadeshia, could wriggle his way into the top flights of society, and the peerage, through merit alone.

More immediately there was the puzzle of where Bhadeshia's wealth came from, and how soundly based his finances might or might not be. Betts pondered deeply for several minutes, put the machine on 'hold' and reached for the phone.

'When Geoffrey was here' – the distinctive voice of Lady Howe rang out above the hum of the crowd – 'we put together a little booklet about the place. Yes, we do miss it. Well, who wouldn't? It's gorgeous.'

Elaine had to agree. She had found a lone copy of the brochure on the marble table in the hallway. The chances of her ever becoming Foreign Secretary were remote, but the opportunity to enjoy the current incumbent's hospitality at his official residence at 1 Carlton Gardens was not to be missed, even if the occasion was merely a reception for the friends, committee and sponsors of the forthcoming ball for the European Union of Women.

Outside the porch, television lights were switched off; the society paparazzi melted away. On a quiet night for news the presence of several recently elevated figures had caused a faint flurry of interest, but no more.

Carlton Gardens was not only very attractive but felt like an elegant home. No wonder, Elaine reflected, the Howes had given up their London flat with alacrity in favour of the grace-and-favour residence at the top of this lovely house; then, on his being turfed out of the job six years later, had made such a fuss at the ghastly thought of a return to Morpeth Terrace.

In a moment she would be surrounded by people clamouring to shake hands. Apart from herself relatively few Ministers had come, though there were plenty of *arrivistes*. The Prime Minister was not expected. The Foreign Secretary was in Brussels, where he seemed to spend most of his time these days.

While Elspeth Howe hugged and enthused, Elaine slipped away. A few moments later she found herself upstairs in the blue drawing room with its remarkable Persian carpet, the double doors thrown hospitably open into the smoking room and the white salon nearby.

'It's a Tabriz, and we really shouldn't be walking on it,' a familiar voice murmured at her elbow. 'Still, it's probably put up with two hundred years of punishment, so a few more crisps and peanuts won't make much difference.'

'George!' she laughed, delighted to see him. His height, his lean spare looks, made her catch her breath. Suddenly the evening took on an improved aspect. 'What are you doing here – is your firm a sponsor? Do you know all about carpets, too?'

'No, but I know a little.' He took her arm and steered her to the less crowded end of the long room. He pointed at her feet. 'Here's another – a Fereghan. Glorious colours – wouldn't you adore living with something like this?'

She looked at him and wondered, fleetingly, what he might be asking, but his demeanour was guileless as he squatted down and ran his palms over the fine-patterned silk. If this was a game, she needed to score points too. She spotted a small marble bust, similar to one on the staircase in the Commons near her office.

'And that's William Pitt. I bet he disapproved of all this extravagance.'

'He didn't know anything about it, Elaine. He died in 1806 before this place was built. Aren't you people supposed to know things like that?'

She growled good-humoured dissent at him. How odd it was, meeting her lover here like this, in public, unannounced. The thought came unbidden, as they stood face to face, that she would have liked to explore the rest of the house with him hand in hand, find a chamber with a big bed and quietly close the door.

This was not the same as her previous affair. Had Roger Dickson walked in at that moment her heart would have leapt and a flush come to her cheeks; only with a great effort would she have avoided stammering, or revealing how much she knew about the Prime Minister, how much she still cared for him. The fear of discovery – the risks both had run – had flavoured the four years of their liaison. Sexuality had played an important role, but also significant had been the shared conspiracy of two outsiders at Westminster, she the woman and he from a poor background, as well as their mutual need for reinforcement and confidence-building, and their awareness of all they had had in common.

With George matters were simpler. For a start there was no real problem about disclosure. She was divorced and so was he: two adults, with no ties, nobody to hurt. Discretion obliged her to say nothing about him to anyone, not even to hint at his existence. As far as the outside world was concerned she was celibate, as MPs without current spouses were expected to be. She sensed that George preferred it that way. A dignified reticence, almost self-preservation, was very much to the fore in his character. In one sense, he was operating against his instincts in taking her out at all; how fortunate that his gentlemanly manner never hinted that he might be doing her a favour.

But his caution made sense. Nobody in public life needed to be reminded how unremitting the unwanted attentions of the press could be. She would never have contemplated an escort whose next action might be to talk to the papers, who might be willing to admit that yes, it was he, and it was she, together on a bench in the park or holding hands in the darkened theatre. Despite her good looks, Elaine's well-known face, so much a part of both her public and private persona, was a severe disability when it came to forming relationships. She was all too aware, and deeply disheartened by it, that many men would not come near her.

It had to be admitted that she had changed also. She was no longer an ingénue but successful in her own right. Left behind was the assumption that she had to live her life through men, or indeed through anybody else. Since her only child was grown and independent she was free to choose her own entertainments. In fact, her assumptions were much closer than previously to those of her male colleagues: the dominant priority was her job and career. She would shy away from anything which might interfere.

Yet here she stood near George, and wanted very much to touch him. George, with his slightly mocking brown eyes and deep bass voice, his enthusiasms and vigour and courtesy: he was an escort of grace and reliability – the kind of man one could lean on – and utterly desirable. But he was not the love of her life. Not yet.

The two paused together by the side door and surveyed the crowd. In the centre a deal of noisy chatter rose, its focus a small dark man in an irascible state.

'We sponsored the champagne and it looks as if the new Lord Bhadeshia has had a glass too many,' George remarked drily.

'It's understandable – he had a real pasting in the tabloids today. Apparently he's been using violence against the blacks to run his operations in East Africa – at least, that's the implication. Nasty stuff: you don't know what to believe.'

George nodded. 'And trust *Panorama* to jump on the bandwagon. They're going to make a documentary in which he will feature. We had them on to my office this afternoon asking for an interview, but the fact is I hardly know the man. It appears he gave my name as a contact who would speak up for him.'

Elaine regarded him curiously. 'And did you agree?'

'Of course not. I tend to run a mile from publicity for a start, as you know. Your talents with the media are not mine. I grant you that in his limited dealings with me he's been above board, but how could I give him a clean bill of health when I haven't the foggiest idea what he gets up to elsewhere?'

Elaine frowned. 'He probably suggested you because of your good standing in the city.'

'Thank you, Elaine. And I intend to keep it.' His voice was almost testy.

She watched as Jayanti waved his arms in agitation, a glass of champagne slopping in his hand. He had spotted a junior Minister from the Foreign Office and charged alarmingly in that direction, words of protest on his lips.

'His body language is wrong. All that excitability makes him look guilty,' she remarked quietly. 'It makes me sad – we are so exclusive in this country, so suspicious of foreigners and what appears to be foreign behaviour. Then we accept for years a liar like Philby, who betrayed everything he was brought up to, simply because he knew how to drop an eyebrow instead of an aitch. Yet the newcomers, these immigrants who've brought real energy and initiative into business, are sneered at in this sort of assembly. I admire them enormously, George – I hate that sort of prejudice.'

George had never stepped outside 'this sort of assembly'. His understanding of the sensitivities of several of those present was slight. He was not, however, about to allow political correctness to warp his judgement. He took her elbow and began to steer her back into the mainstream.

'It's just as much prejudice, dearest Elaine, if we refuse to believe that such individuals can be crooks. There's at least a chance that Bhadeshia's commercial ethics might be a little different from . . . let's say, mine. And now I think you are expected to mingle, aren't you? Any chance of supper later?'

'I've got two boxes – ' she began to protest.

'Fine. Then you can do them afterwards. I'll look out for you in an hour.'

His face had a set which said he would not easily be deterred. Her greatest fear when her husband left, when she deliberately ended the affair with Roger, had been loneliness. That dark monster lay at her door, blowing chill air in whenever she was alone. To spend even a couple of hours with George would mean reading till 2 a.m. to catch up; but it was worth it, to keep that spectre at bay.

'Thank you. I'd like that.'

Pramila was in tears. 'Is it true, Jayanti? Did you have these poor people beaten up?'

'No. At least I don't know.'

Bhadeshia pulled at his tie and sat heavily on the bed. He had achieved nothing at the reception except, as he was acutely aware, to have made something of a fool of himself. He should not have touched that champagne; he had been upset enough without it. An occasion when he should have acquired admirers and allies had turned into a miserable mess.

Pramila raised her head from the newspaper. 'All day the phone has been ringing. Mostly my friends tell me that these Africans deserve it:

223

they did the same to us. But we should behave better, especially now you are a lord.'

Her husband jumped up and paced the room. 'I could not stop it – at least, I knew nothing about it. It seemed like a good idea, to recover ownership of my family's old house. It was very beautiful and would have suited our needs exactly. I mentioned it to the President's assistant. That is all. Then I had a message to say it was ours and the occupants had left. Nobody told me how they were removed. I had no role in it, none.'

Pramila shivered. She could see more clearly than her husband the dangers of being blamed for what was beyond their control; and that in turn came from extending themselves overseas, into an environment with which, despite their history, they were now unfamiliar. Neither Jayanti nor herself would ever have had the stomach for violence, whether in Kampala or King's Cross: essentially peaceable, their first instinct was to avoid trouble.

'What can we do about it now?' she asked, but suspected she knew the answer.

'Nothing. What can we do? We can't give the property back after all this hassle. It is ours now and I have the papers to say so. If necessary I can sell it to help raise capital for the new shops, but it would be a drop in the bucket. And who would I sell it to?'

He stopped. The picture he was painting, though accurate, was bleak and in too stark contrast to his dreams and hopes for the new project. He went to his wife and took her gently in his arms.

'You must understand, my darling, that there will be more rubbish in the press. Sometimes it will be true but not our fault. Mostly it will not be true. Often it is . . . ah . . . legitimate business practice, you know? Hard to explain, but necessary.'

Pramila looked away and sighed. 'You are a good man, Jayanti. You have worked hard and made us comfortable and respected. I am frightened, for the first time. You are to be a public figure. Your every move will be watched. Who is to make allowances for "legitimate business practices" now? Who will give us the benefit of the doubt? Nobody.'

Her husband picked up the newspaper and ceremonially threw it in the bin. He forced a laugh. 'Certainly not the *Globe*, that is for sure,' he murmured.

The year was waking up. Window-boxes were stuffed with multicoloured pansies and wallflowers, in high-walled town gardens wistaria and early roses came into flower once more, and the starkness of trees vanished overhead as their green canopy spread and flourished. Days lengthened and the sun grew stronger: the streets round Westminster filled with coaches and its pavements disappeared under untidy herds of tourists.

A mustachioed figure walked jauntily down the road near Battersea Park checking house numbers. It might have been an estate agent, though the stained raincoat and generally seedy air were no longer so appropriate for that benighted profession now the housing market had at long last recovered.

Jim Betts told himself that, despite a substantial increase in his salary since promotion to deputy news editor at the *Globe*, it made good sense for him to dress down, as he always had. He preferred to be a face in the crowd, observer but never observed. He abjured the Armani suit and the media appearances of an Andrew Neil or Charles Moore; for him obscurity and anonymity were tools of the trade.

His girlfriends took an opposing view. Over the years many had tried to tidy him up – had complained about the faint tide-mark at the back of his neck, or about his not changing his underpants every day. He could not see the point. In Liverpool when he was growing up a daily bath was considered a foppish extravagance, an attitude of which he quietly approved and which had never left him. As long as you smelled clean and could pass, that was sufficient.

Girls, now: in short supply at the moment. Plenty of tarts around, but funds had to be spent on them which he resented. Here he was, a professional man in the prime of life, not overweight – a bit reedy, rather, but some dames liked that – all his own teeth, or nearly, and no need for glasses. Plenty of mileage for the right bitch, surely. The females ought to be queuing up.

Love didn't come into it. James Betts, unloved, unwanted and ignored as a child, had no time for sentimentality. Better to have no ties, and a different girl on his arm each time he entered Stringfellow's. Pressed, he might have indicated a penchant for spending time with a bird he liked, and had taken several women out more than once without demanding sex the first time around. But if the real thing was not quickly forthcoming the friendship would end. Women were for bed, and not much else.

To work. He whistled to himself, a tuneless thin sound, as if to give himself the illusion of friendly company. The Asian articles were having their effect and had been syndicated around the world – or pirated, at least in India, where there had been demonstrations against the British. Betts chortled happily. That his matchless prose had roused a few hundred crazies to fury pleased him no end. The power of the pen, no less. And the TV companies had followed up the theme, though naturally were slower off the mark. He had set the video for tonight, though he'd seen the programme at its press preview. Should keep the pot boiling nicely.

But a top journalist could not let the grass grow under his feet. Even as the last of his Asians articles was being typeset, he was on the trail of material for the next series of hard-hitting reports. This time he would examine several choice government Ministers. It was a couple of years since the most recent batch of scandals. Guards would have been relaxed. It was merely a question of finding the best way in.

For this purpose, PPSs were included. They were on the ladder of government even if not exactly of it. The distinction was blurred, particularly in the public's mind, and so didn't matter. A PPS shared many of the characteristics of a Minister. He would attend departmental briefings and be positively vetted to see secret documents. His twopenn'orth would be invited in discussion; wiser heads would mull over his ideas. Both Ministers and PPSs were appointed by the Prime Minister. Therefore, successful attacks on them were barbs directed at the PM himself. If any were obliged to resign, a hole appeared in the government's armour. Some other poor mug would then be invited to fill the gap, and would arrive at Number 10 to the sound of popping flashbulbs, chest out, panting in eager anticipation. Lambs to the slaughter, the lot of them.

It was a pity many of the current crop of names on the front benches were so dull. There were too few larger than life figures these days. Like Nick Soames, grandson of Churchill, whose mournful battles against his genetic tendency to resemble a large pear were matched only by his jovial good humour. Betts got muddled up between all the Evanses and Joneses in government – making them even sound interesting was an impossible task. Not a single vivid personality or double-barrelled name among them, except in the Foreign Office where blue blood was *de rigueur*.

He might try that lady PPS in the Department of National Heritage – now what was her name? She had spoken out as a Young Conservative in favour of legalising cannabis; maybe she practised what she preached. Or what might Mr Anthony York, PPS at the Department of Health, Welfare and the Family, have got up to in his short life? Betts checked his map: he was nearly there. His destination, York's London home, was the next block.

226

Not married at the age of nearly thirty-four – that was suspicious for a start. Most of the rumours about this one, however, indicated that he was too darned moral for his own good: never met a female up to his standards, probably, and scared as shit to lower them, along with his trousers. Betts paused, congratulated himself on this intelligent turn of phrase and noted it for future use.

It might be easy to set him up. Find a bright capable lady – on the *Globe*'s staff, perhaps, or a student journalist, somebody with a name to make. Had to be a bird with brains and a good head on her – that'd be his type. Better still, if the man could be persuaded to make love in a bedroom wired for sound – even write a few love-letters: however chaste, something could be made of them. Anything for a belly-laugh.

And if by chance Mr York were up to no good he, Betts, would know it in an instant. Guilt would be written all over his face as questions, seemingly innocuous, would be put. Not that the victim would be confronted right away. No, instead he'd be given enough rope to hang himself; his frantic phone calls recorded, his midnight pacing photographed, so that eventually every loving detail would be splashed on the front page for the world to see.

This was it. Betts looked up at the house and noted the neat net curtains, the tidy path. The electoral register indicated that three men lived here, at least on 10 October the previous year, the qualifying date. Two were MPs but for the moment he was only interested in York. Perhaps the third man was a boyfriend? That would be interesting. He stepped forward and rang the bell.

A girl's voice cried out from the back of the house, telling him to wait. A girlfriend? Housekeeper? Cleaner? He wiped his moustache with the back of his hand. The sound of footsteps could be heard along the hallway.

The door opened and Betts found himself staring into a young face he knew too well and had hoped never to see again.

'You!' Karen spat the words out. 'What the fuck are you doing here? You've got a nerve. Go away!'

She was taller than he remembered, more formed, adult. Tight jeans and T-shirt.

'No – don't go. Hello, Karen. I had no idea you lived . . . your name isn't on the register.'

'I wasn't here then,' Karen informed him tartly. Instantly she regretted allowing the reporter to start a conversation. She tried to push the door shut but found it blocked. Hand on hip she glared at him belligerently.

'So what have you come for? If you're looking for my mother she's at the department, as you'd expect. I suggest you contact her press secretary.'

'No, it's her PPS I'm after.' Strictly speaking York was Harrison's gofer, but the discrepancy was minor. 'Mr Anthony York. Is he in?'

'No,' Karen answered shortly. 'He's at work too. Would you mind removing your foot, Mr Betts? Because if you don't I'm going to cause you a serious injury.'

The expression on her face told him she meant it. Betts turned to go, then hesitated. What was the girl doing there? To have a promising line of inquiry disappear so suddenly went against his principles.

'Look, Karen, I don't suppose it'll make any difference now, but I'm sorry – '

The door slammed shut in his face, the knocker rattling in concurrence. Jim Betts pursed his lips in annoyance and trudged back the way he had come.

The overweight lawyer with the shock of white hair heaved himself to his feet and swayed in the direction of his private filing cabinet. His client's voice rose to a squeak.

'I think you should sit down and listen to me!'

Sir John Merriman took no notice. When he had found what he sought he returned to his desk and lowered himself carefully into the extra-wide chair which had been his, as head of the firm of Merriman, Abrahams and Arnold in Fetter Lane for over twenty years.

His client's face was a rictus of misery and fear, but that was true of many who had entered this dusty, book-lined room. On trial here was the frailty of man, his greed, jealousy, cupidity and ignorance. How foolish most of them were, and how scared – not least at the thought of the bill which would inevitably follow even the speediest consultation. Time and again he would advise them not to sue, to forget the insult; or, on the other hand, to bow to the inevitable and apologise. Those who ignored his advice and ended up in court might have even greater cause to worry about the financial consequences. The rules permitted the recovery by a winner of only a proportion of the full costs, while a loser had to bear most of the other side's (probably inflated) expenses on top of his own. Yet Sir John's livelihood depended, as it always had, on a steady supply of injured egos trailing writs for defamation, and the deep pockets which accompanied them.

'I can well understand your feelings, my lord,' Sir John intoned portentously. 'However, I should ask you to consider the question Lord Mishcon puts to clients, and which seems to me to sum up the issue.'

'I do not wish to play games,' Jayanti responded testily. The room was hot and he was beginning to perspire.

'That question is, would your friends believe this of you?'

Jayanti fidgeted in agitation. He did not like the drift of the conversation. 'I don't understand you. Please get to the point.'

Sir John sighed. 'You are being accused, as I understand it, of underhand dealings in your business. Some of your accounts do not add up. The use of violence to repossess your African property . . . not that you would encourage or condone such action, but it is linked with your name. A possible misleading overstatement of your personal wealth to obtain a mortgage for your new house. This is the relevant substance of the articles in the *Globe* and tonight's *Panorama* television film on sleaze, of which we have an advance copy. Am I right?'

Bhadeshia looked at the carpet. 'The mortgage . . . a little exaggeration . . . that is normal.' Then he gazed at his legal adviser, his eyes round and tearful. 'I *have* to put a stop to all this. My wife has become a nervous wreck. My children are being spat at – teased and bullied. Even at a private school! My family . . . my life will not be worth living – '

'You have yet to answer my question – and I must ask you to consider it. Would your friends believe these charges against you?'

Jayanti's head rocked from side to side. 'Yes . . . no . . . What's that got to do with anything? You set me riddles at a time like this. Why – what does it matter?'

Sir John's huge shoulders shrugged imperceptibly. 'Well, if your friends wouldn't believe it, you have no need to sue: your reputation is intact, far more so than I could make it. And if your friends do believe it, or might, then you have a problem which suing won't readily put right.'

The sophistry was beyond Bhadeshia. Sir John waited, then tidied his folder and leaned back. Under the desk he pressed a hidden button.

'Our task today is in the nature of damage limitation. We must test the water and establish whether our opponents are firm under pressure or not. I will draft suitable letters demanding a retraction, an apology and, naturally, substantial damages.'

'But what will you say? Will you insist . . .?'

As he spoke Sir John's clerk entered, tall, thin and lugubrious. The eminent lawyer rose but remained behind his desk. 'Watkins will take you to a more comfortable room and fetch you coffee. If you could wait, my lord, I will get on with it.'

Dumbly Bhadeshia allowed himself to be removed. He glanced back to see Sir John uncap his pen and gaze mournfully at the open file. With Watkins's practised hand resting on his shoulder, Jayanti felt no more an honoured and welcome client but like a convict leaving the dock for the cells.

The microwave pinged.

It was grand, being able to cook your own food; to choose a coloured packet in the supermarket, chilli con carne or shepherd's pie or fisherman's pie, put a fork in the Cellophane to make holes for the steam, remembering to remove any metal foil covers. Then on to a pretty dish, pop it in, and in five minutes there it was, hot and steamy, ready to be eaten.

It made a change from the hospital. Thick white Pyrex plates, never clean. Plastic glasses for water which tasted tainted. Somebody forever screeching in the background. The food was dished up for you, slops and mashed potato whatever the menu claimed, with gravy so stiff you could stand a spoon up in it, and everything too salty.

The prison had been worse. All stodge. No fruit, ever. He'd got fat: the inevitable outcome was a paunch, which slowed him down, and brain cells deadened with ECT and excess carbohydrate. Horrible dirty place, a permanent smell of disinfectant. Open buckets in the cell. If you said a wrong word you were liable to find the bucket tipped over you by morning.

It was so nice to have your own television set. To watch it alone, with no catcalling from other, stupid men. Choose what you liked. Serious stuff, the news, documentaries. Find out what was going on in the world. He could vote now: his name was on the electoral register for the first time in years. A citizen again.

Panorama about MPs and lords. Maybe see her. Elaine. Beautiful: a lovely woman, exactly as a woman should be, not a screaming harridan, but pure and perfect, always immaculately dressed and poised and confident.

Graham Dunn's train of thought made him smile contentedly. He carried his tray over to the low table and settled down on the sofa. He forked food into his mouth, slowly, eyes fixed owl-like on the screen.

Beside him an old *Radio Times* lay open at the horoscope page. He picked up the remote control and pushed buttons until he found what he wanted.

The programme was confusing at times but he had no trouble following its main theme of corruption involving business and politicians. To his relief it was clear that Elaine took no part in it: of course not, she would not soil herself like that.

At last came the moment he had been waiting for.

The screen showed the glare of arc lights outside a handsome white mansion somewhere in London as Elaine emerged from a ministerial car. She was wearing a black coat with a raised collar and a colourful silk scarf at the neck. She paused and smiled at the camera with a quick wave of the hand, then walked briskly across the threshold into a brightly lit hallway. The picture changed to somebody else.

He laughed out loud. He was now certain. She had turned, and smiled and waved. Everybody else would assume she had made the little gesture in the usual course of her duties. But Graham Dunn knew better.

She had done it, with that special secret smile, just for him.

Chapter Fourteen

'And do you wish to be armigerous?'

Jayanti wilted. 'I beg your pardon, sir. What?'

The heavy jowls of Sir Greville Fitzroy wobbled as he enjoyed his little joke. It always worked.

What a lovely job this was. At the age of seventy, after sterling service in the Coldstream Guards and a tedious stretch as a tax barrister, how wonderful to wear the resplendent uniform as Garter Principal King-of-Arms, not to speak of Heraldic Adviser to the Monumental Brass Society and Knight Principal of the Imperial Society of Knights Bachelor: in other words, to be in charge of the nation's heraldry.

'Will you wish to apply for letters patent and a grant of arms?'

Jayanti answered a mite too eagerly. 'Yes, yes. At least, if I am permitted.'

Garter pretended to frown. 'You don't have to, you know. In fact most life peers don't. And there's no need to hurry, either. Lord Denning took thirty years to get round to his.'

He spread his manicured hands on the table. 'For some peers, the cost is a factor. You do realise that the whole hog – arms, crest and supporters – will set you back two thousand eight hundred pounds? No VAT, fortunately. Women don't have crests, so we charge them only fourteen hundred and ninety. We do a special offer of arms and crest alone for two thousand two hundred. It's up to you.'

Jayanti was startled at the tone of the discussion, as if he were seated in a Turkish bazaar instead of an office in the House of Lords. He responded cautiously.

'Perhaps you'd better tell me what's involved.'

Sir Greville sat back. 'You apply formally to the Duke of Norfolk as Earl Marshal. He sends a warrant to me, instructing me to proceed. We discuss what you want. Then I issue you with your patent which you can frame and hang on your wall: that's in vellum with the entire heraldic achievement, arms, coronet, helm, crest, mantling, supporters, motto, orders and decorations in full colour and gold with my signature and official seal. Quite a sight, I can tell you.'

'Golly,' Jayanti muttered.

'The only bit you can borrow from somebody else is the motto – there's no monopoly on that. If you want "Who dares, wins", that's fine by me. The rest has to be original.'

His hearer perked up. 'Lady Thatcher had Sir Isaac Newton on hers,' he offered hopefully.

Sir Greville grimaced. The ribaldry caused by the baroness's taste was a painful memory. 'And a Falklands War admiral. We got that completely wrong: he looked like Captain Birdseye and could only have acquired his four rows of decorations by serving in the First *and* Second World Wars, Korea, Northern Ireland and Bosnia as well as the South Atlantic. Everyone said she should've had a handbag: we'd have been happy with that.'

'But surely', Jayanti protested, 'the coat of arms should be a serious matter?'

Sir Greville shrugged. 'Not necessarily. Geoffrey Howe has a wolf in sheep's clothing; Lord Zuckerman preferred a great ape, while Lord Ackner, who was a lawyer, has two spouting whales swimming hard in opposite directions – barristers in court, I suppose. Grey Gowrie's has black sheep. You have what you want.'

'Perhaps I should ask you for . . . guidance?' The voice was faint. Jayanti was finding the whole business quite overwhelming.

'Well . . . since you're in business, bezants – those are gold Byzantine coins – would be appropriate. And you do import–export, don't you, so how about a ship? Then think about where you come from, and where you live now. Lady Gardner was Australian so she had a kangaroo. Lord Grade combined music with his Russian origins and had a balalaika – a brilliant choice, in my view. Your supporters – the characters on each side – can be anything you want nearly, not only lions and unicorns. Lord Nelson had a sailor, rather as you'd expect. One chap has a Rolls-Royce foreman, while Lord Schon put factory chimneys, a plant chemist and a process worker in his. Your former Party Treasurer, Lord McAlpine, has his gardener with a parrot on his wrist. Only he and I know exactly what that means: all part of the fun.'

He rumbled with genteel amusement, then rose to his feet. Jayanti jumped up. 'After lunch we must rehearse your investiture. Got your wits about you? Good. You'll need 'em.'

*   *   *

The house was a large semi in a noisy road in Hounslow. It was, of course, ideal for the airport; and, Elaine reflected, the rumble of planes overhead, day and night, could not be cause for complaint in a household which depended on air travel for its livelihood.

Nor could Mike afford anything much better. The settlement of their divorce had obliged him to continue paying his share of the mortgage on the property in South Warmingshire which had been the marital home. He made regular if modest contributions to Karen's upkeep and would do so until she finished college. Substantial though his salary as a senior British Airways pilot might be, it did not easily run to the support of two establishments and two more children, especially after Linda stopped work to care for them. The odds were that money was a little tight.

Elaine drove into the driveway and parked. The silver BMW of previous times had given way to a three-year-old Ford Granada. The dent in its wing looked old and the radio aerial had snapped off halfway. In the back, two child-seats took up the space; toys and rugs littered the interior.

As she picked up the gift in its silver wrapping paper and the flowery card she felt nervous. She was too smartly dressed. Her make-up was too elaborate. Quickly she unfastened the big pearl earrings and slipped them into a pocket, then purposefully she walked up to the front door and rang the bell.

'Hang on, I'm coming,' called a woman's voice from inside. It sounded harassed but not hostile. It was several minutes before the door was opened, just as Elaine was wondering whether to ring again.

'Oh, it's you. Come on in.'

Elaine had never met Linda, who had been a member of Mike's cabin crew on long-haul flights. The new wife was younger than herself by about ten years but did not look it. She must have made a most attractive stewardess but her hair was limp and she had some way to go to regain her figure after the latest birth. Elaine caught in herself a tinge of smugness at the favourable comparisons that could be made. Her confidence began to return.

The two women walked through the hall into the living room. A television was playing loudly. Mike was slumped in a chair watching the football. Elaine smiled in wry recognition; that was how she remembered him on countless weekend afternoons when she had been out door-knocking in the rain or battling against the odds to retain her seat and keep her job. How angry his laziness had made her. It was evident that in his new life he was no more energetic than in his old one. She saw him with brutal clarity now that she had no reason to miss him, nor to feel any pang. What he had been for her in their youth, the handsome charmer who had captivated her at university, had completely vanished. The middle-aged man who rose sheepishly to greet her had long since vacated his place in her heart.

Should she kiss him? She took the initiative and did, once, quite affectionately on the cheek.

'Mike – how nice to see you. Thank you for letting me come. You look . . . well.'

They were as awkward as she. There was no angst between the three of them, for no battles remained to be fought; but Mike and Linda's ignorance of the right etiquette in the presence of not only the wronged first wife but a famous person, a Minister of Her Majesty's Government, made them tongue-tied and uncomfortable. Elaine would have to give a lead. She gestured at a chair. 'May I sit down?'

In a few moments tea appeared in mugs with a plate of shop-bought cake. A glimpse through the connecting door showed an untidy kitchen, the remains of lunch plates still in the sink. No dishwasher, of course. No cleaning lady: these would be luxuries beyond their pocket. It struck Elaine forcibly how much her and Mike's lives had diverged since the split. She had had much the better time of it, at least financially; plus an element of control over her life, which the couple before her seemed to have mislaid, if ever they had had it.

There was a flicker of tension in the room. Perhaps all was not well. Had Linda discovered how set in his ways Mike could be? Did Mike get irritated at what was obviously not a well-run household? Whatever the case, it was none of her business, other than to ensure that she did not introduce any further source of conflict. Her voice, hitherto bright and brittle, became gentle.

'I'd love to see Jonathan,' she remarked. 'Is he asleep? And what about your other son? He must be about three now.'

'He's at friends',' Linda replied shortly. She brushed a lock of hair from her face and half-heartedly began to pick up toys, only to put them down in equally haphazard heaps elsewhere in the room. 'Baby's in his cot. C'mon up.'

As she climbed the stairs Elaine began to feel sorry for the younger woman, and sad. For someone who had travelled the world in a glamorous occupation a semi in West London must be a disappointment. The place was hardly vibrant with love and fulfilment. Mike did not seem to be making any more effort in this marriage than in his previous one.

In the smallest bedroom a child was peacefully asleep, curled up on a cot, bedclothes tousled, finger in his mouth. The curtains were drawn but Linda pulled them back so that Elaine could see.

At the light the little boy opened his eyes, focused on the visitor and gurgled. His hand, still sticky and pink from his mouth, reached up to her and she grasped it. A terrible lump came into her throat. The baby closely resembled Jake, the boy that she and Mike had once had, the child who had died.

'Anything the matter?' Linda was a kind-hearted girl. She had been willing to accede to Karen's odd notion of inviting her mother to the christening, though with a marginal private protest that Elaine would seize all the attention. When the tactful refusal had arrived and with it a request to view the new arrival none the less, it had seemed a harmless enough idea. Yet here was the first Mrs Stalker, who still used her husband's name, bent in tears over the cot.

'No – I was only thinking what a lovely baby he is.'

'Karen says he's a bit like she was, according to the photos.' Linda was sympathetic. It must be a hard life, always in the public eye, always on the go. It wouldn't suit her, though she felt nostalgic occasionally for the good times in San Francisco and Buenos Aires, where Mike had seemed such fun. Still, she had angled hard for a respectable husband and her own home and had won both. She had made her bed and would lie on it.

Elaine turned away and blew her nose. She did not feel able to reply or elaborate further.

'Thanks. And thank you for the tea, and the fruit cake. I enjoyed that. And now I must go.'

'Oh! Mike was wondering if you'd like to stay for supper.'

That sounded like the worst possible suggestion. Suddenly it was imperative for Elaine to remove herself as rapidly as possible. She shook her head with a half-smile and headed downstairs. Mike was once again engrossed in the sport on television. He twisted around as she entered, but did not rise as she kissed him once more on the cheek, and gave Linda a hug.

On the doorstep Elaine hesitated. 'I'm glad I came,' she said simply. 'I'm sure you look after him and the children far better than I ever did, Linda. He seems content.'

'Him? He's happy enough.' Linda jerked her head back at the

lounge. 'Was he like this with you? Forever stuck in front of the box, I mean?'

Elaine laughed ruefully. 'He was, actually.'

The two women's eyes met. Briefly they understood each other's lives.

As she headed back down the motorway towards London, Elaine found herself weeping softly. For Mike, who had once had such drive and had lost it. For Linda, who must have dreamed of better, and the hints of weakness in the second marriage. For herself, whose failure as a wife this household represented and underlined. For Karen, whose desire to see her parents reconciled and perhaps even become close friends would be denied. And for the dead child, Karen's brother, who had been the source of such love and pain, when she, Elaine, had been a new, hopeful wife and mother with no inkling of a career, before politics and the public persona had claimed her, so long ago.

While the owner of Bhadeshia's Emporium moved eagerly to practise a stately minuet in the Chamber of the House of Lords his supporters on the Equator faced instead a dance of death, whose outcome would be fateful not only to its immediate participants but to Bhadeshia himself, to his hopes and dreams. Like the eviction of squatters from his African property which had so besmirched his reputation, it was a matter over which he had no control. But neither did his key protector, the President, against whom the action was directed.

Police Constable Joshua Mereginga knew it would be a bad day. Angry dreams had invaded his sleep and he had awoken weeping, to find his youngest child standing over him in puzzled silence. The milk for breakfast had curdled the moment it touched his lips and the old fowl intended for the weekend's main meal had been found dead and stiff under its perch. Someone had knocked his clean uniform off the high shelf on to the dirt floor and messed the blue shirt. That meant he would have to keep the jacket on no matter how hot the day. And it would be searing – as dawn crept inside the hut, the heat and humidity were already enough to send fear into the bones.

The capital had been seething for weeks. Lack of rain meant a poor harvest and exorbitant food prices. Importers and strangers were blamed both for the bad luck and for profiting from it. The President's economic nostrums about free trade meant nothing to hungry people. Nor to Joshua, though he had admired the man when first he was elected. Democracy, they called it, and said it was a good thing; but it did not feed the children.

As he stood in line in the baking sun a trickle of sweat slipped down between his shoulder-blades. The crowd opposite chanted slogans and waved makeshift banners. Behind their barricades they were becoming increasingly agitated. He wiped the palms of his hands on his trouser legs and left dark patches. It was essential to get a firm grip on his night stick: it would be needed.

Next to him stood his sergeant, a massive man who towered over his troop. His heavy face was grim. His hand wandered time and again to the pistol in its holster. The noise from the crowd intensified. Drumming had started, loud and persistent.

The sergeant grunted an order. Joshua offered a whispered prayer. Two men nearby crossed themselves. Night sticks were lifted to the regulation height and angle and shaken menacingly towards the crowd, who shrank back briefly, then jeered louder.

Together, as they had been trained, the line of policemen began to move forward. The sergeant had his gun in his hand and shouted commands at the ringleaders. Behind their line, support jeeps slipped their clutches. A female voice could be heard screaming, somewhere among the rioters, spewing hatred at the police, the President, the foreigners . . .

A shot rang out, high and clear, a loud crack which echoed menacingly around the square. At Joshua's side a fellow officer shrieked, then fell and lay jerkily, blood from a chest wound oozing into the dust.

'Chaaaarge!'

He had no choice. He loped forward, his breath in short rasps, uncertain what he would do next. The noise, the drums, the screams: more shots – the big sergeant was shooting wildly, directly into the crowd, then suddenly, right in front of Joshua, he threw up his hands and fell.

As at a signal the rioters climbed over the barricades and raced for their victims. Joshua saw the man who would kill him, a machete raised in his fist, but felt only surprise as the first blow fell. It was a fate, he knew, that awaited the President he had been so proud to serve – if not that day, then very soon.

Within ten minutes not a single policeman was left alive.

The bodies were dragged round the town and abandoned in a tangled heap in the police station yard. It was from there, long after dark, that a grieving Mrs Mereginga, accompanied by her two eldest sons, collected her dead husband.

* * *

It was a bore, having to fill out claim forms every month. Bits of paper for this, signatures for that, as if he were a travelling salesman required to produce chits for each cup of tea, instead of one of Her Majesty's Ministers and an honourable Member of Parliament merely trying to do his job.

Derek Harrison lit a cigarette and ruminated. The ministerial salary stood at a few pounds over £54,000. That didn't bear comparison with the remuneration of, say, the Chairman of British Gas, who with half a million a year was one of the few people in the country who didn't need to win the National Lottery.

His pay came in two parts – £30,307 as a Minister of State and £24,985 as an MP; it was assumed, though for the life of him he could not see why, that a member of the government could be only a part-time MP, so the usual parliamentary allowance of £33,189 was docked by a quarter. Bloody insulting.

Then there was the car mileage. At 72.2 pence per mile for a car over 2,300 cc it looked generous, and indeed a typical journey home each Friday would generate some £180. Fiddles were, of course, available. Derek envied those lucky Scottish Members who might share a car and the petrol for a 600-mile round trip, then each make a claim yielding £400 a time. And nobody checked up on that claim for mileage within the constituency; if anyone officious ever tried they'd be led a wild-goose chase in the downs and dales of merrie England.

The assistance with the second home was particularly useful – £11,661 and not taxable. Well, it stood to reason: the job demanded that he work and stay in two places. Even a salesman could claim his hotel bills. Harrison could not recall, however, that he had once been asked to produce a receipt for the regular repairs and cleaning costs for the cottage in his patch. As it happened, the place was not mythical – but he wouldn't put that trick past certain colleagues.

The biggest sum was for secretarial expenses – £41,308 and tax-free. One year when he was short of funds he'd resorted to a modest fraud by inventing a part-time researcher and having the money paid into a bank account in Enfield. Couldn't do that now – too well known. Pity he didn't have a wife to employ. On the other hand, the odd impecunious girlfriend was grateful for a little recompense, though on the whole Harrison preferred his women wealthier than himself.

Every sou got spent: it would have been a crime to have left anything in the kitty. The silliest things were passed without a murmur, though he wished that Viking Office Supplies Direct sold better-quality toilet paper.

In all, it added up to a pretty penny. If most people thought their MPs were paid only that miserly £33,000, most MPs knew better. It still wasn't enough. Nobody honest ever made progress in politics *and* ended up rich. A chap must either create his fortune first like Michael Heseltine or wait patiently till the twilight years when consultancies and share options might float in his direction like so much shipwrecked treasure. A few, though, wily and clever like himself, had no desire to struggle in penury but intended to maintain a high lifestyle and garner a little extra, discreetly, along the way.

In which case old pals and business partners were worth their weight in gold. Harrison signed the last chit, inserted it in an envelope for the Fees Office and turned contentedly to the newly minted Bhadeshia share certificate which had arrived in that morning's post.

He would never get it right. He'd stop in the wrong place, trip over, bow at the wrong times. Their lordships, all of whom had executed this elaborate choreography before taking their seats, would whisper. It was said they awarded a new incumbent marks out of ten and would hiss when mistakes were made.

For the first time Jayanti felt scared. He would be mixing with the greatest in the land, the finest brains, men and women of the highest distinction. He did not deserve it. He was not, he knew, a man of enormous intellect. There were moments reading the *Financial Times* when he confessed to himself that he did not understand a word. If his wife wanted to watch television he could cope with *The Bill* and *Golden Shot*; Cilla Black was a particular favourite. But his new acquaintances would be connoisseurs of fine art and culture, of which Jayanti was completely ignorant. Once he had attended a gala performance of *Madame Butterfly* at the Coliseum and had fallen asleep, even though it was in English. He had no higher education, none whatever. He seldom read a book. He had no small talk or dinner conversation.

So how had he made it? Jayanti considered. Backbreaking hard work was the answer. Fifteen hours a day for years, doing the kind of job many Englishmen now regarded as beneath them, in post offices, small corner groceries and off-licences open all the hours that customers demanded. Prepared to trade on a tiny profit others would have turned up their noses at. Willing to serve the roughest areas. Supported by his co-religionists so that banks had neither stake nor share, and in his turn, as his efforts bore fruit, quietly offering finance to others on a word or shake of the hand. It all required a sharp eye and a feel for business, but hardly a degree from Harvard.

Yet that left him vulnerable. Once he stepped outside the community he lost the benefit of the doubt. Here he would be regarded as having something to prove: in this bizarre place, ablaze with its red leather and gold trimmings, he felt his store of resources seriously deficient, at least in comparison with what might be needed.

He wondered whether his desire to become a peer demonstrated his inadequacy. A businessman like George Horrocks, an insider, was exactly the type who would find himself effortlessly in the honours list. Such a man would comment that it was good for his firm, or for the team he led, but care little for himself. He might understand why it mattered so much to a Bhadeshia, yet a Horrocks would privately despise the ambition as worthless.

It was time for the rehearsal. Out of the Moses Room, one at a time, like nervous parachutists jumping over enemy territory. Into the Chamber, stop, bow towards the throne. Turn right, then left, and bow at the Table and at the Woolsack. Lord Archer, his junior sponsor, was in front. There he was, joking away, and turning right instead of left. Jayanti wished he would concentrate.

Kneel – one knee only. Give the Lord Chancellor his Writ of Summons. Back to the Table, put the hat down, take the oath and sign the roll. That was crucial, for everything else, including expenses, followed from that point.

But he was only halfway. Still with Lord Archer in front and his senior sponsor behind, he must process towards the back benches on the government side where he would expect to sit: mustn't forget to bow en route. Sit; put on hats; rise in unison, take off hats, bow. Sit down. Put on hats. Rise, take off hats, bow. Sit down. Again, a third time, not too fast: put on hats. The black tricorne concoctions made all peers look ineffably silly. Rise. Take off hats – hold them over the left breast. Bow. Stay standing.

My God! Jayanti could feel himself perspiring vigorously. Nothing as dreadful had been demanded of him since dance lessons as a child. Back down the steps, bowing in exactly the same places as before – was that a total of ten or eleven times? – to end up at the Lord Chancellor's side, at which point a handshake would complete the ceremony.

Then he was expected to totter the few paces out of the Chamber and head for Tea Room or bar, where doubtless many of his new companions would shortly join him, at his expense.

For a moment Jayanti's heart fluttered and he shivered. The talk of writs and warrants unsettled him. The place was lousy with lawyers. He wished it was all over.

The Red Lion in Derby Gate was a short walk from Whitehall departments and the House of Commons, yet it was infrequently used by MPs. On a summer evening its pavements would be crowded with tourists nursing sore feet and junior civil servants sipping cold lagers. It was a perfect place to meet a staffer from a Minister's office who wanted a quick word before heading home.

Jim Betts put down his Guinness and appraised the anxious young woman seated across the table. Plain, freckled and a bit dumpy; barelegged, with open sandals of the kind once favoured by CND marchers. Possibly a leftie, then. And nervous – that was her second vodka and orange. Betts watched in interest.

'Who did you say you worked for?' he enquired casually.

'The Department of Health, Welfare and the Family, just over there.' The girl seemed to have difficulty pronouncing the name: she was obviously not used to the alcohol. It was not, however, the answer Betts required. He waited.

'Derek bloody Harrison,' she spat out at last. Betts suppressed a smile.

'Not the nicest guy around, at a guess,' he ventured.

'He is not. He's also a crook.'

'Is he now?' Opposite him the girl stared meaningfully into her almost empty glass. He reached over. 'Would you like another?'

Over a further vodka the girl's tongue loosened. Betts heard much which both elaborated his view of Harrison and confirmed the links between him and his close friend Lord Bhadeshia. His companion was reluctant to talk about anyone else, though clearly she reserved no love for her boss Mr Chadwick either. In order not to put her off Betts refrained from taking notes. What he wanted from her, however, would have to be in writing sooner or later.

'How do you know about all this – about the Bhadeshia shares, for example?'

'Derek's so bloody proud of himself he'll tell you. Not in the office, of course,' she added hastily. Her eyes were glazing over. 'In our own time . . . in bed. He's brilliant there.' She sighed morosely and drained her glass, then glared at her interlocutor. 'But I won't talk publicly about that. It would break my mother's heart – she's Catholic, you know.'

'And what do you want out of all this, Deirdre?' he asked softly. 'Is it money? That could be arranged.'

'Not money. And I don't want my name mentioned. I still have a Civil Service career, of sorts. But I'll send you whatever I can. You just print it, and I'll be delighted.'

Karen rubbed her hair with a towel, ran her fingers through to make it stand up spiky, debated whether to apply her make-up before or after a coffee and settled on the latter.

The exercise invigorated her. It was not only that the martial arts class made her feel more confident and assertive; the supervised stretching, the sweat-inducing leaps and kicks which brought suppleness and taut muscles also gave a healthy flush to her cheeks. With a toss of her still-damp head she joined other members of the class in the coffee bar.

'I feel as if I could conquer the world.'

'It's all right for you, a student. You want to try working in the Health Service.'

Helen was three years older than Karen, stick-thin, with a permanent frown and an ever-present cigarette. She was a nurse, currently on weekend shifts in casualty, and hating it. Karen wondered how such a sour personality had managed to choose the most caring of professions, but she kept her thoughts to herself.

'It's not such a cushy life,' she countered, laughing. 'We're forever short of money. Have to survive on shrinking grants and student loans. We have all the exams you have, and more. One of the people in the house I share is a medical student. He has the worst of both worlds, I guess.' She did not mention the occupation of the other residents; if pressed she would have said they worked at something boring in Whitehall.

'Which hospital is he in?' The new voice was flat, the vowels betraying a Midlands origin. Brummie, or nearby, Karen estimated. Their owner was a thickset older man of clumsy movements and nondescript appearance: he seemed out of place in the class. Unnoticed he had carried his coffee-mug over to the noisiest table and hovered at the edge of the circle.

'St Thomas's.'

There was a flicker of interest. 'I know some of those people. I get treated there when I'm ill. What's his name?'

Karen gave the man a hard look. He was a little peculiar. Lachlan might not like the idea of her sharing his name with a stranger. She shrugged. 'What's yours?' she asked.

'I'm Graham Dunn,' the man volunteered and held out his hand. It smelled of soap but did not seem very clean. With some distaste Karen shook it. The skin was papery. 'My name's Karen.' She did not venture any more.

'You live near here?' He was evidently going to be persistent.

'Not far.'

'Me too. I live in a hostel in Jeffrey's Road, but not for much longer.'

'Oh?'

'Yeah.' He looked pleased with himself but secretive. 'My grandad's on his last legs. He's left me his house over Wandsworth way. Bit of a mess, it is, but then he's eighty-three. Don't expect them up and down ladders decorating at that age, do you?'

Karen did not need to feign indifference. 'That's nice for you. Well, I hope you'll be very happy there . . . er, Graham.'

Swiftly she rose, patted Helen cordially on the shoulder and headed towards the changing rooms. At the door she glanced back. The man was attempting to engage the gloomy nurse in conversation, but with even less success.

Montague Spellman OBE tweaked his white gloves, pulled the red tailcoat down over his turkey-cock chest and surveyed the assembly with mingled pleasure and anxiety.

Apart from the Order of the British Empire awarded when he became President of the National Association of Toastmasters, it was a meagre tally of National Service medals that flashed on his bosom. Nevertheless a military bearing was his stock in trade. He lifted his head and stood on tiptoe. His full height would normally have left him still staring up at the average male guest. On this occasion, however, since the supporters of the One Nation group, of which he had never heard, appeared to be diminutive Asian and Chinese gentlemen and their even tinier wives, he could give most an inch or two. That pleased him, and intimidated them nicely.

The Prime Minister was due to attend: his non-appearance was the source of Montague's concern. To proceed without him would have upset his *amour propre*, not to speak of the chairman, the new Lord Bhadeshia and his attractive wife.

Pramila Bhadeshia bit her lip and touched her husband's arm.

'Do I look all right, Jayanti?'

Bhadeshia turned a trifle impatiently, then was halted by the pleading expression on Pramila's face. Her fingers trembled over her silver and gold sari. He could not condemn her as foolish; after all, it was his wife's ambition and courage over the years, not to speak of her commercial acumen, which had brought them both to the Empire Napoleon Suite in the Café Royal, and the grandest event of the year.

The toastmaster hovered indulgently as Jayanti chastely kissed his wife on the cheek and pretended to adjust the embroidered border of her sari. Her dark hair gleamed; drop earrings twinkled with diamonds, and the skin on her neck glowed in the light of the chandeliers.

'You look like a goddess, my dear,' Jayanti whispered.

A messenger hurried in. A hubbub arose as the guests realised that the Prime Minister had arrived.

Bhadeshia hurried forward. 'Prime Minister!' he exclaimed excitedly. 'We were worried about you!'

Roger Dickson tugged at the white tie which had been hastily donned in the Daimler and grunted. 'I wasn't going to let you down – but we do have a crisis on and I may yet have to leave to vote. I trust you're not expecting a long speech from me.'

Secretly Bhadeshia had imagined a major prime ministerial announcement which would have etched both his own name and the dinner in the annals of British history. He hid his disappointment with an energetic shake of the head. Then he brightened: 'But *I* will be speaking, sir, to give the vote of thanks. I will make a rabble-rousing plea for support for you and your government. I hope you will be able to stay for that.'

Roger pursed his lips. To slip away after such a warning might be tricky.

With formidable ceremony and portentousness the toastmaster consulted his list. He held up his hands for silence.

'Prime Minister, my lord, ladies, gentlemen: are we ready? Then I will announce your entry. Thank you *so* much.'

The great doors were thrown open and even Jayanti could not suppress a gasp. The decoration was sumptuous. Down the long wall huge floor-to-ceiling mirrors reflected a thousand sequinned gowns, shimmering saris and shalwar-kameez, and jewels of every hue. The circular tables were a feast of hothouse roses, gold and white menus, elegant crystal glassware and heavy silver cutlery. The porcelain was white, almost translucent, with the crowned 'N' for Napoleon III whom the salon so oddly honoured. The whole effect was gloriously excessive. Jayanti held his breath in awe.

The evening would make a lot of money. Each meal cost £50 per head without wines, but many present, especially the Muslims, did not drink. The liqueurs, the flower arrangements, the specially boxed chocolates, cigars, the printing, the tombola and the pre-dinner reception had been paid for by intimates and colleagues whose smiles shone happily from the pages of the souvenir brochure. And not a soul had entered this room without forking out at least £250 per plate for the privilege: the surplus should be £200,000, maybe more . . .

The meal passed in a dream. Jayanti absorbed the compliments as dish after dish brought coos of delight: the Michelin star was well deserved. The mixed wood mushroom salad perched in artichoke leaves with pumpkin-seed oil dressing was reassuring to vegetarians present. The smoked haddock which followed was delightfully British. The noisettes of lamb with truffles and cream took into account the needs of both Muslims and Hindus, though he wondered whether the chef had ignored his instruction to leave out the Madeira. By the time the iced Armagnac soufflé appeared, its heart-shaped creaminess set off with candied orange peel and prunes soaked in yet more brandy, Jayanti didn't care whether anybody would be offended. The cheeseboard was on its way but he could not manage another mouthful. Coffee next, then the speeches.

He leaned forward and coughed. 'Prime Minister?'

Roger had been listening to Pramila's chatter and had discovered a great deal more about the Bhadeshias' background than his office had been able to ascertain. It sounded rather better than those articles in the *Globe* suggested. Lady Bhadeshia's appearance was a bonus. Yet he could not ignore for ever the nudges from her husband on his other side. With genuine regret the Prime Minister fixed a smile on his face and turned.

'I must congratulate you. This is a marvellous function.'

Jayanti waved a hand at the throng. 'So many people were involved – I cannot take any credit. Your presence, sir, has made such a difference.'

'You must be looking forward to your investiture in the House of Lords. Have you set a date yet?'

Jayanti tried to be modest and failed; pride shone nakedly from his face. 'A fortnight's time.'

Waiters moved deftly among the tables. Jayanti hurried on. 'There is a point I must put to you, sir. At once. All these unpleasant press articles against me and my family and business. Other Asians too. And on television. It is most unfair and they are telling lies. Can't you stop them?'

Roger reflected grimly that if he could tell the media what not to publish the whingeing criticism of his own administration might be a preferred starting-point. Iconoclasm had become a way of life for broadcasters and journalists, who then debated in all innocence why their audience felt so little confidence in public office holders. Increasingly his job felt like a mug's game.

'I wish we could, but this is a free country. We can't tell the press what to do. More's the pity,' he added feelingly.

'Surely they have to print the truth?'

Roger raised an eyebrow. That was a naïve question. 'You could sue,' he suggested unhelpfully, 'but I shouldn't. It'd cost you a fortune and draw renewed attention to stuff you'd rather have forgotten.'

Jayanti opened his mouth to protest further, only to find Montague's whiskers tickling his ear. 'Ready for the loyal toast, sir?'

The toast; the permission to smoke; the five-minute comfort break which led to an undignified rush for the toilets; the stragglers who slunk shamefacedly back to their places as the Prime Minister rose to his feet – Jayanti, in a daze, knew he would relive every detail to his dying day.

'I am delighted to be present, and to honour Lord and Lady Bhadeshia,' Roger began, 'who represent the best in the British Asian community.' His gestures invited his audience to applaud. Filled with excellent fare, bonhomie and love of their fellow man they responded warmly.

'We are proud that this is a multi-racial society – probably the most successful multi-racial society in the world.' That was what the press release said, though it was perhaps a slight exaggeration. Roger ploughed on, with every ounce of sincerity he could muster. 'But that confers obligations on the government. Every citizen in this country should be treated equally. No man or woman should have to suffer from discrimination in word or deed. That is the law. If necessary we will strengthen legislation and its enforcement to ensure that *all* our citizens can live and work in peace.'

A fine sentiment, Roger reflected. Not that any fresh proposals were in the pipeline. Peppering the Lords with a few more worthies would have to suffice – especially if they could lay on a do like this. Gracefully he concluded his remarks and sat down. He had sung for his supper; and been briefed to expect in return a handsome donation.

Bhadeshia's pulse pounded in his throat. A sackful of mail had arrived on the announcement of his peerage, mostly from people he had not known before. Enquiries about the East African project had inundated the office. His bank manager had been impressed and had extended his overdraft. What a vast change it made, to be a name instead of a nobody: no longer an interloper, but a trusted mover in the highest ranks of society. And all it had cost was a little money he could easily afford, paid over to the party in power.

'Mr Prime Minister!' Jayanti was conscious that his voice, as ever when he was nervous, had risen to a squeak. Try as he might the frantic treble persisted. He clutched his notes and paused, sweating.

'We have much to celebrate today! The economy was in the grip of higher inflation – a lot of firms were going to the wall – unemployment touched three million – everything was very bad!'

A sardonic look had crept on to the Prime Minister's face. The problems described were hardly a cause for celebration. He hoped the speech was not going to turn into one long moan.

'But now we have government with prudent policies! The unemployment is coming down every month and now stands at only two million. Balance of payments is improving! Exports are on the up! Growth rate better than all counterparts in Europe!'

Under stress, though he had written down every word, Jayanti had lost his grip on English grammar: both definite and indefinite articles were proving elusive. To his despair his accent was becoming more pronounced with every word. Fortunately most of his listeners had the gist and clapped politely.

'I should like to mention, Mr Prime Minister' – he bowed in Roger's direction – 'that in my opinion there are a lot of Asians in the wrong parties. They should all be Tories!'

The Prime Minister laughed and banged the table with the palm of his hand in approval.

'Other parties have made a lot of false promises. I tell you it is all wrong. Asians want to buy their own properties – want to have their own enterprising businesses – want to give best education to their children – want to preserve their own culture and tradition – '

Yes, thought Roger silently, I can see that; and I can also see that

that's where the problem lies. Yet by trying to preserve in aspic an unchanged tradition, British Asians denied the aspirations of the next generation. No wonder so many like Bhadeshia had worshipped the blessed Margaret – she had made their ambitions, with those of other self-made men, entirely respectable.

Loud 'Hear, hears!' rang around the room. Jayanti, dancing with emotion, jabbed his finger in the air. 'There are over sixty-five marginal seats in which Asian vote is vital. The sooner they come into the party the better!'

'Well said,' Roger called out, and banged the table again.

'Because by temperament all Asians are Conservatives!'

That was his *coup de grâce*. Panting, Jayanti acknowledged the thunderous applause. Light bulbs from a hundred cameras flashed. Then he remembered and reached inside his jacket.

'I have here a presentation for you, Mr Prime Minister. Cheque is made out to Conservative Party. Please, I beg you take it. It is for . . . a quarter of a million pounds!'

The noise was deafening. Jayanti beamed, his task done. The Prime Minister's sharp hiss of breath told its own story. All over the world well-dressed men at dinner tables handed cheques to heads of government. From the United States to Malaysia, from France to Taiwan, money changed ownership both openly and in secret. In most countries far more was expected in return than any British government had ever, or possibly could ever, offer. Had Jayanti made his contribution contingent on a suppression of the *Globe* he would have been wasting his time. That he expected help in future from the important man at his side was undeniable. Whether it could be delivered remained to be seen.

At last the assembly rose as one to its feet and the Prime Minister moved away, the cheque safe in his breast pocket. Eyes ablaze with triumph, Jayanti held court, a dazzlingly happy Pramila at his side.

At the edge of the admiring circle stood a portly man, cigar clamped between his teeth, who was known as a shipping magnate. As the crowd thinned the stolid figure moved forward.

'You presume too much, brother,' the man remarked smoothly, 'when you say all Asians are Tories by temperament.'

'Surely it is true – ' Jayanti began. The man held up a hand and half smiled.

'Some of us, as you know, are trying to persuade our brethren to join the Labour Party. We had a big crowd for the dinner we gave for Tony Blair. It was *very* successful.'

He puffed his cigar in challenge. Jayanti felt his blood pressure rise. 'You only do that because you have no faith – you think Labour will win the next election. You are an extremely cynical man.'

'And you're not, I suppose? If you thought your wonderful Mr Dickson was about to collapse, how much would you – or anybody else – be handing over? The Tories are of interest to you and these worthy people' – he indicated the departing backs – 'because they're in government. What they do seriously affects our daily lives. But change is coming.'

'They are my friends!' Jayanti was nearly hysterical.

'Really?' The fat man chuckled, as if he knew something Jayanti didn't, then turned ponderously and waddled away.

Roger Dickson rolled over restlessly.

'You were not at your best tonight, darling,' his wife murmured as if she felt it necessary to state the obvious. 'I think the job is changing you. You can't plead tiredness every time, surely.'

'Thanks a lot,' he muttered. He felt for his slippers and padded to the adjoining bathroom, where he washed himself with a flannel. By the time he returned to the darkened bedroom his wife was asleep, or pretending to be.

He sat for a few moments on the edge of the bed and brooded. Then he rose and went into the next room where he sat down at the old carved desk with its many small drawers and secret compartments. The cheque from the Café Royal had already been dispatched to the Party Treasurer and had passed from his mind completely. He switched on the lamp.

Caroline was right. His performance in bed had become perfunctory and incomplete. Infrequent, too. The fact was, he was too weary after a long day and a big black-tie dinner to take any trouble, and not sufficiently attracted to his spouse to be more than marginally aroused. Since she was the epitome of the loyal and supportive parliamentary wife, and had confessed to him that she relished her public role as the partner of the Prime Minister, it was unlikely that she would make a fuss or contrive to add to the difficulties of his life. So there seemed little need to bother much; and, the truth was, he didn't.

He had married her because she was suitable. More than that: she was perfect for his needs, he the rising star from a poor background in Brixton who had dreamed of some day entering Parliament and becoming . . . who knew what? . . . important, recognised, admired. It was his nature to be wary of love, anyway. It was love that had got the girls down his street pregnant and tied them into poverty. It was love that had obliged a decent young man to marry his girlfriend against his better judgement, then see the meagre weekly pay packet vanish into the Freeman's catalogue and fish and chips on a Friday night, with no chance of escape or betterment. By contrast it was a wise choice that had brought him to the altar with Caroline, daughter of his boss at the bank. She had made the play, he had seen his chance. Their home life was a model of affectionate conformity. And it was ambition, and luck, and guile, which had led to the door to Number 10 as the nation's leader.

Roger bowed his head. In the past there had been love-making to make his heart sing, with Elaine Stalker. Her image floated into his mind and he stifled a groan. The blonde hair; the lovely flashing smile, the carefree, cheeky air which brought her features so alive. The dancing hazel eyes whose mockery during foreplay could make him gasp with excitement. The things she did, dammit: the touch of her hands on his belly, the taste of her mouth on his own, the sensation of her lips and tongue as she explored his nipples, his navel, his most sensitive parts, as she released him from the pressures and restraints of the day. Her knowledge of his worries, the nuances of their joint world. He could not talk to his wife about his career, not in the detail which Elaine would follow. He could not explore his wife's private places as he had with his lover, knowing what gave the most exquisite pleasure, for Caroline would frown at the wrong moment and draw away, calling all that 'silly' or worse.

Elaine had looked sad recently. Her marriage was long over; a contact in the whips' office had mentioned that she was squired sometimes by a George Horrocks, without realising the twinge of misery the news had caused its hearer.

He had been deeply in love with her. He had known that at the time. Yet he had never told her and had deliberately been vague about his feelings, though she had been open about her passion for him, a devotion which had sustained him for four years. In some ways the affair's intensity had carried the roots of its own destruction, for had the two been more laid back it might have been possible to continue, casually, from time to time. But a love like that demanded space for itself which neither in the end – both married, both under intense scrutiny, with divided loyalties – could easily give.

He would tell her. He would let her know how he had once felt. How he still felt, if truth were told. Who knows, he thought savagely to himself: some day I will not be the incumbent in Number 10. I will then be free, if I wish it. Maybe Caroline would then want her freedom, or would not care if I had a discreet personal life, as long as she was not publicly humiliated. That is the way of these MPs' wives. They are team players. But then would Mrs Stalker still be available? Maybe I should make sure of it. Maybe I should write her a letter.

He opened a drawer and found sheets of his printed notepaper. His mind cleared as he began to write: the prose flowed, unaccustomed words of love and admiration, sexual descriptions which filled him with desire even as they took shape on the page, terms of endearment he never used to his wife. He did not hear Caroline come silently to the door. She gazed at her husband's back as he scribbled, then returned to their empty bed.

At last it was finished. He signed it with a flourish and placed it in an envelope. After some hesitation he wrote her name on the front, then sat staring at it in the lamplight.

All at once he felt utterly exhausted. He could not send it, of course. At least, not yet. But nor could he destroy it, this missive which encapsulated the sweetest moments of his life. It had to be put away somewhere safe.

He knelt down and fiddled with a key. The housekeeper who had worked in Downing Street for years had shown him gravely on his first day how everything worked, but with no need of the information he had forgotten most of it. The key caught and he grunted with triumph. The drawer slid out; behind it was another, a tiny box which he had to reach for. He placed the letter carefully inside, reassembled the drawers and locked the outer one. It would be secure there.

He moved heavily towards the bedroom. It was as if he had spent the last hour with Elaine, and she had whispered to him and comforted him. Now he could sleep.

Chapter Fifteen

The best idea, first thing in the morning, was to wriggle cosily down under the bedcovers, turn over and carry on snoozing; yet it was never possible. With a groan Elaine half rolled, half fell on to the floor, killed the alarm and headed, eyes still closed, for the bathroom.

When she had first arrived at Westminster she had been appalled at the constant tiredness induced by fifteen-hour days six days a week, exacerbated by the dearth of social life other than in the company of those equally fascinated by politics. Gradually she had learned to pace herself. MPs had the recesses at Christmas and Easter in which to recover, as well as four almost unbroken months free from August to November. For a member of the government, however, it was another matter entirely.

The realisation had hit her with a shocking ferocity: Her Majesty's Ministers were permanently on duty. A snatched few hours at home could vanish the instant a crisis threatened, while the longest rest any Minister (especially junior ranks) might manage was a fortnight. Those with a European brief would be lucky to stay in Westminster three days a week, while conferences and sessions on the Continent ate up spare days and weekends. Young children did not recognise their fathers, spouses drifted into petulance and despair. The result was an air of bewildered exhaustion, particularly during the hot months. Yet the treadmill could never be eased. One summer a beleaguered Prime Minister had ordered his tired team off for three weeks' holiday in the hope that no government was good news. During their absence the opinion poll gap widened to over 30 points. The experiment was not repeated.

As she blearily brushed her teeth Elaine remembered it was Tuesday. That meant her first engagement was not until 10 a.m. She let out a low whoop. Moving quickly, she pulled on leotards and trainers, grabbed her smart day suit and shirt and drove off to the House of Commons gymnasium.

The car park was in the courtyard of the old Scotland Yard building in Whitehall, renamed Norman Shaw House after its architect. It was still forbiddingly blackened on the outside, and its refurbished interior retained a depressingly institutional air. The basement, cramped and low-ceilinged, had found a particularly welcome use. At this hour of the morning it was packed.

Gingerly Elaine stepped over heaving bodies on blue mats and started her warm-up. The routine eased stiff joints and loosened cramped muscles. She began to concentrate. Six minutes on the gyrobike had her panting hard; the previous week she had skipped a session, an omission for which she would pay. As she settled on to the rowing machine the sound of high-pitched conversation from the office made her look up.

'It is very important that I should be fit for my new role!'

The voice had a strong accent; Dave, the senior instructor, tried to respond soothingly but the other man interrupted.

'I need a severe programme – not something namby-pamby. I used to be very fit, you know. Played cricket for my school. So none of your easy rubbish, do you hear?'

Heads turned, eyebrows were raised. In a club crammed with over-grown egos, one unwritten rule was to leave them in the lockers outside. Elaine bent and rowed rhythmically. She had no intention of pulling a muscle through being distracted by this idiot, whoever he might be.

Dave emerged in his navy tracksuit, clipboard in hand, an anxious expression on his face. Behind trotted a little dark man in brand-new white shorts and Aertex shirt, still arguing vociferously. Together they toured the machines and with unbounded patience the instructor demonstrated how they worked.

Elaine was standing by the water fountain and wiping her face when suddenly the man darted up and held out his hand. She groaned inwardly. Another useful gym rule was the absence of formality: if members had any spare energy a mumbled 'Morning' might be offered, but no offence was taken if it was not.

'Mrs Stalker! How delightful to meet you again. Are you a member here? Do you come – '

She cut him off almost brusquely. 'Yes, I come as often as I can. Glad to see you here too . . . er . . .'

'Bhadeshia – Lord Bhadeshia,' her companion supplied proudly. 'I am entitled to join. I must get myself in good shape. Important work to do now.' He stood back admiringly. 'I can see where your own good figure comes from, madam,' he added.

She nodded without answer and drained her paper cup. His body language had not improved since the party at Carlton Terrace.

Bhadeshia, dismissed but not abashed, continued to interrupt the steady grind of the gym for another half-hour, then happily took himself off to the showers.

Forty minutes later, blonde hair still damp at the nape of her neck, Elaine emerged through the black archway and deposited her sweaty kit in the boot of her car. She felt refreshed and relaxed. The department was only a few yards away; her office overlooked the courtyard. It was an arrangement convenient enough to maintain her attendance with fair regularity. At times she knew it kept her sane.

Minister of State Derek Harrison, hands in pockets, was walking jauntily through the back entrance as she reached it. He had probably gone to the House first to deal with constituency mail. On second thoughts, maybe he too had arranged his first official appointment for ten. The light in his eye suggested that wherever he had been before had pleased him.

'I've just seen a friend of yours,' she remarked as they fell into step. 'Mr Bhadeshia. In the gym, lording it over everybody – literally. I know he's a good supporter and I'm sure he's a decent sort but he does make himself look silly at times.'

'Can't help it – no point in my telling him.' Derek stood to one side as Elaine opened a door for him. She was, after all, his subordinate. 'He's a bit excessive, but that's his way of showing off. His business operations are doing well. Mind you, some of the credit is mine, you know.'

Elaine sighed inwardly. If Derek's arrogance needed massaging this morning she wished he would choose somebody else to do it. 'Really?' she said loyally.

'Oh, yes. He has interests in East Africa. The banks here were less than enthusiastic at supporting him, more fools they. So last week I got him a big grant from the overseas aid people. Some programme for the development of infrastructure in areas ravaged by war. Four million quid, to start, and more where that came from. Not bad, eh?' He winked at her.

She stopped, puzzled. '*You* did? Why? What's it got to do with our department?'

It was his turn to be surprised. 'What? Here? Nothing at all. But a word from one Minister of the Crown to another – or, in this case, to the official concerned – works wonders.'

Harrison dropped his voice. 'If you were marginally more . . . friendly,

Elaine, you'd have valuable contacts too. Look at this. Bet you haven't one like it.' So saying he slipped off his watch, appeared to weigh it in his hand, examined its face and its engraved back with elaborate admiration and put it back on. Elaine caught a glimpse of the crown on its white dial and the name Rolex.

'Thanks for the suggestion, Derek,' she replied with as much dignity as she could muster. Her mouth trembled. She walked past him, entered her own room and closed the door.

It was several minutes before the shaking stopped and she was back under control. What she had just heard was the most blatant corruption. Of course the Overseas Development Agency would have checked and found that the projects did exist and were not fraudulent, and that employment and valuable progress could result in a desperately poor country. An application for ODA funds might have succeeded anyway, though perhaps not for such a generous amount. The banks, wary of risk, were seldom as keen as proprietors demanded. All that was understandable, and could be justified. On the other hand, while Elaine was unaware of the secret shareholding registered in a tax haven which had also changed hands, what Derek was up to in bringing pressure to bear on hapless civil servants was to her brutally obvious. His actions could be neither defended nor ignored.

Yet what could she do? It had been on the tip of her tongue to remind him, with a measure of sarcasm in her voice, to declare the expensive present in the Register of Members' Interests. But Ministers were not supposed to accept *any* such gifts: declaration did not confer innocence. Not to declare, however, was worse, for it left Harrison open to the accusation not only of using influence for gain but of a cover-up. It was bizarre that he appeared ready to boast quite recklessly about the whole strategy, as if he assumed that nobody in Whitehall would object. His moral sense must be seriously defective. Then the notion of Derek with a moral sense of any kind made her laugh ruefully.

Should she discuss it with anyone? Had Roger still been her whip and her lover that would have been easy. She would have trusted him to use such information effectively but with discretion. The fact remained that recent administrations had lost an extraordinary number of post-holders through scandal. If Derek Harrison carried on waving that watch, he'd soon follow. Each resignation weakened the government and rendered its eventual downfall more likely. It made her furious, when she allowed herself a moment's reflection, to realise that she might lose her seat simply because some of her colleagues had been such fools.

But to discuss meant to tell. That would be – the only description which occurred to her came from school – sneaking. Obscurely she was conscious of an honour code, however twisted. If she told, *she* would be treated as the transgressor. Whistle-blowers won no praise. It would be whispered she was after Derek's job. Certainly she was – but preferably not by those means. Derek would have to trip over all by himself. Given his stupidity and greed, that was increasingly probable.

Jayanti Bhadeshia's next visit was to his tailor, where he collected three excellent new suits with matching silk shirts and ties. How easy it had been to open an account at Gieves and Hawkes; how much smarter than, say, Harrods. The firm knew how a man of position should dress. Young Mr Gieves had worked for John Major's office. On the night of the Tory leadership contest in 1990 the winner's duff neckwear had made Mr Gieves wince. Thus Mr Major greeted the nation as its new Premier in his staffman's tie, a suitably dapper number in striped navy and gold.

Thence to the Carlton, for lunch. The club in St James's had long been the heartland of Tory political life. Lord Bhadeshia's recent application for membership, endorsed by sponsors of the greatest distinction, had been accepted with only a modicum of delay. Had he been female it would have been a different result, though many traditional London clubs, helpless in the face of falling revenues, collapsing fabric, spiralling costs and fierce competition, had been obliged to lower their standards and admit women.

The dignified atmosphere of the main dining room, with its chandeliers, crisp linen and ancient retainers, though intimidating to a newcomer, thrilled him. Across the room Lord Rees-Mogg was eating alone, a newspaper propped up on the cruet. Jayanti bit into a quail's egg dusted with pepper and gazed around, hoping somebody would notice him. He did not have long to wait. Sir Peter Aubrey, Party Chairman, nodded agreeably from an adjoining table. The chairman of the Catering Committee, a former Minister, brought over his guests and gracefully introduced them to the new peer. The air of ease was all-pervading, and suited everyone who breathed it.

It never occurred to Jayanti to decline the approaches of those who, before his honour, would have ignored him. The whole point of seeking preferment was precisely so he could join their ranks. That they should be so privileged he took for granted. Every society had its elites. Rather than harbour any misgivings about his previous exclusion he counted himself fortunate to live at a time and in a place where the climb to the top was relatively unbarred and open to the most humble, as his own rise amply proved. That was a mark in the nation's favour.

Nor did he jib at the method of his elevation. In most such cases, money was involved. Whether it was the purchase of land and titles from King John or Elizabeth I or Lloyd George or Roger Dickson, it was much the same. Princes needed funds: commoners would oblige, in return for nobility and the chance to leave the common herd behind.

A large figure loomed over him, breathing heavily. It was Sir John Merriman, his lawyer, long a member of the club, who placed by his plate a single sheet of fax paper.

'I don't wish to disturb your meal, my lord, but I have been advised that this will be in tomorrow's *Globe*. When you have a moment, I think we ought to have a word about it.'

Jayanti began to read, then let out a howl of pain. Around the tables fellow diners looked up in surprise. Such a cry had not been heard from a member since Churchill announced he would vote against the Munich agreement in 1938. That man had never shown much loyalty. Frowns furrowed fine brows; a newspaper was rustled in disapproval.

Sir John straightened. 'My office, tomorrow morning, ten o'clock?' he enquired. It sounded like an instruction.

It was like a spaceship, Betts reflected, straight out of *Star Wars*. On each side, towering twenty feet into the air and beyond his sight into the roof space, extending a hundred yards from the double doors, the steel megalith of a modern printing press hummed powerfully. No moving machinery was visible but the silvery skin was warm to the touch and vibrated gently. Apart from himself and the process technician the place was devoid of human life, except at the furthest end of the building where bound bundles of newspapers tumbled into brawny arms and were loaded into pantechnicons for distant delivery.

'Bit different to the old days.' The printer jerked a thumb. 'Computerised now. German, most of it. Makes you think.'

'I remember the rows and stoppages,' Betts concurred. It was wise to avoid the word 'strike'. 'We journos claimed to be afraid of no one – except the printers. You chaps had a total veto.'

The man glanced up, pride on his face. 'You couldn't do it now. In those days printing was a skilled job – and keeping those old presses rolling was a secret art, I can tell you. All done much the same way since William Caxton. This baby's from another planet. It doesn't need us. I could programme it for a week and skedaddle. We produce forty-two different newspapers here – got to keep the monster busy. Now, what can I do for you?'

Betts could have waited till the first edition had appeared in the upstairs newsroom but curiosity had overcome him. 'Just want to see how my follow-up piece on our Asian chums has turned out,' he answered casually.

The printer flicked through a copy. Even the ink was high-tech and rarely stained the fingers: a source of regret, for to his mind a man should bear the marks of honest toil. 'Great stuff, Jim,' he remarked. 'You know, we should turn those buggers round at Heathrow and send them straight back to Calcutta. The crime in our area you wouldn't believe – fights and gangs all hours of the day and night, and it's always the blacks. My mother gets really frightened. If there's a National Front candidate in my area next election, he'll get my vote.'

The sole reaction which might have troubled Jim Betts was no reaction at all. He relaxed. 'And what if there isn't one?'

The printer chortled. 'Then I might just set Hermann here to run without my assistance for a bit and have a go myself. Time we British stood up for ourselves. Rule Britannia and all that. Can't have the buggers taking over, can we?'

'We should defy them!'

Pramila switched off the breakfast news on the television and banged her small fist on the table. Behind hovered the fretful figure of her mother; her sister Lakshmi sat slumped on a kitchen chair, weeping noisily and fanning herself with the remains of the *Globe*. Bits of the newspaper, torn up in despair, littered the floor. The front door, barricaded, was subject at frequent intervals to loud knocks from rowdy pressmen.

'How can they say this of my husband? It is not true. He is a man of the highest integrity. Oh, this is too much!'

Lakshmi sat up. 'Defy them is right. We should not hide our faces. But how?'

Pramila paced agitatedly about. The letter-box rattled; a wheedling voice called her name and requested two minutes to ask a few simple questions. She ignored it. Then she smiled, and put both hands together in a triumphant gesture.

'A week on Monday is the date for the investiture. It will go ahead, and Jayanti will walk head high to his place in the House of Lords. The usual practice, I am told, is to give a lunch beforehand, but we will do better than that. We have many good friends to consider. We will have a party that night.'

'A party? Where?' Lakshmi dabbed at her eyes.

Pramila considered. 'It must be in a very glamorous place. Maybe Lady Porter will lend us her beautiful penthouse, now she is living abroad? But no, that would not be large enough. I know! The Roof Garden in Kensington, if it is free – it belongs to Mr Branson and is available for hire. Perfect for a summer evening. We will have that. Hundreds of people, from Asian and British communities. All the government – we will invite the lot. Newspaper editors – oh, indeed. Television presenters – Mr Paxman, Mr Dimbleby. *Both* Mr Dimblebys. Maybe we should ask the Duchess of York, if she is in England? Champagne. Canapés. Supper at ten – that will suit MPs after the vote. Carriages at two a.m. The event of the season!'

Lakshmi clapped her hands. 'Wonderful!' She giggled. 'That will show these dreadful people, won't it?'

But Pramila was not listening. The celebration would demand the rapid placement of orders for catering, drinks, security, printing – already her brain was working furiously. The activity would distract her from the ghastly intrusion on her doorstep. As she reached for the phone she muttered savagely to herself; she would ensure that the tabloids and the gossip columns, friendly or not, would soon have something spectacular to report.

'This time it is not acceptable. You have to stop them!'

Jayanti was aware that his voice had risen almost to a shriek. The dusty room at Merriman, Abrahams and Arnold was again stifling. Perspiration beaded on his brow; he wondered if the solicitor, vast, urbane and imperturbable as ever, turned up the thermostat to discomfort chosen clients, or whether every visitor risked heatstroke indiscriminately.

Sir John pondered. According to the file before him nothing had gone right for Lord Bhadeshia since the day his peerage had been gazetted. The lawyer raised his half-moon spectacles and balanced them on his nose.

'Would it help, my lord, if I outlined the essence of the current allegations against you?'

'Yes, yes – get on with it.' Bhadeshia collapsed back in his seat.

'In the first *Globe* article some weeks ago, at which we made a mild protest, you were accused of somewhat underhand dealings in your commercial activities. The *Panorama* programme repeated these charges – the violence in East Africa, the alleged mortgage deception – but added little, rather as is their wont. But today's newspaper suggests you might have been puffing your company's shares, and that you obtained a substantial grant from the ODA under false pretences. That is far more grave.'

'It is terrible – terrible.' With a moan Jayanti buried his face in his hands. Sir John twiddled tactfully with a letter opener. Jayanti sniffed, blew his nose and tried again. 'I *have* to sue. To put a stop to all this. Or my business will collapse.'

The lawyer shuffled through notes and cuttings. 'So: did you give a personal guarantee of a million pounds against the loan from Barclays Bank?'

Jayanti nodded unhappily.

'And did you have the funds immediately accessible to fulfil that promise, if necessary?'

'I have my house. That is worth a million, easily.'

'The value of a property is a matter of conjecture in the current financial climate, my lord. And is it yours – unencumbered? Or does it really belong to the bank – a different bank?'

There was no reply. Sir John ploughed on.

'And have you been encouraging the purchase of your company's shares, using money borrowed from the company, in order to increase their value? A technical issue, but nevertheless it is illegal under section one hundred and fifty-one of the Companies Act . . .'

Jayanti slumped in his chair, lips pressed together.

'Then it is my duty to warn you, my lord, that you face something far more troublesome than damage to your reputation. By all means issue writs, even try for an injunction. But from what you have just said matters have gone beyond that.'

His client was not with him. Perhaps the approach was still too indirect. Sir John spoke the next few words very clearly.

'It appears on the face of it that you may have come close to defrauding the banks – one of them, at least, and possibly several. And your other shareholders. The Stock Exchange will take a dim view. So, I fear, might the Serious Fraud Office.'

Bhadeshia stared around wildly. 'No – I haven't defrauded anybody!

261

I had to be a little expansive to get the house loan, but that is normal. And ODA were keen to help once they knew about my project. As for the shares bought by my relatives – so what? Anyway, I can pay the banks and ODA back, once the project is a success . . .' His voice tailed away.

Sir John continued as if his client hadn't spoken. 'In which case I have to inform you that you may be embroiled in far more than a libel suit or, indeed, a civil case for recovery of funds. What you might be facing is far more serious.'

The senior partner leaned forward and clasped his hands together on the desk, his lower lip thrust out. If he was correct then his client was a man of straw: no fees would come from Lord Bhadeshia's pocket. It was unwise to waste too much time on him.

'I'm referring, Lord Bhadeshia, to . . . criminal charges.'

Bhadeshia's eyes darted around as if expecting the heavy hand of a police officer on his shoulder any minute. A great sigh escaped from him, as if he had always feared that the world would conspire to ensure that his dreams could never be realised. He knew himself to be basically a good man, not a rogue. He had sought only the best for his family, for his name. He had worked so hard – how he had worked, without complaint. He had supported charities, employed those in need, given money without stint, been a bit of a soft touch. He had aspired, as his heroine Mrs Thatcher had urged, to fortune and to recognition: both had been within his grasp.

'And now, my lord, if you will listen carefully, I will outline your options to you.'

It was fortunate, everyone agreed, that the introduction of Lord Bhadeshia took place at the same time as two other peers, who seemed to be enjoying themselves rather more. True, the gallery was filled with brightly dressed Indian ladies whose fluttering silks were like so many butterfly wings, and overawed men who chattered inappropriately and pointed; a forbidden video camera had disappeared under a sari before an attendant could confiscate it. But despite so many supporters he hurried away too quickly from the Peers' bar, leaving many of his new colleagues with their *amour propre* wounded and their glasses empty.

Press pictures the next day would show the new baron, his eyes troubled, engulfed in red velvet and white ermine. His ears had disappeared under a black tricorne hat which made him look like an extra on Captain Hook's pirate ship. His sponsors, similarly attired, posed gamely with him for the cameras, since nobody knew the validity of the *Globe*'s attack, and for the moment nobody wished to find out.

Jayanti forced himself to be cheerful, but was conscious that glances both condemnatory and curious followed him everywhere. Even the policeman in the Peers' Lobby, usually the soul of correctness to all their lordships, fell silent as he approached and gave him directions with an unsmiling nod.

Outside it was worse; the commissionaire guardian of the main Lords entrance, normally the most jovial of men, glared down at the new peer.

'I shouldn't go that way, m'lord,' he said bluntly. 'Lots of press waiting for you there.'

Jayanti peered around. 'My car is in the Abbey Gardens car park over the road,' he explained weakly.

The attendant took pity. 'Leave it there, it'll be safe. Go back inside. I'll wave in a taxi. Where are you off to – Kensington? Right, leave it to me.'

When the cab came, an ordinary black London taxi, Jayanti felt acutely the humiliation of climbing inside. As the cab swept into the traffic, light bulbs flashed in his face. The cabbie, a tubby Cockney, glanced back, his interest aroused.

'I've carried you before, haven't I?' he enquired.

Jayanti had no idea; he did not make a practice of noting the features of London cab drivers. Habit, however, was beginning to assert itself. 'I am Lord Bhadeshia,' he started, the tone still proud. It occurred to him suddenly that it might be better to keep his identity a secret, but it was too late. The cabbie chuckled.

'Bhadeshia, eh? I've been reading about you . . .'

Twenty-five minutes later it was a harassed and confused man who emerged from the taxi at the side entrance to the Roof Garden Club. The driver had been unmerciful. Only a desire not to lose the fare had stopped him following up the most pointed questions with his personal views on the passenger's alleged behaviour. He would dine out on the tale for many a long day.

As soon as the late vote was over Roger Dickson headed grimly along the back corridor behind the Speaker's Chair to his office. For a moment he read, standing, then sat heavily and slapped the newspaper down on his desk.

'Christ – not another!'

From the front page of the first edition of the *Globe* gazed back the self-important face of his Minister of State for Health, Welfare and the Family. If the tale in many column inches was even partly true – and the photographed extract from a ministerial letter marked 'Confidential' to the ODA showed it was no fantasy – then the only welfare Derek Harrison had been looking after had been that of his friends and himself.

The Chief Whip sat forward in his armchair, his fingers cradling a glass of whisky and soda. 'I have checked: the editor is prepared to stand by the story,' he remarked. 'The other papers will splash it by morning. Of course he won't say where he got the letter, but we've long since given up making a fuss about leaked Whitehall documents.'

'No point. To haul editors before the Committee of Privileges merely makes us look complete prats. It doesn't seem to matter whether the press use honourable methods to obtain their material. The ends justify the means these days.'

'And our Derek made sure that Mr Bhadeshia had the means.' The Chief Whip shifted. He wondered at what point the repeated falls from grace would touch the Prime Minister himself; or would this man retire at a time of his own choosing, his character unblemished but his government's reputation in shreds? 'The Opposition are sure to make a fuss at Prime Minister's Question Time tomorrow. What will you say – will you back Harrison? Pity you've only just made his accomplice a peer. Puts you on the spot a bit.'

You, not *us*. The distinction was not missed by Dickson, whose glance in the Chief's direction was laced with suppressed fury. 'Where is he?'

'Right now? At the Bhadeshia party, I believe. With a hundred or so other Members, showing solidarity and blaming a hostile press for the row as they quaff the best champers, no doubt. You were probably invited – we all were.'

'Get him. And Ted Bampton. In my room at Number Ten in half an hour.'

There were, Betts saw, notable gaps. The evening may have been billed as the event of the year, but Lady Thatcher was busy elsewhere, Lord Tebbitt had pulled out at the last minute, Lord Parkinson had developed an urgent meeting and Lord Archer had decamped to the Bahamas to write his latest bestseller. The entire Cabinet had politely declined. The

Party Chairman did pop in but was pulled out of a back door by a worried aide the instant the first newspaper had been thrust into his hand.

The video of the life and achievements of the new Lord Bhadeshia had been cancelled; the plans – outlined with so much excitement by his wife a few days earlier – for the couple to enter in triumph to a crescendo of trumpets as the last scene played on a giant screen had come to nought. Worse, an appearance on *Desert Island Discs* scheduled for the following week had been deferred: the nation would never know Lord Bhadeshia's taste in music or his habit of singing in the bath. Of all the snubs, Jayanti felt this one most keenly.

The party, however, was not yet over. Jim Betts leaned on the fluorescent silver bar, sipped his fourth glass of champagne, and lifted a smoked salmon and caviar canapé from a passing tray. His attendance was official, standing in for his boss, whose name was on the invitation card. His own name, emblazoned in the byline on those articles, might have guaranteed exclusion, but his face was unknown. For once he was neither gatecrashing nor obliged to work, though his journalist's instincts did not miss a detail.

The low room was crowded and hot, its bluish light ethereal and sexy, making white shirts and dinner jackets glow and fade as their wearers moved between tables. The butterfly garments had been replaced by silver and sequins. The Bhadeshias darted about kissing everybody. Many MPs were there including several junior Ministers with spouses or girlfriends, glad of an opportunity of a night out at somebody else's expense. Elaine Stalker had brought her daughter, who was dancing away in a skimpy red dress at the far end with Fred Laidlaw MP. Their housemate, Mr York, was not around – not a party man in this sense. Elaine was talking animatedly to a tall, older man who was a stranger to Betts; his eyes narrowed. Fresh articles were already forming in his brain. Satisfied, he headed out of the atrium into the roof garden.

Had Betts had any romance in his soul he would have responded at once to the delights of a lush country garden under moonlight with paved walks and lawns, fountains, several pools, an ivy-covered wall, ducks and flamingos, all on a floodlit rooftop in central London. Created when the occupants were the upmarket department store Derry and Toms (Pramila had eaten lunch there once years before), on the demise of the company the roof garden had been taken over by a private club. The strange location was perfect for slightly louche events and much favoured by London's gay community, who adored its exotic atmosphere.

Betts strolled slowly and watchfully, letting the cool night air make him feel more drunk than he really was. He kept away from the flamingos, which he did not trust. It had been a marvellous few weeks for him; soon, however, it would be time to consider his next campaign and its possible victims. It was odds-on that several were present tonight, given the way one or two of them were cavorting about. How easy they made it.

As he came past one of the lighted doors a young couple bounced out in front of him, laughing – Karen Stalker and Fred Laidlaw; but after a few moments Laidlaw declared himself cold and returned indoors, promising to save a table place.

'Evening.'

Karen turned around. It was a fabulous bash, far better than anybody could manage in college. Cheeky of her mother to ask if she might also attend, but Lady Bhadeshia had been graciously hospitable, indeed keen that a few younger guests should come.

She saw a few feet away, his champagne glass at a slight angle, a man of roughly the same height as herself but some years older. Betts's dinner jacket hung loosely on a frame kept thin by cigarettes, one of which rested limply in his fingers, its tip red and smoky in the dark. The moustache was better trimmed than she recalled, the gingerish hairline receding but the hairstyle relatively tidy.

Betts saw before him the young woman after whom he had once lusted frantically and whose refusal and its aftermath had nearly ruined his career. What it had done to her life he did not consider, nor ever had. Karen was fresh, smart as a lick of paint, bright-eyed, though the eyes as she recognised him clouded with suspicion and dislike. She was ripe as a peach. And, if he were not mistaken, she belonged to no one else at present, with the possible exception of Mr Laidlaw. What she needed, Betts decided, was a real man: like himself.

'We meet again,' he continued easily. 'You weren't very nice to me last time, Miss Stalker, when I came to your place. I'd no idea you lived there. You still at that address, by the way?'

Karen stopped herself from answering his question. Where she lived was none of his business. Her voice was frosty.

'Can I help you, Mr Betts? I'm getting cold and I want to go inside.'

'Help me? Oh, yes. You could, a lot. You look lovelier each time I see you, Karen. I haven't forgotten that you were special for me once upon a time. I could still feel the same way – if you'd allow me.'

The proposition was so bare faced that the girl was caught off-guard. But like the lonely housewife who knows as an unwanted caller hisses obscenities in her ear that she should put the phone down at once, yet continues to listen, Karen lingered.

Betts took a step forward and smiled ingratiatingly. 'There! I'm not so horrible, am I? Big success, these days. Likely to get my own news editor's job before too long. Worth knowing, Karen. How about it?'

Karen gazed coolly at the man who had raped her so many painful years before. She should lead him to the parapet and throw him over, for everything he had done to her and had threatened to do to her mother. The breeze ruffled her hair and brought with it calmness and dignity. There was no point in being as unpleasant or as unprincipled as he.

'Well, James. The answer is no.'

'I should like to know why you took it upon yourself to push Mr Bhadeshia's application for this grant. And I want every detail, Derek, however unedifying.'

Roger Dickson perched his backside on an ornate table and glared at the group seated before him. He had deliberately chosen a formal state chamber for the interview. Only the table lamps were switched on, giving the room a gloomy, conspiratorial atmosphere. His face glowered: his mood could not be mistaken.

On an ivory-silk sofa sat the Chief Whip with the Party Chairman, his face creased with worry. In an armchair, head thrown back defiantly, lounged Derek Harrison. Ted Bampton sat upright on a chair, his glass untouched in his hand, his mouth turned down grimly.

Bampton wondered if it was his fault. Had he been hard enough on Harrison? He'd laid down the law and tried to stop the man being a complete fool, but to no avail apparently. This mud would stick to the whole department, himself included. Uncomfortably he wondered if a more experienced Secretary of State might have spotted trouble sooner and more quickly nipped it in the bud. He would know better next time.

'I'm waiting.' Dickson drummed his fingers on the table.

'I know him – and he's Lord Bhadeshia as from this morning, in case you've forgotten.'

Inwardly Harrison was fuming. He could see no point in pretence or argument. They were all in this together, and therein lay his best chance. The arrogance of his tone brought exchanged glances; behind him Bampton shook his head in disbelief.

'Did he pay you?'

'I've been looked after, yes. What of it?'

'Steady on, old chap . . .' the Party Chairman felt obliged to protect the Minister from his own stupidity.

Harrison had been drinking at the party and had downed the undiluted Scotch offered on his arrival. He deeply resented the cloak-and-dagger effort that had whisked him away to this ridiculous inquisition. The press had used a leaked letter, probably by subverting somebody in his office. That was in itself reprehensible and should have brought his colleagues into supportive line on his side, yet it did not seem to be happening. 'I said, what of it? I'm not the only one. Everyone does it. Can't afford to survive otherwise.'

The Chief Whip intervened smoothly. 'Permit me my curiosity. Why Bhadeshia? Couldn't you have picked somebody a little . . . more suitable?'

Harrison did not miss the hint. He might still ditch his business partner and, in so doing, defend himself. Some long-buried decent instinct nudged him.

'Makes me sick,' he muttered. 'Just because Jay's Asian. It was the same with Asil Nadir. And Robert Maxwell, I'll bet. Take their money – oh, yes. Fawn over them. Shower them with titles and honours. No, not give – sell them. Then when things go wrong, boot 'em out. Prejudice, that's it. Race prejudice. *And it's wrong.*'

Roger Dickson grunted impatiently but the Chairman was anxious to sound sympathetic. 'That's right. Like the Rothschilds last century. Paid for the Suez Canal shares. Disraeli thought the world of them – '

'Thank you, but this is no time for a history lesson. Nor does it justify, or explain, what Derek has done – which plainly he does not deny.' Dickson wondered what had possessed him to appoint the chap to the job. If that was to be his defence it ran the risk of incredulity on the part of its hearers. That Bhadeshia's sense of exclusion, which he had obviously communicated to his erstwhile friend, was genuine and might well have underpinned the whole affair was dismissed by Roger without further consideration. Right now his government's reputation was all that mattered.

Dickson stood and stared down at Harrison, who was examining his own reflection in the glass in his hands. Drunk, or doped perhaps, the man seemed divorced from reality.

'Sorry, Derek. You have twenty minutes to offer me your resignation. There's some House of Commons notepaper on the table. The Chief will help you draft it.'

Harrison jumped up angrily. Somebody was to blame for this mess but it wasn't him. The person in charge, then. He jabbed an accusatory finger at his leader. His voice had the edge of recklessness.

'John Major used to let his Ministers stay. He'd back 'em. What they did in private was their own affair, he said. You're sacking me, or as good as. What's the difference?'

Roger Dickson rose to his full height, eyes hard. The lamplight on his silver-streaked hair made it look like a halo of ice. 'The difference', he said coldly, 'is that I am *not* John Major.'

He took a deep breath, finished his own drink and pointed to the alcove where a writing desk waited.

'And you, Mr Harrison, are no longer one of my Ministers.'

The mother understood and couldn't get out quickly enough. The sister set up a soft wail which, after a little practice, he found he could exclude from his conscious mind. But his wife, aware in an instant that he had been hiding things from her, turned her pent-up fury on him, and that was the hardest. Seated next to him in the back of the Jaguar as it sped first home for hastily packed luggage and then to the airport, she screeched angry questions and rained repeated small blows on him, until he felt battered and helpless.

Where had he gone wrong? Why was it so blameworthy to ask a distinguished colleague, the pliant Mr Harrison who had always given him such sound advice, to speak on his behalf to purse-holders in the ODA? He had asked Mr Horrocks to recommend him at the Tarrants Bank board meeting and nobody regarded that as a crime. And what in heaven's name was so wicked about rewarding a close friendship by the allocation of a few shares? Nothing at all, in truth. He could see the point about the purchase of large blocks of shares by his son Varun and his friends, but they had merely allowed over-enthusiasm to expose their activities. The boy still had a lot to learn. As for giving Derek an engraved watch, it was too trivial for words. To exclude Ministers from such tokens of regard and affection was ridiculous. The British were mad, if that was their approach to business. And their press was appalling and should be curbed. No wonder they'd lost an empire.

Pramila was sobbing at his side. In Terminal Four as he waved tickets and passports Jayanti suddenly feared she might refuse to accompany him. He took her hands and implored her, as the mother of his children and his wife of over twenty years, not to abandon him. There was only one way to calm her. In a moment of weakness he promised her that their flight was temporary, to enable him to obtain further funds. However flimsy an excuse, it gave both a face-saver. She dabbed her eyes, lifted her head and followed him through the darkened terminal.

In one last fling he had booked first-class seats on a credit card which would be cut off within days. As the Boeing 747 heaved itself into the air above Slough, then settled for the long flight towards the sun, Jayanti kicked off his shoes, stretched his legs, removed his jacket and handed it to the stewardess. The food would be edible, the wine excellent. The chance to indulge at that standard might not present itself again for many a day.

Chapter Sixteen

It was sultry – oppressively so, with a hint of thunder in the air. A leaden sun sent steely shafts of light through double-glazed windows which could be neither opened nor shaded. The glare moved unstoppably over wood and metal, leaving them blistering to the touch. After its passage papers curled up and drifted to the floor. Dust danced and shimmered. It was almost too hot to move.

Elaine abandoned any pretence of coolness, removed her linen jacket and hung it on the back of her chair. She bent over the red file once more, annotating points with a pink marker pen. Nearby two piles of green folders awaited her attention – letters written by MPs and others of sufficient importance to command a ministerial response. In Bampton's absence on holiday she had his to sign as well as her own. Promotion to the job left vacant by Harrison did not seem to have reduced the paperwork at all.

Elaine did not hear the door of her office open. Not until a shadow fell over her desk did she look up, startled.

'I'm so sorry, Minister of State.' Martin Chadwick smiled oleaginously, but placing himself so quietly before her had been a game. 'I wanted to check how you were settling in, and if there was anything we could do for you.'

You could start by not creeping around, Elaine thought crossly. Chadwick looked a little odd. He must have been to the dentist. His front two teeth had been capped, giving him a rabbity expression which sat uneasily with his superior manner. She glanced around before replying.

'Thank you – there are one or two things. Can we get rid of the ashtrays, for a start? It *is* Whitehall policy to have smoke-free offices. I prefer it that way, whatever my predecessor felt. And I'd like a long mirror in the dressing room next door – would the budget run to one?'

Chadwick did not make a note. A sign of his higher intellect was that he needed no memory aids. He acquiesced smoothly. 'I'm sure that can

271

be arranged. And we have some portable air-conditioning units arriving tomorrow. I'm sorry it's so unpleasant in here.'

The listed buildings in Richmond Terrace had been saved from developers in the mid-eighties and refurbished at an official cost of over £38 million. The crowning success of Norman Fowler's tenure as Secretary of State for Health and Social Security had been to beat off the Secretary of State for Education's competing claim to the new premises. Excellent insulation, modern lighting and thick carpets made the accommodation cosy in winter. In a heatwave it was ghastly.

'Shame it wasn't included first time,' Elaine commented. 'Typical. Who was responsible?'

'The PSA.' That told her everything. She grimaced. The Property Services Agency had been one of the great bogies of the old administration, with an incompetence which was legendary.

Chadwick cleared his throat to obtain her attention. 'The new Parliamentary Under-Secretary would like a word, I believe.'

'Sure. Show him in. And could we have some sandwiches and cold drinks? Prawn mayonnaise on brown bread for me.'

It had not taken long to eradicate every trace of Harrison. As the news of his resignation hit the press tapes, Elaine's name was announced alongside as his successor, complete with a potted biography. Her replacement as junior Minister had followed within half a day on her recommendation as endorsed by Bampton. She wondered whether, when eventually her own career ceased, she would be dispatched as efficiently; or whether she might leave behind some monument or action of which she might be proud. Enoch Powell had warned that all ministerial office ended in tears. Was it too much to hope that hers might be the exception?

The door opened again. Chadwick, who had apparently appointed himself Elaine's minder pro tem, ushered in the tall figure of her new subordinate.

It was Anthony York. For a brief moment he and Chadwick were together in the doorway, face to face, bodies close. Anthony blushed furiously, lowered his head and pushed his way inside.

'Something peculiar, almost sinister about him.' Elaine indicated the now closed door. 'I wouldn't trust Mr Chadwick an inch. Yet he's one of the ablest Dep Secs around, so it's said.'

'Pity we can't choose our staff as they do in America,' Anthony agreed as he sat down. He seemed flustered; Elaine took it to be the heat. 'I wanted a quick word, Elaine. I was surprised and honoured to be given your post when you were promoted, and I am delighted to be working with you. Your old staff are sad to lose you. Is there anything in particular you would like me to do?'

She considered. 'I just hope we can work together as a team rather more than I did with Derek, that's all. Here's an example: I've been asked to speak at the annual conference of MIND, the mental illness charity. It isn't till next spring but we should start to think about it as an opportunity to change our approach. I feel twitchy about our community care policy and would like to start edging the department around to my point of view. Frankly, I think we've closed too many hospitals. The result is mentally sick people sleeping on the streets or getting themselves into trouble. Derek wasn't interested. Are you?'

Anthony examined his fingers. 'Mental illness – yes, I'd agree with you. There's not much help available. Doctors aren't that sympathetic, or knowledgeable.'

Elaine nodded vigorously. For several minutes the two Ministers discussed themes and how the monolith of Westminster received opinion might be shifted. A plate of sandwiches covered in clingfilm arrived with a litre carton of tepid orange juice. Both were hungry; Elaine ate the lettuce and tomato garnish as well. She wiped her fingers and sat back.

'Well, Anthony, it's a great pleasure to have you in office with me. For the first time since I arrived here I've enjoyed a discussion. Are you specially interested in this subject?'

Her companion drained his glass and without responding immediately gathered up the remains of lunch and removed the tray to a side desk. He paused, hands in pockets, and looked out of the window towards Parliament Square. He was a handsome man, Elaine decided, polite and stolid, though there was a charmless awkwardness about him. He did not seem, to use a phrase common in her daughter's generation, at ease in his skin. She was so intrigued by his manner, with the thought in the back of her mind that this was also one of Karen's closest friends, that she did not realise he had been silent for several minutes.

Anthony gazed at the anonymous mass of people who passed below. Judging by their clothes they were on holiday, mostly, and free from constraints, rules and frustrations other than their next destination, the next meal. Most were contented, yet others would have suffered desperate unhappiness as he had. A few, perhaps, knew the meaning of clinical depression; some had this misery yet to come, for themselves or

273

a member of their family. He had a duty to each one. Elaine was right; and she could be trusted.

He returned to his seat and faced her. 'Yes,' he said simply. 'I have some personal experience of mental illness.' And so saying he removed his cuff-links, unfastened his watch and rolled up his sleeves a few inches. Then he held out his arms, palms up, fists clenched, towards her.

She saw the bluish marks across the wrists and gasped.

When he was sure she understood he rolled down the sleeves. 'Nobody knows – my parents do, of course, and our family doctor, but no one in politics. Certainly not the whips, nor anyone at Newbury.' He spoke quietly, a tremble in his voice. 'It was ages ago – at school. I was being ... bullied. Driven crazy. This seemed the easiest way out.'

'But you've had no trouble since?'

There might have been the slightest hesitation before he shook his head.

'Then well done. You must have had a terrible time, but you've come through it. And made a huge success of your life.'

Anthony began to demur but she leaned forward and touched his hand. 'To me that demonstrates strength of character, not weakness. Your secret is safe, if you wish to keep it a secret – and that might be best. I'm delighted to have you with me.'

'Wowie!'

Karen climbed out of the Peugeot and ran to the sea wall. The sunlight hit her with full force, but it was welcoming and luxurious. Its heat played at once on her bare shoulders and arms. Before her delighted gaze the great sweep of the bay at La Baule extended for miles to left and right. The sands were dotted with umbrellas, brightly coloured towels and bare torsos. At ten in the morning it was inviting; by three it would be packed.

Behind her Fred in a multi-hued shirt more suited to Hawaii than southern Brittany hauled luggage out of the car. He paused for a moment and looked up, shading his eyes. 'Not bad,' he conceded. 'Anthony has taste. And we've got the apartment to ourselves for a week while he's sweltering in London, poor sod.'

'Lachlan's coming out on Thursday, remember,' Karen corrected him, 'so we'll have to keep the place tidy.' She relented and came to help.

It had been Anthony's suggestion that the four should stay together for a month of the parliamentary recess. Aware that his resources were greater than theirs, he had taken upon himself the rental of a flat overlooking the sea at a spot in France where he had enjoyed childhood summer holidays. The cost was much the same, he had reasoned, as if he went alone, which he did not relish. The others could contribute for housekeeping and food, and pay their own travel fares.

The large flat was airy and clean. Karen quickly allocated the biggest bedroom to Anthony and took the smallest herself. She stripped off the crumpled clothes in which she had travelled and donned a one-piece swimsuit; then on second thoughts replaced it with a bikini. A T-shirt, shorts and sandals completed the outfit and with a towel, suntan cream, sunglasses, a few francs and a paperback of *A Parliamentary Affair* borrowed from her mother she was ready.

'C'mon, Fred,' she commanded. 'If there's a hole in the ozone layer I want to see it. Let's go.'

In a few minutes their rusty French was in action as the two arranged a month's hire of deckchairs and a green canvas beach tent which would provide the sole shade on the baking expanse of sand. Karen ran around squealing with delight at each new discovery. Showers and a café were to hand; visitors were mainly French and English. The place had a natural, friendly air. The type of aggressive German tourist who might have made their lives a misery obviously preferred more glamorous locations.

At last she laid out her towel, tugged off her shorts and pulled the T-shirt over her head. Fred kept his eyes averted and pretended to read the English newspaper he had bought that morning. In the distance a French youth in tattered shorts pushed an ice-cream barrow energetically from one potential customer to the next, yodelling his wares in fractured franglais. A sea breeze stirred little eddies of sand.

Fred could smell the sun cream as Karen spread it liberally on her thighs. Then the open bottle was thrust under his nose.

'Would you do my back, please?'

He swallowed hard. This was the moment he had been waiting for – had been dreading. He kept his voice steady.

'Sure. Turn over.'

Obediently Karen rolled on to her front and pillowed her dark head on her folded arms. Fred squatted down beside her and squeezed a hillock of cream between her shoulder-blades. His fingers tingled; already her skin was hot. With as firm a motion as he could produce he smoothed the cream along her shoulders and down her spine, massaging the bony ridges to make her giggle. He wondered if she realised he could have done the job a lot more quickly. As he worked she wriggled and sighed in contentment. Her rump, well muscled and firm, reminded him of an audacious landscape – he found himself imagining how it might be to ride up and down those curves and slide deep into the crevices. The faint hairs on her thighs and forearms stirred under his efforts and made him catch his breath.

To finish the task Fred slid his fingers under the back strap of the bikini. With an impatient gesture Karen reached behind, undid the clasp and tucked the ends forwards under her breasts. Shocked, Fred sat back on his heels; it was a second or two before he could start again. He knew that if his hand slipped he would touch that soft whiteness under her armpits. The public beach was not the place. He made one last hesitant pass and patted her as done.

'Thanks. You're good at it, Fred,' she murmured sleepily. She did not offer to reciprocate. He could not tell whether she was teasing him as she closed her eyes.

He had not expected this chaotic churning in the region of his heart so soon into the holiday. It was agony to be in such close proximity to her young, healthy body, one which he had tried more than once to make love to, and had failed merely through his own crassness. Yet she was too sweet-natured to make him deliberately uncomfortable – he could manage that all by himself, simply by gazing under his lashes at the tanning flesh only a few inches from his own.

Karen lay still, apart from her gentle breathing. Fred had a sense that he had been dismissed and that she would not respond if he started a conversation. She was totally in control but, as he squinted up at the sun and realised he had left his sunglasses in the car, it was evident that he was not. Feeling disturbed, yet with the conviction that he ought instead to be enjoying his predicament and might do if he figured out how, he stretched out on his own towel and began to brood.

George Horrocks, however, was thoroughly enjoying himself. He was, he had long recognised, a natural enthusiast and thus a misfit in a world crammed with cynics. He was never happier than when sinking his teeth into a topic, whether at work or at play. Like today, even if only two journalists and local TV had materialised. It was the devil's own game pulling publicity for stunts in August.

It had been the same throughout his life. His army career had been a quiet success because he had immersed himself in it and risen through energy, application and intelligence. Likewise, when he cooked or entertained the results had to be of the highest standard. No half-measures crept into his kitchen. If that meant the postponement of a favourite dish because the right ingredients were not available, he would do so without a qualm: George would never get caught out serving *pêche flambée* with tinned peaches for lack of fresh white-fleshed fruit.

Friendship required steady cultivation too: he never took it for granted. George was assiduous in offering and accepting invitations, while attendance was always followed by warm notes of thanks so that he was ever the most welcome of guests.

The care was apparent even in his love-making – though George would not have dreamed of discussing the matter with anyone. It had to be competently done. He would have been distressed had he not been certain that his partners, such as they were, found his approaches a pleasure, and that his technique left nothing to be desired. Indeed he took such pride in his skill and (in private) his looks that it threatened to make him a little vain. That fault served only to keep him good-humouredly and literally on his toes. Other middle-aged friends may have given up or been ordered back to the gym by doctors worried about spread girths. For George, to stay in rude physical health was central to his approach to life: if you were going to live at all, you might as well do it *properly*.

For decades the army had been his love, but after commanding his own regiment – the top job open to him by the time he reached his mid-forties – only a plateau of boredom beckoned. He had left without a backward glance. Several civilian posts which did not appeal were politely declined; but without activity he was frustrated.

Early one morning he had found himself in a hotel room trying to obtain BBC 1 in an area notorious for poor television reception. To his surprise the delivery from his bedside set was clear as a bell. The service was provided on local cable.

Impressed, he had picked up the remote control and begun to explore. He discovered he could gain access to no fewer than forty-one TV channels including BBC, ITV, CNN, the Parliamentary Channel, Sky and the main satellite services, with five more in other European languages and one in Punjabi, as well as twenty-three radio stations. Automatic video recording of any items missed was possible. He could watch every moment in Parliament should he wish, which was more than parliamentarians in their Commons offices could do. He could see sport in a dozen countries and the news in more.

The astonishing scope of the thing had attracted him, and he had turned to the information booklet on the bedside table. It reminded him of his time as a young soldier learning the rudiments of short-wave radio on an old set: even then, the technical details kept him fascinated for hours. These days the consumer did no more than press a button.

And all, the hotel manager informed him, without the inconvenience of aerials and dishes, which were in the process of being removed. Would he like to see? George needed no persuasion. Soon the two men were on the roof of the hotel as a cool wind ruffled their shirts, watching while workmen struggled to dismantle rusty equipment. Together they pondered the new pollution-free science in which fibres thinner than a human hair could carry thousands of phone messages at once. George had a sudden romantic vision of towns and countryside devoid of ugly metal and telegraph poles and served by invisible underground systems. As the millennium approached, it felt like the dawn of a new age.

That had done it. Still talking animatedly to the manager he had descended the stairs, headed back to his room, picked up his address book and reached for the phone. Not long after he found himself invited to join the board of Prima, a new American-backed company which had won the cable franchise for the Midlands area near his home. A year or so later, on the retirement of the original chairman, the promotion of George both as a committed advocate for the medium and as a man of the highest reputation was assured. He had found his niche.

That was how he came to be standing in the shade of a large blue marquee and enthusing to the assembled dignitaries about the wonders that would accrue to those of their citizens who opted for the new technology, as soon as His Worship the Mayor had switched it on.

'It's future-proof,' he heard himself saying. 'It won't become obsolete. It's quick, it's clean, it's silent. We can connect just about everything you like once a household has opted for Prima: phone, fax, television of course, stereo. Use it for your computer modem – great for small businesses. If you've more than one television you can use them independently. Overall it'll cost you less. This is the twenty-first century, ladies and gentlemen. The impact will be as huge as the advent of the motor car, as dramatic as the spread of electricity itself; and you are part of it.'

'Not sure I want our grandchildren watching sex shows from the Continent – Red Hot Dutch and that,' the mayoress muttered to her husband. He hushed her. The whole notion of satellites whizzing around above his head filled him with wonder and terror. His socialism, such as it was, came from a detailed perusal of the works of George Orwell. What malevolence might be possible if it all fell into the wrong hands?

George touched the mayoress's arm respectfully. 'We don't broadcast that sort of thing,' he murmured. 'There's a market for it, no doubt. But I feel sorry for people who have to watch it. Suggests they don't get much of the real thing, doesn't it? Although we did a survey to find out what viewers got up to while they watched TV. You'd be surprised.'

The mayoress cast a glance at the portly figure of her husband and sniffed.

The group was led into the switching hall. Grey cabinets were opened to exhibit complexities of wiring twisted and coiled like so many nerves or intestines. Lights winked, monitor screens flickered. The chief engineer, white-coated like a surgeon, hid a screwdriver behind his back and shook hands. Councillors and hacks nodded with incomprehension as George explained how the signal was received from every broadcasting station, converted to Prima's frequencies, then sent to subscribers down the thin yellow wire which disappeared into a large black pipe by their feet.

Suddenly he halted in mid-sentence. His eyes swivelled to the monitor. 'Turn it up,' he told the engineer.

Elaine was alone in a studio a hundred miles away talking straight to a remote camera, doing her best to defend the government in some minor crisis. Her performance would be seen by a million people on the lunchtime news. Extracts would replay that night to a far larger audience. If the issue was significant the very sentence she was mouthing would find its way into press files and profiles. A pithy comment might end up in her obituary. Yet she had no idea George was observing her. It made him shiver.

He knew her, as nobody else present did. *They* saw a public figure, a symbol. The mayor was already uttering noisy imprecations about the government. Elaine was disliked by thousands who had never met her simply because of what she represented. If people bumped into her in a street they would assume they knew her and launch into disputes and heated denunciations. She must find it burdensome to be targeted like that. It was inevitable given the government's persistent unpopularity; and given the extraordinary power of television to make the remote familiar.

Yet she was a good woman. Not ordinary: ordinary people did not aspire to become MPs, let alone government Ministers. A pity, therefore, that so many turned out to be merely average or worse once in office.

'Right cow, that one,' observed the mayor.

George frowned. The pressmen moved closer to catch his response.

'I think she's better than most. Easier on the eye, anyway,' George murmured. That produced a cackle from the mayor and a snort from his consort. 'Now, Mr Mayor, time to go outside. We haven't any ceremonial scissors, I'm afraid – too old fashioned altogether. But we do have an extra-large switch. Would you be so kind . . .?'

With aplomb George led the way, and the remainder of the occasion passed off without incident. But his mind was seething.

Why did he feel so guilty? Had she been a fellow officer accused unjustly he would have leapt to her defence. Yet in her case his protective instincts were as nought. Just because she was a politician he had avoided the issue. He'd been disloyal, and his only positive remark had been sexist: that made him doubly angry with himself. The exchange had tarnished his mood.

He resolved to phone Elaine and ensure he spent an evening with her. He would make it up to her somehow.

It would have been quicker to fly to Nantes, but the service was infrequent and Anthony liked trains. Not any old train, of course. The elegant pointed nose of Eurostar promised rapid action once the meander through the Kent countryside was over. The Channel Tunnel itself took less than thirty minutes, leaving him with a slight disorientation: the voyage to another country ought to be more momentous. If it became mundane, would the political barriers dissolve too? Did they matter, anyway?

As the train emerged into the sunlight and smoothly picked up speed, the surface of the cup of coffee on the small table before him hardly shimmered. In less than an hour they would arrive in Paris, where he planned to stay for a couple of days. Then he would carry on by the TGV Atlantique. The others would collect him at Nantes for the short drive to the sea.

Anthony gazed out of the window. He ought to resist the temptation to think of life as a journey, travelling God knew where. He had not anticipated being a Minister so soon, nor in such circumstances. Harrison's amorous escapades had been the talk of the Commons since the chap had been elected. Instinctively Anthony disliked Derek's attitudes to women. That he'd come a cropper sooner or later was expected, but that it should not be over a woman was a surprise. Anthony was grateful that the incident had propelled him so quickly into office, but the realisation that he was thus assumed to be morally superior to the person he replaced made him queasy.

Derek had spoken briefly in the House in a personal statement but (presumably on the advice of his lawyers) had kept his mouth firmly shut thereafter. He had made it plain he had no intention of resigning his seat and intended if he could to clear his name. While warrants were out for Jayanti Bhadeshia's arrest on several charges the ex-Minister was required only as a material witness. Any charges of corruption might implicate other parts of the government. To everyone's relief, therefore – other than those who had lost money – the view was taken that prosecution of Mr Harrison himself would not be in the national interest.

Anthony pondered. Derek's riposte to his critics had hinged on motivation – his, and theirs in condemning the ignoble Lord Bhadeshia. He had wanted merely to assist an honest entrepreneur engaged in commercial activity which would be helpful to an under-developed country. Because of the man's origins he had been refused finance by institutions in London, quite unfairly. The ODA had seen the force of the arguments, which had been put without inducement or favour (many doubted that, but nothing could be proved). Construction contracts would have gone to a British consortium. Exports would have been boosted. Derek declared he could not understand the condemnation of actions so transparently worthy, unless racial intolerance was in play. As he spoke, his side of the House had growled approval.

Herein lay, Anthony guessed, the greatest gap between politicians' perception of their activities and the public's judgement. To Derek or Elaine, or most of their fellows, what mattered was whether a person aimed to do good or harm. If the motives were sound, then however disastrous the out-turn the individual expected to be forgiven. Even that studied neutrality which stemmed from laziness or indifference could be claimed as a virtue. Only when an office holder set out deliberately to do damage or had his own secret agenda – like the former defence Minister Alan Clark, who did not believe in free trade except in love and armaments – would disapproval be right.

The public didn't see it that way. They couldn't care less about a man's purpose – they didn't believe what most politicians said, anyway. What mattered were the *results*. To be honourably earnest might impress other politicians but for voters it was insufficient. It was outcome which counted, and little else.

The train slowed; a hiss in the air and a deep Gallic voice over the intercom announced Paris while the scenes outside were still rural. Anthony reached for his jacket and bag.

The only conclusion he could arrive at was that within its confines he had to try to fulfil his new office as well as possible. A phrase came to his mind. *Do, or not do. There is no room for 'try'.* What he achieved might not be entirely within his control but he would be judged on that and not on his simple desire to do the right thing. The transition from backbencher, where he merely talked about ideas, to Minister, where he was charged with carrying them out, was enormous. The responsibility weighed heavily as he rose to leave the train.

'I can't.'

'Why not? I haven't seen you in a month.'

'Because I'm busy. I'm the only senior Minister on duty.'

'So? Does that mean a sixteen-hour day every day, even in recess?'

'Yes. Sorry, George, but I have to finish this box. Otherwise there'll be some explaining to do when Ted returns.'

'You going to get any holiday at all?'

A sigh. 'When Ted's back I can take a few days off. Not now.'

'Not good for you. Your brain will soften. You'll make worse decisions unless you take time for yourself. Tonight, for example.'

'No – there's a bid for me to do *Newsnight*. That's at ten-thirty.'

'Cancel it. Get a backbencher to do it. Postpone it.' She hesitated.

'Elaine?'

'Yes?'

'*I love you.*'

Silence.

'Come and have dinner with me.'

'Oh, George – '

'Or shall I come to your place? I could bring a baby chicken roasted in honey with salad and a bottle of chilled wine. Instant meal, ready in a trice. Don't hang up on me! Say yes.'

He had never before told her he loved her. She had not heard the words from a man for a dreadfully long time. The new knowledge hung in the air between them.

'Do you mean it?'

'Certainly.' He did not repeat himself or expand further, but she was weakening. A note of triumph had crept into his voice.

'Tonight, then. I'll say no to the BBC. My place, about eight. And forgive me if I'm a bit flat, will you? It's been a lousy week.'

'Thank you. Sancerre or Meursault?'

She laughed at last, wistfully.

'Just you, George. That's all I want.'

Fred stepped out of the shower and gingerly patted himself dry. With the towel wrapped around his middle he stood in the lounge, back to the mirror, and strained to examine himself over his shoulder.

'Serves you right for not putting sun block on properly, you idiot.'

'But I'm striped!'

Karen, grinning but sympathetic, pulled him into the fading light near the window. Fred had caught the full force of a strong sun. His failure through a sudden shyness and lack of nerve to ask his companion for help meant angry red areas on his fair skin wherever he had not been able to reach.

She fetched sunburn lotion and began gently to apply it. Fred jumped as the cold fluid ran over his skin but submitted dolefully.

'Bend down a bit.'

Fred was a little taller than Karen. He sagged at the knees and hung his head like a naughty schoolboy, arms limp at his sides. She reached up and smoothed the lotion over his neck and shoulders. He winced as her fingers passed over sore protuberant bone but relaxed as the medication took effect.

'Turn around.'

Dutifully he obeyed. She had already bathed and changed into a sleeveless blouse and a clean cotton skirt. The flushed tan on her cheeks made her look exotic. In the darkened face her hazel eyes were warm and steady but something new stirred in them.

'Anywhere else, Fred?'

Her hand moved lightly on to his chest, then dropped slowly to his navel and rested on the twisted knot of his towel.

'Wherever you like, Karen . . .' His voice croaked and he cursed himself. Why was he such a clown? If his back wasn't so painful . . .

She laughed and pulled slowly at the towel, her knuckles grazing his belly where the reddened flesh turned to white. The fabric dropped away and fell to the floor. Calmly she capped the bottle and discarded it on the heap.

She stood before him, hands on hips, and examined him up and down with a mocking air, but with genuine affection in her gaze. She tilted her head at him and ran her tongue over her lips. Then before he could back off she lifted his organ in one hand and rested it there almost in curiosity.

Her other hand, still creamy, began to brush it softly and repeatedly along its length. As it grew under her encouragement she watched with amused delight. His breath came in short bursts as her movements became more rhythmic.

'Not in trouble there, Fred, are you?'

'No, but I will be if you carry on doing that.' He suddenly asserted himself. For a brief second he closed his eyes and prayed that this time, at last, they would really make it together. And, as an afterthought, that it would be quite as fantastic as he imagined.

He opened his eyes to find Karen still looking at him with merry anticipation, a broad smile on her face. Firmly he grasped her hand. 'Come on.'

'*Une salade de gésiers, s'il vous plaît. Et une bouteille de vin rouge de table.*'

He would not dream of eating gizzard at home. In fact he suspected it was banned under some health ordinance or other. Yet at the Coupe d'Alsace round the corner from the Boulevard Saint-Michel the small pieces of spiced meat were a delicacy. The strange taste, the unaccustomed freedom, the wine, the warm evening air, gave him a heady sensation which was entirely pleasurable.

Yet he wished he were not alone. Perhaps he should have persuaded Karen and Fred to travel with him, or even Lachlan? He had reflections he would have liked to share. Alternatively, in an expansive mood induced by alcohol, he could have been, he knew, a relaxed and interested listener. He had never been really drunk and had no idea how far he could go or how his behaviour might alter. But solitude, all at once, did not seem so perfect a substitute for companionship.

It was Paris; it was summer. The locals might have cleared off for their *fermeture annuelle*, not to return till September, but many students remained as well as visitors. Across the room one couple were more engrossed in each other than in the food. The young man was thin and eager, the girl wore shorts exposing long tanned legs which to Anthony seemed curiously unsexy. In the middle of the main course the girl rose and flung herself on her boyfriend, sitting on his lap with her limbs entwined around his body. For several moments they engaged in passionate kisses and only stopped when the waiter enquired laconically if they had finished their meal. Then she returned to her seat and they continued eating.

Anthony frowned. The episode excited him, but not for the reasons he might have expected. He had not found his heart thumping because he yearned to be hugged by those thighs. It was the boy's face, the hunger in it, the moist mouth. He ordered a cognac, and sat, watched and waited.

Elaine sucked the wishbone between her teeth, dropped it on her littered plate and contentedly licked her fingers one by one.

'How do you do it, George? You only phoned me mid-morning and here you turn up with a feast.'

'Been slaving over a hot stove ever since.'

'Don't you have a job to go to? How come you get the time to do this and I don't?'

He grinned sheepishly. 'I cannot tell a lie. I popped into Harrods. Ideal for busy grafters like you and me. You sounded as if you needed some home comforts. What a mad life you lead.'

'I suppose it's because there's nobody to stop me these days.' She spoke quietly. With George there was no point in coquetry. When he was ready he would lead; if he wanted to talk, or to encourage her to do so, she could not hurry him. It was a surprise to realise she was adjusting to the rhythm of another person's preferences – and how much she liked it.

He snorted. 'Why don't you put your foot down? Why can't you say "No" and "Sod off" more often, as you did tonight?'

'Part of the culture, I suppose.' She reached for her glass after George refilled it. 'I could say it's my conscience – I'm not happy to stop until all the stuff's done. But that's an impossibility – no sooner do I empty my box or the diary tray or clear the folders off my table than they're simply replaced as if by some evil magic. And I'm terrified that the file I've not read will be the one with the biggest row boiling up inside.'

'You have to prioritise. Or get your staff to do it for you.'

Elaine pictured the ubiquitous Chadwick and pulled a face. 'That takes a while. It needs confidence between civil servants and their Minister, both ways. The officials hate it if we veto their pet schemes on political grounds. We get furious if they dig their heels in and say something won't work. That's creative tension, if you like, but it's wearing.'

She rested her chin on her hand. 'It's so damn competitive, too. I got this position through a fluke. That won't happen again. The next move up, if it comes, will follow some pretty detailed scrutiny. I can't afford any hint that I don't pull my weight.'

'I heard your hours in Parliament were going to be reduced. Didn't it happen?' George retained a healthy scepticism about the operations of Elaine's workplace.

'No – on the contrary. We're supposed to finish at ten p.m., but that's been the rule since the Fenian filibusters of the last century, and always practised more in the breach than in the observance. But Wednesday morning sessions in place of Fridays are driving Ministers scatty. We used to have a single debate on Fridays so only one responder was needed. Now there are half a dozen subjects chosen by ballot. We can't manipulate that. Each one requires attendance by Ministers from various departments. Better for backbenchers, awful for us.'

Her lover sat back in his chair. Beside him the sliced Cox's apple was half eaten. All that remained of the St Maur cheese was the dark ash rinds.

'What did you mean by the culture? It's a practical matter, isn't it?'

Her laugh was hollow, her face sad. 'We're like Japanese salarymen. Supposed to slave away for the sake of it, useful or not. Much of what's in my box is rubbish, but it takes a stronger character than me to tip it out on the floor and walk off.'

'Might do them all good.' George was looking at her.

She drained her glass and giggled. 'I could imagine Bampton trying that. He's made it – he's in the Cabinet. But I couldn't, as a woman. Can't complain, see? He'd immediately accuse me of not coping. Weak, useless. Can't get into fights with the civil servants for the same reason. So, my sweet, one cultivates an air of competence even as one collapses from exhaustion. All part of the pretence.'

He leaned across the table and took her hand. 'There's no pretence here, Elaine. Have you enough energy left?'

He had not said again that he loved her. She wondered if she had misheard, or whether it had been a ploy to gain her attention; or whether in a few moments she might find out more.

She stood up and moved around the table. He rose and pulled her gently to him. Raising her hand he kissed her still-sticky fingers. 'You taste of honey,' he said, and led her to her bed.

It was time: for them both.

Karen had long since put behind her any residual fear of men.

286

Militant feminists might scream that every man was a potential rapist but, as a judgement on most of the males she knew it simply did not ring true. In Fred's case she was certain he was incapable of forcing any woman against her consent. On two occasions – on New Year's Eve and later, again at the house – he had accepted her demurral with grace and dignity. If she was to break her duck with a decent bloke, this was as good a moment as any. It was time to give Fred his chance.

Not that she loved him, other than as a friend. When it came to comparisons, Anthony, with his aura of power and assumed authority, was a more alluring figure. Karen was not the first woman to be fascinated by ambitious men. Looks alone could not explain the amorous achievements of the most successful Lotharios in the House of Commons, if power itself were not the aphrodisiac.

But the hours spent in the lazy sun lying at this young man's side, virtually unclothed, almost touching, had had a considerable effect. She had found herself glancing sideways and surveying him. He was not well muscled – quite thin, really, and not hairy – but that gave him a boyish innocence which was both reassuring and . . .

A stark-naked Fred, his body patched in red and white, thighs clenched, took Karen by the hand and walked into his bedroom with that ungainly gait of a man with a full erection. The girl moved more easily, undoing her blouse on the way, until by the time Fred had reached his bed and was rummaging in his bedside locker she stood beside him, naked to the waist.

'Fred.' There was a sweetness in her voice. 'I am so fond of you. You know that, don't you?'

The box of condoms was in his hand. Shaking, he tried to extract one but the silvery packets slithered through his fingers and cascaded on to the bed. She hid her mouth behind her hand but her eyes danced. He dropped the box with a muttered oath and reached for her, pushing her down on the bed.

His mouth was upon hers, and then on her breasts, and she moaned as he found first one nipple and then the other. Her skin tasted of sun and the salt breeze, and had a natural perfume he would never forget. In response her back arched upwards; she murmured his name and her fingers stroked his head. He told himself he must not come too fast, that foreplay was everything, that his partner must also enjoy it if there was ever to be a second go. He reached under her skirt and found the surprisingly wiry hair and the intimate place, already moist, and slid his trembling fingers inside.

287

Karen remembered she had turned him away twice: now she must help. She half sat up, undid the skirt fastening, wriggled out of the garment and kicked it away, her panties following, until the warmth of her flesh was there underneath his, touching his trunk, and her limbs began to spread out beneath and around him.

'Put it on, now,' she urged. He knelt up as she moved more securely further up the bed. His hands were shaking uncontrollably as he fumbled in desperation.

The girl took pity. Without a word she relieved Fred of the pale flimsy object and pushed him over on to his back. She had seen films; she had rehearsed this moment in her mind. Deftly she rolled the condom up and placed it over the tip of his penis, then with a swift sure movement rolled it down. And caressed him, holding him in one hand like a joystick – and before he could resist, her other hand flat on his belly, she raised herself over him and slipped him inside her.

As he began to move, the fiery skin on his back rubbed against the sheet and burned first in furious protest, then in added screaming fervour. It did not take long. With a yelp of pure pleasure he came, and his hands reached up to cup her breasts. As he did so she whooped and arched her back in her own climax. He pulled her down on top of him, and held her very close, full of joy at life, suffused with admiration and adoration for the panting girl whose arm was now flung in abandon across his body.

'We did it! Oh, wow – hooray!'

'We did, Fred. What a love you are.'

Gingerly she eased herself off him. Fred raised his head and indicated with pride the silvery sheath in his groin. 'You know how to take these things off, too, then?'

She reached for a box of tissues. 'Carefully, I believe.' As she did so she laughed and so did he. For several minutes they lay close and nuzzled each other. Then she eyed him up and down and grinned broadly: already he was beginning to stir. 'We could use a lot of these this week.'

He reached for a packet and began to peel it. 'We could indeed, Miss Karen. Roll over . . .'

Anthony was not sure how it had happened. That he was drunk was more than likely; he had not eaten much that day other than the salad and some cheese but he remembered draining the last of a bottle of wine and a couple of brandies.

The young man with the black hair and dark eyes had entered after him and sat alone at the table vacated by the amorous couple. Anthony was not conscious that he had still been casting glances in that direction, though the man's beauty was striking. Spanish, perhaps, or at least Mediterranean. Not British, of that he was certain; and therefore the man was usefully unaware of his observer's identity.

The young man smiled and raised his glass. After a second's hesitation Anthony returned the salute. Both were in casual clothes, Anthony's rather more expensive: a polo sweater, slacks, a light jacket for the warm evening. As he pushed the cheese plate away a chair scraped. The man stood by his side. He was tall and slim and smelled faintly of a musky male perfume.

'*Vous êtes tout seul ce soir, comme moi, je crois?*'

The voice was low and melodious. It would have been wiser to say no, he was not alone, that he was waiting for a friend: the fellow would have shrugged and gone away. There had been no salutation, no '*Bonsoir*'. It was as if the stranger had already assumed an acquaintance.

Impulse. A crazy feeling. On holiday, away from prying eyes, caution thrown to the winds, far from rules and obligations. A brief friendship, a chance merely to practise his French, entirely innocent. An adventure: no harm could come of it, if he were careful. Anthony had summoned the waiter, ordered more wine and as casually as he could motioned the young man to join him.

From that point onwards events were a blur, until he found himself once more alone back in his hotel room in the Rue du Sénat. Anthony flung himself down on the bed fully dressed and groaned out loud, as he had done barely thirty minutes before. But then he had been unclothed, and so had the stranger. And in the space of that half-hour Anthony had learned what certain other people do, and where it hurts and what soothes and what eases the movement and how the pain is relieved and released, all against a background of weird music and whispered phrases of synthetic love, from a man he had never met before and never wanted to see again.

With a bitter gesture he wiped his mouth against the back of his hand. He could still taste that tongue thrusting against his: it was, he realised, the first time he had ever been kissed sexually. He had responded so eagerly that he had drawn blood from the man's lip. There had been blood elsewhere too, faint marks on his own shoulders and buttocks from whatever the man had used on him – a cane, was it? – and the leather belt from his own trousers. Then Anthony had clung to him and had cried out in mingled ecstasy and terror. Now he felt horrible, unclean.

The shower was cold. Savagely Anthony wrenched at the tap, which came off in his hand. Scalding water rained down on him; his back stung. He stayed in as long as possible, the water slicking his hair down his face, then stepped out and pulled on a dressing gown, leaving the shower still running.

Then the tears came. Back on the bed he curled up like a child and cried himself to sleep.

Chapter Seventeen

Elaine put down her tray and smiled across the table at her daughter. 'It would appear', she remarked drily, 'that you had a splendid holiday.'

Karen's tanned face opposite, her eyes bright, skin glowing with health, told its own happy tale. A substantial plateful of curried chicken and rice was disappearing into her mouth with astonishing rapidity; a slice of lemon cheesecake waited on the side with a large pot of tea.

The Strangers' Cafeteria in the House of Commons was known to all those worked in the Palace of Westminster as the 'staff caff'. Its offerings were basic, wholesome, plentiful and cheap. Despite the apparent formality of dark panelling and scrolled plasterwork, the large room was a haven of friendliness. Tea urns hissed, plates clattered; sauce and vinegar bottles graced the tables. Police and security men in shirtsleeves carried their fish and chips into far corners. Secretaries smoked and gossiped. Research assistants on meagre salaries, thin as rakes, bent hungrily over dollops of cottage pie followed by roly-poly with custard. Best of all, nobody took the slightest notice of an MP with a guest, though Members had their own room, smaller and smarter but with much the same cuisine, next door.

'You look as if something's happened.' Elaine was not about to be inquisitive, but if her daughter wished to confide she would have a ready listener.

'How can you tell?' Karen giggled. 'It has, actually. Or rather, *he* has.' Her head tilted, teasing. 'You know him; he works not a million miles from here.'

'Anthony?' Elaine's eyes rounded. 'I knew you were keen on him, but – '

'No, not him. Guess again.'

'Haven't the foggiest. Another MP? I'd have thought you had more sense.' Elaine frowned. 'He's not married, is he?'

'No, he's not. I'm not *that* stupid.' Karen caught the shadow of pain on her mother's face and dropped her gaze. 'Sorry, Mum. I didn't mean that.'

'Don't apologise. You were right.' Elaine paused and looked out of the window. Although it was early autumn and still warm, a blustery wind had kept most diners off the Terrace. Karen's judgement was far sounder than her own. She turned back. 'So, who is it, then? Don't keep me in suspense.'

'Try one of the other chaps I live with.'

'Fred? Good Lord. I didn't think he had it in him.'

Karen laughed again. 'Neither did I, but he has now. Been reading the manuals, at a guess. Got quite a technique – '

Elaine spoke sharply, but with a chuckle. 'That's enough. I don't need to know the gruesome details, thank you.'

'He's getting quite keen. I think he's in love with me.' Karen preened herself, pushed away the empty curry plate and started on the cheesecake. Watching Karen's evident enjoyment as she picked at her own salad Elaine envied her daughter's calorific capacity. A similar meal would have defeated her before halfway.

'And you?' Elaine prompted.

Karen's mouth twitched thoughtfully. 'I like him, of course, but I don't think I want to marry him. Maybe I know too much about the life of MPs and their families. It's not as if I were a starry-eyed researcher, for whom MPs are madly glamorous. He's sweet, and lovely in bed, so we'll carry on as we are for a while. If he starts getting romantic I may have a problem.'

'He's the sort who might,' Elaine warned. 'Don't hurt his feelings.' She suppressed an urge to remark tartly on Karen's willingness to make love when love was absent. Her curiosity surfaced. 'So what happened with Anthony York? Did you two just never get together?'

The girl munched cake for a moment. 'We did, but it was most peculiar, Mum. Something is *wrong* with him. He's mixed up quite badly inside, somehow. At La Baule, on the beach, with everybody cavorting around practically nude, he wouldn't take his shirt off and sat in the shade reading a book. At least he pretended to read. Most of the time he stared out to sea and looked so . . . sad and confused. He didn't say much either. I can't make him out.'

Elaine was not about to divulge what she knew about Anthony's unhappy background. Her remark to him, that his subsequent success was the more admirable, was sincerely meant. The scars on his wrists did not make him unsuitable in any way as her junior, though she felt a distinct sense of relief that he was seemingly no longer in her daughter's sights. To see Karen involved with somebody with such a past would have caused her anxiety. Yet his well-being was her concern, as it was Karen's.

'He's been a bit odd since he came back from leave,' Elaine mused. 'Hyperactive, almost – working terribly hard. Yet the moment the talk veers towards anything personal he clams up.'

'There weren't any nightmares on holiday either, which was unusual.' As Elaine raised an eyebrow in surprise, Karen told her about the disturbed nights in Battersea, though hesitating noticeably over the details. Her mother guessed what might have happened but thought better than to enquire. She was unsure she wanted to learn that her daughter made a habit of slipping into strange men's beds. Karen continued, 'I was worried that he might have bad dreams in France, but he slept like a log: impossible to wake in the morning. A bit dopey in the daytime too.'

'Maybe he's started taking something to help him sleep.'

Silence ensued. Neither wanted to consider the implications of one of Her Majesty's Ministers becoming dependent on drugs. It occurred to Elaine that perhaps Anthony's inconsistent hyperactivity might have a similar cause.

She pondered. In the weeks since his return the junior Minister had made no attempt to renew the former favourable contact and had shied away from further gentle probing. It was as if he were warning her that the subject was closed. 'Before recess I thought we might become quite close: he seemed to trust me. Now it's gone. It makes me uneasy. I'd rather he asked for help, if he needs it, than rely on pills.'

'I don't think he'd know how to ask for help.' Karen pushed away her plate. 'Anyway, although he's my landlord I have other fish to fry. Possibly too many for my own good, in fact. D'you remember that awful journalist, Jim Betts from the *Globe*?'

Elaine frowned, then shook her head. She knew little about her daughter's early history and nothing at all about the rape that had happened over four years earlier. The name was vaguely familiar, since it appeared regularly over the sleazier stories in the *Globe*; other than that, she would have been hard put to summon up a face to match it.

'What of him?'

'He's hanging around too. Phoned and pestered me a couple of times. But I think he's after dirt on the MPs I live with: that's his kind of journalism. I wouldn't touch him with a bargepole, so don't fret.'

'If you do see him, even just to talk, do be careful.' Elaine rose to go. Half an hour she had told the office. A nagging sensation of too much left unsaid disturbed her.

Karen flushed, then laughed lightly. She knew far better than anyone what Betts was capable of. 'Yeah, Mum, I will.'

'Like a honeypot to the bees, that's you,' Elaine commented as they walked together to the doorway, but there was pride and love in her voice.

Under the table Anthony drummed his fingers. He felt tense. The pulses in his skull beat faster and with a fiercer intensity than he was used to: the rhythm was frightening. But without the benzedrine he would be dozy, as he had discovered for much of the time on the beach; and without the nitrazepam he could not sleep, but relived that night in the hotel room, each moment of it, right down to the entering, the exquisite pain, the relief . . .

No. He must *not* remember that. It had been madness. Completely out of character. The whole affair disgusted him to the core. Worst of all, with a complete stranger. He had offered the man money, which had been accepted with a whisper of thanks and an offer to see him again, but any such notion was completely out of the question. And what they *did* – it was forbidden and decried everywhere, in the Bible, in polite society. Yet alone at night as he lay tossing and aching for sleep, his face buried in the pillow, Anthony felt those skilled hands creep once more to his buttocks and force them apart, felt first the fingers, then was it an instrument? . . . and at last . . . *that* slide into him. He realised he dreamed about it, had always dreamed about it. Before the night in Paris he had maintained a kind of virginity and had pushed other pictures, lurid and exciting though they might be, from his mind. Yet it had happened. He had let it happen. Not only allowed it, but asked for it; and wept as he asked, as the young man made certain that consent was given, freely: begged for it, in fact . . .

The sound of genteel laughter floated into his consciousness. Around the departmental table somebody had made a joke. He had missed it and could only join in a half-second too late. The meeting of Ministers and officials moved on, but across the room Chadwick was staring at him curiously. He was being watched. He would have to be watchful himself. He stilled his hands and slipped them into his lap, raised his head and gazed around almost defiantly.

At the other end of the table Martin Chadwick was performing a double act. Part of him was indeed noting the facial revelations of Mr Anthony York. The main part of Chadwick's brain, however, was supporting the Permanent Secretary in his exposition of the possibilities for the department in the forthcoming Queen's Speech, and the likely depredations of the Chancellor in the Budget which would follow in November.

Money was very tight. On the other hand, the still-new department's value needed to be enhanced. The combination of necessity and penury created an intriguing conundrum.

'We could abolish the health authorities: that'd stir the pot nicely, and save money.' Chadwick's tone was helpful.

'What good would that do?' growled Ted Bampton. 'Upset a lot of people, that would. All our friends. People we appointed for their political purity. And loyalty.'

Chadwick pressed his fingertips to his mouth and delicately cleared his throat. His professional code prevented him commenting on any sentence that contained the word 'political'. 'I only suggested it because you frequently ask exactly what the health authorities do, Secretary of State.'

'Doesn't mean I want 'em abolished.' Bampton glared at the adviser. 'I don't know what *you* do, Chadwick, but it doesn't mean I'm about to abolish you.'

A titter went around the room. Chadwick was grudgingly admired, but not liked.

'Oh, I don't know, Secretary of State,' Chadwick responded. 'Were you to present me with the same deal as the Treasury chaps, I might be tempted.'

'What's that?' Bampton looked up, uncertain whether to welcome or deplore the possibility of losing Martin Chadwick.

Chadwick shrugged self-deprecatingly. If Ministers wished to be distracted from the agenda, that suited him fine. 'The Secretary to the Cabinet wants to lose eight out of twenty-four Under-Secretary posts and fifteen out of sixty-four Assistant Secretary posts. Since these are senior positions, the terms are generous. An Under-Secretary aged between forty and forty-eight would take on redundancy five and a quarter times his salary as a lump sum, of which the first thirty thousand pounds would be tax-free; and of course his pension at age sixty, which is index-linked. Plus a lump sum of fifty-five thousand pounds on that date too. Also tax-free. That's it.'

'Blimey! I wish somebody would make me that sort of offer,' Bampton muttered.

Chadwick decided to rub it in. The information helped remind everyone present why the cleverest in the nation still chose the Civil Service and not, like Bampton, industry or politics.

'And were I over forty-eight I would be able to draw an annual pension of twenty-five thousand pounds right away, while the tax-free lump sum on my sixtieth birthday would be increased to sixty-six thousand pounds.'

Elaine Stalker leaned across the table. 'You've worked it out, Mr Chadwick. Let's assume you were eligible for the Treasury scheme. Since you're . . . what? . . . about forty-five? . . . how much would you get, in total?'

'Right away? About three hundred and fifty thousand.'

'Christ.' Bampton glowered. 'Amazing what you can do with other people's money, isn't it?'

The Permanent Secretary quickly intervened. 'But he's not eligible, and as a new department we are short of staff, not overmanned. So shall we move on, Secretary of State?' He flashed a look of annoyance at his deputy. They would have words later.

Chadwick smiled to himself. How he loved showing these peasants up. He let the discussion wash over him for a few moments. His attention was caught again by the fingers of the junior Minister opposite, which had crept back on to the desk and were fiddling in a distracted fashion with the papers before him.

He allowed himself to stare coolly at Mr York. As a connoisseur of the unusual, Chadwick could tell a mile off who was at ease with his sexuality and who not; and whether a little experimentation would be welcome, even if the suggestion had been spurned the first time.

Chadwick had long felt himself doubly fortunate. To be well married, and contentedly so, was not a camouflage but a significant part of his own life. It was not simply a matter of status or fear of the opprobrium that diminished any open homosexual's chances in the government service, though officially discrimination had been abandoned. Unlike gay couples, he could father children and was blessed with a family who would bring joy for years to come. Chadwick had no intention of coming to a lonely and loveless death, possibly from a horrible disease. On the contrary: he fully anticipated dying after a highly respectable old age, surrounded by weeping children and grandchildren, his hand held lovingly by his grieving wife, from whom his dark side had been totally hidden. His name would be honoured. He would not be a source of controversy. Not ever.

Yet there was something infinitely irresistible about a good-looking younger man, especially one with breeding and education. Bisexuality had its delights too. Poker-faced but with a slight sardonic twist to the lips, Chadwick ensured that Anthony was aware of his scrutiny. It amused him that the Minister was discomforted. If the pictures flitting through that handsome troubled head had anything to do with sex, Chadwick would be happy to oblige.

'Helsinki! It's such a God-forsaken place. Do I have to?' Bampton was speaking, exasperation in his voice.

Chadwick reflected with mild contempt that once again Mrs Stalker had up to now largely been left out of the conversation. The omission was more noticeable since Harrison had gone; the latter's double act with Bampton, which had sounded at times like a conspiracy to keep Mrs Stalker out of the frame, was no more, while Mr York was too new and junior to take his place. So Bampton did most of the talking himself. The rest of his team did little more than form an audience. Mrs Stalker seemed restless with that role.

'I'm afraid so. We must send a Minister to the Congress; it'll be the first occasion it's been held in Finland since the country joined the European Union.' The Perm Sec was grave.

Bampton pointed, rather rudely. 'Elaine?'

She responded swiftly and with a thankful grin. 'Sorry. I'm at the Conservative Women's Conference that day. Been promised for months.'

'Then it'll have to be you, Anthony. Think you can handle it?'

Anthony was hesitant. Ministers present from other countries would be of higher rank and probably far more experienced. 'Me? If you want me to, Ted. I'll do my best.'

Bampton motioned at the officials. 'Somebody'll go with you to guide you. Who'll it be?' A couple of hands were raised. For them Helsinki was a welcome jaunt. Bampton made a note.

'Thank you, Mr Chadwick. Now look after him, won't you?'

Nick Thwaite, news editor, thrust a long fax at his deputy and laughed out loud. 'So what do you make of this Peter Tatchell, then, Jim? Isn't he a gift?'

'He's a prat, but I'll hand it to you, he produces great copy.' Jim Betts ran his eye down the paper. 'Some new names here,' he commented. 'One or two are seriously litigious. If we print this we'd be treading on eggshells.'

'Broken reputations and torn cassocks, more like.' Thwaite reached for his coffee. 'I don't mind being sued as long as we have evidence we can produce in court. Mr Tatchell may be aching to tell the world about his gay acquaintances in high places, but we have only his word for it.'

'Can't you just see him in the dock as a material witness? Describing the spots on a bloke's back in detail, or the size of his dick. Entertaining, that.'

'But unreliable. Remember that big fish you landed – Sir Nigel Boswood? Queer as a coot. But we had the rent-boy, and he had the photos. So there was no case. Open and shut, you might say.'

The two laughed lewdly. Thwaite continued, 'Look, I've no ethical problems about publication. It's a practical matter. As a newspaperman I accept that the private lives of individuals are . . . a matter of intense public interest. If not, the gory details wouldn't help us sell newspapers, and they do.'

'And we'd be performing a public service too – some of these shirt-lifters are such shits: hypocrites, every one.'

'But Tatchell and his peculiar pals have their own axes to grind,' Thwaite warned. 'They're not simply in the business of "outing". They're after revenge. I can see why – among the names here some are loud and nasty in condemnation of gay rights. That doesn't prove they're queer. It'd serve 'em right, though, if we did print the lot. In a twisted way I'm almost sympathetic.'

'You'll have me wondering about you next, Nick.' Betts examined the list with more care. As he reached the end he sucked his teeth. 'Well, now, here's a new boy. New Minister too. He's a definite possibility.' He pointed.

Thwaite peered over his arm and whistled softly. 'My, my. Do you think Tatchell's merely guessing, simply because the chap's not married? Worth a little homework, I think, Jim.'

'Absolutely. I'll get on to that. I know where he lives.' Betts rose with a broad grin. 'I even know who he lives with – and none of them's hitched. I'll enjoy this one, Nick, thanks.'

Anthony waited till ten minutes after the meeting when all who had attended had safely dispersed. He knew from ministerial diaries that Bampton had no engagements for a couple of hours. A phoned request for a few minutes of the Secretary of State's time received a curt assent. Soon he found himself seated formally at the other side of Ted Bampton's desk.

The Cabinet Minister had not bothered to stamp his personality on his office. On the mantelpiece stood two photographs of himself and his family, one in evening dress with his wife in shapeless blue silk, the other in casual clothes with Jean and the girls, posed under a tree. Anthony surmised they came from election addresses, the only publication over which a politician has total editorial control. The prints on the wall were gaily coloured impressions of Mediterranean scenes, possibly brought back from holidays. Bampton seemed to have avoided, or vetoed, the ubiquitous sepia tints of British castles and ex-Prime Ministers: a mark in his favour.

'What do you mean – you don't want Chadwick to go with you? Why ever not?' Bampton lit a cigar and puffed for a moment, then tipped ash into a saucer. 'Come on. I'm listening.'

Anthony sat marginally more upright and steadied his gaze. 'I'm not sure he's the right official for this trip, Ted. I'd rather take ... say, my own Private Secretary.'

Bampton shrugged. 'Well, of course you can take him, but he's not the departmental expert. Chadwick is. Do you two not get along – is that it?'

Anthony was struggling. His cheeks flushed and his hands twisted together. Bampton, who in his business days could spot trouble a mile off, frowned.

'If that's the case you'd better explain to me why not. You're supposed to work with all the civil servants, not pick and choose. What's the problem? I can't deal with it till I know.'

'I ... I can't tell you exactly. Only that it would not be a good idea to send him. If he goes, then I shouldn't.'

'Really?' Bampton drew out the vowels slowly. He put the cigar between his teeth and rolled it back and forth, once. His eyes narrowed and he surveyed the embarrassed young man, letting his inspection roam over the well-cut suit, the white-knuckled fists, the knees pressed tightly together.

So that was it.

Bampton would not have demeaned himself with any active homophobia, any more than he would indulge in sexist remarks about women. In Huddersfield both were standard fare in pubs and clubs, along with racist jokes and a general agreement that all but male white heterosexuals were lesser breeds. It was in part distaste for such boorishness and the waste of energy it entailed that had pushed him into greater efforts than his contemporaries in both business and public life. If he, his ilk, his principles and his preferences were to be judged superior to others, then it had to be a genuine superiority, not merely one shouted by drunks after closing time.

He did not know any queers, not properly, and didn't want to. It was hard to imagine chaps like Chris Smith, the Islington MP, or Matthew Parris, the prize-winning *Times* columnist, doing anything sexual with anybody, let alone with each other. If a man did not fancy women then in Bampton's book it was wiser for him to stay celibate. Anything else was asking for trouble.

That was also the best course for any man who could not manage to fall in love with a suitable lady, marry her, have children by her and stick with her, as he had. Nobody took that route now. The world had become a soulless place of short-term liaisons, where adultery was normal practice and nobody *tried* any more. And they wonder why the kids go bad, he concluded to himself grimly.

He put the cigar down, leaned his elbows on the table and gave Anthony his full attention. His voice was low and cool.

'Has Mr Chadwick been propositioning you, is that it?'

'What? No, nothing like that . . .' But Anthony's flustered denial told its tale. Bampton pursed his lips.

'I don't want to know about it. Take some advice, lad. Find yourself a good girl and get hitched. You're a bit long in the tooth to be still single. Whatever the urges, they can be satisfied in marriage. At least, that's my view.'

Anthony was scarlet. His mouth opened and closed but no sound came out.

'And we'll hear no more nonsense about Mr Chadwick. He's going with you to Helsinki, and that's that.'

Anthony trudged miserably back to his office and for half an hour pretended to read the preliminary briefing for Helsinki. The typed paragraphs swam before his eyes. His coffee was cold and bitter but he did not want to call for a fresh cup. Quickly he slipped a small white pill on to his tongue and swallowed it with the remaining black liquid.

That trip to Finland could not take place, not as it had been planned. If he found himself in a foreign hotel with Chadwick nearby he knew what would happen. Or, rather, he was sure he could guess the start of it. The man would drop hints at him throughout meetings and dinner much as he had that morning. His gaze would be direct, friendly and discreet. The communication would not be so obvious that others would notice; or, if they did, it would appear that a distinguished older civil servant was anxious to assist his junior Minister on his first foray into international negotiation.

But those glimpses across the table held terror. They told Anthony everything. Chadwick had not been permanently repulsed in Brussels. On the contrary: having waited till the incident was long behind them, he proposed to renew his efforts at seduction.

Anthony felt his mind start to clear. On a notepad he began to doodle. The letter 'A' stood for himself, 'C' for Chadwick. An arrow eastward pointed at 'P': Paris. He could return to the Coupe d'Alsace, if that was what he wanted; but doing it with a stranger seemed the worst option and was open to blackmail. Yet, between Chadwick's first approach and his second, Paris had happened and could not be undone. In Anthony's baggage for Helsinki would be packed a bleak awareness of his own desperation and how it might be alleviated. A large 'B' in a square box stood to one side: Bampton, his boss, who disapproved of the whole business but was incapable of sympathy. No wonder Ted had a reputation for being a tough guy who lacked sophistication; he seemed not to understand how anyone else functioned at all.

Anthony drew a circle several times around the 'C', then almost involuntarily, without breaking the line, pulled it around the 'A' like a lasso. With an oath he threw the pencil down.

Who might he turn to? Whom could he trust? Elaine, his immediate superior, would, he was sure, show more compassion than Bampton. She would not laugh at him, nor suggest impossible solutions like marriage. But to confess to her required admitting both the threat from Chadwick and his own inability to ignore it. That also meant blackening Chadwick's character as well as his own. Furthermore, unless she took his place on the delegation she could not assist, not without a complaint to someone else such as the Perm Sec. In any case, she seemed to have her own battles with Bampton. Better not to involve her at all.

Was there someone at the Battersea house – his cousin, maybe? Lachlan's psychiatric knowledge might be invaluable and as a doctor he was sworn to confidentiality. Anthony began to chew at a fingernail, then stopped himself, crossly. Lachlan was part of the family, but had never been taken into his confidence. These revelations would be a terrific surprise. And to embroil him might be to abuse his friendship.

Medically trained or not, Lachlan wasn't his doctor. He'd simply suggest that Anthony seek specialised help.

As for confiding in Fred, the idea was ludicrous. Karen, too. There'd been a time when that might have been possible. She knew more than most people but had never betrayed him. Karen suspected something was up – he had seen her observing him more than once. But the moment had passed, had it ever existed. And Karen was newly wrapped up in Fred. That he might be the subject of earnest analysis between Fred and Karen in bed – it had probably occurred already – filled Anthony with humiliation and shame. He had no urge to put flesh on the bones of their suspicions, nor to listen to any more superfluous advice.

But if he did nothing . . . the trip was only a few weeks away, soon after the Party Conference. And if he evaded the threat at Helsinki it would surface elsewhere: there would be many opportunities to come.

His head hurt. He passed a hand over his brow and was surprised to find his palm damp. What if he went, and Chadwick made his advance?

Anthony covered his eyes and face; behind his hands, his mouth opened wide as if he would cry out but nothing came. He saw himself at a distance. A black pool lapped at his feet. The water as it touched him left a scum. From its surface came a smell of decay; yet he ached to tear off his clothes and jump in . . .

Did that mean he was gay? Anthony struggled, horrified, then with a huge effort forced himself to consider the odds. He did not *want* to be: he wanted to be a straight heterosexual, though it was clear now that he wasn't. He strongly deplored homosexuality and always had – was on record with his disapproval. Gay sex was unnatural, a perversion, though he recoiled from categorising other people's proclivities in offensive terms. He was simply not *like that*. He had never felt attracted to boys at school – indeed had been repelled by the touch of human skin. That, surely, had been the problem with Karen, and girls generally: he didn't like touching or being touched. It wasn't that one gender or the other was the more repellent. All physical contact had made him recoil – at least until Paris.

It had not occurred to him, ever, to ask why that should be so. His innate reserve left him wary. That was how he was brought up. His parents had reared two offspring perfectly well in a calm, controlled atmosphere; he could not remember a single occasion when his mother had cuddled him, while his only direct contact with his father was an occasional bluff handshake. His sister, a more demonstrative character, would fling her arms around his neck, but accepted that such was not his style.

Perhaps he was one of those people for whom sex didn't matter much. He certainly wasn't like Harrison with his undiscriminating appetites. Anthony could easily imagine himself instead in a celibate world – in medieval times he would have been content as a monk. Then his strange urges could have been chastised with a hair-shirt or birchings. As a penitent he'd have been stripped and tied to a post or held down, as brother monks chanted prayers and waved incense at him . . .

Anthony gasped: the thought of being beaten, whatever its objective, filled him with intense excitement. As he heard the cane swish through the air towards his flesh he could also feel the erection. Pain had become not a punishment but a sexual release in itself.

Beside him the phone rang shrilly. Cursing he picked it up. It was his Private Secretary.

'I am so sorry, Minister,' the voice murmured, 'but he insisted on speaking to you himself. It's a Mr Jim Betts of the *Globe* newspaper. Says it's urgent. A press release he's just had. Shall I tell him you're busy?'

'No, put him on.' An inquiry about the latest health statistics might be a useful distraction.

The phone clicked. 'You're through.'

'Ah, Mr York? Good afternoon. Betts here. This won't take a moment.' The accent was Liverpudlian overlaid by several years in London. The effect was not pleasant. There was a pause.

'Yes, Mr Betts. How can I help you?' Anthony let his voice lift in impatience.

Betts cleared his throat. It sounded as if the journalist was flicking through sheets of paper. Anthony was about to speak again when suddenly the question came, loud and clear.

'Did you know, Mr York, that your name appears on the latest list of homosexuals to be outed by the gay group Outrage? Do you have any comment to make? Mr York – Mr York . . .?'

Karen heard the door open downstairs and the heavy footfalls on the stair. From the direction they then took it must be Anthony.

He was early; usually he didn't come home in the late afternoon, not since he had joined her mother at the DHWF. On a normal weekday it simply wasn't worthwhile, not with votes and late-night adjournment debates at the House.

If her landlord wanted a drink or tea he could presumably make it himself; there was no need for her to go down. On the other hand, it would be polite and friendly to be in the kitchen when he entered it, which would presumably be his next move. He had been looking so peaky lately. It worried her that anybody near her should be unhappy, especially when her own life had taken such a positive turn.

But she was home to work. The essay she was writing had reached a tricky point. Far better to finish it, then go downstairs.

As Karen debated lazily with herself, Anthony's bedroom door slammed. He retraced his steps and in a moment had gone, banging the front door behind him. He could hardly have been in the house five minutes. She heard the car door open, then close.

Puzzled, she rose and peered out of the window and watched as Anthony put the car in gear and drove off at speed, heading back towards the river. Before she let the curtain fall she glanced down the road. Another car's lights, quickly switched on, caught her attention. It was parked on the other side about thirty yards away. It too moved from the kerb and came past. It seemed to be following Anthony. As the second vehicle briefly drew level with the house she recognised the driver.

Jim Betts.

It was almost dusk. He would have to move carefully in such unfamiliar surroundings. Above him the darkened tree branches, still in heavy leaf after the summer, rustled in the wind. In the distance street lights began to glow orange: down there, in respectable households, curtains would be drawn, televisions switched on for the evening news. Out on the bleak hillside in North London, however, the air was dank. Litter blew around. A dog barked repeatedly several streets away and was not silenced. It was a God-forsaken place.

He sat in the car, engine switched off, the window half wound down. Other cars pulled up, engines purring, then drove past, through the gates and further down the hill. Their drivers peered furtively at Anthony. Some mouthed a word. One waved and tried to attract his attention. Each car had only one occupant.

From the pub came the noise of raucous laughter and music. Jack Straw's Castle, it was called. Along here two centuries ago highwaymen waited as the stagecoach, filled with exhausted but wealthy travellers, made its way towards London. Perhaps the criminals had hidden under the same trees. The pub's lights were inviting but he would not enter. Whatever was in his psyche, whatever distortion or madness he might be subject to, the answer did not lie indoors. Not tonight.

A small white van drew up in front of him. In the fading light Anthony, nonplussed, could just distinguish the logo of the local health authority. A muffled figure emerged and set up a folding table and chair beneath the largest tree. He removed various smaller packets from a box, laid out a clipboard and a couple of pens, placed a pair of spectacles on his nose and began to serve himself from the contents of a Thermos flask.

Anthony pulled on a jacket, tucked a woollen scarf around the lower half of his face and locked the car. Hands in pockets, he walked slowly towards the table.

'Evening. You want some condoms? They're free.'

The muffled figure was a bearded man in a grubby purple anorak. The smell of tomato soup rose incongruously as he sipped, hands clasped around the mug, seeking its warmth. The spectacles gave him an owlish look. Anthony did not reply.

'We give them out, see. In the evenings. Safer sex. It's all right, honestly. The police know we're here and they won't bother us.'

'Ah. I see.' Anthony wanted him to go on talking.

'No, you're OK here. It's a long time since the Met chased the boys around the Heath. Not unless there's trouble. Here, take a few.'

A gloved paw was held out, its contents hidden. The man smiled up at Anthony, an open, pleasant expression on his face: a professional helper. Anthony thrust his own hands deeper into his pockets and shook his head.

A tall man in a light-coloured coat and leather trousers walked past them. In his lapel was a mauve badge. He did a sideways shuffle, exchanged a muttered greeting with the health worker and accepted the offer of condoms. For a moment there was eye contact between Anthony and the newcomer, who paused for a moment as if to judge his intentions, then shrugged and disappeared down the hillside.

'The badge – what's that?' Anthony gestured at the retreating back but kept his face hidden.

'HIV awareness. It means he goes in for safe sex and is AIDS-aware.'

'Does that mean he has AIDS?' Anthony was incredulous, then checked himself. A person's needs didn't change just because he had contracted the virus.

'Maybe. More likely not. It means he can be approached by men who have. He doesn't mind, see. Sets their minds at rest that they won't infect anybody else. Sets other minds at rest that he won't pass on an infection. Not just HIV, either.'

'My God,' Anthony muttered. These were worlds of which he had no knowledge, despite his position in a health department. Behind him he sensed rather than saw other men arrive, mostly in cars which were parked neatly under the trees and who walked down out of sight, singly at first, then paired off. Several stood quietly as if waiting for somebody.

The man in the anorak twisted around to get a better view of his interlocutor. 'You're new, aren't you? No, I don't want your name. You'd be surprised how well known this place is all over the world. We had one guy last week who'd come straight off the plane from San Francisco. Took a taxi from Heathrow and found a partner less than an hour after landing. He'd read about it in a contact magazine.'

So had Anthony.

An edge came into the man's voice. 'You're not press, are you? 'Cause if you are you're not welcome.' He turned his back with a huffy air.

'No – no, I'm not press. I'm just . . . not sure, that's all.'

The man laughed softly. 'Few of us are, to begin with.' He rose and held out his hand to Anthony. In his fingers was a small white card. 'You might find it helpful to call this number. It's the London Lesbian and Gay Switchboard. Advice and information, any time, day or night. Good people – '

That was the last thing Anthony wanted to have found in his pocket. The man stood there, smiling, his hand out in friendship, spectacles glinting dully in the reflected light from the pub.

Anthony suddenly felt violently sick. So this was what it meant. Out on a chilly hillside in a public park. With strangers whose face he could not see, his own face hidden. A phone number to talk to more strangers. No names, no recall, no comeback. No pride, no love, either. Only shame and furtive fumblings and the sudden thrust, crying out, then a wiping, readjustment, the tidying up of clothes before stumbling away. The morals of dogs, serving each other in tumbled semi-nakedness. Desperate, urgent, dangerous. Horrible.

No!

With a great yell he upended the table, sending condoms, Thermos, papers and pens into the air. As the health worker protested, Anthony turned on him in fury, then stared in astonishment. This was no longer a seedy man in a purple anorak. Instead a tall hooded black shape strode towards him down a rain-sodden pathway. Within its cloak several shapes shimmered, merged and separated, all of them familiar to him. He did not need to ask the apparition's identity, he had always known it – the prefect at school with his clammy hands, the whispering youth in Paris, the old man in the lane, whose visage he had never seen. The voice was too easily recognised, the invitation too gross, too tempting. It was Chadwick . . .

Anthony screamed as he formed his hand into a fist and thrust it blindly at that dreadful spectre. He heard the crunch as spectacles broke on the bridge of the nose and the squeal of fear and indignation. He lashed out again and the cry turned to a shriek of pain. Then others came running, shouting; he was shoved to the ground and found himself pinned down in the mud. Somebody sat on his arm, twisting it back as if it would break. As he struggled, the pressure increased. At last he gave up and lay panting but still.

'Bloody 'ell! What's goin' on 'ere?'

'Fucking homophobe. Asking questions. Jesus. I can't see.'

'You all right, Carl? We'd better get you to casualty.'

'Anybody know the bloke?'

'Somebody take Carl here to the Royal Free. I'll get a statement from him later.'

'Lord, what a mess.'

A heavy hand was laid on Anthony's shoulder. 'Right, matey. Let's be having you. Up, now. And no more punches.'

Anthony found himself hauled upright. A torch was shone into his face. His sodden scarf was dragged roughly from his mouth. He blinked away dirt.

'Now who the hell are you, and what do you think you're doing lashing out at people going about their lawful business?'

The thickset police officer was as tall and solid as Anthony. His glare was direct and angry. Behind him the injured man, nose and mouth streaming blood, was being comforted by friends and helped into a car. The man with the mauve badge moved in the shadows nearby, his profile in the headlights pale and grim. The crowd of men surged, frightened and upset. The revving of engines bore witness to those who had no wish to be discovered at such a scene.

The policeman sighed. 'Right, mate. Hold out your hands for the cuffs. It is my duty to warn you that you do not have to say anything, but it may harm your defence if you do not mention when questioned something which you later rely on in Court. Anything you do say may be given in evidence.'

'Oh Christ.'

'Right.'

'Christ Almighty. Is it on the PA tapes yet?'

'Oh, aye, Chief. There was a reporter on the spot in seconds. They listen to the police radios.'

'Tipped off, probably. Looks as if the *Globe* man was there and saw it happen.'

'Set up?'

'Who knows? Doesn't matter, anyway. Our chap shouldn't have been anywhere near Hampstead Heath. At least, not that bit. And not without good reason.'

'Where is he now?'

'Rosslyn Hill police station. In the cells.'

'Bloody hell. What's his story, then?'

'Haven't the foggiest. Maybe he was doing research for the Health Department.'

'That'd be original.'

A pause. The Chief Whip in his office at Number 12 could be heard issuing rapid instructions as the Party Chairman and Jackson, Anthony's whip, conferred in the whips' office.

The Chief returned to the line. 'Has he been charged yet?'

'Yes. Affray and actual bodily harm.'

'Not gross indecency or anything like that?'

'No-o. Kept his trousers on. Seems he laid into one of the other blokes there. Unprovoked. The chap may lose an eye.'

'Christ. Somebody get on to his parents, will you? We don't want them finding out from the press.'

'Too late. They beat us to it.'

'Oh, hell. Anthony York, of all people. I'd rather he was gay: that at least we could defend – his own business and so on. Though if he was charged he'd have to resign. But queer-bashing . . . nobody can wave that away.'

'Shows you never can tell.'

'Chief, we have to issue some kind of statement.'

'We have to, indeed. Any ideas?'

Chapter Eighteen

'But did he proposition you in any way?'

Anthony shook his head.

'Or offer you anything?'

'No . . . yes. A card for the Gay Switchboard. He was trying to help, that's all.'

Sir John Merriman shifted his weight in discomfort. Police chairs were not designed for well-padded posteriors such as his own. His client was not being co-operative. The man seemed bowed down by shame and remorse. The lawyer longed to tell him to sit up and look him straight in the eye, as he would have to do in the magistrates' court in a couple of hours' time.

'That gives us something to work on, at least,' Sir John murmured and made a note. 'We could claim you believed he was about to molest you. Then it's self-defence, though it's a bit thin.'

'No – no.' Again Anthony shook his head.

'So what exactly do you suggest, Mr York?' An edge of sarcasm crept into his voice.

'You don't have to invent anything. In fact I'm not sure why you're here. I intend to plead guilty.'

'I shouldn't advise it.' The solicitor sighed and closed his file. 'Makes it much harder to say anything in mitigation. What is this – do you want to be punished, is that it?'

There was no reply.

'I saw it happen!'
TORY YOBBO iN GAY PUNCH-UP SCANDAL
Dramatic resignation after arrest

by *Globe* Deputy News Editor JIM BETTS

The latest scandal to rock the Tory Party exploded in the gloom of Hampstead Heath at seven o'clock last night. As darkness

descended, junior Health Minister Tony York was arrested by
police and charged with causing an affray. He spent the night in
the cells and will appear in court this morning. It is expected that
bail will be granted.

York resigned his post at midnight in a dramatic phone call to the
Prime Minister, made from Rosslyn Hill police station. He had
been in office only ten weeks. His court appearance can only add
to Roger Dickson's current troubles.

For York was chosen specially for his squeaky-clean image to replace
Derek Harrison, the flamboyant former Minister who was sacked
in the wake of the Bhadeshia scandal after allegations over his
links with the corrupt financier.

Luckily for Dickson the Commons is not sitting, though Opposition
spokesmen last night were quick to demand its recall. In the
words of Anne Malcolm, Shadow Minister for the Family, 'That
department seems to be falling apart. Is there a curse on its
incumbents? We want an inquiry. We demand to know what
the government is going to do to protect gays in this country
from yobbos like Mr York.'

The lurid prose continued on several inside pages; space was filled out
with library photographs of the ex-Minister mainly taken at the general
election beside a large head-and-shoulders shot of Betts looking suitably
solemn.

This reporter happened to be on the Heath as the incident blew up.
What exactly the new Minister was doing there in the first place
will be for him to explain, but the fight took place in a spot
notorious for homosexual pickups.

Perhaps it is significant that, only hours before, Tony York's name
had appeared on the latest list of men accused by the gay activist
group 'Outrage' of being closet homosexuals. It is not the *Globe*'s
practice, along with other responsible newspapers, to publish
unsupported smears. But in this case we believe our readers have
the right to know.

I saw it all happen. I have told police that I saw Tony York approach
a young man, later identified as 25-year-old Carl Rosenberg, an
outreach worker for the Hampstead and Highgate Health Authority.
Mr Rosenberg was in attendance in his official capacity, handing out
leaflets and free condoms. He is to be found on the Heath most
evenings. His role has been dogged by controversy. A statement
issued on his behalf accused Mr York of . . .

Jim Betts refolded the newspaper and hugged himself. There was something immensely satisfying about the demolition of yet another Tory Minister's career. He hoped the article, with its nuances, exaggerations and deliberate minor inaccuracies – he'd never heard the man called 'Tony', for example, but it sounded much more camp; nor was York a direct replacement for Harrison, but so what? – would really annoy the PM, the Chief Whip, the Party Chairman and all the other uptight party functionaries.

Serve them right. That's what happened when politicians set themselves up as guardians of public morality. That's where 'Back to Basics' got you.

Anthony York had been trouble writ large. Betts recalled with glee the look of horror on that copper's face as he, Betts, had announced the culprit's identity. A government Minister, no less. Their prisoner had been treated with kid gloves after that. One of the charmed circle. Charmed no more.

Betts picked up the phone. Pictures were on their way from the York family home showing the shocked faces of Anthony's parents. It was believed the accused would head off there after being bailed, but just in case staffers were on alert at his Battersea address and at the gateway to the House of Commons. Betts would cover the court appearance himself, though the *Globe*'s legal affairs reporter was pissed off at being elbowed aside. Two photographers were lined up, one at each exit. Even if the bleeder climbed a chimney to escape they'd get a shot of him doing it.

As Betts rubbed his hands in pleasure a face appeared around his door. 'Congratulations, Jim.' His boss was envious. 'I don't know how you do it. That's another scalp to you. And you're a key witness, too. How did you manage to be there at the right time?'

'Been keeping my eye on that berk. It was obvious he was going to do something stupid sooner or later.' Betts was laconic. He was after Thwaite's job, but did not intend to reveal too much about that, either.

Thwaite sidled inside the small office and helped himself to one of Betts's cigarettes.

'Have you figured out yet why this government seems so accident-prone? Ministers have been falling by the wayside like they've been sprayed with poison gas. Don't they realise we're watching them?'

'Well . . .' Betts pulled on his Silk Cut and sucked the smoke deeply into his lungs. These mild blends didn't have the kick cigarettes used to have. He pretended to think, but political analysis was neither his forte nor his passion. 'I suppose, once they're appointed, office is such a cocoon that they get to think they're invulnerable. And the kind of bloke who gets embroiled in politics in the first place must be a risk-taker by nature. Otherwise why would anybody bother?'

'For you, Jim, that's profound.' Thwaite teased without malice but Betts grimaced. 'There used to be a concept of public service. What about that?'

'Not any more! That's old hat. These Ministers are time-servers. Anybody wise would seek a simple job with a contract of employment and a pension. These chappies do exactly the opposite. They deliberately choose a risky environment. From this year to next they've no idea whether the government will survive or if their next step will be the dole queue. Even between elections, on average Ministers last barely two years, you know. Look at them – performing monkeys, every one. Don't tell me that's normal behaviour.'

'So give 'em half a chance and they'll act like the loonies they really are?'

'Right.' Betts had tired of the conversation. He suspected that in a subtle way he was being patronised. 'Now, if you don't mind, I've some articles to write. On what might have been going on in Mr York's peculiar mind, for example. On the gay conspiracy in Whitehall which even the Prime Minister doesn't know about – there isn't one, but there will be by the time I've finished. The other lot are worse. The country'll be overrun with homosexuals if Labour wins – teaching it will become compulsory in schools. We'll scare the pants off our good-living hetero readers and make life hot for the nation's queers for a bit. OK?'

'Fine, Jim. Nobody writes it like you do.' Thwaite kept smiling. Inwardly he shivered. He hoped he would never be the target of one of his own newspaper's campaigns.

Phone lines buzzed as MPs, deprived by the recess of their usual gossip, shared their prejudices and relief that this time some other poor fool was in the frame.

'He was being attacked. He must have been.'

'Anthony? Always so po-faced. Remember his maiden speech – all about family values.'

'It's usually that sort. Butter wouldn't melt. At least you know where you are with a Harrison.'

'Not the first time this has happened on Hampstead Heath. That young chap from the north-east. Hexham, wasn't it?'

'Yeah, but he was caught screwing. Bit different!'

'*He* said it was childish. Not what I'd call it.'

'Broad daylight, that one. Beats me why they do it.'

'God knows. Maybe they can only get it up when somebody's gawping.'

'Some of us wish we could get it up at all. What a waste.'

'You had a phone call yet?'

'Who, me? What for – character reference?'

'No – don't be daft. Who's going to take his place? There has to be somebody. That's a busy department.'

'Health, Welfare and the Family. Ghastly. I'd prefer a real job like defence or transport.'

'Well, it won't be me. I'm too outspoken for my own good. And they'll be looking for somebody absolutely whistle-clean.'

'Narrows the field, doesn't it?'

Roger Dickson waited until the dumpy woman who brought the coffee had set it down and arranged the cream jug and sugar at his elbow. As the door closed behind her he pushed a plate of biscuits towards his Secretary of State.

'Have one. It's taken me a year to persuade the kitchen that Hobnobs are not a drain on the economy.'

Ted Bampton shook his head but helped himself to coffee. He longed to light up a cigar to calm his nerves but the Prime Minister's views on smoking were too well known to defy. Although it was his Parliamentary Under-Secretary who had quit office in disgrace he had an obscure feeling that he himself was in the dock.

'So do we know what happened, Ted?'

Bampton shrugged. 'I've not spoken to him. Bloody stupid, if you ask me.'

'He had strong opinions. My office were up early this morning and have briefed me on one or two things he's said in public.'

Dickson tossed over the photocopied pages of Hansard marked with fluorescent pen. The Cabinet Minister glanced through them, blew what in less polite society might have passed for a raspberry and handed them back.

Dickson decided to rub it in. 'For example, in the debate on the Matrimonial Bill, he set himself up as a proper little Mary Whitehouse. "We should set a moral tone," he says. "I for one disapprove of many aspects of today's society." And later: "We should at all times be in the business of raising personal and moral standards."'

Bampton roused himself. 'Plenty of us would agree with those views,' he growled.

Roger could feel himself growing angry. Not only had he lost another member of his government in as yet unexplained circumstances, but the chap in charge of one of the most sensitive departments of state held similar views.

'Those, Ted, are the excuses of the fanatic through the ages. That sort of thing leads anti-abortionists in America to kill clinic workers. In the UK we've had animal rights campaigners picketing ports to save calves that would otherwise go for dog food, and putting lorry drivers in hospital as they did it. It's yet another version of the end justifying the means, don't you see?'

'No, I don't.' Bampton defended himself with some asperity. Why on earth was the Prime Minister, at this moment of all times, spouting left-wing philosophy? 'And I don't see what it's got to do with Anthony York, either.'

'Let me put it this way, then. What the bloody hell was he doing on Hampstead Heath beating up homosexuals? Was it some kind of personal crusade? Trying to clean the place up – was that it? Appointed himself a morality policeman?'

'God knows. You'd have to ask him. But it wasn't his style. He wasn't demonstrative like that. Very buttoned up. Kept himself to himself.'

'So was it a . . . a brainstorm? Had he been acting in a peculiar way lately?'

Bampton pursed his lips. 'Not exactly. But he was taking time to settle. Didn't get on with the civil servants.'

Roger raised an eyebrow. 'Be more specific. Was he having rows with them, or what?'

'Couldn't say. But he'd had a word with me, yes.'

Roger sat back. He was beginning to understand. 'So he tells you he's having difficulties. All the civil servants – or only one or two? And you, of course, were the soul of sympathy.'

Bampton shuffled uncomfortably.

'Oh, so you weren't all that sympathetic. Told him to stop snivelling and pull his socks up, did you?'

'Look, Roger, you can't nanny them the whole time.'

The Prime Minister's eyes became steely. 'What about Harrison – did you know he was in cahoots with Bhadeshia?' Bampton shook his head.

'Tell me, Ted, do you ever spend any time with your Ministers, other than the absolute minimum? Do you ever just sit and chat with them?'

'Can't see why I should. They have their work to get on with and I have mine.'

Dickson frowned. Although Bampton was several years his senior he allowed himself to sound cutting, like a headmaster with a floundering pupil.

'You've lost two Ministers in the space of a couple of months, Ted. Your department is patently not a happy place. I originally asked you here to get your suggestion on York's replacement. Before we agree any names, I must tell you that you need to try harder with your people. You're supposed to create a team – everyone pulling together. Naturally there'll be problems, personality clashes and the like. But you should know these individuals backwards, their strengths and foibles, and be able to anticipate trouble. It shouldn't hit you between the eyes. Preferably not once – and certainly not twice.'

Bampton was about to open his mouth but thought better of it. He had heard such sentiments long before as a young factory manager after a prolonged strike. In the manner of the times it had been attributed to rampant trade unionism, not to poor management. How could it be his fault if something similar occurred here too?

Dickson leaned forward. 'You have one excellent Minister left in Elaine Stalker. I hope you're looking after her better than the two you've managed to lose so far.'

Bampton reacted indignantly. 'Mrs Stalker can look after herself perfectly well. I must take issue with you. Babying grown men and women is *not* part of my job. Most of all, not her. Roger, you know my views on women MPs and the like. If you want to move her elsewhere I'd be willing.'

It was on the tip of the Prime Minister's tongue to lambast Bampton's misplaced belligerence. The unhappy expression on his Minister's face, however, suggested he had gone far enough. He murmured non-committally and moved on to the question of a substitute for York.

The exchange left him deeply uneasy. He brooded on how he might arrange to have a word with Elaine, if only to warn her.

His face was everywhere – plastered over the tabloids, particularly the *Globe*, but the *Daily Telegraph* had it prominently on the front page with an almost verbatim report of the committal procedures occupying the whole of page three. *The Times* photo was larger but its inside story smaller; it would make up for that, however, on Wednesday when Bernard Levin would thunder about the irrelevance of the doings of minor government functionaries. The *Financial Times* speculated on the effect of the resignation on interest rates. In the *Daily Mail* Linda Lee Potter blamed the parents. The *Sun* had a 'Kiss My Arse' competition adorned by Anthony's features. The *Independent* forgot all about it and the *Guardian* spelled Anthony's surname 'Yorke'.

Journalists and cameramen had tried to board the train with him, but transport police, used to football hooligans, had efficiently confined them to the platform. Some ran from carriage to carriage searching for him, pressing their noses to the windows. Anthony locked himself in the toilet cubicle. At last the train moved off and he felt it safe to emerge.

The first-class carriage was not crowded. Anthony chose the seat facing front nearest the door. He wanted to be quickly away when the train drew into Bristol. A pile of newspapers lay in front of him along with a book. For a few moments he tried to concentrate, head bowed, but the discordant noises in his head took over. He turned the paperback over and, as was his wont, stared out of the window.

The backs of houses flashed past, first in tight terraces, their roof lines dissected by firebreaks according to the law in London since the Great Fire, their narrow yards littered with bicycles, old cars and discarded rabbit hutches. Then came net-curtained older semis in the suburbs, their gardens varying from the shabbily paved over to the immaculate. As the train picked up speed through dormitory towns the houses were newer, built of red brick like skinned flesh, clustered together with minute gardens. The product of eighties greed: the bearers of negative equity. Some of those properties, Anthony reflected sadly, would represent a loss to their unlucky owners till well into the next century. From his vantage point he could see the tops of foliage turning yellow at the edges. By the time his erstwhile colleagues arrived at the annual Conference the branches would be bare.

His next appearance in court would occur on the Monday of Party Conference week. The story would be all over the press again like a mud-tide, blotting out the careful news management devised by the spin doctors, blanketing important statements, infecting the whole assembly. Thus on the Tuesday he, Anthony York, would dominate the nation's affairs, not Ted Bampton, who had planned to announce the new department's policies with a great rhetorical flourish. Before this, Ted might have merited a warm welcome and a standing ovation. Not now. Anthony slipped down a little in his seat and wished he could disappear altogether.

He could not grasp clearly what had taken place. He had not slept since his arrest but had lain awake, eyes open, staring at unfamiliar ceilings. Both body and mind felt completely numb as if dosed with an anaesthetic which had not yet worn off. He wondered dully whether, when it did, he would feel a resurgence of the old frantic worries. Churchill had known what he'd called 'black dog', but had emerged each time full of bounce and optimism. That was a kind of manic depression well recognised among great men, who were spurred on to acts of huge achievement as if fearful that their next snake-filled pit could be their last. Anthony doubted whether he himself would ever feel anything but listless again.

In which case, what was he good for? His had been the shortest ministerial tenure in living history; he had made himself a laughing stock. He would never achieve high office. The best he could expect, years on, might be a vice-chairmanship of the party – and even that would produce sniggers. More immediate considerations intruded. The thought of the hate mail which would flood in left him near despair. Nor could he consider running advice bureaux for months yet, if ever. If he could not summon up the courage and vitality to tackle the most mundane tasks for his constituents, could he continue as an MP?

How limited his activities would have to become. It occurred to Anthony bitterly that never again could he be the first to leap to help someone in difficulties: he would hesitate even to assist somebody across the road, for fear of the sentence beginning, 'Aren't you . . .?' The nightmare would not be over with his sentence; it would have just started.

'Good afternoon, ladies and gentlemen. The buffet is now open for tea, coffee, hot chocolate, a selection of beers, wines and soft drinks, sandwiches . . . The buffet car is situated towards the front of the train between first and second class.'

The twanging West Country accent reminded Anthony that he had eaten nothing since breakfast in the cells. His appetite then had been non-existent but the hours since and the gently rocking motion combined to make him almost hungry. He fumbled in his pocket for coins and rose from his seat.

The moment he arrived in the narrow corridor of the buffet car he knew it was a mistake. Four large men in T-shirts and donkey jackets were leaning on the bar cradling beer cans and chatting to the young steward. Anthony surmised from the cement dust on their clothes and hands that they were construction workers. From their manner it appeared they had been drinking for some time. As he entered the men turned around curiously.

'Well, what 'ave we 'ere?'

'City slicker, don't touch, Harry. No offence, mate.'

'Maybe 'e'll buy us a drink.'

The four looked at him hopefully. Anthony coloured but ignored them. He gestured to the steward. 'A coffee, white, please. And what sandwiches do you have?'

A hoot of laughter greeted him. 'Wot *send*-witches do you *heff*. Love it!' The leader took a step forward. 'Well, mate, don't, then. We're on our way home – just finished a big job at Staples Corner. Two months early so we've big bonuses coming. In a mood to celebrate. So wotcha name, then?'

It was clear the men expected him to spend his journey at the bar like themselves. The steward bent his head and muttered his wares, then handed over a ham sandwich made in a factory the day before and a plastic cup of coffee.

One of the men was examining Anthony carefully. He reached into the back of his jeans and brought out a rolled-up newspaper. He peered again at Anthony, then unfolded it and nudged his neighbour, who suddenly straightened and pointed.

'Ooh, that's right. You know you're a dead ringer for that politician, this one 'ere? That raving queer wot got arrested wiv 'is finger up somebody's bum. You're not 'im, are yer?'

In his haste Anthony nearly dropped the coffee. Stuttering excuses he stumbled out of the buffet car and back to his seat. After a moment, to his horror, the door slid open and four faces appeared above him.

'It is. Blimey.'

'Don't touch. 'E's probably got a disease.'

'Don't fancy that, do you?'

'Should be put in prison. They all should.'

'Cut it off!'

'Probably 'asn't got one!'

This last sally was greeted with raucous laughter which caught the attention of the other occupants of the first-class carriage. Once it was realised that the banter came from four solid-looking drunks, discretion became the better part of valour. Heads slipped behind newspapers. No one would come to his aid.

Anthony found himself breathing rapidly. If he acknowledged his tormentors that would only encourage them. If he pretended they did not exist that might goad them further. He began to feel apprehensive. What might they do, on a train with open carriages? He looked up: he could reach the emergency handle. But that would bring the train to a screeching halt and attract precisely the kind of official censure he was desperate to avoid. The louts would claim they were having a harmless bit of fun. Given his new reputation, nobody would believe his version. He might even face further charges.

Sticks and stones. The worst they could do was gabble obscenities. Those he could and should ignore. Easier said than done.

Anthony gagged. The sandwich was cold, the ham slimy. In his ear the builder was crooning a love song, rolling his eyes to the suggestive lyrics. Anthony kept his eyes fixed firmly forward but prayed inwardly. My God, was it always going to be like this – a target for public ridicule, as if he had no feelings left? It had taken John Profumo thirty years' hard labour to recover his reputation – but then he had been a Cabinet Minister and had lied to the House, neither of which was true of Anthony. Minor miscreants such as Keith Best or Eric Cockeram, who had quit Westminster after buying more privatisation shares than the law allowed, had vanished from sight. But infamy for an incident like his own would last a lifetime.

He shoved the remaining sandwich back in its plastic wrapper and finished the coffee. It would not do. He should not be considering merely the impact of his action on the outside world, or of its reaction to him. He was a self-starter. He had his own code. Sooner or later he would have to come to terms with what he had done. His sternest judge would be himself. Judge, jury. And executioner.

The continued commotion had at last brought the senior guard, a small dark man with a pronounced accent.

'Now then, gentlemen! This is the first-class section. May I see your tickets, *please*.'

With great deliberation he examined each ticket. Everyone knew what was coming next.

'You must return to your seats. You are not supposed to be in here. They're not bothering you, are they, sir?'

Anthony did not reply but the trembling of his hand on the table

320

was sufficient. The conductor moved swiftly to shoo the men out. A muffled conversation and much chortling could be heard behind him in the corridor. Then the door swished open once more.

'Ahem!' The conductor adjusted his cap and pulled out a notebook. 'Mr Anthony York, is it? Yes. I've been reading about you. Would you be so kind as to give me your autograph?'

At the station his parents waited, his father poker-faced and gaunt, his mother wringing her hands and crying. He had told them not to come, that he would take a taxi, but the imperative of family duty had overcome their fears. Their presence made him feel grateful. Someone would stand by him, even though there was no chance of their understanding what had happened, or why.

His heart sank. The press were also present in droves – not only the locals, whom he recognised from better days and who approached apologetically. Stringers and freelances galore, their camera flash-bulbs popping, mini-recorders at the ready, faces hard, scrambled for a foothold on the platform. Three television crews, the sound booms swinging wildly overhead, cameramen with portables on shoulders and blind to everyone else, elbowed, shoved and trod on feet. The naïvety of the station manager, or maybe a private willingness to see a criminal humiliated, had permitted this invasion. Anthony stopped, appalled, at the phalanx of bodies which barred his way.

Two young women from rival radio stations leapt at him and shoved microphones under his chin.

'Mr York! Mr York! Have you any comment to make?'

'What were you doing . . .?'

'Are you a homosexual . . .?'

'What do you say to the remarks of John Redwood . . .?'

Anthony had no idea what Mr Redwood might have said and was unsure that his activities were any of the man's business. Mouth set, he shouldered his way through, parents in tow, aware that the following day's photographs would show him scowling and bitter.

Someone pulled at his sleeve and would not let go. He swung brusquely around. A leering face thrust itself into his.

'Going to land a punch on me too, were you? Go on, then. Pete, you got the camera ready?'

*　　*　　*

321

They were everywhere – hanging over the gate to the house, in a neighbour's drive. Several scruffy cars in the pub car park revved and made to follow as his father drove past.

'We have spoken to the local police and have a number to call if it gets too intrusive. They were helpful.' His father manoeuvred around the pressmen and scraped the side of the car against the gatepost. Flash-bulbs popped. 'Damnation.'

'They'll give up eventually.' Anthony could think of nothing else to say. In a family in which real discussions never took place conversation was limited to details. 'They'll find somebody else to harass.'

Behind him his mother sobbed once, then gulped, caught her husband's glance in the mirror and buried her mouth in a handkerchief. Mr York sped up the drive and parked with a scrunch of gravel.

In a few moments the three stood in the hallway, removing coats and shuffling their feet. No words were spoken. With a look of reproach his mother handed him a pile of messages in her meticulous handwriting: she had not known to take the phone off the hook. Now it began to ring shrilly. Anthony suddenly felt exhausted, picked up his bag and headed for his room.

'You all right, Elaine?'

'Oh, Betty. Thanks for calling. Yes, I'm OK. For once it's not my name in the papers.'

'I feel sorry for the poor bastard. Whatever he's done, trial by press is far worse.'

Elaine agreed wholeheartedly. Should she ever face a similar inquisition, Betty Horrocks as chairman of her Conservative Association would be the first person approached for a comment. The wealthy widow held a place both of authority and of affection in Elaine's life. As George's sister-in-law she was almost family, though in a crisis Betty would revert to her public role as Elaine's most prominent supporter. Both sensed that this phone call could be a kind of rehearsal, a search for the right form of words. Both hoped the practice would never be needed.

'He was shaping up to be a very good Minister,' said Elaine. 'It's such a shame. Terrible timing too.'

Betty grunted. 'There's never a good time. Will you be affected?'

'Well – it looks as if the post may be left vacant for a while. No appointment's been made. We've no legislation coming up this year and the budgets are under control. So it may be just me and Ted working together.'

'That good news or bad?'

Elaine considered. 'Good, in that I'll carry more responsibility. Bad, in that I'll have more work to do! But I can have a new PPS. It's my choice and I need someone I like and trust. I think I'll ask Fred Laidlaw to do it. He's a decent lad, keen and capable but with a lot to learn.'

'He's not gay, too, is he, Elaine? I don't want to sound suspicious, but – '

Elaine laughed heartily. 'Oh, no, Betty. Fred's not gay.'

A couple of weeks passed; press interest waned. Anthony found he could breathe more easily, provided he kept to the house and garden. He had tried a walk further afield but had been startled by a cameraman who jumped at him out of nowhere. The postwoman scuttled up the path, shoved dozens of letters scrappily through the box and pushed off again as fast as her legs could carry her. Many of the missives were written on green paper, the handwriting ill formed and ignorant. Anthony threw them unread into the fire.

A former university woman acquaintance was reported in the *Sunday Sport* as saying he was sexually inexperienced and incompetent. He could barely remember her and wondered how much she had been paid to utter the words put into her mouth. His friends seemed to have gone to ground except for Lachlan, who, badgered by Betts, had angrily informed the world that his cousin was a far better man than any of his detractors. Fred had kept his head down, no doubt embarrassed at his unexpected good fortune, which Anthony did not begrudge him. Nobody else had a word to say in his defence.

Sir John had arrived in a limousine, entered the hallway ponderously and mumbled apologies to Mrs York, like a doctor at a house where a patient had died. All was well for the forthcoming court appearance. It would be brief. A conditional discharge, a fine, damages were mentioned. The young man, Mr Rosenberg, had recovered and was trying to persuade the police not to press charges: it was of course too late for that, but his attitude would count. Indeed, he was willing to come privately and talk, if that would help. Chastened by such forgiveness Anthony shook his head.

Yet he absolutely did not want to appear in court. The formality and inevitability of the process appalled him. To hear the charges read out, the bald description of what had taken place, would raise once again the questions he had so far successfully evaded. How could he face with equanimity those accusers – the beard and spectacles, the burly policeman – and the grey figure with the mauve badge, seated like a ghost in the public gallery? And, worse, the media, the commentators, the gay campaigners harrying him to come out – each demanded of him something he could not give: an account of himself which made sense.

Then there was his own Conservative Association. Reassured by his mother that Mr York was unwell and could not appear for a while, the officers had postponed the post-mortem until the day after sentence. He would then be obliged to respond. It would be like a second trial, but without the dry ritual of the criminal court. At the executive committee meeting, if strong words were needed they would be said. His dishonour would be dissected in minute detail. He wondered if there was some way he might refuse to come, then realised that such discourtesy would simply compound his crime in their eyes. He had no choice, and no words to put them off. His fate would be in their hands.

Yet he had no fight with them; indeed, he hardly knew them. He hardly knew anybody. Not that he wanted to talk. On the contrary. In the weeks since the events his mind had been like a great lake, with nothing as far as the eye could see, no distinguishing feature, the surface by turns black or purple or green but entirely murky and impenetrable. He preferred to keep it that way. The only possibility of calm lay in floating motionless on the surface and resolutely refusing conscious thought.

But the court case entailed his emergence in public once more. There was no way it could be postponed. He would become a public victim all over again – fresh meat to be thrown to the hounds. The sound of weeping began to hum inside his head, as it had at Battersea when the tension had begun to mount, when Karen had found him. As the days passed Anthony found himself increasingly agitated. It was not to be faced. It was not.

He had taken several tablets but their effect was transitory. He slept fitfully and when he awoke it was dark and quiet. He could not remember dreaming, but this time he found himself not in the wind-swept lane nor on the Heath as he had feared but in his own room. It was not raining, nor windy. The silence seemed almost welcoming. The whimpers in his head were still there but fainter. His mind was clear, peaceful.

He rose, pulled on a dressing gown and went over to the bedroom window. Outside all was still. The sky was free of clouds. A bright half-moon cast shadows as his eyes adjusted. The black silhouettes of trees bowed gracefully like old friends.

He ought to take another pill and go back to bed. With a glass of whisky – that would make the drug work more quickly. The alcohol was downstairs. His mother would not allow him to carry a bottle to his bedroom: to her, imbibing in company was just about acceptable but to drink alone in his current state of mind would be dangerous.

He tiptoed down the stairs, avoiding the step which squeaked, entered the shrouded drawing room, found the cupboard without turning on the light and poured himself a finger of spirits. His nocturnal wanderings amused him. Deceiving his mother was a game. That was foolish: nothing that had occurred had been her fault. He drained the glass and poured another, larger this time.

The tension in the house was dreadful; his parents' unhappy faces oppressed him deeply. It was obvious he could not stay with them much longer. His only other home was in Battersea and that would mean a return to London, to neighbours who would stare and murmur, or not know what to say to him. What could he do? Where could he go? The scenes in the train and on the station haunted him. He gripped the glass to stop himself trembling, then examined his fingers with curiosity, turning his hand this way and that. The reporter had been right: he had wanted to lash out, longed to see another face crumple beneath his fist. Was that to be his response from here onwards – violence, instead of the carefully modulated argument which had been his stock in trade? Whom would he hit next? A constituent? A man in the pub? His father?

A statement would have to be crafted soon ready for the court. Why had he done it? The question had been put to him so many times but he was still at a loss to answer. How could he explain that he'd been fighting off ghosts? They'd think he was mad. Perhaps he was.

The whisky was soothing and seemed to guarantee that the horrors could be kept at bay. The noise in his head was no louder. He poured another drink and began to pace the room. One glass-fronted cupboard held books, another pieces of his mother's Crown Derby, a third his father's fishing trophies. Anthony half smiled as he peered at the medals and cups. As a small boy he had sat on the river bank and watched in admiration as his father fiddled with lines, flies and bait, then rose, cast and settled down to wait patiently for hours on end. The water was deep down by the weir. His memory told him vaguely that there had been some conversation between them, desultory perhaps, but still a form of communication. He could not remember what they had talked about.

The room seemed stuffy. It was still two hours before dawn. A stroll down the garden to the length of river which edged it would be pleasant. He might see a kingfisher as it got light. He could take the bottle with him and finish it there. That wouldn't be possible in daylight – some snapper on the far bank might be waiting with a telephoto lens. How unusual, to go for a walk without being molested. He chuckled grimly. It seemed he had become a thing of the night.

Anthony opened the back door softly and tiptoed slowly out, shutting it behind him. To his own surprise he no longer felt hostile to the press: they had a job to do; it was his own fault if he had given them something to write about.

He was angry with himself for being so stupid. Perhaps he should have taken up Elaine's invitation to talk further, for she at least had been kind to him. He was not impressed with Bampton. Had the man listened to his efforts to ask for help and responded, none of this might have happened; but he, Anthony, must take responsibility for his own actions and not blame others. In any moral code that had ever made sense to him, he was the master of his own fate.

He sat down by the river bank and lifted the bottle to his lips. A sudden plop in the water startled him, but it was only a foraging night animal. In a distant tree an owl hooted. A flutter above his head may have been a bat investigating him as an intruder. He waved it sleepily away.

He trailed a finger in the black water. Its ripples intrigued him; so simple a matter, so complex and uncontrollable. The moon moved behind a cloud and it suddenly became darker. He liked it like that. He did not want it to get light again, ever.

The water lapped lazily at his feet. In its surface he could see stars reflected. Their perfection had no end; their existence was pure, inanimate, without thought or conscience. How very different from his own life, so muddied with confusion and weakness. Was the human state always to be thus – to understand what should be, but never to have the capacity to achieve it? To want something, and in wanting to know for certain that he could only aspire, never attain? He understood happiness, he was sure. But he had never felt it, never had it in his grasp. And now he never would.

The bottle was nearly empty. The sky had begun to lighten, a fraction, in the east. It would be daytime soon, with a return to all the misery, the torture of being. It would be better to stay here.

Here. In the quiet, alone but for the reeds and the trees which could not think or comment or condemn, where nobody and nothing cared who he was, or what he had done. Here. Now.

Chapter Nineteen

For most significant events the inhabitants of the Palace of Westminster have a standard response. Marriage was greeted with teasing, sometimes with concern, even commiseration: a man must marry, though preferably only once if he were to keep his constituency officers content. Births, frequent among the younger Members, met with admiration that a fresh dynasty was under way. It would have been bad manners to ask such a parent when, if ever, the family might spend time together, unless of course the Member happened to be female.

Death was different. The immediate reaction of most MPs was relief that it wasn't their own; given the punishing effect of long hours and open bars, subsidised restaurants and excessive stress, this response was understandable. Diaries would be consulted for attendance at funerals and memorial services, secretaries instructed to send floral tributes. In the Commons Library the obituary pages of *The Times* and *Telegraph* would rustle, especially now that their writers were so deliciously frank. Then the Honourable Members would reach for the nearest copy of *The Times Guide to the House of Commons* to check the most important fact about any departed colleague: the size of his majority and the vulnerability of his seat.

'We'll have to attend, of course.'

Bampton spoke gruffly and shuffled his feet. Elaine nodded, her face miserable.

Nearby other figures milled gloomily in Members' Lobby. It was the first day back. The Party Conference had been overshadowed by the tragic news that the body of promising young junior Minister Anthony York had been found drowned in the river at the bottom of his parents' garden. He had left no note. There were no signs of a struggle. The post-mortem had revealed no congenital heart disease or other problems which might have precipitated a collapse. That the victim had been drinking heavily was suppressed for the sake of his family.

Of course it was *possible* that Anthony might have taken his own life, but that would have been the unhappiest conclusion. Those who chose to commit suicide tended to do it more brutally, as if to punish all who remained as well as making the outcome quite certain. They left behind not bewilderment but guilt. Nobody wanted that. Thus the coroner was likely to return an open verdict, which would satisfy no one but suit many.

The charges against Anthony were set aside. Carl Rosenberg tried to contact the Yorks to express his grief but they would not respond. Their postbag was too full of virulent letters gloating that their only son was dead.

A memorial service of some kind had, however, to be arranged. St Margaret's Westminster, the parish church of the House of Commons, was duly booked and the Speaker would attend. Tickets could be obtained from the Speaker's trainbearer's office. The service would be conducted by the Speaker's chaplain, as it was for all MPs. Since it had become known that Anthony had been in some kind of dispute with his boss Ted Bampton shortly before his death, it was felt wiser that the lesson should be read not by Bampton but by the Chief Whip.

'I liked him very much. I shall miss him.' Elaine spoke quietly. Bampton, mindful of the Prime Minister's dressing-down, searched for appropriate words but could find none.

The pair were joined by Derek Harrison, tanned and fit as if he had enjoyed a long lazy summer. 'Pity you didn't like him a bit more, Elaine,' he remarked breezily. 'Attractive single woman like you. Oh, I know he was a bit on the young side, but it might have avoided a lot of trouble, mightn't it?'

Elaine whirled around in fury. 'You are such a shit, Derek.'

Harrison laughed and wagged a finger. 'Now, now. You should be nice to me, Elaine. I'm standing in the '22 Committee elections next week. I'm told I've every chance.'

The notion of Derek officially representing 250 backbenchers and thus wielding considerable influence over Ministers through innuendo and intimidation did not improve the thoughts flowing through Elaine's brain. She made herself smile at him. 'You have a big following, have you?'

'I think so. Enough.' Harrison returned her smile confidently. 'I shall take a particular interest in the affairs of the department, naturally. Willing to support you in every way, my dear Elaine.'

* * *

Roger Dickson ran his eye down the densely typed paragraphs and frowned. He tapped a Biro on page four, then addressed the handful of occupants in the Cabinet Room.

'Another one. We really could do without these cases. Murder of an innocent member of the public by a deranged man who should years ago have been locked up, followed by a report by a distinguished QC which blames gaps in the government's community care policy. Everyone knew the killer was dangerous, he says, but nobody took effective action. Some of the so-called professionals involved were clearly blithering idiots. He seems to think we can be held responsible for every clinical decision taken in our name. Unfortunately, that's the public's view too.'

The full Cabinet was not present. Instead the DHWF team sat opposite: Bampton, Elaine and a nervous Fred. Civil servants had been excluded but the politicians were not alone. Beside the Prime Minister sat an earnest young man from the Number 10 Policy Unit and a new junior secretary called Alice, who discreetly took notes but said not a word.

'They're hoping to use the story to show that we don't spend enough,' Bampton growled. He tried to sound belligerent but Anthony's death overlaid everything. In the middle of all this misery party politics felt like a dirty trick.

'Of course they are. What do you propose to do to counter their argument?' Dickson's voice was neutral but his eyes were hard. He avoided looking at Elaine.

Bampton produced a sheet of paper. 'I've prepared a letter to send to parliamentary colleagues. It will explain that the total amount available nationally for social services spending, including community care, has almost doubled from three point six billion pounds a year three years ago, to six point four billion in the current year. Even allowing for inflation that's nearly a fifty per cent increase. Much more rapid growth than any other area of local authority spending.'

Elaine added ruefully, 'This was supposed to be a cheaper option as well as better. It was touted as saving millions compared with the cost of those dirty old hospitals. Hasn't turned out that way.'

The policy adviser agreed. His task was to add a few suitably defensive lines to the Treasury's Weekly Brief for Ministers. 'It's the local councils which make most noise. They run the community care programme, not us. We give them the money, ring-fenced so it can't be spent on anything else, but still they demand more. Aren't they persuaded?'

'They're mostly Labour. Or Liberal Democrat,' Bampton observed sarcastically. Advisers were wet behind the ears these days. 'That's what happens when one party's been in power nationally for ages: the other side wins everything else. There *aren't* any councils under our control with these responsibilities – except Westminster and Wandsworth, plus Buckinghamshire, which we tried to abolish.'

That gave pause for thought. Fred ventured what seemed to him the obvious question. 'I don't suppose there *is* any more money . . . ?'

'Now you sound like one of them, not one of us,' Roger chided. 'There's usually a bob or two in the pot, Fred, but this year it's gone to keep Ulster Members sweet, to subsidise franchisees of private railway services and to pay off all those gays and lesbians we sacked from the armed forces. It's called choosing priorities.'

Bampton snorted as Fred subsided. The younger man was puzzled. Nobody seemed to be 'choosing' anything. Someone decided the budgets, but if the studiously blank faces around the table were correct it wasn't anyone present. If not them, then who?

Roger pressed his fingers together. 'The inquiry chairman wants changes in the law. We also face calls for compulsory medication for those outside hospital. Is any of this feasible?'

'In the simple sense that we could get legislation through the Commons, yes,' replied Bampton, for whom the idea of tedious evenings guiding a complex new bill through its committee stages did not appeal one bit. 'But what difference would it make? We have the power now to compel the barmy to accept medication but in practical terms we have to incarcerate them to do it. Since we don't have too many spare places, and few where a violent patient could safely be housed, it's a bit pointless.'

'I hate to feel there's nothing we can do,' Roger mused. 'Elaine, any ideas?'

It was on the tip of Elaine's tongue to suggest bluntly that, if their analysis was correct, further psychiatric hospital closures should be halted and plans made to open fresh units as a matter of urgency. More staff both inside and outside the hospitals would also be useful. But that was not how tricky issues were handled. It would help if such radical and obvious proposals could be made not by a single individual such as herself but by a powerful group. The question shifted, therefore, to how such a group might be brought into existence.

'We could try the usual old chestnut,' she offered. 'Since an inquiry has already taken place, and indeed it's not the first, perhaps we should set up a committee. A working party of Ministers if you like, Prime Minister.'

'A Cabinet committee would carry more weight. I was thinking on the same lines.' Roger sensed that Elaine might have worked out some answers. 'The Lord President will chair it and you'll be a member, Ted. We'd better have the Financial Secretary to the Treasury too, to keep you in line. My office will put out a press release. You can have *carte blanche* to investigate the problem of these roving maniacs terrorising our citizens. Except that I'd prefer to manage without changes in the law, and – '

'And?' Ted prompted him with a half-smile. He could guess what was next.

'And there's no more money. Not a penny. Happy?'

Dr Lachlan McDonald wrinkled his nose at the reek of tobacco, vinegar and unwashed bodies. Under his feet the carpet was grubby and suspiciously damp. The stuffing spilled out of the armchair, horsehair smelling of mould and decay. He wondered what state the toilet might be in and decided to wait.

The communal lounge of the hostel at Jeffrey's Road, Lambeth, was not his idea of the finest consulting rooms, but as a conscientious practitioner it was his duty (and part of his training) to visit his charges wherever they lived. This was particularly true when the question at issue was whether the individual had adapted well to circumstances beyond the hospital and was ready for discharge.

Lachlan observed with approval that the man sitting opposite him was the cleanest object in the room. He scrutinised the dark blue blazer, grey slacks, shirt and tie for signs of wear or discoloration but could find none. Only the tobacco-stained fingertips revealed other obsessions, though the man was not smoking now.

'Well, Graham, you seem to be doing well. You certainly look fine.'

'Thank you, doctor. Keeping up appearances matters. It all helps with the rehabilitation.' Dunn spoke as if choosing his words with care. He avoided the familiarity which those in authority so readily, and infuriatingly, assumed with him.

'The community psychiatric nurse comes in regularly? You've been getting your injections?'

Dunn shifted. 'I have, but they make me a bit dozy. Now that I'm much better I'd prefer something lighter.'

Lachlan consulted the notes. 'Yes, I thought that might be the case. I brought you some tablets which you might like to try. But you must take them regularly, or you run the risk of a relapse.' He handed over a small bottle and explained the medication.

Dunn listened and nodded slowly. After so many years he reckoned he knew more about the different treatments, their power and their side effects, than the medics. Chemical straitjackets, most of them, and nasty in their own right – people got addicted, even died taking them. But it was unwise to reveal the extent of his knowledge. Doctors hated competition.

'Do you have any long-term plans, Graham?' Lachlan asked kindly. It was hard to believe that the mild, pleasant person in the scruffy armchair had been accused of several knifings when in a violent rage, or that he had been described by one police officer as 'very dangerous'. It was too easy to label patients early on, then fail to recognise a successful recovery under way.

'I think I'll stay here for a while. It isn't the nicest place, but at least I'm close to people who know me. I have a little money and I'm looking for part-time work that won't affect my benefits. I've stopped smoking – well, almost. I'm going to classes to get fit and I've lost some weight. It's one day at a time, isn't it?'

Lachlan suppressed the suspicion that this recipe sounded a little too pat. Mental patients were often cunning. Dunn's assessments showed he was of normal intelligence and could be highly plausible. On the other hand, it would be folly to put a willing person off. He was prepared to give Dunn the benefit of the doubt, in the absence of any evidence to the contrary. Anyway, he could not hang around to probe more deeply: Anthony's memorial service was due to start in an hour. He smiled encouragingly. 'Keep fit? Where?'

Dunn shrugged as if self-deprecating. 'Oh, I do Tai-kwondo. No, don't worry. It's just self-defence stuff – nothing aggressive, but I enjoy it. In Battersea.'

'You'll be finding yourself a girlfriend next.'

Dunn's eyes flickered but he kept his head down. 'Yes, doctor. A good idea. I might well do that.'

He began to rub his hands together in that old compulsive gesture. Then he stopped himself, and laughed softly.

Elaine was shown to her place, two rows from the front. On one side of her Bampton slumped, a hymn-book unopened in his hand. On the other Karen, neatly dressed in a black suit, was bolt upright and pale. Across the aisle sat Fred, looking older, with other members of Anthony's Commons set.

Before her were ranged the family, backs bowed. His sister Harriet, who resembled her mother rather than Anthony, had two big-eyed children and a husband in tow. Aunts and a grandmother huddled together. At the first notes of the organ, as the Yorks settled into their pews, whispers from those nearby noted the resemblance between Anthony York and his father and murmured at the grief of his mother. From under a black velvet hat her grey hair straggled, untended.

There was no coffin. The remains had been cremated in a ceremony two days before attended only by close relatives. The press had been deliberately misled as to the time and place and had turned up to find an empty churchyard. The ashes would be scattered in the meadows he had loved. There would be no stone, no plaque.

Elaine blew her nose and glanced around. The Prime Minister was not present, but was represented by the Chief Whip. Only for a more senior Minister, or a particular personal friend, would Dickson make time to come. Elaine wondered whether, had it been her, he would have attended. Would the mask have slipped long enough to reveal that he knew her and cared for her? With a slight shake of her head she dismissed such notions. It was wiser not to speculate.

The church was full; plenty of anonymous well-wishers had turned up, including a gaggle of leather-jacketed bikers, whose shambling arrival produced jibes about Anthony's secret vices. Patiently it was explained that he had helped a motorbike club faced with complaints about noise; they had as much right as anyone else to pay their respects. Elaine surmised that others included representatives from the constituency and from charities and causes with which Anthony had been associated. And, anxious not to cause any offence, the bearded health worker he had attacked slid quietly into a seat at the back.

Without the co-operation of the parents the chaplain had been at a loss to devise a suitable service. He did not know the dead man personally. That a lesson might be driven home had not, however, escaped him.

'Deliver me from all mine offences: and make me not a rebuke to the foolish' came the rolling tones.

The congregation sighed and looked down. It might be Psalm 39, Elaine reflected resentfully, but these were hardly words of comfort. She felt unutterably sad.

There was a rustle in front as one of the family moved forward. The young man stood facing the worshippers for a moment as if in prayer.

'That's Lachlan,' Karen whispered. The American accent when it came lent breadth and dignity to his address.

'Anthony was my cousin, and my friend. He was, in any terms that make sense, an honourable man. He believed in service, he believed in duty . . .'

As he spoke, the man he described came back with a rush to everyone present. Elaine gave up any attempt at self-control and wept. Beside her, tears glistened on Karen's cheeks. Mother and daughter clasped hands tightly.

Lachlan moved back to his seat. The organ began to rumble for the final hymn. The worshippers rose for the last time.

> Dear Lord and Father of mankind
> Forgive our foolish ways!
> Re-clothe us in our rightful mind,
> In purer lives thy service find . . .

They didn't come much purer than Anthony, Elaine thought savagely. That was the trouble. She had the distinct sensation of Anthony's presence, sombre and cool, deploring with his friends both the tragedy and its causes. If she turned around he would be standing there in his dark coat, staring ahead. He had let himself down. He died because he set himself standards that were too high, impossible for him to reach. His death was an accident, no matter what happened exactly.

> . . . Where Jesus knelt to share with thee
> The silence of eternity,
> Interpreted by love . . .

The silence of eternity. Never to speak, or be heard. Never again to explain or justify or persuade. Never to communicate: that meant for MPs like herself and Anthony, Bampton and Roger, nothing, the end of existence, for ever. She was certain Anthony never wanted that.

The last verse: she could not join in any more. Around her voices soared, high and floating.

> Breathe through the hearts of our desire
> Thy coolness and thy balm
> Let sense be dumb, let flesh retire;
> Speak through the earthquake, wind and fire,
> O still small voice of calm,
> O still small voice . . .

The mourners came outside into winter sunshine and stood about hesitantly. With Karen beside her Elaine paid her respects to the family, then lingered. She had an obligation not only as Anthony's closest colleague but as a recognisable presence to acknowledge the shy greetings of strangers. A few words were exchanged with the bikers, who trudged off towards their parked machines pursued by photographers. It was a relief to hear a familiar voice.

'Tragic business all round.'

'Hello, Betty. What are you doing here?'

Betty Horrocks pulled her fur-collared black coat closer around her. In her hat with its tiny veil and the discreet diamond brooch she looked correct and dignified. 'Known the family for years. Mrs York's some kind of second cousin by marriage. Anyway, my curiosity overcame me; and I thought maybe you and Karen could use a little support too.'

'Thank you. You're right. I feel so horribly guilty about the whole thing. If only he had asked for help – if we had responded – he might still be alive.'

'If only we had known about his old troubles.'

'*We did.*'

Both Karen and Elaine had spoken together. The three women stared at each other in surprise. Elaine took the lead. 'I knew he had a history of mental instability. He told me. But that doesn't mean he was about to go off the rails again. And, though I tried to get him to talk, after the summer he clammed up. I wish now I'd tried harder.'

'And I knew he was having problems with . . . personal relationships,' Karen continued cagily. There were too many journalists around to speak openly. 'He was a mixed-up guy. I wish I'd sat him down and got him to relax and confide. Or asked Lachlan for help. God, what a mess.'

Across the square Big Ben began its long peal. It was twelve noon. Elaine kissed Betty and gave Karen a hug.

'I must go. I've a speech to write about our wonderful mental illness policies. The temptation to mention Anthony in it is strong, but perhaps I'd better not.'

She walked quickly away.

Betty watched her retreating figure, then turned to Karen.

'Your mother's looking tired. Working too hard, probably, though with the upheavals in that department it's hardly surprising. The place seems jinxed.'

'There's nothing to prevent her overdoing it now,' Karen mused. 'I mean, when I was at home, and Dad, she *had* to stop sometimes.

But now she's on her own . . .' She hesitated. It occurred to her that Betty might be reluctant to touch on the subject for fear of hurting her feelings. She took the plunge. 'What Mum needs is a man.'

Betty chuckled. 'She's got one. My brother-in-law. He's quite keen on her.'

'George? Yes, I know about him. Been going on over a year now, hasn't it? What's he like?'

'Haven't you met him? Goodness, aren't they a pair of dark horses? You should. After all, if they do get together he could end up as your stepfather.'

The shocked expression on Karen's face made the older woman pause. She laid a hand on the girl's arm. 'How would you feel?'

'I . . . I don't know. To be honest, I'd never thought about anything like that. It's not because I'm so close to Dad – I'm not. He's so wrapped up in his new family that I hardly figure, but I don't resent it. I suppose it's simply that the idea is so new.'

Betty's practical nature reasserted itself. 'Then you should get to know George. If he's the right man for your mother you'll like him. Leave it to me.'

Slightly shaken, Karen laughed. 'Betty, you're a wicked old matchmaker.' But she put her arm round her and gave her a cuddle. Betty as a step-auntie was a comforting thought.

Fred was hovering. Betty took the hint and after exchanging a few polite words with the young MP headed for a taxi.

'I'd like to offer you my arm, Karen, but everybody would notice,' Fred observed wryly. 'You busy, or can we walk somewhere? The moment I go back inside I have to start being official again, and I don't feel like it just yet.'

Her failure to help Anthony still oppressed her. Karen realised that she would never again dismiss appeals from friends so casually. 'Sure,' she responded easily. 'Let's go along the Embankment towards Cleopatra's Needle. If we're careful we can avoid the press – they've plenty of material for tomorrow's papers.'

The two strolled quietly, without touching, away from the church and crossed Parliament Square near the House of Commons car park. They walked up Westminster Bridge Road by the new Tube station, then left at the top, past the landing stage which in summer would be swarming with tourists. As Westminster receded behind them Fred glanced quickly about, then slipped Karen's arm through his own.

He had expected to reflect with her over Anthony's death, and what might have been in their friend's mind at the time. He started to share the Lobby gossip about what exactly the chap had been doing on the Heath, but Karen was not interested and shook her head. Nothing whatever in her make-up permitted any levity about Anthony's death; it seemed to her dreadful that anybody could make jokes out of it, or any of the events that led up to it. She seemed preoccupied and troubled.

Fred switched to another subject. Anthony's will, recently published, had shown him to be relatively wealthy. Apart from small bequests, his parents would receive everything. The ownership of the house was an issue for them both.

'I think I'll try to buy it – his people might give me a reasonable price. If they're difficult I'll have to go elsewhere. A parliamentary salary doesn't run to properties in Battersea, I'm afraid.'

'We may have to move, then.' Karen tucked her scarf in more closely against the wind. She chose a stone bench and sat down, with Fred huddled up beside her. 'Lachlan will be going home before long, so he doesn't count. I doubt if the Yorks will take any action until he's gone. You'll be OK. That leaves me.'

There was silence. Fred bit his lip. What he planned to say weighed heavily on him. The words he had rehearsed seemed utterly inadequate: once more, as so often with Karen, he feared he would most probably make a complete fool of himself.

On the river a barge laden with rusty containers wallowed sluggishly as it headed for Tilbury. Once this part of the Thames had been solid with traffic, but relatively little now came this far. The rumble of cars along the Embankment provided a protective barrier to their conversation and created an illusion of privacy. Behind them fractious children in quilted jackets were being propelled along by tired mothers. Opposite sat the concrete monstrosities of the National Theatre, Hayward Gallery and the Museum of the Moving Image, depressing lumps of tasteless grey concrete. On the bridge to his right a solitary male figure walked steadily, head down against the wind. In St Thomas's Hospital neon was ablaze through every window, as ever; somewhere inside under those lights, cancer was being excised, a blood transfusion was under way, a brain tumour had been diagnosed. Life went on, and death, whether Fred opened his mouth to speak or not.

He moved closer and took Karen's hand. 'You don't need to worry about where you're going to live, Karen. You can stay with me.'

He felt a responding squeeze. 'Thanks, Fred. You are sweet. We'll have to see. I mean, you can't be seen shacking up alone with a spare bird just like that. You have your reputation to consider. Maybe we'll advertise for a flatmate, or somebody at the House may want to come and share.'

'No!' To his horror it was clear that Karen's mind was running along a completely different groove. 'That's not what I meant at all.'

She turned her face to him, bewildered. 'Sorry. Don't get cross. Then what did you mean?'

All the fine words, the protestations of love, vanished into thin air. Aghast, he sat for a moment with his mouth open. Karen turned away, her gaze following a seagull which circled over the water a few feet away. The man on the bridge had reached Boadicea's statue at the Westminster end. The seagull's cry seemed to echo the anguished wailing in Fred's own breast.

'I . . . Karen . . . can't you see? Am I that awful – that it doesn't occur to you? I want to marry you. There. Now I've said it.'

Breathing heavily he slumped back, chin thrust down into his coat.

'Let me get this straight,' the girl said slowly, her gaze firmly on Fred's face. He could not lift his eyes to meet hers. 'You want us to set up house together? As man and wife?'

Fred nodded dumbly. Now was the moment to tell her how wonderful she was, how much he wanted her, what a gap she had created in his life that only she could fill. The words would not come.

'Well . . .' Karen was dubious. 'In the first place, Fred, I'm still a student. I'm nowhere near ready to get married yet. Settling down, to be frank, was not on my list of things to do this year. Second . . .' She glanced at him sideways. How could she tell him how bizarre the idea seemed? Not that she had any objections to Fred himself. He would make an excellent husband, of that she had no doubt. He was straight as a die, kind and devoted to her. He would be faithful, and loyal. He was great company, even when he was rattling on about his job, and increasingly exciting in bed.

But Mrs Fred Laidlaw? An MP's wife? It was bad enough to be an MP's daughter. At least that was a temporary matter, in the sense that as she developed, her umbilical cord with her mother was shrinking. To choose to marry Fred, on the other hand, would be to tie herself to a political man for the rest of her life, with all the restrictions that would entail. The whole suggestion made her recoil.

'You won't have me because you don't love me, I can see that,' Fred muttered gruffly. He pulled his hand away from hers and shoved it deep into his pocket. 'And you're probably right – I'm not up to much. But I love you, Karen, I really do. I've thought about it a lot. I was going to ask you anyway, but this awful business of Anthony's death has brought it to a head.'

He turned to her, his face creased with anxiety. 'Please don't say no. Please, just think about it. If you prefer I won't mention it again. But the proposal is there. Whenever you want.'

He jumped up to bring the dreadful exchange to an end. 'I have to get back. Are you coming this way? Of course not – LSE is further down. God, I'm so stupid.'

Reluctantly Karen rose at his side. Her heart was in as much turmoil as his, but for different reasons. She did not trust herself to speak but kissed him softly on the cheek. That made things worse: awkwardly he tried to put his arms round her, but she slid away, and set off rapidly towards the Strand.

The man who had walked across the bridge had witnessed the parting of the young couple, who appeared to have had some kind of tiff. The girl looked vaguely familiar. He realised after some thought that she attended his Tai-kwondo class on Tuesday nights. Perhaps he would mention to her next time that he was sorry she had had a row with her boyfriend. Not that he was interested in her himself, of course. His lady love was closer to his own age, and much more beautiful.

She must not visit him in that horrible hostel. For the moment it was both convenient and convincing; but as soon as he was in his own place he would invite her. She might need a little persuasion, but given time she would come round. Then the happy times could commence. He had waited long enough.

He stopped at the empty bench and ran his fingers over the seat where the warm bodies had raised the temperature of the stone. How strange the traces that human beings leave behind. An infra-red picture would show for at least another half-hour, even in chilly weather, that people had sat here. He smiled to himself. He never felt the cold.

Many changes were coming. He rummaged in his pocket and pulled out the bottle of tablets. For a moment he turned the bottle over and read the label carefully, his lips moving with the words. He no longer needed them. With a flourish he tossed the bottle in the bin, and walked calmly away.

Chapter Twenty

Ted Bampton sat on the edge of his bed in his underpants and muttered grumpily to himself. In his state of undress the ravages of the years were all too apparent. Rolls of white flesh engulfed his middle, sparsely covered by chest hair like grey sheep's wool. The brown-mottled shins, the spindly, under-muscled limbs and the pendulous near-breasts bore witness to days spent behind a desk and evenings cradling a pint or attending political dinners. As she examined him covertly from the bathroom his wife Jean was troubled. It was not true that only women aged badly. In unfavourable circumstances men did too – faster, and worse.

'Where are my clean socks? I thought I put 'em out last night and now I can't find 'em.'

Jean came into the bedroom wiping her face on a towel. She nodded at the bed. 'You're sitting on them.'

Bampton grunted, shifted, found the socks and pulled them on. Wordlessly his wife pointed around the room at the fresh shirt, the brushed suit, the tie and braces, hung up ready. As he groped for a handkerchief and hunted for his keys she moved quietly to help with his tie.

'Something's eating you, Ted. What is it?'

'That bloody referendum. I think we're going to lose it.'

She stood back in shock. 'Surely not. The Prime Minister wouldn't have called one if he thought he'd lose.'

'You have more faith than I, sweetheart. Or more sense than any of us. Winter's a stupid time to have a vote, anyhow. We called it to unite the party and we've failed catastrophically – they're all over the place. And, as de Gaulle complained when he lost his last one in 1969, the electors appear to be voting on a question which is not on the ballot paper.'

The tie was straight. Jean patted her husband's shoulders as she might a lump of warm dough destined for the oven. 'I don't follow you.'

Bampton checked his wallet and pulled on his jacket. 'We thought the issue was whether the United Kingdom should join the single currency.

You know my views on that – I hate the whole idea, but if it's there we must join. Can't get left behind. But the nation is busy weighing up the government and finds us wanting. I feel like a gladiator in a Roman arena waiting for the thumbs-down. Any minute.'

As he kissed his wife on the cheek she smiled wanly. 'I don't pretend to understand, Ted, but if you tell me I should vote for it I will.'

'Good girl. We could do with a few more like you,' Bampton grunted approvingly. It was not his way to express affection to his wife, even when they were alone: except in bed, and then not often. Their loyalty was solid enough not to require constant reinforcement. Yet this morning felt different.

The doorbell rang – his Ministry driver, as ever on time. Ted picked up his red boxes, his back hunched and tired. 'The aggro is coming from women voters. I wish they were more of your mind, Jean. You're a good woman, you know that? You don't argue with me and mess me about, not when it comes to my job, and I don't interfere with you. You know your place – running things here in the home, bringing up the girls, and not bothering yourself with silliness outside. Why can't the rest be like that? Makes life much easier.'

Jean laughed, a slow reassuring chuckle. 'Because women don't know their place any more, and many wouldn't be content to live the way we do. More fool them, I suppose. But it suits me.'

At the door he turned. 'I suppose we're a bit old fashioned, the pair of us.'

'So what? We're more typical of couples in this country than the feminists would believe. And the happier for it.'

'Thank God for that.'

'Off you go, Ted. Will you be late home tonight?'

Jim Betts had to confess that he would be heartily glad when the European referendum was over and done. He could arouse not a scrap of enthusiasm for either side. Both lots seemed crackpots with an element of the sinister. The desire of the antis to remain big fish in a small pond was natural: tiddlers in a puddle, more like it. But they seemed to think all the advantages of the Common Market would continue regardless, including the attraction of Britain for Japanese money, even if the country pulled out. On anybody's guess that was unrealistic. On the other hand, Heath and his acolytes hoped to be more than mere minnows in a Brussels fish-tank. Most politicians lived to tell other people what to do, whatever their cant about individual freedom. Power-mad, the lot of them.

It was much easier to write about their personal lives. Jim Betts was well aware that he had made his reputation with ripe prose and riper situations, for some of which he took credit for setting up in the first place. His conscience did not cost him a wink of sleep. What if a sharp eye and a quiet word in the right place led to the rental of an empty basement in a Minister's home by a convicted prostitute? The fool should have kept his house to himself and not been so greedy. And how about the arrangement with a foreign polo club owner to photograph Prince Charles in the shower room? But a bloke who waltzed naked in front of hotel windows shouldn't get too upset to find himself full frontal in the newspapers. Pity only the Germans had published the royal flush. It might have done wonders for the Prince's popularity.

The era of exotic living seemed to have waned among MPs. These days they got involved not in toe-sucking sessions with out-of-work actresses but in altercations with anti-motorway demonstrators, after which they resigned with alacrity. One or two had even started to resign over issues of principle, an alarming development. The latest scandal involved payment to peers to ask questions, though why anybody should bother was beyond the wit of man.

Maybe that relentless scrutiny really had driven the Members into good behaviour, or at least to greater caution. Maybe they were so poverty-stricken that their entire free time was taken up earning an honest copper writing novels. Or perhaps they were just smarter at covering their tracks. The political world would be a dismal place if that were so, and he might have to work a lot harder.

What of the chap at the top – how vulnerable was he? Betts brooded, chin on hands. The fact was, Roger Dickson was a stupendous liar, cheat and hypocrite. He might appear to be the devoted family man, but in a previous incarnation, not that long before, he had had a lover, and one not so far from home. In the House of Commons, in fact. She was a Minister herself now, which made her trebly interesting, though it seemed likely that the affair was finished. Only he, Betts, knew about it. But he could not see how to prove it.

Yet did that matter? If he spread a little pitch, would it not stick? He chewed his moustache. His scruples suggested he must be getting old himself. Once he would not have hesitated – the details would have been all over the front pages before you could say 'Scoop!' But that was before the deputy news editorship, the large car and the comfortable expense account. A place on the board was hinted at, as soon as Thwaite retired. To publish a story he could not substantiate would lead straight to a libel case – Dickson would not hesitate. The *Globe*'s owner, in pursuit of respectability, had become a member of the Press Complaints Commission. Betts would be out on his ear sharpish.

He sighed, then brightened. There was always entertainment to be had. Reflections on both Anthony York and Dickson's erstwhile paramour nudged his thoughts in a single direction. He pulled out a small black book and began to flick through its pages.

In the few moments before the debate began, Elaine seated herself on the dark green leather to the left of the dispatch box, tidied her skirt over her knees, adjusted her earrings and reminded herself to smile, but not too much. The black-eyed remote cameras opposite, slung beneath the public gallery, were on watch. The rules covering Commons broadcasts gave editors nightmares. Obliged to provide a mere record of events and to discourage demonstrations, controllers were not allowed to cut away to Members who were not speaking or to perform a quick swivel to an interesting noise in the gallery. Nevertheless Ministers and front-benchers were always on show. Should she grimace or wriggle or scratch her head, a million people would see.

Both floor and benches were littered with crumpled papers from the previous business. Beside her the whip rose, bobbed to the Deputy Speaker and murmured the time-honoured formula: 'I beg to move, that this House do now adjourn.'

With a buzz of relief Members sauntered out and headed for bars or clubs or home. There would be no more votes. Only fanatics would stay behind for a debate on the most insignificant issue of all to the Commons: the provision of child care for Members and their staff.

Derek Harrison slid along the second bench and bent low behind Elaine. His presence startled her and she caught her breath.

'You answering this, Mrs Stalker?' he whispered in her ear.

'Not exactly. No Minister needs to respond – it's the House's business, not the government's. But I'll listen and intervene if necessary.'

'Personal interest, then? Not planning any more children, are you?'

Elaine twisted round to find Harrison's face only a few inches from her own. His skin was slightly oily and smelled of that morning's aftershave, mixed with cigarettes and, faintly, whisky. A tuft of hair in his ear was black and springy. She recrossed her legs and smoothed her hands over her thighs.

'Why, Derek – is that an offer?'

He snorted and moved away. For a brief moment Elaine reflected wistfully how pleasant it would have been to work in an organisation where intimidation and bullying were frowned upon and perpetrators got the sack. She longed to develop a sense of humour about it, or a capacity to turn the other cheek. At Westminster the only way to respond to people like Harrison was as she had just done, which for her was an effort and out of character. Yet to her disgust he had been triumphantly voted on to the executive of the '22 Committee, the return of the prodigal, as if its politicians wished to celebrate in public the values so many held dear in private.

Alan Beith, MP for Berwick-upon-Tweed for over twenty years and chairman of the House of Commons Commission, gazed ruefully as the audience dwindled. Short, verging on the tubby, cheery, the very essence of the Methodist lay preacher and former politics lecturer, he knew his task was to persuade the House not to vote for child care but merely to think about it.

'The usual way in which new or extended services are provided to the House . . .' he intoned.

Elaine counted heads. Apart from the Deputy Speaker and Harrison, Beith was the only other man in the Chamber; ten women Members, mostly Labour, had settled down in isolated clumps to listen. She wondered what had happened to the younger male MPs who had small children. Gone home to help bath them and put them to bed? Fat chance, in most cases.

A Labour woman MP, smartly dressed, neatly coiffed and ambitious, was on her feet. 'We have come a long way since October 1979 when Mr Patrick Jenkin, then Secretary of State, said on BBC television, "If the good Lord had intended us to have equal rights at work He wouldn't have created man and woman."'

'I wouldn't be so sure,' came a deep growl behind Elaine. Harrison had clearly decided to stay and make trouble.

Next it was the turn of a Conservative. The floor was taken by an older distinguished MP, Member for a Midlands urban seat for thirty years. Dame Mathilda Matthews was no friend to the reformers; on the contrary.

'There are at least five reasons why I am against this proposition,' she began alarmingly. Elaine observed the stolid body in its expensive but cosy knitted suit, the gaudy jewellery, the over-heavy make-up. When the dame had entered the House it was a huge achievement for a woman. All the more disappointing that she appeared so unwilling to help others.

'Our workload gets inexorably heavier and most Members need more space than ever before for their filing cabinets, computers and papers. It is extraordinary to suggest that there is some wide-open space that could be used for a crèche. We are here to work.'

Elaine listened unhappily. Dame Mathilda was in full flow, her ample form quivering with righteous indignation. 'Babies and toddlers would be noisy and costly!' she cried. 'We would need a permanent crèche all year round. We could have a thousand children, babies and toddlers in this place!'

'Might talk more sense than you!' came the cat-calls, followed by hoots of derision from Opposition benches.

Baffled and heaving, the dame eventually gave up. Elaine suddenly realised why it was so hard to make progress. There would always be Dame Mathildas who would support the enemy's case and in so doing give credence to the male presumption that the dear ladies were unsuited to rational argument.

Another Labour speech came and went. At last it was Harrison's turn. He rose and elaborately adjusted his cuffs as if the entire discussion was a joke. His voice floated silkily.

'What I principally object to is the collectivisation of child care around the place of work. It is an Orwellian picture. I say to the proposal, "No, no, no."'

As Elaine fumed silently, the whip nearby sighed, checked the clock and opened his blue folder. Without bothering to hide it from the Minister he wrote, 'Harrison – calm, convincing.' Then with a crisp movement the file was snapped shut and replaced on the bench. The business of the day was over.

As the Rover slid away from New Palace Yard, Elaine kicked off her shoes and lifted her legs up on to the seat. In front she caught the eye of Sheila, reflected in the mirror.

'It's my own fault. I shouldn't allow the neanderthals to get under my skin like that.' Elaine had been describing her encounter with Harrison. Her accurate imitations of both him and Dame Mathilda had made her driver laugh out loud.

'It's harder in some ways for women today,' Sheila mused. At the entrance gate to Parliament Square the vehicle waited until a police officer stopped the traffic. 'When I was young a mother only worked if she had to, and there was more sympathy.'

The two chatted easily on the short journey to Elaine's flat past the windows of the Army and Navy store. It was a long time since she had walked home. With red boxes tucked beside her the official transport was justified, and security demanded it, but the shared conversation at the end of a long stretch was ever welcome. It took the place, Elaine realised, of the loving exchange which had once occurred between her husband Mike and herself, that pause before bed that put the day's work in perspective and used to prepare her for sleep.

'Minister, you'll have to do without me for a few days. I'm on leave tomorrow,' Sheila announced as she pulled into Elaine's street. Something in her tone made her boss look up.

'Everything all right?'

'It is now.' Sheila sat quietly. 'My old man died during the night. I heard this morning. I could have gone right away, but there was no point – the funeral isn't till Thursday and his mother is coping beautifully. I'll be back next week.'

Elaine put a hand on the uniformed shoulder, which sagged as she squeezed it. 'I am so sorry, Sheila,' she said softly. 'It wasn't a surprise, though, was it?'

'Yes and no.' Sheila's voice was nearly inaudible. 'Of course we'd been expecting it any minute. But still – when I get to his ma's, that'll be it. He's gone. Never see him again. I suppose that's why I didn't fly there immediately – wanted to get a bit used to the idea, like.'

With a brusque movement she got out and held Elaine's door open for her. Elaine slid over, her head bent. Boxes were lifted out and deposited at her side. Minister and driver found themselves face to face awkwardly on the pavement.

Sheila shrugged. 'Well, I'm a widow lady now. On my own. You and me both.' She uttered a short laugh full of desolation. The lamplight showed tears glistening on her cheeks.

Elaine bit her lip. 'It's not the same. Mine is still alive. I could bump into him any time. And I know he's well and happy. Without me.'

'Maybe that's worse,' Sheila muttered. The women's eyes met. Elaine put out her hand. For an instant the two clung to each other as equals and friends.

A sense of unseemliness asserted itself and both were embarrassed.

Clumsily they separated; empty words were murmured. Then Sheila climbed into the Rover and, staring rigidly forward, drove away.

'I can't put it off any longer. I have to get this speech for the MIND conference rewritten and submitted for clearance, then sent out as a press release. So what exactly am I to say?'

In her office at the department Elaine faced a group of unhappy advisers. Several distinguished faces, familiar to readers of *Care Weekly* and *Social Work Today* but unknown to a wider audience, sat opposite, their expressions glum. At her side Private Secretary Fiona Murray took notes in a large ruled book, the idiosyncratic method favoured at the Civil Service College. Chadwick impassively occupied one end of the table. Directly facing the Minister was the formidable Miss Clarkson, short, dumpy, harassed and kind, a red scarf at her throat and earrings adangle, who led the mental health team.

'But Minister – we're nowhere near agreement for a new line on these hospital closures.' Miss Clarkson leaned forward anxiously. The first, rejected draft speech lay on the table. She pushed away an empty coffee-cup. 'The inter-departmental working group set up by the Prime Minister has met several times. However, we can make no progress against . . . er' – she sought for a suitably tactful term, and gave up – 'complete obduracy by the Treasury.'

'But the community care programme is costing us a ruddy fortune, and it doesn't work!' Elaine thumped the table in frustration. 'People slip through the net every day. The wards are full to bursting. Seriously ill patients have to be turfed out early to make room for the next batch, who happen to be worse.' Officials dropped their eyes and shuffled papers. Some at least, she suspected, sympathised. That did not mean instant acquiescence. 'Those are not just my views. They're the conclusions in inquiry after inquiry. Usually when somebody's been *murdered.*'

Miss Clarkson winced. 'Minister, we have taken on board your private wish to halt the closure programme. As you know, we do not all agree with that view. Care in the community is helping a great many people to a more normal life. However, you do need to appreciate the way these budgets work.'

'I'm listening. Tell me.' Elaine allowed herself to sound belligerent.

Patiently Miss Clarkson attempted to elucidate Health Service funding: 'providers' and 'purchasers', 'health authorities', 'boards', 'trusts' and 'fund-holding general practices' littered her sentences. Elaine felt her eyes glaze over.

'All I know is that I'm tired of explaining away twenty thousand more well-paid managers in the NHS in the last five years when old ladies are sleeping on trolleys in corridors and mentally ill patients are roaming the streets.'

She glared around to see who would wilt under the onslaught. Most shrank from her gaze. A reputation for fierceness in discussion did her no harm, she reckoned: like Margaret Thatcher, she sought only a solid basis of facts from those who would dispute with her, and was ready to be convinced. But not by the woolliness on offer this morning.

Miss Clarkson waffled gamely for a few minutes but refrained from comment. Whoever had dreamed up the complexities which baffled the Minister could answer for them, not her.

Elaine sighed. 'Look, the MIND people are in favour of the closure of most of the old mental hospitals. Some of their supporters have had horrendous experiences in psychiatric hospitals and I don't blame them. But in truth they're not happy about *any* form of compulsory treatment outside either, which is our best alternative. They claim that strong medication carries risks too, and that's correct. I can see that patients are people first and have rights; but I can't see how leaving them untreated protects those rights. Or those of anybody else.'

Fiona nudged her elbow and pointed down the page.

'And my secretary reminds me that I am obliged to take a decision before the end of the month on the closure of St Kitts. It's in the constituency next door to mine. I'm under pressure to pay a visit. I've been before, but years ago. Any guidance there, please?'

Chadwick cleared his throat. 'The land has already been sold, I'm afraid, Minister. The developer is pressing for vacant possession.'

'Bloody hell,' Elaine muttered. She raised her head. 'Then I will go. At least I can take responsibility.' She resisted the temptation to ask why a ministerial signature was required if the matter had been sewn up. 'We have, I assume, created superb new facilities to rehouse the patients? That is our policy.'

'There are hardly any patients left there,' Chadwick sidestepped neatly. 'We've been trying to close that place for ten years. It's had no money spent on it and much of the building is unusable. You remember the fuss about the new hostel? Well, that was part of the replacement.'

'It houses only thirty men, all officially temporary residents. The hospital held . . . oh, I don't know why I bother.'

350

For a moment she felt close to tears. Miss Clarkson came to her rescue. 'Minister, there is an opportunity in this speech to voice . . . shall we say . . . misgivings. We will prepare a fresh draft for you. The Secretary of State must see it, of course. Shall we put it in your box tomorrow night?'

With a heavy heart Elaine brought the discussion to an end. As the experts were shown out by Fiona, Chadwick returned to the room and sat down quickly beside her. He indicated the rejected draft.

'Do you want it leaked? Might help establish your position.'

She recoiled, shocked. 'I don't think I heard that. If I'm to get a shift in policy I'd rather do it properly. Open and above board. Preferably with the full approval of the Secretary of State and Prime Minister.' His face was expressionless. 'Thank you for trying, though. I appreciate it.'

Chadwick rose and moved languidly to the door. 'You know I have no views on policy – that's for Ministers to decide. I just don't want any more trouble in this department. You're an excellent Minister, if you don't mind my saying so. You'll weather this storm. Probably by saying less rather than more.'

With that he slid out of the room and shut the door.

Elaine sat for a while longer and brooded. Chadwick's hint was timely. It would be far better to make a bland speech. It would be sounder politics to shut the damned hospital at once without going anywhere near it. The best approach was as in warfare: heads down, not poking up over the parapet, not with lethal ballistics whistling around. She sensed how little she might know. The developer was probably a supporter of the party with a handsome donation in the pipeline. That wasn't corrupt – merely an indication that he knew which side his bread was buttered. A Labour government would close the hospital too, but the land would go for a car park or soulless municipal flats. The patients, voiceless and usually voteless, counted for nothing.

Derek Harrison helped himself to a peach from the large fruit display and bit carefully into its yellow flesh. In January they must have come from somewhere exotic: Chile, or South Africa. The picture of dusty farms under a southern sun brought a wistful memory. What a pity the regime in Jo'burg no longer needed caring right-wingers like himself and John Carlisle. The years had long passed when a powerful speech against sanctions led to free palm-fringed holidays in the sun. These days it was pay your own fare to watch the rugby or nothing.

He was reduced to lunching with British businessmen with a line to spin. At least he could name his location: the linen-covered tables in the airy conservatory of the Lanesborough Hotel at Hyde Park, the most expensive in town. The tinkle of its central fountains covered all indiscretions. Lazier Members of the House did not get this far. He wiped his fingers on a napkin and pushed away his plate.

'Now you didn't invite me here simply to tell me the gossip, Giles.' He smiled.

The substantial gentleman opposite in a well-cut suit twiddled with his coffee-spoon. 'You're an important personage now, Derek. Oh, you were before, as a Minister. But you can roam a little more widely. Though, as it happens, my interest is in your former department. The health side. A piece of real estate. Used to be St Kitts Hospital. Know where I mean?'

Harrison screwed up his face. He could not remember any details at all, but he would be the first to admit that his perusal of departmental papers during his period in office had been at best skimpy. 'Go on – I'm listening.'

A waiter hovered, offered coffee, cigars, brandy. Derek hesitated briefly – it was only lunchtime – then accepted a cigar. His host followed. For several moments both men puffed contentedly as the fragrant smoke hid their faces.

His companion bent the match and tossed it into a saucer. 'It's empty now apart from a few gaga types who are due to move any minute. The problem is your friend Mrs Stalker. Got cold feet, it seems. Won't sign to close it.'

'You're interested in the development?'

A shrug. 'Not directly. As chairman of the health authority I have to be careful. But we need the funds released – the revenue. The bills won't wait on that lady's scruples.'

'What are you going to use the money for? I mean, it helps if it's for more eye operations and the like.'

'It is.' The chairman reached for a heavy glass ashtray and knocked his ash into it. 'But I also have a new administrator at seventy-five grand, and fourteen board directors at ten each, and there's my honorarium – and we've around thirty more bods doing accounts and reports and the like we didn't need when that closure was planned. We're talking a million revenue shortfall this year, Derek, unless I can get a transfer of funds. Pronto.'

Derek Harrison examined the glowing butt of his cigar. 'Interesting,' he murmured. Then he grinned at his friend. 'Leave it to me.'

*   *   *

He wished he were taller. It was a huge effort to see what was happening over the crowded shoulders in front of him. The air was chill; breath hung on it like frost. The muddy ground beneath his feet slithered and he could get no foothold on the wet grass. A woman in a dirty green coat slipped and grabbed hold of his arm but he brushed her off. He was glad he had brought his protection. It might be needed.

The shouts were spasmodic at first – only the union organiser in front with his megaphone, trying but failing to whip up a frenzy. Police in yellow Day-glo jackets looked bored but adjusted the straps of their helmets tighter under their chins, their gaze sweeping the crowd. A superintendent in a tight uniform larded with braid barked orders into a mobile phone. At a guess fewer than two hundred people were present, but their continual movement in the narrow entry road to the hospital made their numbers difficult to judge and tricky to control.

As the afternoon light faded, spotlights were switched on, blinding in their sudden intensity. Television cameramen milled around for editing shots. A presenter smoothed his pale hopsack jacket and grimaced with distaste at the dank edifice behind him, where weeds grew out of gutters and windows were cracked and boarded up. He had no desire to go any further and particularly not to meet any of the hospital's remaining occupants.

The union organiser pushed forward, was singled out, interviewed and encouraged to denounce the government. Young women in red plastic macs and impractical short skirts clutched microphones in cold hands and prodded demonstrators into articulation. Photographers arranged giggling groups with their placards in the doorway. 'SAVE ST KITTS' was to be the message on the following morning's front pages.

The Minister was due at three. Tension rose and shouting began. At five minutes to the hour the main hospital doors opened. To loud cheers out came a phalanx of male psychiatric nurses in off-white tunics accompanied by workmen in boilersuits, dinner ladies in check aprons and cleaners swinging buckets and mops. Behind them, after a suitably pregnant pause, emerged the doctors, male and female, in white coats. The new groups swelled the massed ranks and started a ragged chant. The police superintendent stepped back, spoke rapidly into his phone and began to look alarmed.

Half a mile away the ministerial car slowed.

'Oh Christ,' Chadwick muttered. He put the car phone back in its

353

cradle and turned to Elaine. 'There's a big demo. Blocking the front. Looks a bit ugly. The police advise you go in the back way. They've prepared an entrance through the kitchen. Can you climb through a window?'

Elaine's pulse started to race and her mouth went dry. Beside her Fiona Murray shrank into her coat.

'No, that's not on,' Elaine responded quietly. 'We've come to listen and we can hardly do that if we skulk about.'

In front Sheila, returned early to duties, stiffened and slipped the car into a lower gear. Chadwick and Murray exchanged glances. Neither dared demur from the royal 'we' so readily assumed by Her Majesty's Ministers. Had officials had their way, the forbidding pile looming before them, its portals flanked by protesters, would long since have been razed to the ground.

'Then the police advise that you get inside quickly, Minister, for your own safety.'

'Oh, they're exaggerating,' Elaine made herself say. 'What are they bothered about – nutters among the crowd? People affected by the closure are upset and I can understand that.'

It was clear from his face that Chadwick was genuinely worried. She responded to his concern. 'I'll be careful. But I'd rather do it my way.'

The Rover turned into the driveway and edged cautiously between the lines of demonstrators. Elaine knew she must not hide herself: she sat up straight, set her face in a smile and undid her seat-belt ready for a speedy emergence.

Dunn could just see her if he stood on tiptoe. She was searching the crowd for him and he waved frantically and called to her. At last she beamed brightly at him from the back of the car. She was looking lovely.

As the car door opened and Elaine got out the shouts rose to a crescendo. Most were unsavoury, some obscene. Dunn gasped at the foul language and abuse screamed over his head. 'Stalker! Stalker! Out, out, out!' and '*Kill the bitch!*' came from somewhere in the mêlée. As if by signal the yells were followed by a hail of over-ripe tomatoes. Most seemed to miss. Then one appeared in a fist near his ear and was more accurately aimed: it hit the Minister with a firm sound and splattered over her dark coat, to a roar of delight from the crowd. Once she was in range more began to fly. The superintendent moved to her side and took her arm. Through it all Elaine grinned determinedly and waved, but after a moment's hesitation she headed straight for the sanctuary of the main door, nearly hidden from sight by burly policemen.

There was a crack and fizzle and Dunn's eyes began to water – somebody must have thrown a stink bomb or a firework. The yells in the front became tinged with fear. Behind him somebody pushed hard, then another, and he found himself being shoved forward. His feet scrabbled for a hold and he almost fell.

A woman's voice was screeching in his ear – some dreadful things about Elaine, terrible words which derided her beauty, her probity, her character. Criticisms which he, Graham Dunn, knew to be totally untrue. He lurched away. Full of anger he reached into his pocket.

It was after a tour of the desolate empty wards, her heart still thumping, face white with strain, that Elaine sat down at a table with the staff who had not walked out to listen to their pleas. The discussion did not last long. Chadwick was motioned away by the superintendent with a sombre look. He returned and waited respectfully until a break in the proceedings, then whispered urgently in Elaine's ear. What he murmured to her made her pick up her papers, nod curt goodbyes and move rapidly to the door.

As the car purred out of the hospital grounds Elaine craned her neck. A drizzle obscured the windscreen. The remaining demonstrators stood around disconsolate and weeping. An ambulance was parked askew on the turf, its doors wide open. Paramedics in bundled anoraks knelt in the pool of light from its headlamps, the rain silvering their hair. On the ground lay the body of a middle-aged woman in a dirty green coat, her fingers still curled around a soft tomato. The dark stain on fabric and earth told what the police had already established: that she had been knifed, once, fatally in the neck, probably by somebody in the crowd.

'You weren't listening to the play. In fact I don't believe you took in one word. Was it that murder?'

Elaine shifted in the taxi and nodded unhappily at George. He checked that the cabbie's eyes were firmly fixed on the wet night in Charing Cross Road. Gently he pulled her into his arms to comfort her.

'Yes, in part. That poor woman – she meant no harm. Her son had worked there twenty years and was about to lose his job, that was all. But I can't help thinking about myself. It makes me feel that the knife could have been aimed at . . . well, me. Demonstrations are bad news – you never know who might be in there. It's scary.'

'If you'd avoided the crowd, you'd have been called a coward.'

'Right. But better than being a dead hero. Or heroine.'

George took her hand and rubbed it absent-mindedly. 'Nobody outside sees those risks. I certainly didn't. It's not only the IRA, is it? You're a target for everyone.'

She laughed ruefully. 'Part of the job. Part I've come to hate. I get really frightened sometimes.'

He turned, concerned. 'Cheer up. You're doing very well. I see more of you on TV than in the flesh and you always come across wonderfully. I want to tell everyone that I know you: I feel so proud.'

'Don't. It's all an image. Sometimes I feel so confused. I don't know any more what's real, what's me, and what's make-up or lighting or lines-to-take. That visit was a case in point: I wanted to help, to show somebody cared, but when I think it through I went to salve my own conscience. The public verdict will be different – that a Minister got her just deserts and that poor mother didn't. I feel so badly about it, but there is nothing I can do or say that doesn't make things worse.'

'You can talk to me.'

But Elaine was speaking almost to herself, her voice bitter.

'I feel as if I am vanishing. D'you know, I long to make my own speeches, not phrases concocted by somebody else. I dream of saying "I agree!" when an interviewer makes a hostile point, instead of batting it airily away. I yearn to tell the truth for once. It's not easy.'

'But you're still enjoying the job, surely? You're getting on better with Bampton, aren't you?'

Elaine's silence told him. She sighed and continued, 'It's fiendishly difficult to make any worthwhile impact, that's the problem. Easy if I simply mouth the same old policies, but then what's the point of being a Minister? Ministers are supposed to have power, yes? That's what everyone thinks. Yet here am I, powerless to make changes in key areas I understand and care about.'

Her face as she spoke seemed haunted. George squeezed her hand and was silent.

'As for Bampton . . . To shift policy I need the active support of my boss, which I don't have. He neither trusts me nor knows how to work with me. He'd be much more comfortable with another man – he and Derek got on fine. Ted seems to have no confidence in my judgement. My own fault, probably.'

'What on earth do you mean?' George was now thoroughly alarmed.

'*I* can't grasp what makes *him* tick. If I did, I could persuade him.

But if I make a suggestion he rubbishes it. If I give an instruction he'll countermand it. I never seem to get the benefit of the doubt. This hostility is becoming a vicious circle and is creating a terrible atmosphere.'

'Are you sure you're not just feeling sorry for yourself? You do work crazy hours, Elaine. It's easy to get matters out of perspective if you're exhausted.'

To his relief she giggled weakly. 'Woody Allen once said that just because you're paranoid it doesn't mean they're not after you.' She paused, then carried on, choosing her words with care. 'Let me give you an example. A month ago I was asked to do a long interview on the Dimbleby show – you know, Sunday lunchtime. I was unsure: my critics say I'm on the box too much and Ted feels overshadowed. So I told him I reckoned it was much more appropriate for a Secretary of State. Ted got quite shirty, said I wasn't to decide his television appearances for him, and that I must accept. As it turned out I was right to be reluctant – colleagues have been quite snide about it.'

George was curious. 'And if you'd said you were keen . . .?'

'He'd have insisted that he do it.'

'Heavens. Sounds like you have indeed figured out how his brain works, but it's not attractive. The sole consolation I can offer is that it happens in business too – usually, as you've guessed, when a boss is challenged by a more effective subordinate and doesn't like it.'

'Especially if the underling is a woman? Even if that is categorically not her intention?'

'Absolutely. No bloke likes to be shown up by a female. It's still a man's world, Elaine.'

The taxi slowed as Elaine indicated the entrance to her block of flats. Both emerged under a big umbrella and George paid, then escorted her up the steps.

'Do you want to come up – coffee, or whatever?'

The offer was made out of politeness and increasing habit, but it was obvious that she was tired. He shook his head.

'I won't. But listen, Elaine. You don't have to be stuck this way. There is another world out there in which people lead civilised lives, get to bed at reasonable hours, earn respectable money, have friendships and loves and success based not on lies and hypocrisy but on hard work and talent. If you want to leave any time, I can help you, make introductions. You don't have to be a Minister – or even in politics at all.'

She leaned her face against the wet door-jamb. The soft patter of rain on the umbrella sounded like whispered words from afar. She shook her head.

'I don't think you follow me, George. This *is* my life. I chose it years ago. You can't get into politics at all unless you decide quite early and go for it single-mindedly. I've never done anything else – a bit of teaching, that's all. To pack it in would mean giving up everything I believe in – *everything I am*. It would mean giving up: not simply abandoning a career, but also tearing up my credo that a good person *can* get things done, can make a difference. I look at some of the' – she searched for adequate descriptions – 'some of the self-centred bastards and fools and incompetents and downright crooks who head for Westminster. They're outnumbered by the nice guys, but the latter are much less effective. I tell myself that good must win in the end, and that I must stick it out. If I resign, somebody better might well fill my place. More likely it'd be another Harrison. That's why I stay and battle on. But God, it makes me weary.'

George stroked her hair and turned a damp curl around his finger. He had not planned what came next, though he had known for some time that it would happen. Not on a wet doorstep, not after a melancholy exchange, had been his intention, but after a wonderful dinner, a loving conversation and bed. But it was not kind to leave Elaine alone and distressed. If he accepted her half-hearted invitation to come up, he would only be a nuisance. The red box behind the flat door would command more of her attention; she would not relax until every paper inside it was read, annotated, signed. Thus the doorstep it would have to be, with the night rain dripping slowly off the umbrella down their necks, hiding on her drawn face what he suspected were tears.

'My dearest girl, I love you very much and I am deeply troubled to see you so unhappy. It doesn't have to be like this. Think about it. And while you're at it . . .'

He hesitated. Did he really want to? Was permanent entanglement with Elaine entirely wise? She was a public figure, an icon and an Aunt Sally, blamed for deaths and tragedies, an exemplar both admired and reviled. Her internal world was minuscule and shrinking, and apparently not of great significance to her. This was a woman who performed in public daily for the sheer love of it; would that not be anathema to a very private man? Despite his strictures against Bampton, how comfortable might he himself feel as her official partner, forever in her shadow and no longer a person in his own right, teased by his male friends as the lady Minister's bag-carrier?

He looked down into her eyes, which were half closed against the weather. She swayed slightly against him and his heart went out in pity and love. This was Elaine, whose body he knew so well, warm and round and wholesome. This was the woman who had brought gaiety into his otherwise dour life, whose femininity was a constant joy. This was the battling spirit whose intelligence and dogged persistence had brought her to high office, whose sweetness of soul had protected her through pain and desertion. She was formidable; and beautiful; she was a great prize. Millions of people whom she had never met trusted and liked her. He should do the same.

He drew himself up to his full height.

'Elaine – will you marry me?'

'Oh George . . .' She began to laugh wanly. His expression told her he was serious. For several moments there was silence.

Elaine took a deep breath. 'Marriage was the last thing on my mind. I think the world of you. But to be honest I'm not completely over Mike or . . . the other one, my ex-lover. That still hurts, a lot. And given the mess I made of being wed I'm not sure I'm cut out to be a wife – certainly not the conventional kind. I'd treat you as badly as I did him. Anyway, I have more than enough on my plate right now.'

It was not every night that a fine man proposed. Feeling slightly ridiculous, but conscious that her response was more than a little ungracious, she reached up and kissed George on his cheek. Her finger traced the faint mark her lipstick had made.

She reached in her bag for her key and unlocked the front door. 'I'm not the remarrying kind, George,' she said. 'At least, I don't think so. But don't go off me, will you? Apart from my daughter you're the best thing in my life, by a streak.'

George had never imagined the possibility of a refusal. As the door opened and Elaine disappeared under the hall light and up the stairs, he did not move or speak. Twenty minutes later, as another taxi dropped off late-night travellers, he was still standing there under the umbrella, the rain staining the shoulders of his coat, his greying hair slicked to his neck, his face grave and sad.

Chapter Twenty-One

The '22 Committee was in an ugly mood. Alerted by gossip in the tea rooms and speculation in the morning's press, over 150 Members crowded into Room 14 – a telling contrast to the sixty or so who normally turned up on Thursday evenings. With self-important saunters they ran the gauntlet of reporters in the corridor outside; then the door was firmly shut.

The chairman smiled warily as he waited till each MP had found a seat. If Sir Tom Reynolds had learned one thing in his years in the prestigious committee chair it was that backbenchers, at their best a bastion of disciplined Britishness, could be fearsome when they felt like it. He rose and cleared his throat.

'I call for the whip on duty to give us the business for next week.'

Johnson, the Deputy Chief Whip, stood. He was uneasy. Members looked too pleased with themselves. In his immediate vicinity sat the executive, elected by their fellows to give voice to the authentic grumbles of the backwoodsman: their faces were studiously innocent. But in front sat the most recent to join their ranks, Derek Harrison, in a new suit, and a tie with a dashing navy stripe, who exchanged whispers with his neighbours. His confident demeanour alarmed Johnson. Something was up – something beyond the control of the whips' office and thus impervious to their twin powers of coercion and patronage.

'On Monday there will be a debate on the Criminal Justice (Scotland) (Lords) Bill,' Johnson intoned. The three Scots present mournfully made notes in their diaries. Since the party's representation north of the border was so thin, others would have to be press-ganged to help. Johnson peered around. Perhaps Harrison as a former Minister . . .? A detailed brief would be placed in the whips' office so he wouldn't have to strain himself with research or originality. But as Harrison, his consultation ended, sat up, Johnson pursed his lips. Whatever that one was planning it wasn't to help the current administration.

'There will be a three-line whip at seven p.m. *and* at ten.' A groan went

360

up. That meant no evening off; no opera, no theatre, unless a chap was prepared to miss half the last act. 'There will be a two-line on Thursday at seven.' Much better. Members with pairs smirked. Brief questions were put, then Johnson resumed his seat. The chairman rose again.

'If there are no further questions, I'll thank the whip on duty and ask if there are any notices of motions. Yes – Mr Harrison?'

It was clear this was prearranged. Harrison stood to loud applause from strategically placed friends: not clapping, but the traditional banging of the flat palms of hands on desks with a chorused bellow of support. The whip kept his expression impassive as Harrison began to speak.

'First, Sir Tom, I think we should congratulate those involved in the successful "No" campaign on the referendum . . .' 'Hear, hear!' came the roar of response, accompanied by further prolonged palm-banging. In the corridor, primed as to the likely timing, journalists checked their watches. The noise lasted a full minute.

Derek grinned. That roar had done its work. The suggestion floated by Number 10 that a second referendum might be held to reverse the result, as had happened in Denmark, would now be dropped. The '22 had just expressed a strong view to the contrary, which no party leader dared ignore.

'But in truth, Sir Tom, I wanted to turn to a quite different matter which threatens us.' Colleagues settled down, though many present knew what was coming.

'I am deeply concerned, as we all are, at the proposals from the latest report of the Nolan Committee,' Derek declared. Another rumble supported him.

Lord Nolan's committee had been set up by a previous Prime Minister who had found it difficult to believe his own Members might ever be seriously on the make. Its instructions had been to examine allegations of 'sleaze' which had entertained and shocked the nation for several years, and to recommend means of avoiding such problems in future. It had, however, set about its task far too thoroughly for some.

'Not only have ex-Ministers been banned from paid positions with companies linked to their former departments, which causes *genuine* hardship for some.'

'Right, tell 'em, Derek,' growled a voice at his side. Both men had been barred from lucrative directorships once Lord Nolan had seized the bit between his teeth. Harrison hoped he looked martyred, but saw that most of the '22, who were never likely to have the chance to dig their snouts into the deepest troughs, were not over-sympathetic. He hurried on.

'Far worse, it appears that we're to be banned from any links with so-called lobbying companies. That will mean Members are expected to give up a great deal of time to important issues – Sunday trading, for example, or the Channel Tunnel Link – yet work for free. Nowhere else in the country are people obliged to toil for goodwill alone. I think we should make it quite clear, behind the scenes, that such action would be *intolerable*.'

'Absolutely right,' the man behind him commented audibly to another. 'What'll we do if we can't be parliamentary advisers? It'll turn us into paupers, that's what.'

'Drive good men away, it will,' a companion concurred. 'Look at us. Too busy to earn a decent living outside, can't turn a quick penny inside – what's the place coming to?'

Derek had not finished. His voice became deeper. 'But there is a far more grave proposal which we should fight with all the power at our command. That is the idea that the activities of parliamentarians should be regulated by an outside body – even subject to law.' He surveyed the packed room which, shocked and hushed, hung on his every word. 'Since time immemorial this House has regulated itself. It makes its own rules – often harsher than outside. If any Member transgresses, it is for the House and its committees to investigate and put right. To abandon this time-honoured system – the Committee of Privileges in particular – would mean the total loss of our cherished independence.'

A sigh of agreement emanated from almost every throat.

'We must ensure that the existing arrangement is preserved and that no short-term, short-sighted solutions to recent . . . ah . . . difficulties be allowed to emerge,' Derek continued. The chairman was signalling to him that his time was up. 'Whatever the public think, we know that such trivial matters as "cash for questions" or the acceptance of hospitality, even at the Ritz Hotel, are blown up by a politically motivated press to discredit us. We've already tightened the rules on declaration of interests. MPs declare jars of honey and free golf club memberships – it's reached ridiculous proportions. If Parliament is to restore its age-old reputation we should be – *must* be – permitted to discipline ourselves.'

That went down fine with his fellow backbenchers. Johnson bowed his head in acknowledgement. Harrison's skill had to be recognised – he had scored two hits in as many minutes. Not that it would wash with the voters. The old whip reflected gloomily that MPs' standing depended not on whether their transactions went unrecorded or how they were reprimanded, if ever, but on their behaviour in the first place. If those present could not grasp the widespread disgust at their receiving money in circumstances which amounted to bribery and corruption, then no amount of rule-tweaking would enlighten them. Or stop them, either.

As the committee broke up and Members began to surge towards bars and dining rooms or home, Harrison paused in the corridor, surrounded by an avid group of journalists and acolytes.

'Yes, I think that'll be the end of any talk of joining the single currency,' he remarked breezily. 'Do I think that'll result in Britain being left behind? I hope so – I'd rather be poor but proud with the pound, than have the German Mark in our pockets. We want elected politicians to run this country, people like us, not faceless foreigners.'

His attention was caught by Ted Bampton, who had emerged from another committee room and begun to stride away down the corridor. Deftly Harrison extricated himself and made off in the same direction. As he caught up, he glanced over his shoulder: the press had found other quarry. He put a hand on Bampton's arm.

'A quick word, Ted.'

Bampton turned. 'Derek? What can I do for you?'

Harrison lowered his voice. 'Sort out your Minister of State, that's what. She's holding up an important deal by her refusal to close that hospital – the one where the murder occurred in the middle of a demo against her. There'll be more trouble, mark my words, if it isn't shut at once.'

'I don't know why she's that bothered.' Bampton was wary. He had liked Derek and enjoyed a good rapport with him; in his private view, the man's sacking had been dreadfully unfair. With Elaine, on the other hand, he was permanently uncomfortable. Matters had not gone as far as open warfare, but he could not trust her one inch not to do or say something stupid.

'No good reason, you may be sure. She's trying to show you up, Ted. Make you look uncaring while her own image with the public is all sweetness and light. You're the main sufferer, you do realise?'

Bampton frowned. If Derek was hinting that his subordinate would go further and align herself with his enemies – and Ted, like most political animals, took it for granted that he must have some – then he was prepared to listen. He was fed up making excuses for her, and

363

answering questions from the press on the wilder remarks she had made. 'She's quite a favourite of the PM's. And a bit over-sensitive to criticism. Have to handle her like a new-born baby.' He patted Derek's arm. 'Anyway, thanks for letting me know. That's useful. Buy you a drink?'

Not exactly arm in arm, but with an evident degree of closeness, the two men headed unhurriedly down the stairs.

Betty Horrocks drove cautiously into Tesco's car park, threaded her way past shoppers pushing awkward laden trolleys and stopped ostentatiously in the corner spot. Within a few moments Elaine arrived and parked in the next space. Clipboards in hand, the two women lounged against their vehicles and waited.

Betty pulled her scarf tighter round her neck, raised her nose to the wind and sniffed appreciatively. 'Spring's in the air,' she announced. 'Can't you smell it? Daffodils and crocuses and fresh green leaves. Lambs in the fields. Love it.'

'Better than canvassing in the rain,' Elaine agreed. 'How many helpers do we expect today? The candidate for the council seat, of course. Our lone YC – here he comes. Anyone else?'

Betty hid her concern. 'I've had eight promises, but you know what people are like on a Saturday afternoon. Racing and rugby on the box. And everybody's shopping – we might do better simply handing out leaflets at the store entrance.'

The Young Conservative, James Turner, approached and shook hands. Elaine took in his solid Warmingshire frame, his honest expression, the youthful solemnity. Back in the fifties, she had been informed, the YCs in South Warmingshire could gather three hundred for a dance, though a faithful band of barely thirty would volunteer for political activity. So much for history. She craned her neck and searched over the tops of cars for more familiar faces. It was ten minutes past the hour. Nobody else was coming.

'Let's get cracking,' she suggested. 'Can't hang about. James, you take the evens. Betty and I will do the odd numbers.'

Together they began to walk down the street. Elaine reminded herself that Chairman Mao had begun his Long March with a handful of companions: by the time it was over he had conquered China. The reflection pleased her.

How tough it was to keep grassroots politics alive when nobody else felt like it or could see the necessity. The great political parties were mass movements or they were nothing. Door by door, in a marginal seat such as her own, each vote was contested, persuaded, convinced or lost. The most invaluable ingredient in democracy was shoe leather.

Half an hour later the candidate for the forthcoming local council elections caught them up with profuse apologies – he had forgotten, he said. Betty pursed her lips and wordlessly handed him a canvassing sheet. It would not do to berate him; it was so difficult to get anyone to stand who could put two words together and wasn't a raving fascist that one had to be grateful.

Elaine swung into a steady rhythm and was soon tingling and warm. Open the gate; up the path or across the lawn, ring, smile, introduce herself – though that was not necessary at most houses. Ask not how the individual would vote *this* time since many would not say, but how he voted *last* time, and whether anything had happened since to cause a change of mind. That gave the punters the chance to moan, but at least the canvassers would emerge better informed. Even as she received polite refusals she still enjoyed the magic of participation, the possibility of influencing events, albeit in a minuscule way. The news so gleaned was not uniformly happy. The Sunday newspapers next day would emblazon on their front pages the government's wavering support. She knew it before they did, on every doorstep.

As dusk came the team called it a day. James, stoical and cheerful, bade a respectful goodbye and moved off. The candidate shivered, looked at the darkening sky, muttered an offer to do more during the week and followed suit. Elaine watched their departure, then bent over the car bonnet, calculator in hand.

'This ward voted eighty per cent for us at the general election, we know that. Well, they've forgotten – or pretend to. Barely half the households we've seen claim to have been with us last time. Of those, a fair proportion say they see no reason to change their minds back to us again. We have a guaranteed thirty-two per cent here, Betty. Bit bleak.'

'Not enough,' Betty agreed. 'Never mind – mustn't give up.'

She patted her MP affectionately on the arm and left. Less energetic, she was chilled to the bone and longed for hot cocoa with a drop of rum. It had been on the tip of her tongue to ask what Elaine was doing for the remainder of the day but she decided against it. A quiet evening in front of the television would thaw her out. If her numbers came up on the National Lottery that'd be thrilling. She began to dream how to spend the money.

Mario Vargas wiped the bar slowly, methodically, then emptied the lone ashtray and refilled the bowl of peanuts. The shoppers' tea crowd had drifted home. Pre-theatre couples were finishing gin and tonics and would soon wander out into the night. Several of the older members had headed in the direction of the dining room, which at the weekend would be echoing and poorly patronised. The only customers left in the bar, who at a guess were settling in for a session, were two middle-aged gents who seemed to have nowhere else to go. He hoped they would not become maudlin or start talking politics to him. He was not in the mood.

'Don't mind if I do.'

As the whisky glass was raised to the optic, George realised it was his fourth of the night. 'Make it a double?' his friend enquired convivially. George nodded.

The two men moved down to the end of the club bar. This was not his normal haunt on a Saturday night; and George could only vaguely remember the portly man at his side who claimed to have served with him in Cyprus. Philip, wasn't it? George attempted a calculation. He must be in his mid-fifties. Looked older, with that sweaty red face, thinning hair and straining shirt buttons: time had not been kind.

'How's the wife, George?'

George gulped the whisky too quickly and coughed. 'Wife?' he asked blankly.

'Yes – Marjorie, was it? Margaret? You used to get letters from her. Bit besotted, you were – we caught you once in your bunk with a book of love poetry, trying to find something suitable to write back. Don't you remember?'

George struggled. 'There was a lot of joshing from the lads, that I do recall. I must have been very young.'

Philip put a fist into the peanuts and stuffed them into his mouth. 'You did get married – I think I was invited but couldn't go. Not still the missus, then?'

'No.'

'I'm on my third,' the man confided. 'You learn a lot about the ladies as you go through life, but it's not always congenial. Bloody women!'

'I'll drink to that,' George muttered, and drained the glass. With an unobtrusive movement Mario refilled it.

'You see,' Philip theorised, 'these women, they don't know what they want. Starts off lovey-dovey. A woman needs a home, security, kids. A name. Not keen on sex, most of 'em, but they'll oblige in return for a position in life, see? Mrs Philip Horne. That's what it said on the Harrods account. What more could a fellow offer?'

'Never satisfied,' George mumbled. 'You give them your all and it's not enough.'

'I don't bother these days.' Philip reached for the fresh drink. His sticky fingermarks on the crystal were like a child's. 'Stick to girlfriends. Nothing permanent. Good night out in return for a bit of the other. Keep 'em happy with flowers, perfume. It works. I'm having a bit of fun for once in my life.'

George contemplated the idea, but casual relationships had never been his style. He eyed his companion. 'So what went wrong tonight, then? How come you're not out gallivanting with some pretty girl half your age?'

'Ah, there's the rub.' The man sighed theatrically. 'The age factor. Gets us all in the end, you know. I took her to the races Wednesday. Cheltenham, big day out. Me in best bib and tucker and the dolly very fetching in a new hat. At the paddock there were more eyes on her than on the horses. Big lunch, champagne, the lot – well, I'd made a killing on those relaunched Baring's shares. Mid-afternoon she's vanished. Gone off with the winning jockey in the three-thirty. Twenty-two years old. Shan't put any more money on him, I can tell you. Or her.'

George stared gloomily into his drink. 'Been on my own a long time,' he murmured, half to himself. 'Didn't bother me. Then I met . . . someone special. Now I can't bear to go home alone.'

'I've got a few phone numbers, if that'll help,' his companion suggested. He began to rummage in his jacket pockets.

'Thanks, but that'd make it worse.' George made up his mind. He put the glass down on the counter and fastened his jacket with a slight hiccup. 'If I stay here the whole night they'll have to carry me back. I think I'll go to a movie. Something violent and bloody to match my mood. Coming?'

He felt restless. Nearly everything was ready. The bolt on the big gate had been fixed. The kitchen and living room were tidy and warm: the fridge was well stocked. Pity the hot water boiler was so unreliable – he could not afford to get it fixed yet. Down in the cellar one or two small jobs remained. He hoped the cellar would not be needed, but it was as well to be sure.

He stood in the middle of the carpet with the television on loud and watched as lottery balls fell down the Perspex tube, one by one, to the roar of drums. Stupid people. Everybody in the hostel had bought tickets, queuing up excitedly on Saturday afternoons and then glued to the box. Not him: he was above trivia. And it was a waste of money. You shouldn't trust to luck. If you wanted something in life it was better to work for it. Or take it.

As the programme finished he paced around, then with a sudden movement switched off the set. The blue vase on top rattled precariously. He had planned to stay in but the surge of furious energy which now engulfed him made that impossible.

In the kitchen he opened a deep drawer and pulled out the knife. It had a heavy black handle and a fine broad blade, clean as a whistle. He ran a finger along its edge and winced as it cut the skin. For a moment he stood and watched curiously as the blood welled up on the gash. Then he sucked at the wound till the flow stopped.

Time to leave. He pulled on his coat and scarf, though he did not feel cold. And gloves, of course. On an impulse he returned to the kitchen, took down her picture from the wall and stuffed it into his pocket.

The Rover glided to a halt outside the ministerial entrance to the Department of Health, Welfare and the Family. Elaine wondered if it had been wise to start the week with Derek Harrison's voice on BBC Radio.

She was not surprised that the Radio Four *Today* programme, with its aggressive interviewers and devotion to the murkier byways of British politics, had become a target for criticism even from the BBC's own boss John Birt. Whatever serious events might have occurred elsewhere – a government fallen in Italy, a financial crisis in Japan, an earthquake in Argentina or riots in Singapore – the cost of foreign correspondents had deprived producers of access to anything not in English and not near London. Thus the previously unheeded twitterings of the Members' Tea Room were transformed into a daily cacophony belted out on the airwaves, elevating their subjects to an undreamed-of significance and devaluing Parliament itself far more quickly than had any combination of Brussels, referenda and sleaze.

'No wonder the voters don't trust us,' Elaine mused. The weekend's round of meetings in the constituency combined with the dismal response on the doorsteps had depressed her. It was clear that politicians of every party as a genre had sunk to an all-time low in public esteem.

'We have news just coming in about a murder . . . '

Elaine hesitated. Some instinct told her to listen. She motioned to Sheila to turn up the volume.

'. . . A woman's half-naked body has been found in bushes at the back of Finsbury Park station. Forensic medical examination indicates it had been there since early Sunday morning. She appeared to have been the victim of a knife attack. Police believe she was a local prostitute and are appealing for witnesses . . .'

Elaine shivered. 'They take such risks, those women,' she muttered. Sheila nodded wordlessly and held open the door.

The memory of Derek Harrison's voice and the image of the bundled corpse unsettled Elaine. It was only after two cups of strong coffee and a considerable effort that she was able to concentrate on the matter which demanded her urgent attention: the speech for the MIND conference, which was to take place at last the next day.

Anxiously she paced around, speech in hand, then walked into the small dressing room next to her office. It was dominated by a black leather armchair and the long mirror installed after her request to Chadwick. She pushed the mirror into the corner of the room and closed the door. Now she could rehearse in peace.

'I am delighted to have this opportunity to be present today. The work of MIND in making mental illness more comprehensible to the general public, and thus its sufferers more acceptable, is widely admired.'

She paused and scribbled. That was clumsy. Civil servants were never engaged for their ability to *write*. A far more valuable skill was a talent to obfuscate, and in so doing never to offend.

'You have campaigned long and hard for old hospitals to be closed and replaced with high-quality community care. In that respect you have overturned prejudices and helped bring about tremendous social change . . .'

She liked that bit. It would lead easily into the government's actions, particularly the expenditure of vast sums of the hearers' own money. It was still quite in order for government achievements, even under an ostensibly tax-cutting regime, to be lauded in terms of money spent: inputs. Nobody had any idea how to measure output. What might that mean?

And did good modern care need hospitals or not? Elaine had no more idea than most of her predecessors. The research, commissioned to support latest practice, naturally did just that. Her instincts might move her in the opposite direction but she had no support, could quote no papers. Yet she yearned to get the policy right. That could involve a simple announcement that she would close no more hospitals. St Kitts could be the first for reprieve. If the department wanted a ministerial signature on the closure papers they could seek one elsewhere.

A soft tap came on the door. Elaine sighed. Her confusion was unresolved, but there was no more time. Tomorrow she would have to busk it a bit, and hang the consequences.

Fiona Murray poked her head discreetly around the door.

'Sorry, Minister, but there's a Detective Inspector Morris here from the CID. It is urgent.'

Elaine handed her the sheets of paper. 'Can you organise coffee, please, and get this lot retyped? Check it, make sure Miss Clarkson is at least marginally content, then send it upstairs to the Secretary of State for clearance.'

Inspector Morris was a dark-clothed figure with a sombre mien. He waited quietly in the doorway to the outer office until Elaine invited him into the room. He was tall and slim and for a fleeting moment she thought it was George, oddly transposed to her presence. George had not been in touch since that conversation in the rain. There had been no time: with a guilty pang she realised she had barely thought about him. She motioned the policeman to sit as coffee was served.

'What is it this time, inspector?' she enquired brightly. 'Middle East terrorists? Animal rightists? Or an international spy ring in South Warmingshire?'

The inspector half laughed. His voice was very deep. 'No, Mrs Stalker.' In front of him he placed a large brown envelope. Out of it he took a polythene bag with a tied-on label and removed from it a folded piece of tattered coloured paper. He smoothed it out methodically on the table before pushing it over to her. 'Do you remember this article?'

It was the astrology piece in the *Radio Times* which had so irritated both Elaine and the inhabitants of the house in Battersea. She examined it, puzzled. 'It was some time ago . . .' she began doubtfully.

The inspector pointed. 'Can you see what's written in the margin? It's a bit faint.'

She turned the piece of paper and screwed up her eyes. Her lips moved silently as her finger traced the ill-formed letters. Then she pulled her hands away as if bitten.

The policeman leaned across the table and retrieved the evidence.

'Yes, you have it,' he commented laconically. 'It says, "Die, bitch, because you are not so beautiful or clever."'

Elaine found her voice. 'Is it directed at me? Does somebody want me dead?'

'It may help to know where we found it.' Morris raised his cup to his lips and sipped slowly, his eyes on Elaine. Her face told him that she knew nothing whatever. His duty, therefore, was simply to warn her. 'It was on the body of the girl we found this morning in Finsbury Park. She had had her throat cut – a single wound. We think it was probably directed at her.'

'What? Was she killed because she *wasn't* me?'

'We don't know, Mrs Stalker. But somebody is making a comparison of sorts. We've briefed your security staff here. One of my team is on the way to your local police station to talk to people there. We need you to be particularly careful. The same applies to members of your family and your close associates.'

'Oh, no. My God.' Elaine felt drained. For a few moments the inspector spoke softly to her about extra vigilance and the need to check alarm systems both in London and at home in Warmingshire. In return she handed over Karen's address and her former husband's, and after a moment's hesitation those of Betty and George.

'Thank you. We are dealing with a fairly nasty character, I'm afraid, so you must take no chances.' He paused. There was no need to upset her unduly – yet if she were sufficiently alarmed she might be better protected. He pointed at the writing. 'Did you notice?'

'Notice what?' She peered over to get a better look.

'Our friend has weird habits. This message is done with a fingertip, not a pen or Biro.'

Elaine felt herself go cold. 'Yes?'

'I am sorry, Mrs Stalker. As far as we can tell, it's been written in the victim's blood.'

After the police officer left, Elaine called in her staff and, without revealing the more gruesome elements, issued brief instructions. Faces drawn, they went about their tasks for the rest of the day in unusual silence. The matter would have to be kept quiet. Nothing whatever would appear in the press about the direct connection between the dead woman and one of Her Majesty's Ministers. To publicise the link would advertise the lunacy, which might delight the criminal and invite further bizarre acts. It was vital to protect information useful to the criminal inquiry were a confession obtained. Nobody could accurately make up details like that.

Elaine sat and brooded. A murder, close to her. Two murders, in fact, if one counted that poor woman in the crowd at St Kitts. Both women, both killed with a single blow. Both with a knife. She shivered. Despite the heating the room felt chilly.

She was beginning to wonder whether George hadn't a point. Was the game worth the candle? Did she have the right to put herself so at risk, let alone her daughter and those near to her?

George had been trying to reassure her that she had a value other than in politics. She had rejected his comments out of hand, but of course he was correct. She could do useful work outside: she would never starve. Worthy charities would welcome her intervention, and might offer her employment. George's business friends would take care of her. Or she could return to teaching, or even local government, where the pressure was less and the sense of achievement in many ways greater. She would survive. But not, it appeared, if this maniac got any closer. She felt panicky. Who was he? What did he want?

Fiona appeared at the door and coughed discreetly. 'Minister, are you very busy? Your daughter is here. You're not due to see that delegation from Esher until noon, so you've plenty of time.'

Elaine checked her watch. 'Has she eaten? Then put the Esherites off till one-thirty and get us both some sandwiches. And wine, please, I think – I could do with a drink. If I don't have time for my daughter, particularly today of all days, then I've got my priorities wrong. Send her in.'

As Fiona was leaving the room, Karen pushed past her and rushed in. She hugged her mother, but the anxious look on the girl's face added to Elaine's pain.

'Mum! What's going on? I was hauled out of a lecture by the dean. The police didn't say much. They said you'd tell me . . .'

Mother and daughter moved instinctively away from the large polished table to less formal armchairs at the other side of the room. Karen kicked off her shoes in a gesture unconsciously similar to Elaine's and curled up. Her mother motioned her to silence as Fiona brought in plates and a bottle. In a few moments the girl was munching a ham sandwich and accepting a glass of white wine.

'So what's happening? The detective said you're connected in some way with this dead body. Did you know her?'

Elaine shook her head. 'Not personally. But there was something which suggested that I or those near me might be in the firing line, a bit.' She stopped. How to tell a daughter about unknown terrors? Karen had never taken much notice as an adolescent when her mother had tried to warn her about the pitfalls of adulthood. The child had insisted on making her own mistakes. She had suffered for it, with what had amounted to a breakdown and a spell in hospital, stomach-pumped after a botched suicide attempt. Elaine was acutely aware that the girl had never revealed the source of her misery then. The only explanation must be that it had involved her parents. The time was not yet ripe, however, to unnerve the youngster.

'Anyway, we have to be more careful. Don't let strangers into the house. Best of all, don't be alone in there.'

'That could be difficult.' Karen reached for another sandwich. 'There's only Fred and me now. Bit like being a married couple.' She chuckled. Her mother looked as if she could do with cheering up. 'Which is what we practically are. And if Fred has his way we will be.'

Elaine stopped eating. 'What – our Fred? The PPS here? I hope he hasn't been taking advantage of you.' Her eyes narrowed as Karen burst out laughing. 'Or is it the other way round, miss? Have you been manipulating him to your own ends?'

Karen's dancing eyes met hers and both succumbed to giggles. The girl was relieved: her mother's miserable face had cut her to the quick. 'Manipulating? In a manner of speaking, you could say that. But he wants to marry me, Mum. I mean! Can you see me as an MP's wife, opening bazaars and clinging to my hat? Poor Fred. He's quite besotted.'

Elaine's jaw dropped in surprise. Karen related the conversation on the Embankment bench in the shadow of Cleopatra's Needle. At last Elaine's practical nature reasserted itself.

'You could do worse,' she remarked thoughtfully. 'He would be considerate, and the fact that he's devoted is a plus, not a problem. Anyway, what's wrong with the idea of you as a conventional wife? I did it long enough.'

'No, you didn't,' her daughter corrected her. 'You never were the little wifey, obsessed with shopping and housework and babies. You were always *working*, the whole time I've known you. With just as big a job as Dad. And it was absolutely clear to me as a kid that your career was at least as important to you as I was – more so, often.'

'My God,' Elaine whispered for the second time that morning. 'Was it really that awful? I didn't mean to neglect you – it's just the way my stupid mind functions.'

Karen shrugged. 'It wasn't awful at all. It isn't now. It was frequently fun being your daughter, in fact. I could get to the front of the queue at the cinema at home. When I was little people would give me sweets – even money, sometimes. Boys didn't like it, that's true. They thought I'd talk politics. But then I wouldn't spend time with anybody who bad-mouthed you anyway, so it panned out fine.'

'I think I owe you an apology,' muttered Elaine. 'There is clearly a side to your life of which I've been completely unaware. If my being famous or so engrossed with myself has caused you grief I'm so sorry.'

'Don't be silly, Mum.' Karen held her mother's hand for a moment.

Outside, Big Ben was striking noon. Elaine waited till the chimes ceased. 'You don't have to be a conventional wife either, Karen, sweetheart,' she said quietly. 'You and Fred should talk it through. Don't say yes unless you're sure. But it's for each couple to decide how they want to live. Most women work; most women today are equal partners, more or less, with their men, at least in decision-making if not in earning power. Even Cabinet Ministers' wives do their own thing. The constituencies don't like it, but so what? And you'd not be a hindrance or handicap to our Fred. In fact, you'd be the making of him.'

Karen licked her fingertips contentedly. 'He thinks so too. But would it work the other way round? I mean – do I *need* to get married? Is there any point in it? I can have everything I want through my own efforts: I don't need a man to provide, as women used to. I can earn a living. I'll pay taxes in my own name. I can buy a house, and have my own mortgage. And car, eventually. I'll have my own pension, and pay for it. I can travel and see the world. I'll compete on equal terms, have a good job and a grand old time. I don't want kids yet, though I suppose I'll go broody some day – but not for ages. Even then I can have them without a piece of paper and gobbledegook at an altar. So come on, Mum, tell me, why bother getting married? What's the point?'

Elaine shifted in her seat, then realised her daughter, though musing out loud, was seeking answers. She leaned back, wineglass in hand, and stared at the ceiling. It was blank: there were no easy solutions written on it.

'I've been asking myself the same thing in recent days,' she responded slowly. She sat up and looked straight at Karen. 'Ever since George asked *me* to marry *him*.'

374

It was Karen's turn to be startled. 'What? George Horrocks? Ooh, Mum. What did you say to him?'

'I said no. Now I'm wondering whether that was wise. And whether I've put him off for good, which would make me very sad.'

There was a moment's silence as both women digested the shared news. Elaine spoke first. 'What do you think of George?'

'Dunno. I've not met him properly. But now I understand why Betty said I should. If you like him, Mum, you carry on. I won't stand in your way.'

'Thank you – though nothing would, if I intended to go ahead. But I've exactly the same worry as you. The question I can't resolve in either my head or my heart is whether I wish to be a wife again, with all the complicated baggage-train of conventions and misunderstandings that implies. If you love someone, you don't make calculations like that – you fall in love and get married; or, as you rightly say, just move in, open a joint account and share the washing-up. Yet experience suggests that a more hard-headed approach, almost a trade negotiation, might be better for the long run. On the other hand, how could anybody human be so cold-blooded, faced with an attractive, charming and loving man?'

Karen gazed shrewdly at her mother. 'Do you love him, Mum?'

Elaine parried. 'Do you love Fred? Or are you simply very fond of him? I take it he's keen on you. And presumably has hidden talents – which I don't want to know about,' she added hastily.

'He's learning,' Karen remarked coolly, which made her mother blink. Then, 'One thing's for sure. They both love us, don't they? Or they wouldn't have asked us to marry them. What a pair we are, we Stalker women. I think I could grow to love Fred in time, but not yet. That's the answer to your question. But you haven't answered mine. Do you love George? Or not?'

If I lost him . . . Elaine allowed the picture of a world without George Horrocks to float before her eyes. The doorstep to the flat would have been empty. No umbrella would have been held to protect her; the rain would have slid down the back of her neck without hindrance. Indeed, there would have been no theatre visit either – no quiet drinks, no delicious suppers at his house, no hands caressing her thighs in his bed. A colder, lonelier world, with the fear that some day a card would inevitably arrive inviting her to George's marriage to someone else.

Elaine rose and crossed to the window overlooking Whitehall. Karen joined her and put an arm around her mother's waist and her head on her mother's shoulder. The two leaned on each other gently like sisters, each with an empty glass in her hand, and considered the past, and the future.

'Yes,' said Elaine simply. 'I do love him. I don't think he knows how much; and neither did I, till you prodded me.' She bowed her head. 'God help me. My marriage to your father failed because I put my job first. I'm in danger of losing George in the same way, but quicker. Do we have to? Isn't there some middle way? We don't want to be old-fashioned wives, yet we need to be loved and secure in the most traditional fashion possible. I can't see the way out.'

'If you love him that's a start. At least Fred and I have time on our side.'

'Get on with you. George and I aren't in our dotage yet.'

'But you're not getting any younger, Mum – '

Elaine gave her daughter a playful push. The discussion had reached its natural end. 'That will do, miss. Now I have people to see. Thank you for coming and cheering me up. God, what a day. There's one thing I'm quite sure of, though.'

Karen was gathering up her bag and jacket. 'Mmm – what's that?'

'That I love *you* very much, and am delighted you're my daughter. If anything happened to you, I don't know what I'd do.'

Chapter Twenty-Two

Elaine opened her eyes with a start, certain it was not yet time to get up, but panicky and fearful. For several minutes she stared at the darkened ceiling in complete incomprehension. A rivulet of sweat trickled between her breasts; her body felt feverish. Then she threw off the duvet and sat up.

There had been a noise. She stayed still and listened. Outside the weather was miserable, dank and windy. A gust rattled the window – was that it? She was thirsty; she rose and entered the kitchen, opened a cupboard for a glass, turned on a tap. The fridge motor rumbled into life and made her jump. Inside it a plate rattled. Still groggy she reached into the fridge and rearranged the contents, then picked moodily at a piece of cheese. It might give her bad dreams, but she did not care.

No psychiatrist was needed to tell her what was the matter. Her brain began to churn again, as she knew it had in those moments of fitful sleep. The image of George's face on her doorstep intermingled with press pictures of the dead girl and her own fingernail as it traced the line on a crumpled piece of magazine of the murdered woman's dried blood. If only George were at her side, he would coax her out of this misery. If George were present, however, she would not feel so disordered.

She mustn't let herself become afraid. Inspector Morris had his job to do. Maybe he had had to warn other women featured in the media that this maniac had an obsession with them, too. Perhaps the lunatic liked blondes – Helen Mirren, or Felicity Kendall, women whom she resembled slightly. She had not thought to ask and was uncertain whether such knowledge would have made her feel more secure or less.

Nobody realised the hidden dangers facing prominent women. To be targeted directly by a nutter, an irrational person who could become a danger to herself or her family or (because of his twisted mind) to an imagined rival or a critic, was a permanent worry. It had happened to Monica Seles when a man had lunged with a knife and disrupted the champion tennis player's career. It had happened to actress Jodie Foster and led to an assassination attempt. More than one actress had had to resort to the courts to fend off an over-zealous admirer.

What would she do, if she found herself in such trouble? The advice was to stay cool and avoid confrontations. The safest course was exactly the opposite of her instinct to stand up and fight for herself – it was better to attempt to win the person's trust, and in so doing to disarm him. Even unwittingly, over a period of time loyalties could shift. The phenomenon, she had heard, was dubbed the 'Stockholm syndrome', after the Sveriges Kreditbank robbery in 1973, when a remarkable realignment of affection of victims towards their captors took place. The befriending didn't have to be real, but it had to be convincing.

Elaine's teeth chattered. She returned to her bedroom and sat down, shoulders slumped. An early start to the day loomed, with a smart turn-out and preferably a sparkling performance, yet she felt terrible. She ran her fingers through her hair: it was dry, straw-like, the ends split and lifeless. A much-needed appointment to keep the fading locks blonde had had to be postponed.

What had also disturbed her slumber had been the recurrent demands of the MIND speech. It could no longer be ignored. The bland phrases of the agreed text, jumbled, ungrammatical and disorganised but with fragments of coherence – like the conversation of an Alzheimer's sufferer, she recognised grimly – jarred in her head. *These were not her words, not her sentiments.* Did she have to say them?

The window-pane rattled again, suddenly, loudly. Elaine gave a little cry. That was not the wind, surely, but a pebble or gravel. Briefly she debated whether it would be safe to check, then shook her head crossly. She pulled up the window and leaned out. A blast of cold air hit her. Nobody was visible in the poorly lit street below, only a swirl of litter from a torn binbag. Yet the notion persisted that the disturbance had not been entirely imaginary.

There was nothing more she could do. She shut the window, crawled back into bed and tucked the bedclothes tightly up to her chin. She tried to breathe deeply and rhythmically. If she gazed long enough into the dark, sleep, however episodic, would come.

As the train lurched around a curve Martin Chadwick braced himself, bent across the table and whispered as loud as he dared.

'Minister – forgive me. I don't wish to disturb you. Have you read today's press cuttings yet? You should. Especially the piece in the *Globe.*'

He pushed the photocopied bundle across and glanced around distastefully. It was all very well for the Minister to come over public-spirited and insist on taking the train. First-class rail travel offered certain advantages, he would admit, especially in such wet weather. Quite decent coffee in white cups. A proper tablecloth with silk flowers perched in a little vase. A free *Daily Telegraph* for those passengers who, having paid over £70 for their tickets, were too mean or rushed to buy a paper. The chance to stretch one's legs and to use the loo. A magnificent breakfast, had the Minister not turned up her nose at slices of bacon, black pudding and fried potatoes, a disdain Chadwick had felt honour-bound to imitate. No: what irked him was the presence of other passengers, those whom Transport Minister Steve Norris had memorably called 'dreadful people'. They were dreadful because they were *listening.* The Rover, however cramped, bore no risks that someone might overhear his elegantly phrased advice.

'You trying to warn me – are the papers nice or hostile?' Elaine began to turn over the pages. The extracts had been delivered early to her flat but she had had no time to read any.

Chadwick grimaced. 'See for yourself, Minister. Page fourteen.'

Obediently Elaine found the right page and began to read the editorial out loud.

STOP THIS VANDALISM NOW!

As police today stepped up the hunt for the murderer of good-time girl Yvonne Pasari (23), whose naked body was found behind Finsbury Park Tube station on Sunday morning, fears grew that a new serial killer could be on the loose.

Inspector David Morris of the Metropolitan Police confirmed, 'There are definite similarities with a series of attacks some years ago. We are checking forensic evidence.'

In the early eighties, the killer of several women, two in London and one in the Leicester area, was never found. Police think it possible he has been in prison in the interim, or in a mental institution.

The *Globe* sees grave cause for concern. It is time to change the rules over who is let out and who is locked up. To ensure public safety these killers must be put behind bars for good – and that means, *for ever.*

Think of Jonathan Zito in 1992. A harmless musician was knifed by paranoid schizophrenic Christopher Clunis. Or the case in 1993 when hostel worker Georgina Robinson was murdered by an inmate who had gone shopping. He returned with the knife he used to kill her.

Those maniacs' previous violent history was on record. No action was taken. The slaughter of innocents was the result.

Nobody could claim that Yvonne Pasari was an innocent. Hers is a familiar tale of abuse, rape and neglect followed by prostitution. She had been on the streets since the age of 13. She ran risks every night of the week. But that does not mean she deserved to die at the hands of the latest Ripper. Nor do we want to see another die at the same hands.

The answer is obvious. To every normal man and woman in the country, but not to our politicians. *Lock 'em up and throw away the key.*

What will happen instead? Take today, for example. In Birmingham, Minister Elaine Stalker is due to address the annual conference of MIND, a pressure group for the mentally ill.

Will she tell them that the policy has gone too far? Will she put public safety first? No. Instead she is planning to confirm the closure of one of the most respected mental institutions in the country, the prestigious St Kitts Hospital in Leicestershire.

Over 400 patients will have to leave, yet no new provision has been made. Instead they will be cared for 'in the community' – with all the risks that entails. Eighty trained and experienced staff are set to lose their jobs. Some are broken-hearted at leaving the place where they have worked for decades. Many will quit the NHS, their skills lost for ever.

And that's what will happen to the patients too – they will disappear into our cities and housing estates, some to become homeless, some to beg, some to sink into depression and even commit suicide. And others to commit serious crimes and end up in prison.

That does not have to happen. Instead the *Globe* calls on Minister Elaine Stalker to restore our trust in this government.

Come on, Elaine. Announce today that St Kitts will stay open. Tell us the money will be found for its refurbishment. That the trained nurses and doctors can keep their jobs. That its work can continue. And that we can sleep easy in our beds.

There will be no more restful sleep for Ms Pasari. Tonight the prostitutes of North London walk in fear of their lives. Tomorrow it could be a respectable woman. It could be your wife, your mother, your girlfriend, you. Write to your MP now.

'God, that's a dismal start,' Elaine muttered. 'Whatever my view on St Kitts it's hardly "prestigious". A dump, more like. And where did they get these figures? There aren't anything near four hundred patients there.'

'From last year's annual report of the hospital trust, I expect.' Chadwick shrugged. 'Before the most recent run-down. The staff numbers are a bit out too, but then I'd expect the unions to exaggerate. That's probably their source.'

The clip did not include the photographs of the demonstration at St Kitts and its tragic aftermath, but Elaine could imagine what the double-page spread looked like.

She bit her lip. The grime on the train window, the slanting rain outside, obscured the landscape from view and reinforced her unease that she did not know where she was heading. 'You anticipating strife in Brum?'

'The police will be out in force,' Chadwick replied grimly. 'You open the conference so you're the first speaker. We've indicated that you won't take questions –.' He held up his hand as Elaine began to protest. 'I know it's your preference to be open, Minister, but these are the instructions of the Secretary of State. This closure is a delicate matter.'

That was news to Elaine. She searched Chadwick's face but learned no more. Her disquiet intensified. Without further conversation she opened the file marked for the day, took out her revised speech and forced herself to concentrate.

Keith Quin MP had had a good Parliament, so far. The short, balding, somewhat overweight Labour Member for Manchester Canalside had entered the Commons in 1987 full of fire and brimstone, determined to grind Thatcherism into the ground. In that, he had to admit, he had not yet succeeded, though his spirits were rising as he sensed that change was at last in the air.

A decade or more and two lost general elections behind him, battle-scarred and hardened, he had altered his views five times on Europe, voted for John Smith, Tony Blair and the abolition of Clause Four, first derided then embraced grant-maintained schools and learned to denigrate Arthur Scargill, thus demonstrating a knack of always being on the winning side. Like many of his fellows he had absorbed some tough lessons, not least the value of patience.

One more push should do it. For the voters, especially the bulk who counted – the English – liked Mr Blair. Poor Michael Foot, he of the wild eye and exotic diction, had never been taken seriously. Neil Kinnock had been worse, with his Welsh accent. John Smith had a more reassuring style but nevertheless was a Scot. But nice Mr Blair was so profoundly and obviously *English*, with his tidy London house, his barrister wife (did Welsh MPs have barrister wives? Keith thought not, on the whole) and bright children at good schools, that the public were charmed. Whether in the end that would translate into victory remained to be seen.

The current disarray on the government side was a big help, but it was also a puzzle. Keith knew little about the workings of the Conservative Party, except that it appeared a streamlined and wealthy machine compared with his own, which was manned by a handful of gloomy activists, most of whom he distrusted intensely. The Tories seemed to have more fun, more style. He pictured flowered dresses and big hats at garden parties at which champagne was quaffed and large cheques discreetly proffered. Yet Conservative Central Office no longer bothered to conceal the £16 million overdraft run up years before with no visible means of repayment. That left virtually nothing in the kitty to fight the next election, a thought which made him hug himself with delight.

For Keith, deep-down, a mystery remained. With all those natural advantages of schooling, breeding and inheritance, how could the Tories have made such a God-awful mess of things?

His current task was to exploit that mess in one particular instance. He walked jauntily down the Library corridor and pushed open the door to the Speaker's offices. The first room was empty, but steam curling from a half-filled coffee-cup on the big desk indicated life nearby. Above his head Big Ben chimed nine-thirty. The bloody thing chimed constantly; enough to drive you crackers.

Would he like to be Speaker, some day? He pondered briefly. No, all that ceremony and gobbledegook was not for him. He'd gratefully accept junior ministership under Mr Blair should it come his way, or failing that prop up the Kremlin Bar with chosen cronies for the rest of his career. It wasn't a bad life.

'Can I help you?'

The Speaker's trainbearer was a small, trim man. He knew everyone from his vantage point at the Speaker's left elbow: each day his head would bob up and down, his hand scribble furiously on a notepad, as Members rose in their places to indicate they wished to catch her eye. In quieter moments he manned her outer office. The job required both discretion and cynicism, but not humour.

With a flourish Quin produced a piece of typed script.

'Yes,' he said importantly as his listener waited. 'I want to put down a Private Notice Question. For this afternoon. For the Department of Health. Am I in time?'

The official glanced at the clock. 'Just. The Speaker likes PNQs before ten so you've squeaked in. It'll be considered at noon, then if she agrees the subject will go on the annunciator soon after.'

'She will accept it, surely?' Quin looked anxious.

'If it's an emergency, and significant, and not a prank, yes. The Minister then has to come hot-footing it here to answer at three-thirty. What's it say?'

Quin squared his shoulders, smiled and read: '"Would the Secretary of State for Health please tell the House . . ."' He finished the sentence and grinned. 'That should set the cat nicely among the pigeons, don't you think?'

The lights were too bright. They blazed down and blinded her. Her retinas were jagged with green and red. Her pulses were pounding: the rush of blood into her brain, rhythmic and urgent, made her nauseous. She wanted to shield her eyes, but any such gesture would produce an instant reaction from the banks of photographers. Every time she moved her head or blinked, light bulbs flashed, camera motors whirred. Their editors needed a frown, a moment of despair or confusion, to liven the front page.

She felt disorientated; lack of sleep made her light-headed, with a hint of hysteria under the surface. If she could not see her audience she could not judge their reactions, whether warm or hostile, nor gauge how to win their approval against the odds. No wonder the Nazis used fierce light for interrogations.

'Madam President, ladies and gentlemen,' she began, but halfway through the first paragraph she faltered and had to take a sip of water. Behind her on the platform a chair creaked.

She glanced up. Photographers jostled. Click, click, click. Words were coming out of her mouth but mechanically, without her usual verve. 'We are making progress,' she heard herself say. 'Safeguards are in place . . .' She passed a hand over her eyes. The momentary blackness was worse than the light.

The text was swimming before her, hidden by purple blotches. With an effort she persevered and stared at her notes. Their spare print was too faint. Her eyes began to water but she dared not reach for a tissue – the Minister wiping her eyes, almost in tears, would make a devastating picture. She tossed her head as a dog might, and took a deeper breath.

She didn't normally suffer from stage-fright. What was happening to her? Then the lines resolved themselves and suddenly she was looking once more at the morning's news story, the names 'Clunis' and 'Robinson' in bold headlines; and the face of the dead mutilated prostitute stared up at her from the lectern.

She had to get through this speech. It was the one agreed. Its sentences filled the anodyne press release even now being handed out by Mr Butler, the press officer, though each copy bore the rider 'Check against delivery'. It set out as had a dozen other speeches she had made with mounting distaste the correct policy, agreed and refined over years. It was not her place nor in her power, she now realised, to alter it. The working group of Ministers had met once or twice, but in the absence of any political will a reversal was impossible. Neither the drive nor the groundwork to make a considered judgement were available. Nobody but herself was in the least interested.

Why had she ever wanted to be a government Minister? What crazy urge had stimulated this ambition? It had started with altruism, of that she was reasonably sure – the desire to help others, after the death of her child. That was compounded by the huge pleasure when a speech was applauded, or when a case she had pursued succeeded, or when a new approach she had advocated proved popular. And she had thoroughly enjoyed the publicity, even orchestrated it, at least to begin with. Like most Ministers she had been gratified when her picture or a quote appeared in the press, sure that here was evidence she was doing her job properly. But not any more. If Chadwick was right and she was a good Minister, why did it bring her such distress? If George was right and she could fulfil herself outside politics, why did she continue to obey the rules, particularly when she was utterly certain, as she was today, that a mistake was being made?

What price loyalty – to the Prime Minister, to the party, to Ted Bampton? Somewhere inside her pounding head she heard a hollow laugh. The Prime Minister had not turned out to be a great deal of use to her apart from the original promotion, but that was no surprise: she could not expect favourable treatment. Their affair was long since over. As for the party, it was hard to be loyal when each month fewer of the policies enunciated by its main spokesmen made sense to her or to the electorate. If the sum total of the loyalty she could offer was to keep her own counsel on other colleagues' briefs, that did not restrict her action on her own.

And Bampton? At the thought a sour taste came into her mouth. It was clear from Chadwick's comment on the train that instructions had been given behind her back. The realisation that a fellow politician might use a civil servant – part of the opposing army – to keep her decent instincts in check was galling. Working for Ted had turned out to be a miserable experience.

It was entirely her own fault. She'd not been the great success she had hoped. Not matched up to her own expectations, nor anyone else's. Not shown that skill in getting on with people, so essential in the distorted world of politics, with even those she heartily disliked like Derek Harrison. Her natural honesty in such murky waters counted against her, not in her favour.

Only two pages left. The passage about St Kitts loomed. The audience was restless: her ambivalence had communicated itself. In the front row journalists watched her intently, then wrote in bursts. She could anticipate their verdicts. The Minister's speech did not go down well: a wooden performance, a lack-lustre stance. Rifts within the department. The Minister in a straitjacket, told by her boss to stick to the line. Bampton had wagged the finger and insisted: no imaginative comments, no jokes, no wisecracks. Mrs Stalker looked as if she wished she were anywhere else on earth. That last, at least, would be true.

With a little shake of defiance she raised her head.

'I mentioned earlier my admiration for your campaign for the closure of old hospitals,' she said. *This was it.* 'By and large you were right. But the public has expressed concern that we might have gone too far. So have sections of the tabloid press.'

A clatter of disapproval rolled around the delegates. Elaine raised her hand to calm them. On the front row Butler the press officer, looking alarmed, flicked through his text as he searched in vain for the Minister's new words. She felt a sudden surge of excitement, of freedom.

She squared her shoulders and continued: 'As a rule, as you know, their opinions and mine are not close. In particular I deplore their depiction of the mentally ill person as always dangerous or violent. That is wrong and unacceptable.'

A ragged spate of clapping broke out. Strong words, the taking of sides, was what they had come to hear, not the mealy-mouthed insincerities of most government speakers.

Elaine paused, glanced behind at her boats and put a metaphoric match to them.

'I am not therefore bowing to any emotional pressure, nor to any ill-informed populist campaign, when I say that I have some sympathy for the view that we have shut too many hospitals.'

The applause faded and a murmur took its place. Emboldened, exhilarated, she drew herself up to her full height.

'I am therefore announcing today that I will not be closing St Kitts Hospital in Leicestershire. The reason is that I am far from convinced that sufficient alternative provision has been made. It will have a five-year reprieve. I will invite the health trust to consider how its work can continue until Ministers are so satisfied. Till then St Kitts stays open, and I wish it well.'

Dimly behind the lights she was aware of noise and catcalls but she no longer cared. With a few anodyne sentences she finished and stepped away from the microphone. In a moment, after perfunctory thanks had been uttered, Chadwick hustled her down steps and into the back room.

He slammed the door shut. On the other side of it she could hear Butler fending off raised voices from both angry delegates and an eager press. She felt light-headed, pure, happy.

Chadwick's face was like thunder. 'Well, Minister, you've done it now,' he remarked coldly. It occurred to Elaine that he had been given strict orders to keep her under control and would himself be carpeted on their return. 'Am I right in thinking that new policy was entirely your own idea, or did you manage to get clearance between New Street Station and here?'

Elaine was donning her coat and gloves. 'I don't think you should speak to me like that, Mr Chadwick,' she responded calmly. 'I said what I knew to be right. Anyway, it's done now, so I shall merely invite my colleagues to support me. Most of them don't give a damn.'

An assistant sidled in and handed Chadwick a note. He read it and snorted. His voice when he spoke again had a triumphant edge.

'Well, Minister, you'll have a chance in a couple of hours to find out. The Opposition have put down a PNQ about the closure of St Kitts and the Speaker has accepted it. You'll be explaining yourself the moment you get back. I wish you luck.'

The ministerial car was waiting at Euston at the end of the platform well away from the press. Once in the back seat Elaine sat silent and gazed unseeing out of the window. Chadwick spent most of the journey mumbling in Whitehallese into the car phone.

Several requests were relayed for press comment but Elaine shook her head. At the dispatch box she could defend herself, but by then the whips would have been at work rallying support. The last thing the Prime Minister needed was the weakening of another member of his government. The tabloids and the editorial in tomorrow's *Standard* would sing her praises, though that was not why she had done it. She had gambled, but it was hardly an earth-shattering revolution. After a slight wobble and a row with Bampton, she would be safe.

And after that? She pushed her mind beyond the worries of recent weeks. Her stand on St Kitts made her feel different, more confident. It had cleared her conscience: she had done what she could to avenge the life of that poor dead girl, however remote the link. Were she to be hauled before the Chief Whip to be ticked off, she would seize the opportunity to request a transfer in the next reshuffle. She had had enough of Bampton, his arrogance, his belligerence, his lack of courtesy, his picky criticisms, his failure to trust her. She was sick to death of having to explain herself when other Ministers received the benefit of the doubt, probably simply because they were men. If the government meant what it said about promoting women then it could start with her.

The thought occurred that maybe she should circumvent the problem and ask to speak to the Chief Whip herself. She might also call George, apologise for her miserable manners to him, and ask if he'd like supper.

One thing was for sure, she had no intention of doing her boxes, not tonight. If necessary she would plead illness or overwork. She needed the night off, desperately.

That her reflections were not entirely rational, that she was dog-tired just beneath the surface, made her smile wanly. That she had by her wilful actions confirmed Ted's lack of faith in her was a consideration pushed to the furthest reaches of her mind. She snuggled down inside her coat, leaned her face against the glass and drifted into central London in a doze.

'Whaddya mean, it's been stolen?'

Wholesale greengrocer Calum McCafferty, otherwise known as

'Mr Spud', and thirty years in the business, shoved his unshaven chin into the twitching face of his delivery man. 'How can you lose a van? Wha' happened?'

'I tell you, I was only gone a minute. I was delivering potatoes to the mini-market on the corner of Blake Street. I took the last bag in round the back and got the geezer to sign. I come out – and it's gawn.'

'But why in Christ's name would anybody wanna steal a van half full of carrots and cauliflower? Ciggies, whisky, yeah. Prize antiques: that I could understand. But veggies?'

'It was a good van. Unmarked. Maybe somebody wants it for a robbery,' the younger man offered helpfully.

Calum's eyes narrowed. 'Oh, aye. One of your mates, was it? Going in for a bit of ram-raiding, are we? It'll end up smashed to smithereens. Worthless – a write-off. Bloody 'ell.' He sighed heavily and brooded, then brightened. Provided the insurers were satisfied, a smaller van would be adequate in future and he could pocket the difference.

He grunted at his assistant. 'I'll get on to the insurance company. You'd better have your tale pat when the assessor comes round. Meanwhile turn your tiny brain to this question – how'm I going to get three ton of best Spanish onions out to my customers in the next couple of hours?'

The Secretary of State crashed his fist down on the table. Coffee-cups jumped. A file slithered to the floor. Above his head chandeliers shimmered in sympathy. At his side, his face a mask, stood Martin Chadwick. In the background hovered Miss Clarkson, eyes blinking, earrings dancing in agitation. Of one fact there was not a shred of doubt: Ted Bampton, pacing around his office, was apoplectic.

'No! You did the exact opposite of what you were expressly told to do. You departed from an agreed and cleared text. You made it up as you went along. You've caused endless headaches in this department and elsewhere. And you want me to support you?'

Elaine, her back to the mock fireplace, returned his stare calmly. She felt serene. The lunchtime news had been full of her morning's exploits. Her picture was on the front of the *Evening Standard* – 'MINISTER DEFIES PARTY LINE ON CLOSURES.' Her office had been bombarded with requests for interviews. The public perception of her defiant act matched her own – that she had done what she believed in, despite enormous pressure to conform. The main result of the fuss would be to enhance her reputation. The Prime Minister, if begged to get rid of her by this red-faced monster now dancing attendance before her, would simply move her to another department. Thus she would have killed two birds with one stone.

'I don't see why not. It's only one hospital closure. Not a significant place, though it's close to my patch. I've hardly reversed years of policy – most of the hospitals have long since vanished and been replaced by supermarkets. If this gives us breathing space to rethink what we're doing, that'll be a good thing, surely?'

'That's not the point. Are you nuts, or what? You went behind my back. You've upset one of our keenest supporters in the health authority. We've got developers demanding millions in compensation. And what the hell for, Elaine? So you can set yourself up as the Mother Teresa of the NHS, is that it?'

His face was turning purple. Elaine felt a twinge of alarm.

'I was merely trying to do what I thought was correct. It was my brief, after all – nobody else's. And I will be happy to defend myself this afternoon in the Chamber.'

'No, you bloody well won't. I'm answering that PNQ, not you.' Bampton wiped his mouth with the back of his hand and glared at her. 'You'll stay put. In the department. Don't budge, don't go anywhere. Certainly not to the House. And keep your big lip buttoned, do you hear?'

She took a step away from the crude fierceness of his malevolence and found herself with her back against the wall. Behind him Miss Clarkson was wringing her hands in silent sympathy. Elaine recalculated rapidly. The situation must not be allowed to deteriorate any further.

'Ted . . .' She held out her hand in supplication.

'What?' He spat out the word.

'I . . . I'm sorry. I seem to have set you against me. That was not my intention.' She paused, then was silent. Common sense and ambition together told her she should withdraw the St Kitts closure, and tell him so now, at once, if Ted was to be mollified. He was a key player in her career and she should not have so heedlessly embarrassed him. But she could say no more.

He waited, then shrugged. His voice was gruff. 'We all do lots of things we don't mean, Elaine. But if I were you I'd sit here quietly for a while. And seriously consider my position.'

Derek Harrison made no attempt to hide the bounce in his step as he walked towards Members' Lobby a few minutes ahead of the Speaker's

389

procession. He was not surprised to find his sleeve touched by several hacks, notebooks at the ready.

'So what does the 1922 Committee think of all this?' a voice hissed. The Liverpool accent was unmistakable.

Derek turned. 'Ah, Jim. Well, I can't speak for the whole executive, naturally. We have a meeting later today, then a few of us will go and see the Chief Whip.' That did not sound weighty enough. 'And the PM, if necessary.'

'Stalker's been told to keep her bloody mouth shut. Bampton's answering the question,' Betts continued, never taking his eyes from Harrison's face. He was rewarded with the faintest hint of a smirk.

'Really? I wouldn't know about that. Maybe the Secretary of State wishes to declare his unshakeable support for his Minister of State's judgement.'

Betts laughed. 'And pigs might fly. Thanks, mate.'

'It will be on in five minutes, Minister,' Fiona murmured respectfully. 'If you want to watch, you'd better come now.'

A dreadful tiredness had overtaken Elaine's post-speech euphoria. As she climbed the short flight of stairs to the press office, the sole place in the department wired up for the Parliamentary Channel, her legs felt like lead. It was only with an enormous effort that she held her head high as she entered the room and took a chair.

Two press officers slid into seats on either side – like warders, she suddenly realised, detailed to ensure that she made no contact with the outside world. They nodded curtly and averted their eyes. Fiona, quietly solicitous, brought her a cup of milky coffee and, most unusually, a small side plate with a slice of cherry cake. Nursery fare, suitable for sick children.

Prime Minister's Question Time was nearly done. Normally she would be seated in the row behind Roger, near the civil servants' box, dressed in a smart suit of an eye-catching colour. Constituents would tell her proudly that they'd seen her and would look for her in the same spot every week. Instead Fred Laidlaw, her junior Minister, was seated there, and looking anxious.

Not that it was the best location if one wanted seriously to follow the proceedings. Usually she was deafened as the voices of the protagonists were routinely drowned out by barracking. On the other hand, sometimes she could hear more than the microphones would pick up – the nastiness about Opposition Members, the sexist comments, the crude imitation of female squeaky voices and of any regional accent which dared show itself on the other side.

Her curiosity was vaguely aroused. How totally different it looked from the viewpoint of the camera compared with being there. The broadcast made the proceedings seem more dignified and mannered. With a *frisson* of amusement and old love she noted the slight bald patch on the top of Roger's head, where normal cameras seldom caught it. She wondered if he knew.

Keith Quin perched on the edge of the front bench like a turkey-cock, aquiver with energy. His right hand clutched a sheaf of papers. He watched the Speaker's face.

'Right! Time's up,' called the Speaker, for all the world like a northern barmaid.

The Prime Minister subsided thankfully, then shifted to make room for Ted Bampton. Miss Boothroyd peered over her glasses. When she was satisfied that everybody was ready, the circus could continue.

'Private Notice Question – Mr Keith Quin.'

Keith rose to his feet a mite too quickly and knocked over the glass of water his leader had recently poured. He decided to ignore it.

'With permission, Madam Speaker, I would ask the Secretary of State to answer the question of which I have given him private notice, namely what's happening to St Kitts Hospital?'

The unaccustomed informality of the question and Quin's grin brought chuckles around the benches. The water dripped on to his feet. Ted Bampton rose at the dispatch box, hitched up his trousers and waited for silence.

'Madam Speaker, in order to put paid to any speculation I must tell the House that press reports are incorrect. There has been no reprieve for St Kitts Hospital. It will be shut down in the near future. Arrangements are being made . . .'

Elaine turned freezing cold. In fear she gripped the edge of her seat. The press officers beside her did not move a muscle.

She had expected that Ted would bluster, would circumlocute, would be at his politician's best. He might express regret that mild misunderstandings had occurred. But there would be no question that he would defend her vigorously as a member of his team and stoutly declare his faith in her, at least in public. To do otherwise would call into question his own judgement, not only hers. His language might be lukewarm. He might let it be known that the reprieve was a one-off and did not signal any shift in policy – even that, Elaine could have accepted. Whatever fuss he might make in the privacy of his room, however soured their relationship, in public he would display a united front. That was what leadership was all about.

What she did not expect was this chilling reversal. He had completely overruled her. It was as if every scrap of work she had done, the time and effort she had put in, the high reputation she had gained in so many fields, were as nought. *Ted was wiping her out.* And from his set expression he knew exactly what he was doing.

'What's going on?' she whispered, bewildered.

In the Chamber a roar greeted the announcement. Members leapt to their feet, trying to catch the Speaker's eye, Harrison prominent among them. The Speaker called his name. As the remote camera sought him out he pulled his cuffs, checked his jacket buttons were fastened, and settled his face to studious composure.

'Madam Speaker. May I congratulate my Right Honourable Friend on a most sensible decision. Isn't it a fact that the days of incarceration are over? Haven't we allocated billions of pounds to ensure that something better is available? Isn't care in the community a reality, and one of this government's greatest achievements?'

'Hear, hear!' came loudly and dutifully from those around him. Ted half rose, but Derek had not quite done.

'And doesn't this call into question the future of the Minister of State for Health?' He smiled sweetly and resumed his seat.

Bampton's mouth clamped shut. Through gritted teeth he managed to squeeze out the formula: 'I have complete confidence in every member of my team.' He pointedly failed to mention her, let alone single her out for praise. The message was plain.

'Ah, but *we* haven't.' A voice floated above the baying crowd. Elaine and the television audience did not hear it, but Fred did, and hung his head. And so did the Prime Minister, as he quietly left the Chamber.

'I think, Ted, that I am entitled to an explanation.'

The evening was turning dark. Traffic ground slowly down Whitehall, red tail-lights winking. Bampton's office had no curtains but the lamps were switched on, angular branches of upturned neon which cast a surreal light not quite bright enough to read by, as if style had taken precedence over utility.

The woman who now sat before him almost buried in a large armchair, a weak whisky cradled in her hands, seemed smaller and frailer than the Boadicea of the morning. She looked as if she had been crying. Ted Bampton felt relieved not to be facing a screaming harridan, as he had feared; but the sight of Elaine's haggard face made him think of one of his daughters the day she failed to get into university. The best fatherly advice then had been not to give up but to try again. The same line would not be appropriate on this occasion.

'I couldn't let you make policy on the hoof, you must see that,' he began, and stopped.

'That's not the problem and you know it.' Her voice was becoming stronger. She took a sip of the whisky. 'Ever since we started working together I have somehow failed to win your trust. We have never gelled, have we? Not as a team, not as superior and subordinate. And I have tried, Ted, I truly have.'

She looked as if she were about to start crying again. Ted Bampton shifted uncomfortably. Damn women, always expecting special treatment and never quite making the grade. Except Margaret Thatcher: she had had what it takes. But they only came like that once in a generation. Thank God.

He shrugged. 'Well, I have no trouble getting on fine with everybody else. Has it occurred to you it might be you?'

Elaine looked at him, shocked to the core. 'You want my resignation, is that it?'

Bampton rose and walked away, out of the circle of adversity. He did not reply. It was not his place to tell the lady that she was not fitted for government, but that was his considered opinion. To have said too much would have been deliberately unkind, and he was not that. Instead he stood on the hearthrug, hands thrust deep into his pockets, and for several minutes examined the toes of his shoes with his lower lip thrust out and a hint of impatience.

'Then you shall have it. I can't work like this any more. It is making me so miserable.'

It needed only a friendly or thoughtful word, a whisper of consolation and compassion, to bring her back into the fold. Whatever was broken could be mended. But to do that needed a greater spirit than Bampton's.

Instead he turned and headed towards the door. With his hand on the knob, he paused.

'Right, then, if you feel that way. Take your time. I'll leave you to it.'

She stared at him, unseeing, as tears rolled down her cheeks.

He went out and closed the door behind him with a firm click. As he walked down the corridor he wondered if she meant it. You never could tell with women like that.

The Prime Minister's wife prided herself on knowing her husband rather better than he did himself. That evening some instinct told her to intercept the first editions of the papers and take them up herself to the modest eyrie he kept as his private study.

She was startled to find him stretched out on the old sofa, feet up, though still in his shoes, a drink to hand, eyes closed, and one hand half covering his face. An expression of total desolation suffused the fine features. As she entered the room he started, then slowly swung his legs back to the floor.

'Roger? You feeling OK?'

She handed him the newspapers. He glanced at the lurid headlines one by one and tossed them aside.

'What? Yes. Well, no, if truth be told. This Stalker business. What a shambles.'

'You could have told her to think again.'

'I could, but Ted wouldn't have her back and it would have been impossible to move her anywhere else. Damaged goods, if you see what I mean. Anyway, she was adamant. She'd had enough, she said.'

'So she's really gone? She'll be missed.'

'She will.'

Roger bowed his head and stared deep into his drink. Once long ago he had poured Elaine a whisky, and as he had gazed into the liquid had seen in its swirling colours her golden hair and her laughing hazel eyes. His face clouded and he took a large swallow. A faint sigh escaped from his lips.

His wife seated herself gently at his side and placed a hand on his knee. 'She was somebody very special, wasn't she, Roger?'

He wondered whether to lie. In his public life he lied and covered up the whole time: the role demanded it. Deception was a deeply ingrained part of his world, and part of his self-protecting nature. He had never told Elaine how he had loved her, though the memory had never faded. The letter he had written had stayed hidden and he had nearly forgotten it. Her elevation had come because she deserved it, not because he was biased. The same entirely rational considerations had led him to accept with a heavy heart her handwritten note a few hours before. To act otherwise would have been to expose them both. And that would never do.

To his wife he owed something akin to the truth. He sensed that she knew anyway. Perhaps she had always known. He put his arm around her and kissed her softly on the cheek.

'Yes, she was lovely,' he whispered. 'But she's gone. There is nothing for you to worry about. Tomorrow I have to replace her. Any ideas?'

Chapter Twenty-Three

It had been the utmost in grand modernity. At its opening in May 1906 a double room with private bath cost thirty shillings a night and servants' quarters six shillings. Its proprietor was the first to put a jug of iced water on each table for his American clientele without being asked, the first anywhere to offer a bathroom en suite with each bedroom. It was and remains a masterpiece: the arcaded façade is a copy of the Rue de Rivoli, while the interior with its gilded acanthus leaves entwined over every column, its Carrara marble fireplaces and glittering chandeliers is as fine a celebration of Louis XVI as anything the French court contrived. And all in the heart of central London.

As Karen climbed the four steps of the Ritz's Piccadilly entrance the hotel seemed to her the height of vulgarity. That the original backers (according to the leaflet she picked up in the foyer) were the Blackpool Building and Vendor Company Limited seemed entirely appropriate. She strolled through the main lobby and halted before a sculpture of Neptune with a water nymph. The god's triton was carried at a provocative angle while the lady writhed enticingly around an open oyster shell. The blatant imagery made the girl smile.

Yet perhaps Neptune's avid expression was a warning. In an hour or so she could expect a similar ogle on the moustached face of one of England's top tabloid journalists.

She did not want to meet Jim Betts, but he had pursued her with a persistence which had made her falter. He had suggested dinner at the grandest locations, day trips to the coast, even to Paris on Eurostar. Eventually he had hinted over the phone that he was aware that the house in Battersea contained only half its previous occupants; that, he had continued, implied she was living alone with Mr Fred Laidlaw MP, a young man of impeccable credentials, who was carving out a splendid new career in her mother's old department. Betts announced as well that he had been asked to write an in-depth article about her mother. There were unanswered questions, too, about Mr Anthony York. Now, was she going to co-operate or not?

The tone of his remarks had sickened her. That Betts knew less than he implied was likely; that he would invent what he didn't know, even more so. He was keen to dish the dirt on any MP, indeed any public figure, for that was his chosen role. Through Karen he had a link with several. Her mother had gone into hiding, so she was an obvious target. Betts had also made it clear that he wanted her for herself: probably in part because she had resisted him so far, and that he found irresistible.

The moment had come to accept, however reluctantly, his offer of dinner. The encounter would present a unique opportunity. She could find out what he had obtained or believed about Fred, and put him to rights about their relationship. She wondered if 'just good friends' sounded convincing. She could confirm the good character of Anthony – his decency, his integrity – and counter any speculation to the contrary. And she could mount a fierce defence of her mother.

The worry surfaced that she was being naïve. Years of experience had taught her never, ever, to trust the press. Yet should she turn her back entirely the *Globe* would print whatever rubbish it fancied. She had a duty to perform.

Wistfully she traced her finger down the triton. One more deep-seated fear remained. Her previous sexual encounter with Betts years before had been an occasion of too much trust combined with excess alcohol which had ended in disaster. He had snapped: the result had been violent. Her total reticence on the subject since had been the price of Betts's own silence on her mother's affair with Roger Dickson. Had he ever written a word, she would have shopped him. And, though she could look the man in the eye, still he terrified her. Betts, and that memory of him, were devils yet to be exorcised.

Neptune appeared to wink at her. She would have to be careful.

The Ritz and its glories had provoked similarly mixed reactions in the breast of another guest who had passed her unnoticed and taken a seat at a table under a potted palm.

Varun Bhadeshia was a year or so younger than Karen. He did not have her advantage of university education, but like her was aware of the powers of the press, especially when directed at a parent in the public eye whose behaviour had been less than impeccable.

It was no coincidence that his particular hatred was also reserved for the same person, Jim Betts of the *Globe*. There were others, of course; but Betts was the best known, acknowledged as the hard man of the tabloids, the one who would defend his profession against all critics with vigour and a total lack of concern for the feelings of those he hounded, and then go out and do it again. The journalist's photo, cigarette defiantly to hand, adorned most of his output these days; his byline on a front page would guarantee a surge of sales. If ever the chance presented itself, however, Varun Bhadeshia would willingly confront the man who had in his view ruined his family.

Varun squared his shoulders. He had taken some care with his appearance; the dark suit fitted comfortably on his solid figure. His father had once in an intimate moment touched the boy's cheek and murmured that his good looks came from his mother. The thought of his parents, now so far away and in such disgrace, made him ache. That trouble about the share purchase was behind him: because of his age it had been decided not to prosecute Varun. For him, however, the sense of loss over the collapse of the business was the more acute, since while it existed his father had demonstrated a confidence in him which he had cherished, and which held out the promise of their working closely together in future. None of that could happen now.

Instead he had to earn a living. Discreet inquiries in the community had drawn something of a blank; it dawned on Varun that outside his immediate family his father's blatant courting of the Conservatives and what amounted to his purchase of a peerage was frowned upon. Thus it was with some trepidation that the youngster had approached the chairman of a shipping broker's, a portly man never seen without a cigar, who had an office in Piccadilly and was known as an active supporter of the Labour Party. The reaction, a prompt invitation to a drink at the Ritz, had surprised Varun but it made sense. He had accepted with alacrity and was half an hour early for the appointment.

He ordered a lager and sat quietly, rehearsing in his mind his credentials and his eagerness to satisfy a potential employer. Then, more relaxed, he began to take an interest in his surroundings.

Had Karen glanced from the draped windows of the Ritz through the early-evening sunshine towards Green Park, she might have spotted a man she would recognise – perhaps more than one, though she would have been hard put to recall exactly where she had met the second. But both men knew her.

George Horrocks wrapped his coat closer. A morning at the Prima office, an extended lunch, a couple of hours at the latest Royal Academy exhibition – all had failed to raise his spirits. The breeze which drifted up from the distant lake reminded him that it was not yet summer, despite the camellias and the showy blossom on the cherry trees. In normal circumstances he would not have allowed himself to feel chilled, but would simply have shrugged and prided himself on health of mind and body. But a bare week after Elaine's resignation he did not feel normal at all; he felt devastated.

He wanted to rage at the world, to stop passers-by and harangue them, to extol her virtues and express his pent-up fury that such a stupid matter could have cut her career so short, so abruptly.

Betty had refused, gently, to help. Much as she loved her brother-in-law her first concern was her MP. She explained Elaine wanted to see no one, not even him. Unable to make contact, since her answering machine was taking all the calls in both London and Warmingshire, he had repaired to his club and sought out whatever company he could find. He wasn't bothered that gossips might link his name with hers: it was on record that he was her escort, one of her inner circle, in so far as she had one.

He saw better than most how wide of the mark was much of the public perception of her. The tabloids had had a field day, crowing about her fall and only later bemoaning the loss of one of politics' most attractive personalities. She was described in one broadsheet paper as 'unclubbable'. George knew this to be a bad joke. Elaine was not eligible to join many of the clubs which were home to the cabals and intriguers at the heart of both Tory Party and government: she was a woman. In any case, long evenings dining with cronies dishing the dirt on her honourable friends was not Elaine's style.

George's view that politics was a dreadful way to earn a living had been confirmed by everything that had happened to Elaine. It must be hardest, he realised, on those like her who lived alone. George suddenly realised why family life mattered to so many male MPs. To have somebody supportive at home must be a great joy. Only a devoted wife with limited ambitions of her own would wait docilely for a long-delayed husband and accept his excuses of three-line whips, abstainers and late defections. For outsiders it was a complete enigma, but George could begin to understand. The women believed in their husbands and would win in the end. Long after temptation had faded, the intact pair would enjoy each other's company, bask in the affection of offspring and friends and share comfort for aspirations unfulfilled and mountains never climbed. Both partners benefited.

On the other hand, a lover, male or female, could easily become frustrated by juggled diaries. Why had a date been cancelled, or what could possibly be more important than dinner for two at Simply Nico's? A lover might not hang around for an explanation. The exceptions were those women who dreamed of displacing the MP's wife and becoming wives in their turn. For a few, ambition would be fulfilled; but, for the majority, to be strung along for years and then discarded was the fate which awaited them, and most knew it.

How different was married life from an affair – as different as could be. George began to brood deeply. He walked head down along the pathway between the giant plane trees, the sole species which could thrive in London's polluted atmosphere. Their bark was peeling as it did every spring: large pieces of blackened fibre fell away from the trunks revealing pale green membranes already turning khaki, which would stiffen and darken with age. He ran a hand over his head and was troubled to find stray hairs in his palm. He could not recall a moment before when he had been quite so conscious of the passage of time.

His proposal to Elaine had been bungled, he could see that now. He had not prepared her. Nor had he taken his own offer seriously enough: it had been made almost in a casual way and she had been right to refuse him. How arrogant of him to assume that she would just fall into his arms. He cursed himself roundly.

His mind ran over her response. She was not sure she was cut out to be a wife, she had whispered, and cited the failure of her marriage. The proof of that, he supposed, was that her ex-husband had promptly found a replacement. Elaine had declared herself to be 'certainly not the conventional kind' of wife. He could not argue with that.

With a wrench he also saw that he had wanted to marry her because he hoped to own her, as if she were a wonderful piece of furniture. To see her every day, her golden hair spread out next to him first thing in the morning. To have breakfast at her side – to hand her her coffee, to order two different newspapers so they didn't fight over them, to indulge her preference of radio programme in the morning while he chose the late viewing. To share treats with her: the theatre, a film, a stroll in the park, an ice-cream on a hot day. To roll her over, his hand on her firm rump, and slide his fingers down in the warmth, seeking her and making her laugh and lift into his embrace. Ah, yes. Together. For ever. That would have suited him very well.

What he had not considered, not for a moment, was what Elaine would get in return. To convince her would require him to conduct himself in another fashion entirely. He would have to get inside her mind and soul and work out what it was *she* needed.

He was close to the road. To his left sat the squat pile of Lancaster House; the sound of chatter floated through open windows. Another government-sponsored jolly. To his right Buckingham Palace loomed like a forgotten wedding cake, the upper tiers missing, its fluted architraves slightly grubby as from a thousand fingerings. The Mall, shady and calm, beckoned to his left. It would soon be dusk.

He had ambled this far with no deliberate purpose other than a desire for fresh air, but perhaps his subconscious had been active nevertheless. If he continued across Birdcage Walk, past Wellington Barracks and the Guards Museum he would be in striking distance of Elaine's flat.

Her name was last week's news already. The press rat-pack would have thinned out. There was always other quarry. Maybe she would be home. He could leave a message as he had tried to do several times. He could even emulate the pressmen and camp out, hoping to catch her. A three-line whip was anticipated that night at ten o'clock – speculation had been rife over the narrowness of the government's majority. So if she were home she would have to emerge eventually, or return later. He was determined to talk to her.

It was desperately important that she should know that somebody still loved her. And he did, very much.

The second, shabbier man in the park had come to much the same conclusion.

Elaine was not to be found in her house in the country: he had travelled there. The property had a desolate air. Newspapers lay uncollected on the step. The letter-box was stuffed with post made limp by overnight rain. In the window stood an abandoned vase of tulips, their stems drooping, brown-tinged petals fallen on the window-ledge. A young policeman was on duty at the gate. He had not liked to speak to him. Boredom might have driven the officer to ask awkward questions.

He had hung around the village for an hour. The local publican had polished beer glasses and regaled yet another visitor with tales of how Mrs Stalker was liked in the neighbourhood, but how it had often been asserted that sooner or later the lady's enemies would catch up with her. Asserted, that was, by wiser creatures like himself. Dunn had longed to strike him for that.

He didn't want to find her in the constituency anyway. That was too far. The return journey in the van would not have been impossible, but the shorter the better. She might not see it his way. She might not want to come.

He rummaged in his pocket and gave each of the items there a comforting squeeze. Not long now. The park's well-tilled beauty soothed him and brought him back to the present. He squinted upwards at the dying sun. Might it be possible tonight? What he had in mind was so tricky. There might be press around. He didn't want to get caught and spoil everything.

He raised his head and sniffed the wind as if its mixed odours of hyacinths and petrol would guide him. Then he turned towards the south.

Fred sat hunched in his room in Commons Court and tried to ignore the whine of the ventilation. To have been allocated this office to himself was a recognition of his elevation as a junior Minister, but the niggle remained that a ten-by-twelve cubby-hole with no window was not exactly the best he could do. Still, at least he was almost directly over the Commons Chamber. When the division bell rang he could saunter down the stairs at the back of the Speaker's Chair. It gave him a vicarious thrill to arrive at the 'Aye' lobby as other colleagues came panting from their more glamorous suites in Abbey Gardens. Not everyone qualified for an office on the main site. He ought to be grateful.

It had been especially convenient when his boss Elaine Stalker had worked across the narrow corridor on the smarter, window side. Her room was much the same size as his own, which meant that it was crowded when three people were in it. Yet it had a cachet. Hers had long been a ministerial room. Its occupation indicated a high position on the ladder. And now it was empty.

He groaned and laid down his pen. If he were a proper politician he would have hassled to transfer to that better room. As it was, he was trying to keep thoughts of Elaine's resignation at bay, and failing. Why hadn't she fought? Why the silence – not a peep after that fateful MIND speech? Alternatively, why hadn't she run for cover, backed off, recanted? Even were it true that she had been told to keep quiet, she could still have found a way. She had plenty of friends in high places – why hadn't she activated them? It was rumoured that the PM thought highly of her. She could have survived, had she wanted to. Maybe not wanting to was the root of the problem.

Fred recognised that, if he were ever faced with the choice between obscurity and a job he could not carry out with enjoyment, the former might be preferable. Those who were ambitious enough to rise and stay at the top would take whatever was offered and contrive to make a success of it – or, at the very least, arrange that cronies would declare them a success, which amounted to much the same. Elaine wasn't like that. Such connivance, he felt intuitively, was not her style. Maybe that too was a weakness on her part.

She had not said a word after; she'd just disappeared, probably to the home of her constituency chairman, that stalwart lady Betty Horrocks, whom Fred had met at Anthony's memorial service. Betty would have put Elaine to bed in the spare room, folded her clothes and left her jacket neatly on a hanger. He could picture Mrs Horrocks bringing hot chocolate and aspirin, or Scotch and biscuits, and sitting for hours in her dressing gown, encouraging Elaine to talk. But somehow he felt that was unlikely. Elaine would not have said anything, not to Betty, not to anyone.

Karen had shrugged dolefully when he asked her. Her face had indicated she had been crying, but there was a determined set to her mouth. Her mother, she averred, would confide when she was ready. Meanwhile she, Karen, would go about her everyday activities as if nothing untoward had occurred and she recommended Fred do the same. But she had refused point-blank though politely to sleep with him since, saying she too preferred to be on her own. His exclusion from her innermost thoughts grieved him more than anything else.

The vacancy had not yet been filled. The Prime Minister was taking advice, it was said. A reshuffle was not due till the summer and the PM hated being rushed. The media hinted that an amalgamation of departments was a possibility. The health side, it was pointed out, had for two decades functioned in tandem with social security. These days health authorities and trusts by and large ran themselves and needed less ministerial interference. Such a merger would obviate the appointment of another Minister. So ran the official line. Meanwhile Fred had been discreetly asked to carry on as normal – and should he learn anything from Elaine about exactly what had gone on behind the scenes, what rows had taken place or remarks been exchanged, he should let the whips know at once.

For in the firing line was the Secretary of State himself. The PM had let it be known that he was not pleased. After the loss of two good Ministers in a row, sharp comments were made in the more hostile media about Bampton's fitness for senior office, though it was conceded that the events were probably unconnected.

Yet Ted Bampton was hardly a victim – not unless Elaine made him so. What was missing as yet was the vindictive statement, the howl of revenge, which a Norman Lamont or a Geoffrey Howe had delivered with the express intention of damaging their masters. The press waited to see whether Elaine would oblige. Fred suspected that she might, but in her own good time.

The object of Fred's musings crouched huddled on the edge of the sofa where she had been for hours. Her jeans were crumpled, the shirt was not clean. In her hand lay a scrunched-up ball of damp tissue.

On the coffee table sat the remains of a ham sandwich and a half-drunk cup of soup. The sink held two dirty cereal bowls and spoons. On the draining board were several unwashed mugs alongside an unopened bouquet of dying flowers. There was no point in cooking, while eating out would be an ordeal. She could have ordered a pizza, but Elaine could envisage the delivery boy's face as he recognised his customer. Pity would have demolished her: curiosity was worse. Anyway she was not hungry.

It was six days since her world had fallen apart. Margaret Thatcher had opined on her own forced resignation that it was as if a map of one's life, printed on glass, had been thrown to the ground and shattered. Not only were all the patterns confused but no way existed to restore them.

Margaret had never adjusted. In the years since, she had drifted round the world attending expensive dinners hosted by admirers, ostensibly to raise money for the Thatcher Foundation, though few were clear what that organisation did. Her interventions in British politics had at first been restricted to criticisms of her successors not quite *sotto voce* in private houses, then expanded noisily into her memoirs and world-wide promotion tours. The result was a travesty of a great woman; she seemed to have lost her dignity and sense of purpose entirely.

As for Elaine, she felt numb. She did not comprehend what had happened; only that her dismissal had not been part of any plan. It had been as much a surprise to her as to the press and public and she had been unable to respond. Some Ministers use the weapon of resignation to get their own way; some leave government because the fun has vanished or because of lack of progress on a pet project. What no one else could see was the weary acquiescence, the imploding will, with which Elaine had confronted defeat. She might have fought, and perhaps should have tried. She could, indeed, have insisted on seeing Roger and – what? – as a last resort, perhaps, made veiled threats against him and demanded a move away from Bampton's malevolence. But the dangerous game of blackmail had not entered her head. Indeed, quitting her ministerial career at all had never been on the agenda. When George had hinted that she should consider it if the job no longer gave her satisfaction, she had rejected the notion out of hand, and him along with it.

How could she have so misjudged events? Elaine passed her hand slowly over her eyes. Here was a question to which she had no answer, save that it probably served to confirm her unfitness to govern. She couldn't have been much good as a politician if she could not see that black hole coming. It was all very well being a good communicator: a valuable skill, certainly, and lacking in many colleagues, but not in itself sufficient. Her talents as a populariser, her high level of credibility with the electorate, had brought her to government, but were not enough to keep her there. What was missing was sure-footedness, that ability to sidestep trouble. She smiled wryly. Not that these qualities were in great abundance on either front bench. Yet most of those in high office or hankering after it would not end up trapped as she had been.

Elaine had hardly noticed the press: the numbness had so frozen her that it was as if she had gone into suspended animation. Betty had been wonderful and had insisted on taking her in for the crucial first few days. She responded to no one. The answerphone was left permanently on and she did not listen to the recorded calls.

At the office, according to Betty's report, Diane had fielded every enquiry with brutal efficiency. Sackloads of letters and cards had arrived. Most of the correspondents were sad or incredulous; nearly all were friendly, though Elaine had no way of knowing how much hostile mail had been redirected into Diane's overflowing bin. Intrigued, she had started to read some letters but had been convulsed by tears and soon laid them to one side.

If only she had been allowed to defend herself. That was the crunch. Bampton had told her to keep her mouth shut, had taken her place at the dispatch box, had spoken for her. It was not merely that he had overruled her, though that was bad enough. He had implied by his action that she did not count; that she was incapable of accepting accountability for her own behaviour and was not to be trusted. That hurt. And was wrong. *He* was wrong. But he had destroyed her as thoroughly as if he had taken a pickaxe to her. After that, there was no recovery.

It was getting dark. How long had she been sitting there? It was hardly strange that, preoccupied with recent events, churning them round in her mind in a futile attempt at analysis, she was barely able to focus on anything else. The vote was at ten: after a week's permitted absence her attendance was required, roughly at the hour most civilised people were preparing a nightcap and heading for bed.

A bath might refresh her; then she could start to don the uniform, the tailored suit, the crisp blouse, the dark tights, make-up, earrings, pearls, the slim gold watch on her wrist which marked the minutes, so long and empty, since everything she had hoped for had ended.

She felt groggy and helpless. Yet she would have to face the world sooner or later; delay only made things worse. With a sigh, Elaine rose and trudged towards the bedroom.

'Hello, Karen.'

She had been standing, one foot forward, as she studied yet another lanky maiden whose gilded form adorned the Palm Court area. The sculpture had, she felt, a lamentable mixture of pre-pubescent innocence and voluptuousness. She noted Betts's eyes roaming rapidly over both the inert and the human curves displayed before him.

He made a noise which sounded like smacking his lips. 'You look terrific.'

'Thanks.' She kept her voice cool. The coat and dress she had chosen were simple. His remark told her plainly what was in his mind.

'So – you ready to eat, or would you like a drink first?'

She considered. His manner was almost gauche; he looked younger and tidier than normal. Was she really doing the right thing? It virtually amounted to leading him on, which meant taking a huge risk. She shuddered inwardly. Karen was neither vindictive nor vengeful and would in normal circumstances have shunned all contact with the man. For a moment her resolve wavered.

'Let's drink first. We can look at a menu at the same time.'

A waiter brought vodka and ice for him, an orange juice for her, a bowl of nuts, which Karen began absent-mindedly to nibble, and a set of oversized menus. Another waiter whisked away her coat. The two perched slightly awkwardly on high chairs, their glasses precarious on a tiny marble table.

'A place like this makes me want to turn cartwheels in the foyer,' Karen confided.

'Yeah, it's not my usual stamping ground either.' Betts offered her a cigarette; she refused. He lit one for himself, then sipped his drink and grinned. 'So, how's your mother?'

'Fine, thank you.' Karen was instantly on her guard.

'When can we expect her to make a statement? She can't stay silent for ever. The whole press has been trying to phone her but she won't return our calls.' Betts was watching her. 'What happened, exactly? She must have spoken to you. Had a brainstorm, or what?'

The offensive remark was designed to breach her defences. Karen paused, picked up her drink and examined it carefully as if the answer were written on the liquid's surface.

'She's very down. You have to understand. Leave her alone – you won't get anything out of her, nor out of me.'

Betts wriggled irritably. 'That boyfriend of yours, then,' he suggested. 'Laidlaw. Done well for himself, hasn't he? You two planning to get hitched?'

'No, we are not.' This time Karen failed to keep the annoyance out of her voice. She recovered control quickly: her listener would magnify any clue she gave him. 'It's pure chance that we're the remaining tenants of that house. I have another year and a bit of university. Then I don't know what – I have to get a job, but it probably won't be in London.'

'Don't fancy being an MP's wife, is that it?' Betts gave a knowing leer.

She should answer bluntly that Fred had not asked her, but that would be a lie. Any other response would be an admission. Either would lead to further probing. Karen restricted herself to a shrug and a half-smile, as if the subject did not interest her.

Betts blew a smoke ring and looked disappointed: stonewalling was clearly the right way to deal with him. Karen examined him under her lashes. Perhaps if he failed in all his objectives with her he would cross her off his list and leave her alone in future.

The waiter approached. 'For madam I can recommend the poached quail's eggs with tomato jelly and caviar, or the warm duck tart and foie gras salad,' he urged unctuously. 'Followed by oysters in champagne, or lobster and leeks, if madam prefers. The main course – '

407

'Blimey,' muttered Karen.

The waiter was not deterred. 'Madam might find the fillet of brill to her taste with a crab, spinach and mustard sauce, a speciality of the house, or a roast guinea fowl — '

'You got any beef?' Betts demanded.

'Certainly, sir, two kinds.' The waiter pointed delicately with his Biro. 'Fillet of beef with aubergine, potatoes and morels, or Beef Wellington – that's in a pastry case with the chef's pâté – with creamed spinach.' He paused, then moved away. 'Take your time, sir, madam.'

'What the bloody hell are morels?' Betts spluttered as soon as the waiter was out of earshot.

'Dunno.' Karen felt a twinge of sympathy, then hardened her heart. She put down the menu. 'I suppose it's good value for forty-nine pounds each if you think about it, what with lashings of pud to come. But I don't think I have much appetite.'

'I can afford it,' Betts responded huffily.

Karen folded her hands in her lap. If Betts's real purpose in meeting her was to parade and augment his fund of knowledge about Fred and her mother it was clear he knew less than she had feared. They were not safe – they would never be safe – but he had nothing fresh to impart or he would have produced it already. On the other hand, that glitter in his eyes indicated that his other motive, to worm his way into her own life once more, had become his priority. As far as Karen was concerned, that meant the evening was finished. To settle down to a five-course meal would, however, have tied her to his side for hours. The problem was how to remove herself from his company. She took a deep breath.

'I don't doubt it. But I'd be happier elsewhere. I am sorry but I don't wish to stay.'

Betts began to protest, then with a muttered oath he stubbed out his cigarette, called to the waiter, paid for the drinks and retrieved her coat. She rose and turned towards the main entrance. To her annoyance he fell into step beside her. So he had not given up, yet.

As the pair moved down the lobby they failed to notice the young Asian man who observed their progress at first with vague attention and then with a gasp of recognition. Hurriedly Varun tossed some coins on the table before following them. If Karen did not want to spend another minute with Betts, somebody else did.

*　　*　　*

In St James's it was cooler. Starlings twittered overhead and fought for roosts. Tourists and theatre-goers in groups and pairs strolled by, engrossed in their own affairs. Karen frowned. It would have been better to have emerged at the hotel's other exit near Green Park Tube; however, the early-evening air was pleasant enough for walking, or she might for once take a cab. She could aim for her mother's flat, but only if she could shake off her unwanted companion. To her satisfaction Betts, though still attempting to talk to her, looked cross. She suspected he would try to claim the £100 bill even though it did not nestle in his wallet.

Together they walked briskly down the busy street, past shop windows filled with leather riding boots and top hats. The journalist continued to dig for information but the girl was visibly fidgeting. It dawned on Betts that Karen had no intention whatever of spending the evening with him, let alone planning more intense activity later.

They stopped near the Carlton Club. Nearby a taxi came to a halt, double-parked. Karen looked hopefully towards it. Betts calculated urgently. The girl was not to escape. He grabbed her elbow.

'You know I've always fancied you, Karen,' he murmured. 'Ever since . . . well, you know. I'm sorry I was rough with you that night. I'd had too much to drink. I'm not normally like that.'

Karen made herself give an answering nod. 'Well, thanks for the apology. You took your time about it.'

'So come on, Karen. I'm not hungry. Not for food, that is. Don't go.'

The girl tried to tug her arm free. The taxi pulled into the kerb a few yards from her: its driver appeared to be checking his books. She could simply open the door, climb in and tell him to drive off. Betts could then churn out his lies without her assistance, tacit or otherwise, and she would speak to him no more, ever.

Before she could move a harsh new voice interrupted from behind.

'Mr Betts? It is Jim Betts of the *Globe*, isn't it?'

Betts let go Karen's arm, turned and found a young Asian man standing before him, feet planted firmly, legs apart, hands on hips. He was tall for an Asian and stocky, and he was scowling. Karen stepped swiftly towards the cab but hesitated. She wondered what was going on.

'I'm Betts, yes. Who are you?'

'I saw you in the Ritz. My name is Varun Bhadeshia. Does that mean anything?'

'Never met you in my life.' Betts was impatient. 'Come on, Karen.'

The youth came close and shoved Betts belligerently in the chest. 'You know my father. In fact you wrecked my father's life. Our whole family. You, with your foul articles in your newspaper. I hoped some day I'd find you. Now I have.'

'Oh yeah?' Betts tried to elbow his challenger out of the way but Bhadeshia did not budge. The journalist glared. 'So – whatcha going to do about it?'

His aggression seemed to touch an exposed nerve in Varun. The boy took a step towards Betts, his mouth twisted in bitterness. His voice lifted.

'Mr Betts, you are evil – you are the lowest of the low! A swine!' One or two heads started to twist in their direction. 'I have justice on my side. See – this is what I will do!'

To Karen's horror the young man raised his right fist and before anyone could cry out or stop him aimed it straight at Betts's face.

George had reached the traffic lights at Victoria Street. He glanced at his watch. It was barely eight o'clock. If Elaine was at her flat and intended to emerge in time for the ten o'clock vote then he was a little early. He recognised too that his nerve was failing him, much as he longed to see her. Perhaps it would help if he had a drink.

On the corner stood the Albert, its billboards emblazoned with the statement that it had been *Evening Standard* Pub of the Year. He liked the fact that the frontage was not festooned with bay trees or pretending to be an Italian trattoria: it was self-evidently and reassuringly traditional.

He pushed open the door and stepped inside. For a moment he was startled by the noise and smoke. The place was packed. Just about everyone present, including the bar staff, was younger than himself. But he did not feel in the mood to seek somewhere quieter, and its cheeriness was in its favour. He hesitated over the choice of drink, then settled for a half-pint of beer which he carried to a small corner table; there he sat, sipping and thinking.

The jumbled reflections of an hour before had nearly sorted themselves out. The future looked much clearer. He would press Elaine to take him on, for better for worse. And he would persist until she agreed.

For her, things couldn't be worse than now. Surely she would see that if a man were willing to stand by her in these days of utmost misery he would also be the right person to have around in sunnier moments?

Or would that seem like shroud-chasing? Would she be revolted and get the idea that he was trying to stage a rescue so that she would be grateful? Gratitude was not a sound basis for a relationship. On the contrary, he did not want her to feel beholden to him in any way. He would have to handle their next meeting with great care.

The question remained: what did she need? What did *she* need? George squared his shoulders. She needed him, that's what. All that remained was to find the language to convince her.

It came to him, and he laughed softly, ruefully at himself. In posing the question he had found the answer. In putting her needs before his own, he had become the perfect partner for such a woman.

He knew what he needed – and did not need. He didn't want a conventional wife. That was why he had never found himself in the least tempted by the dozens on offer. They'd have bored him silly. A woman who hung on his every utterance, who saw her role as to act through him and to him, who sought no more than to be a wife and mother – he would have tolerated such a woman but found her frustrating, limiting. He needed a partner with a life and mind of her own, a self-starter with an independent spark, who would not want him around every minute of the day. Who sometimes would not need him at all, and that was hard for many men to accept. Her. Elaine.

A lady like that – he paused. No, he did not want to be her bag-carrier. Somehow he saw that she would not expect that either. But her helpmeet, her companion, her lover – her escort, of course, her *man* – the shoulder to cry on, the soothing caress in the darkest hours of the night: he could offer that easily, and with a full heart.

And if she should refuse a second time his own heart would be empty. But he would go on asking, again and again.

He raised the beer glass and drained it. He did not require another. Amused at his own regained self-control he rose and headed for the door. Her street was a few minutes' walk away.

It was, Karen thought later, a moment she would long savour, as Betts staggered, his hands cupped to his face, a red trickle oozing through his fingers. The blow had landed so swiftly and cleanly that hardly anyone had noticed. A couple of tourists skirted the trio delicately. The cabbie had raised his eyes, then returned to his notebooks. The two men stood facing each other, Varun dancing on the balls of his feet, his fists up.

She should separate them. Neither should get involved in a fight, not here in public. Above their heads a street light switched itself on with an audible ping. It made Betts, half bent clutching his face, look far more sinister than the smartly dressed young Asian.

'You bastard.' Betts lunged at the boy and pushed him hard in the chest. Taken by surprise Bhadeshia stumbled and fell. As he rolled over and struggled to rise, Betts instinctively reverted to his own adolescence in the back streets of Toxteth where rough and tumble with fists or boots was a way of life. Self-defence, it was called. Do it quickly and run. Nobody ever went to the police.

Self-defence against this jumped-up black bugger, whoever he was, would be a pleasure. With a grunt Betts lifted his foot and landed a hard kick in the boy's ribs, then another. Varun cried out and tried to scramble away. The cabbie, disturbed at last by the commotion, reached for his radio.

'Stop it! What are you doing? You'll hurt him. Stop!'

Desperately Karen tugged at Betts's sleeve but his temper was up. 'I'll teach you,' he snarled. 'Paki bastard. You'll sort me out, will you? We'll see about that . . .' And he aimed again to land another blow, but lower down, at the boy's kidneys.

Karen never planned what happened next. She knew she should have tried to prevent Varun's attack but it had come so unexpectedly. Betts's response, however, was uncontrolled and vicious. Her loathing of him rose in her throat like bile. She was secretly pleased the Asian had hit him, particularly since the punch might alter Betts's appearance: it would not be improved by a flattened nose but he would suffer no real harm. What he was trying to do to the boy, however, was different. It looked as if Betts might continue literally to put the boot in till he had landed Bhadeshia in hospital.

She could not let him continue. He *had* to be stopped.

'Look at me!' she commanded. Betts paused and half turned as the boy lay moaning, but his foot was ready for the next assault.

The teacher in the Tai-kwondo class always warned against trying anything other than with a trained opponent. The rear leg axe, for example, could blind a man, or crack a cheekbone: the muscles of the hamstring and gluteus maximus contract on impact to produce tremendous power.

She stepped forward as she had been taught, weight on the right leg, arms upraised to give balance. Then she unleashed the kick, aiming low, and felt the flesh shudder as she hit home: *right in his genitals.*

Betts gagged and doubled over, clutching his groin. With a sob he slipped, to become an ungainly heap next to his victim. For a moment he struggled to rise, then lay, winded and retching, on the pavement.

Karen calculated that Betts would not be seriously injured; she was more concerned about Varun. She reached down to him. 'You OK?'

Warily the young man scrambled to his feet, one hand pressed to his side. With the other he dusted off his trousers as well as he could. 'Thanks. I owe you for that.'

Then he looked up anxiously. The altercation had attracted official attention: in the distance a constable was marching smartly down from Piccadilly Circus, his radio raised to his lips. 'I think we should make ourselves scarce – I have to see a man about a job.' The boy slipped away and vanished into a side street.

It had only taken a few seconds. Varun had a point. Karen must either stay, which meant she had some explaining to do, or leave without further ado.

She felt very shaky. As she turned away it came to her that never again would she be frightened of Jim Betts, or anyone. She it was who had emerged triumphant, not him. He was curled up, his nose swollen, knees tight to his chest, making nasal mewing noises which disgusted her. A little bravado was in order.

'Well, Mr Betts, now you know how it feels. That should put you out of action for a bit.'

She did not flinch when he lifted himself on one elbow and yelled throatily after her.

'Bitch!'

Graham Dunn had hovered for over an hour. It had taken twenty minutes to find somewhere to park but at last he had struck lucky, when a big Mercedes a few yards from the entrance of her block had moved away. Heart in mouth he had run for the van and backed it into the vacant slot. Couldn't be better. Perhaps the gods wanted him to succeed.

A light shone through the curtains of her flat. He was reasonably sure she was there. Her presence so close made his pulse race. Whatever indignities she had put up with in recent days, now she was about to be happy and loved. He, Graham Dunn, would love her.

Only he grasped how she felt, how desperate, how alone. Even the pressmen had abandoned her. He had seen them day after day, a dwindling band, until yesterday there had been no one. Perhaps a stringer had been ordered to keep an eye out for her at the House of Commons, but other than that they had lost interest already. But he would be faithful. Her car was parked under a street light. It would not be long before she would come down the stairs and go towards it. Then he would approach her.

George Horrocks strolled along Victoria Street. Opposite Westminster Cathedral he waited for traffic to clear before he could cross the road. At his side a young girl touched his arm.

'George?'

He turned. The face was immediately recognisable, but was flushed; the eyes were unnaturally bright.

'Karen! Good evening. What are you doing round here at this time of night?'

'Heading for my mother's. I haven't seen her for a while, though we've talked on the phone. I thought I'd go and see her.'

George chuckled. 'Then we're on the same errand.' As they reached safety on the other side he looked more closely at her. 'Are you all right? You look a bit . . . odd.'

Karen sagged suddenly. 'Can I take your arm, George?'

He offered it wordlessly. As she slipped hers through he noticed she was trembling. 'What is it?' he asked gently.

'I seem to have got involved in a fight, down St James's,' she said sombrely. 'I wasn't hurt, don't worry.'

He stopped dead. 'What was it – a mugger? Shouldn't we call the police? The station's round the corner, in Rochester Row . . .'

She shook her head. 'No, George. It was somebody I know. I don't want the police involved.' She took a deep breath. 'I thumped him one: he won't forget it in a hurry. But I feel a bit wobbly, and terribly ashamed of myself too. I shouldn't have done that.'

'Perhaps it will help to talk to your mother.' George was grave. He let the girl lean on him and saw she was glad of his support. Together they walked slowly past the shops. 'How is she, anyway?'

The two talked quietly as they headed towards the entrance to Morpeth Terrace. The side road was full of parked cars but was otherwise empty. Elaine's flat was still over a hundred yards away. As they glanced up simultaneously the light in her window was switched off: that meant she would be coming down the stairs. Best, perhaps, not to confront her suddenly on the doorstep, which might scare her. They slowed their pace. Her car was at this end so she must walk towards them. In a moment they observed Elaine's door open and her figure, a headscarf covering her hair, emerge.

The details, the silly irrelevancies, for ever after stuck in Karen's brain, as if time had stood still. From one window, high up, came the sound of the Rolling Stones, while the smells of a curry floated out of an open ground-floor ventilator. The window-boxes were a riot of blue and yellow pansies. Her mother's coat was dowdy and the scarf was dull and brown, not in character.

It was at that precise moment that a stranger stepped forward. Karen barely took him in: he had been lurking behind a vehicle and not been immediately visible. A man in the street, that was all. A tubby, middle-aged figure, nondescript, like thousands of others in central London. Nobody of the remotest significance.

'Mrs Stalker?'

Elaine shrank, fearful. 'I have nothing to say to the press, sorry.'

'I'm not press. I'm a . . . an admirer. I wanted to say how sorry I am at what happened to you.'

She hardly glanced at him. 'Thank you,' she said, and looked vaguely in the direction of her car. But he blocked her way.

'Would you give me your autograph?' He thrust a grubby book and pen towards her. 'Please.' She sighed and took the items listlessly.

As she scribbled, her head bowed to hide her face, he raised a hand to touch the golden hair on her forehead but stopped himself just in time.

'I love you,' he said.

'What?' Her voice was faint.

'I love you, Elaine. I've always loved you. And', he continued eagerly, for she had not moved, 'I know you love me. I've seen you looking at me when you're on television. I saw you at St Kitts when they threw things at you – that was terrible. I tried to protect you.'

She raised her eyes and looked at him, puzzled.

'Protect me?'

'Yes. The woman who threw that tomato. I sorted her out.'

The boastful pride in his voice brought her to her senses. With a little cry she dropped the autograph book and pen and backed away. But she was too late.

Dunn had darted forward even as she realised the danger. Something hard was dug into her and she could feel its steely edge between her ribs. He grabbed her wrist and shook her.

'You do love me. I know it. I've seen the way you look at me. And I will make you happy, Elaine, I promise.'

'No –' She opened her mouth to scream but no sound came out. He was pushing her furiously. She half walked, was half carried towards the kerb until her shoulders were up against a big white Transit van. He reached across, his body pressed over hers, turned the handles and swung the doors open. She smelled his sweat, his breath, and recoiled in horror.

'Inside!'

She shook her head dumbly. He raised his hand and she could see what had been pressed into her side: its cold steel winked in the light from a window. With the knife's point he touched her throat, a nick, so that it stung. A smear of blood followed the blade and he dipped his finger in it to show her.

'*Inside.* And not a sound.'

From the far end of the street came a distant shout and the noise of running feet. With a loud curse and sudden superhuman strength the man picked her up and propelled her bodily into the interior. She overbalanced and fell back into the void. There was a sudden strong smell of onions. He bent down, caught her dangling feet and manhandled her legs inside the van. One of her shoes came off, bounced on the van's fender and fell into the gutter. He slammed the door shut, raced to the driver's seat, switched on the ignition and with a screech of clashing metal shoved the vehicle into gear.

It was parked too tight. With a curse he revved hard and drove into the green BMW in front, shunting the car forward the necessary couple of feet. Then he swung the wheel, careered away from the kerb, sped off the wrong way up the road and disappeared around the corner, just as George and Karen arrived at the empty spot.

Chapter Twenty-Four

The white van clattered around Pimlico with its engine roaring and headlights full on. In the back its dazed passenger was flung from side to side each time the vehicle lurched around a corner. Soon, however, the vehicle proceeded more sedately. Though the driver's body, visible through the communicating grille, still sat rigid, his white-knuckled hands on the wheel appeared to relax a little.

For several moments Elaine, afraid and confused, wondered if she was in the middle of a strange dream. She could recall fumbling with her door keys in her flat and feeling helpless because they had almost slipped from her fingers, as if the fates were conspiring against her. Then she had started down the stairs. She had stepped into the street, relieved that there was no sign of any journalist, and been struck by cold air which had made her want to turn back inside. There had been a man . . .

Her head hurt where she had banged it on the floor of the van. The cut on her neck stung. She rubbed it and recoiled at the streak of dark blood on her fingers: it was deeper than she had realised. One of her shoes had vanished and her left ankle throbbed. Slowly and painfully she sat up.

The rear of the van had no windows. Some light came through from the driver's section. As street lamps flashed by, the garish neon intermittently lit up her surroundings. She found she had to concentrate to make anything out, and she wondered groggily in which direction they were travelling.

Light bulbs strung out overhead in graceful curves: that was Albert Bridge, surely. So the van was heading south of the river. The speed was steady as if there were yet some distance to cover. Such a route could take them anywhere – down to the coast, or to a ferry across the Channel. What was happening?

There was not much room. The vehicle had the look of a standard Ford Transit. The load area was half filled with sacks, nets and boxes from which came pungent but not over-fresh odours of potatoes, leeks, onions, cabbage and the earthy smell of root vegetables sold the old-fashioned way, still covered in soil. The floor had been partially covered with an old rug: on each side her exploring fingers touched cold metal and tattered greenery. An attempt had been made to create a space between some of the boxes, but it was apparent that a large object such as her own body could quickly be concealed from cursory examination and covered very effectively with the produce.

Elaine's teeth chattered. She reached out to the nearest potato sacks for comfort and pulled what she could reach around her legs. Despite her coat she was terribly cold.

The traffic noises receded. The light filtering into the back changed: now it was mainly the van's own headlights reflected from blackened narrow walls. It was bumping slowly on an uneven surface. Then it stopped.

She heard the driver descend from his seat and close his door quietly. The crunch of footsteps came alongside.

Instinct told Elaine to stay still. Her mouth went dry and her heart thumped so loudly she feared she could hear it reverberate from the ceiling. She tucked her feet under her and sat up as tidily as she could, her shoe in her hand. It was low-heeled and not much use as a weapon, even had she summoned the courage to try against that knife. Bare-footed she could offer little resistance.

The door opened and before she could protest or move the man climbed in beside her. The gleam of the knife, held threateningly but steadily, was a potent reminder. She gasped and touched her throat.

'Sorry 'bout that. I didn't mean to hurt you. You won't get hurt. Just do as I tell you.'

The voice was gruff, flat, as if the words had been rehearsed so many times that any vestige of emotion had been lost. In the dark she could not make out her captor's features but could dimly recall a nondescript face and grubby hands holding an autograph book. She winced as her body weight pressed on the twisted ankle.

The man was fidgeting and muttering to himself. The right hand still held the knife; she could not see what was in his other hand. Then without warning he grabbed both her arms and hauled her towards him. With terror she wondered if he was about to hit her, but in one swift movement he hauled her hands in front of her, wrapped a length of electrical cord around her wrists, pulled tight and tied it, all the while holding the knife. The knot was worked underneath her fists where it would be difficult to reach with her teeth. At once her fingertips began to tingle from loss of circulation. In bewilderment she stared at him but his head was bent.

'Your legs, please, Elaine.'

'I've hurt my ankle.' It was almost a plea.

'I won't tie it too tight, I promise.'

It was as if she were a child hurt after a fall and he a solicitous parent. As he wrapped the flex around her calves the incongruity of his tone struck her and she choked back a laugh. The sound emerged as a whimper and he paused, a flicker of distress on his face.

'I've got to do this. But if you behave I'll take them off when we get home.'

'Home?'

'Yes, it's not far. You'll like it. It's our home, Elaine. Yours and mine.'

Suddenly he lunged at her. His arm was raised and the knife was pointed directly at her face. His voice became harsh. 'No silly business, see? No screams or anything. I don't want no trouble.' She recoiled and shook her head, her eyes wide and terrified. That evidently did not reassure him. After rummaging in his pocket he brought out a roll of brown parcel tape. Clumsily he tore off a long piece and slapped it over her mouth, pressing the ends down firmly across her cheeks and into her hair. The effect, she realised, was that even if she tried she could remove it only with considerable pain. A cry was stifled in her throat.

He leaned over her: she shrank away and fell awkwardly on to her side.

'That's better,' he grunted. 'Won't be long. You sit tight.'

As if I could just clear off, Elaine reflected miserably as the man shut the main doors and climbed back into the driver's seat. The next moment the van backed out of the alley and recommenced its lurching. He was not used to driving it, that was obvious. There seemed to be a problem changing into fourth gear: immediately it seemed important to remember details like that.

Elaine's mind was still sluggish after a week with little to eat and barely any sleep in the twilight hours after her resignation. But she needed her wits about her now. She took a deep breath, nostrils distended. Her heart was still pumping hard and the adrenaline did its work in reviving her. At least she was not going to suffocate even if she was trussed up like a chicken and bouncing to God knew where among the cabbages. And she was alive.

419

How should she react? The practicality of the thought made her want to laugh. It was quickly suppressed. How weird that her first reaction was one of hilarity – was that hysteria? Yet part of her was becoming detached, observing her own behaviour, commenting on it. Perhaps this too was a defence mechanism.

Better to feel angry than afraid. That would be a powerful form of self-protection. Anger would keep her sane. It would be essential to hide the anger, naturally. But if she could conduct a running dialogue with herself, debate rapidly what to do and say; and if inwardly she retained a sense of fury at the violation of being carted off in this horrible van against her will, that was also probably healthy. She must retain her willpower, her sense of self. She would not give in.

That was a decision made. But give in to what? What exactly did this harsh-voiced knifeman intend?

She had missed the vote. That made her smile under the tape but reminded her of its presence. She would have to be careful or the tight stickiness would tear the delicate skin of her lips. With an effort she settled her mouth against the bond and breathed hard through her nose to get a grip on herself.

One arm was twisted under her side and was going numb. She wriggled and rolled over on to her back, but there was barely room to bend her knees. The van bounced over a pot-hole and she heard a muffled oath. She was lying too close to the doors and could not save herself should they fly open. With an effort she pushed herself backwards with her elbows, her bound hands held over her stomach, raised her head and rested it on a large pungent brown bag which she guessed contained shallots. The small round objects rustled close to her ears but made a reasonable pillow.

Who was this man? What did he want? He had talked about 'going home', of 'our home'. He had declared that he loved her; and more peculiarly that he believed she loved him. What on earth could that mean? Was he some kind of nutter? Was this a genuine kidnap? To what purpose?

Of course it's a kidnap, silly, her inner voice whispered. *He'll be after a ransom of some kind. And you know the rules adopted by British governments and police forces whenever hostages are taken: no ransom, no deals. Not even if death is the likely outcome. You're on your own.*

The justification was obvious. If ransoms were paid, as the French had a habit of doing, then more ransoms would be sought. That meant more hostages: it put other innocent citizens at risk. To all such demands

British authorities would say no, on the grounds that a country which resolutely refused to bow to pressure was of no use to criminals. Its nationals, therefore, were less likely to be any value as targets. At least, that was the official line.

So was this man a terrorist? Elaine's brow furrowed as she tried to remember everything about him. The accent was not foreign or Irish but Midlands, Leicestershire perhaps. He seemed to be acting alone. His weapon, which had already been used to good effect, was a broad-bladed knife, not a Kalashnikov. His talk of loving her did not fit with any terrorist vocabulary. He had not barked orders in a military fashion, nor shouted slogans. He had not mentioned politics.

Her pulse quickened in fear. Then if he was working to his own agenda, who the hell was he and what was in his mind? An individual criminal was far more difficult to detect, far more dangerous than a group acting in concert. His name might not be on any list of suspects, his address and whereabouts unknown. An extraordinary terrorist action which hit the headlines throughout the world was one thing; but a lone crackpot . . .?

She would be missed, she was sure of that, but perhaps not right away. The whips would assume she could not face everyone at the vote and had not done the courtesy of alerting them. Her pair might be annoyed that she had made no arrangement with him – if she were planning to slope off he could have gone home too. The majority was thin but should be sufficient. It was unlikely that the government would fall simply because she had not attended. If there were to be a second division, an urgent phone call might be made to her flat but all the caller would get would be the answerphone. No joy there.

Yet she could not just disappear without trace. That simply didn't happen. She had heard a distant shout as the van doors slammed on her – a familiar voice. Somebody running. Not one but two people, racing down the terrace. She had seen no one but had sensed other presences, too far away to help. Surely they would call the police? The hunt might yet be on.

But if this were a kidnap then there was no way of knowing it other than from the criminal himself. She cudgelled her mind for details of other cases. A news blackout was often requested. The result, if it were achieved, could only add to her anguish. The Birmingham estate agent Stephanie Slater who had been kidnapped in 1992 had listened to the radio news on the hour every day for over a week and not heard a whisper about police involvement, despite the fact (which she discovered later) that no fewer than a thousand officers had roamed in the fog to try to catch the culprit. And failed; so that the battered young woman had been returned to her home at dead of night not by the police but in the same red car in which she had been abducted, and by the same driver.

Elaine had read Stephanie's description of her ordeal. The memory of it made her shiver uncontrollably. Yet the girl had endured when others had perished. However paralysed with fear she had stayed cool, her brain working overtime. Early on she had grasped that co-operation with her captor would be the sole means of saving her life – and of bringing him ultimately to justice.

Co-operation. No resistance. *You'll never manage that,* the inner voice said. *When have you ever succumbed easily to anything or anybody? Giving in is not in your nature. Your spirit will not allow it. You will try to escape. You will try to hurt him. You will want to destroy him – and if you don't you will be destroyed. In your own esteem if nothing else.*

No, she inwardly replied. To give in would mean *not* giving in. She would not let her spirit fail her, as perhaps it had when bullied by Bampton. She dragged her knees up to her chin and tried to hug herself but the cords on her numbed arms were too tight. *I'll do whatever he wants. At least, I will try.*

Her independent second mind was getting into its stride. Its reflections, she mused wryly, were going to be both a comfort and a profound irritation. The newest thought was that it seemed oddly appropriate that her withdrawal from public life, with that gnawing desolation and despair which had accompanied her exit and coloured her every moment since, should be underlined by this abrupt and bizarre physical removal. The fact that she no longer mattered might influence the way everyone behaved. It was at least possible that nobody would notice for ages, not even Karen or George. Till it was too late.

She buried her face in the shallots. Whether it was their pungent smell or tiredness or the pain from her ankle and aching body or the deprivation of sleep or a sudden realisation of the dreadful peril she was in she could not tell; but she lay crying silently for some time, eyes open but sightless. *I'll do whatever I have to. I don't have much choice.*

The van was slowing down. Alert again, she listened hard for tell-tale sounds: lorries lumbered in the distance, a cat yowled; it seemed a quiet place. The driver waited as a car passed a few yards away and sat for several moments more until its lights disappeared. Then he switched off the engine and climbed out.

*   *   *

'What in God's name is going on? Who was that?'

George could not keep the fear from his voice. Behind them a street door opened. A slim young man in shirtsleeves emerged, wineglass in hand, and yelped in disbelief at the mangled BMW. Soon he was joined by his guests and a few onlookers disturbed by the noise who gesticulated at the car. None mentioned Elaine. It appeared no one else had seen the incident.

Her left shoe, plain, black and low-heeled, lay in the gutter. George positioned himself over it and bent down swiftly as if picking up a dropped coin. When he straightened up the shoe was in his hand and he hid it under his coat. He turned to Karen, who stood stock-still and open-mouthed.

'You got the key?' he whispered. She nodded. 'Upstairs, then. Quickly. Hush now.'

Without a word she did as she was told. In the flat he closed the door and reached for the phone. She noted dully that he seemed to know his way about.

'What are you doing?'

'Calling the police. Your mother's in some kind of trouble.'

Karen sat down heavily on the sofa. 'Oh, my God.'

The girl's face was white. George decided she had to be his second priority, not his first. He began to talk rapidly in a low authoritative tone into the phone.

The van, from what she could tell, appeared to have been parked in an open yard. Elaine heard the footsteps move away, then the sound of a heavy metal object being dragged across and a loud clang, as if a big gate had been closed.

The footsteps passed back and forth in the yard. The man was muttering to himself. A wooden door banged open, shut, twice. A light was switched on – the yard must be next to a house. Minutes passed. She wondered miserably if he intended to leave her inside the unheated van the whole night. Despite her resolve she was shaking. Held before her as if in supplication her bound hands were turning blue. She agitated them up and down to bring the life back into her fingers but to no avail. The cord cut into the flesh behind her knees and reduced the circulation there, too. Her captor need have no worry about her leaping up and trotting off: her legs would not have carried her.

The door handle began to turn. In panic she shrank away, dragging her numbed legs after her, as if to hide among the sacks. Then the doors were flung wide open and the man stood framed in the glare from a window which left his face in shadow. His hunched figure seemed larger than before, and more powerful. Elaine strained to see his expression, while keeping herself away from the light. She sensed he was scrutinising his booty with interest. He reached to her face and with some gentleness removed the tape, though she whimpered as hair came away with it. Then he nodded in satisfaction.

'We've made it. Well done, Elaine.'

It had to start now, the deception, if ever. She took a deep breath but her voice quavered.

'Well done *you*, you mean. What do I call you, anyway?'

'You can call me Bob.'

The way he spoke implied that it was not his name, but it would do. She wondered if he could manufacture a personality as neatly as a name, and if so whether he would be kind, or crazy, or vicious – or simply mad. And whether she could cope, whichever it turned out to be.

He was not young. A few years older than herself, mid-forties, at a guess. A faint scar disfigured the forehead and gave him a rascally, distorted air – or maybe that was her imagination: most people wouldn't spot it. The hair was thin and grey but had been cut recently. He was clean-shaven, more or less: the chin was covered in light stubble as if he had shaved very early that morning but not since. It was as if he knew how to be dapper when he wanted but had chosen not to be, perhaps in an effort to go unremarked.

He reached out a hand to help her. Clumsily she shuffled forward to the opening, then blushed as she realised her skirt had begun to ride up over her knees. She halted.

He looked at her, puzzled. 'Come on, out. You can't stay in there for ever.'

Modesty would not be in order, it seemed. With another wriggle she was sitting on the edge of the van, legs bound, thighs exposed. A broad ladder snaked down her tights. Bob stood in front of her, one hand on the door handle, the other outstretched. His gaze fell on her legs. A sigh escaped him and he made as if to pull the skirt down but stopped himself. Then he looked longingly at her.

'Not yet. Not here. But thank you.'

With a thump her feet were on the ground and she tried to stand. The ankle throbbed and gave way so that she stumbled. She made herself laugh lightly.

'Sorry. I think you had better untie my legs or I won't be able to move.'

His voice was doubtful. 'You won't try to run away, will you? We have such a lot to talk about.'

'I won't.' The state she was in, nearly fainting, he could have prevented her flight quite easily. It was not worth contemplating. For the first time the knife was not visible but she had no doubt it was close by.

He bent and fiddled with the flex but it took several attempts to untangle his handiwork. His hands felt clammy and awkward. As the ligature relaxed the blood rushed into her cramped muscles and gave her pins and needles. To reduce the discomfort she rose gingerly on tiptoe a couple of times.

Mutely she held out her hands to be untied but Bob ignored them. 'Right.' He indicated the back door to the house. 'Inside. Sharpish, and don't make a sound.'

It was a Victorian property, tall and narrow. The yard was only big enough for the van, which would be hidden from the road by high walls and what she could now see was a large metal sliding barrier to the road. The house's guttering hung loose; an old water barrel lay tipsily on its side. A broken window-box held a solitary geranium. The property had an unloved air, as if over the years it had been occupied by many different souls, none of whom had wanted to be there; nor had any left a mark save the aberrant individual who had once in hope planted the box. The sole light came from the unshaded ground-floor window. There was no number on the peeling paint of the back door.

'This your place?' Elaine kept her voice casual.

'In a manner of speaking. Don't ask too many questions.' He seized her arm and began to hustle her inside.

'No, no. I was admiring it,' Elaine tried, but he did not respond. The door closed behind them.

The back room was a spacious but semi-derelict kitchen which patently had not been renovated for decades. At least it was warm – a gas stove in a corner was switched on. On the drainer several washed mugs and plates had been placed upside-down. A black bin was full to overflowing. A couple of torn tea-towels hung over a string line which stretched from a hook in one wall to another. By the stained sink sat handtowels and, odd in its newness, a bar of soap. A wooden table and several rickety chairs made up the rest of the furniture. Gratefully Elaine sank into the seat he indicated. Turning his back briefly Bob busied himself with an old electric kettle and two of the mugs.

'You like your coffee black with a sweetener, don't you, Elaine?'

She was startled. 'Yes. How do you know?'

He snickered. 'I know a lot about you.' Soon the hot drink was placed before her. She reached out for it with her numbed hands: a sip would revive her. But the liquid scalded her tongue and she grimaced. It would have been easier had she not been bound, she gestured. With a grunt he rose, untied her, took away her coat but then quickly restored the bonds. She was to be in the most obvious way possible his prisoner.

Suddenly she felt very dirty. At the same time other needs were arising.

'Bob, is there a bathroom I can use?'

His eyes flickered. He was obviously wary but said nothing. With a curt gesture he rose and beckoned her to come with him through the hall and up narrow unlit stairs. The climb made her pant and both head and ankle began to throb again. At the top he jerked his head towards an open door: judged by the odour from behind it, it was what she sought. He turned his back, but did not move to return downstairs.

What the hell is this? her inner voice demanded as she shuffled inside the smelly cubicle and managed to sit. A new roll of soft pink toilet paper hung incongruously on a piece of raffia tied to a nail in the crumbling wall. It came to her that Bob had attended to certain key details as well as he could. The entire exercise had the hallmarks of careful preparation. But how far would he go? To her relief he stayed outside but held the door handle so that a slit of two inches remained. When she looked up she caught a glimpse of one eye at the crack. She bowed her head.

What are you doing, asking him politely if you can go to the loo? And letting him stand there, peeking through the gap? See, he's at it now. She started up: the glinting eye disappeared and his bulk shambled a few feet away.

I'm staying alive, that's what, she told herself firmly. The realisation was grim and basic. *At any point he could have stuck that knife between my ribs or slit my throat.* The most dangerous time in any kidnapping, she recalled, was the first few minutes: that was when tension ran highest. From there on, the longer she could keep her captor in a good humour, the better her chances of making it. At any rate, that was the theory.

It must have been an hour since she had opened her own front door.

She raised her arms to see her watch: past eleven. With difficulty she wiped herself and struggled back to decorum.

He was on the landing. 'I must wash my hands,' she said firmly. 'Is there a sink or bathroom?'

'You don't need it,' he responded gruffly and started to go downstairs; but his unguarded glance had shown her the small room on the other side of the landing. It could be no more dire than the toilet and its use might give her a little privacy.

'Yes, I think so.' He turned, a flash of anger on his face. She took a breath and kept her voice as even and neutral as possible. 'It's different for women, Bob. I can see where it is. Is there soap and a towel in there?'

'Don't budge. I'll have to get them from the kitchen.'

He clattered down and could be heard rummaging. She stared hastily around. The hall lamp was high up and broken; an extended ladder would have been needed to fix it, which was presumably beyond Bob's abilities. The place smelled dank. Wallpaper peeled from the roof line downwards, its raddled surface rain-stained and yellow. She wondered if this was a short-life house, let to a housing association maybe, one with more ambition than money. Perhaps nobody knew the house was in use. If that were so, then a check on the electoral register would reveal nothing. She conjectured with increasing anxiety that nobody was slated to pay the council tax; that no landlord bothered to collect the rent. Then in credit lists only old dead names would appear against this address, noted for minor infringements of hire purchase long ago. At the worst, officially nobody lived here. Her spirits sank.

Bob returned, a clean towel over one arm, a fresh bar of Imperial Leather in his hand. Her favourite soap. It was creepy – as if anything more could make her fearful over and above what had happened so far. With muttered thanks she took the proffered items and entered the ancient bathroom.

Again he was outside the door and would not let her close it. 'There isn't enough water for a bath. Bit limited, this place. But in the morning I'll boil the kettle for you.'

In the morning?

Slowly she soaped her hands and face. That was hours away. What did he plan to do next? How was the time to pass? She was exhausted, but could not imagine sleeping in this strange place, in captivity. Did he mean to sit up all night and talk?

That might be the best. Methodically she rinsed her face, shook the drops of moisture as well as she could from her hands and dried herself. The bath was grimy but dry, so she left the towel neatly on its side.

'Good job there isn't any hot water – I'd come out of that bath dirtier than I went in,' she joked as she emerged.

That was a mistake. His voice took on a grating edge again. 'That's the best I can do. Anyway, it's not important.'

She paused enquiringly on the top step. 'It's late, Bob. I'm very tired. Where do I sleep?'

A cunning glint came into his eyes and he began to rub his hands. 'That's up to you. I meant to get a bedroom ready but there wasn't time. There's a basement. Nicer than up here. It has a heater. I've made up a bed for you.'

As she followed him down the stairs a surge of mixed terrors swelled and threatened to unbalance her. She held on to the loose banisters with both hands, still bound. The inner voice was speaking to her, urging her not to compromise herself. This was not a cosy domestic scene: she was not visiting one of the surlier of her constituents. This maniac had deprived her of her freedom and threatened her with a knife. There was no knowing what he might do next. She had to consider her options, and as rapidly as she could.

Escape might be a possibility now that her legs were unbound and sensation restored to them. Her ankle might give way again under pressure – she would have to watch that. Yet how? The front door, of which she had caught barely a glimpse, looked as if it hadn't been opened in years. A huge rusty bolt held it fast at the top. The lock had no key. Above it frosted windows were cracked and half of one pane was missing. But the wood was warped in places; might it be rotten?

The back door was no use. It led out into the yard which she had seen and knew to be well secured. The brick wall might have been scaled with luck, but the sheer metal gate would be difficult without assistance even were her hands free.

The front room door was closed. Houses like these used to have a best room at the front, a parlour. The proud owners would overfill it with heavy horsehair furniture, antimacassars in place, a shiny coal scuttle on the black-leaded hearth; a room used only for Sundays, funerals and visits by wealthier relatives. Sometimes a large bay window straddled the bit of front garden, its window-ledge a repository of treasures to be exhibited to neighbours. Supposing one of the windows were broken or loose . . .?

'Here it is.' Her pondering sharply interrupted, she came back to the present with a surge of despair. The man she knew as Bob was standing by a small wooden door set under the stairs. A single light burned inside.

'Is this where you want me to . . .?'

She could not bring herself to finish the sentence, she who was so articulate, so adept with words. Her breath choked in her throat. He pointed.

In his right hand was the knife.

Deep inside, Elaine longed to cry, but she suppressed the feeling swiftly. Whatever was to happen next she needed to be completely alert.

'Are – are you coming too?' She paused on the second step.

'If you would like me to, Elaine.' His face creased in what passed for a smile.

Her gorge rose in horror. Elaine looked up and found herself staring straight into the man's eyes.

The closeness of his presence meant she could smell him, as she had when he first bundled her into the van. A sweetish, sweaty smell, not unusual in one engaged in massive effort. But it was not an odour of several days; however neglected the house, to her relief he was not too foul in himself. Then she recalled his reluctance to let her use the toilet unobserved or wash her hands, and shuddered.

Life came first. Only if she got out alive could this be brought to a conclusion. She would not let herself be panicked into losing the battle. Fear there was in abundance, but like a soldier she must assess the risks, diminish and avoid them wherever possible, and do everything in her power to get through this night in one piece.

Like a soldier. The memory of George came into her mind and she half smiled. George would not flinch under fire but would strive to do his duty. George would not fear pain, or wounding, though he would not be reckless. With a pang she realised that George would not have the foggiest idea where she was, nor even that she had vanished. He would not be riding to the rescue. Nor, unless she was mistaken, would anybody else, not for some time. This night she was on her own.

The bleakness of her imprisonment made her square her shoulders. Then with a shock she saw that Bob had taken that wistful half-smile to be directed at himself.

The knife was held out, as if not to threaten her but in pride at what it could do. Its blade was broad and shiny – the brightest and best-cared-for thing in the entire house. She examined it almost inquisitively, then recoiled. The tip was stained by what she recognised with horror as her own blood.

He reached out his other hand. Giving a long sigh he touched her golden hair, and let the strands run slowly through his fingers.

Inspector Morris stood in the flat and made rapid notes. 'Don't worry that nobody else saw. That could be useful. Now to this van. Did you get the number, sir?'

George screwed up his face. 'I think it started M one four five, or something like that,' he began, then hesitated. 'It was a greengrocer's van, of that I'm sure. "Somebody's Fruit and Vegetables" was painted on the side. An Irish name.'

'We'll check that out. Sounds as if it was stolen.' Morris spoke into his mobile phone, his tone cool to conceal his worry. 'Right. I need an exact description of the man. Did you get a good view?'

'I think I did.' Karen spoke evenly. 'He looked . . . I can't put my finger on it . . . familiar. I was just wondering if I might have seen him before.'

Morris's eyes lit up. 'Good. If he's been tailing your mother he may well have left clues. Everything you can remember. Both of you.'

The next hour passed in a blur. Karen and George found themselves deep inside Canon Row police station talking to a bleary-eyed artist who, unshaven and tieless, started to make a passable sketch of the man they had so fleetingly seen. It was best, he explained, to do it while the picture was still fresh in their minds. Nobody mentioned the obvious fact that if Elaine were to be found alive and well speed in identifying her attacker was essential.

Calls were made to Betty and to Diane at their homes: both were aroused from their beds and sworn to secrecy. If the abductor had been stalking his victim then he may also have written or left messages. Both women were requested to examine files going back at least two years and to indicate anyone who had aroused their suspicions. 'That means any man who did not have a legitimate reason for contacting Mrs Stalker,' Morris tried to explain, but Diane had cut him off. 'We keep a barmy file, inspector,' she informed him, then pulled on her clothes and headed grimly for the office.

As the charcoal and pastel picture emerged, Karen groaned and frowned deeply. 'Come on,' she cajoled herself. 'Who is it?'

'Might he have come to an advice bureau?' Morris was hovering, notebook in hand.

She shook her head. 'If he had I wouldn't have seen him there. No, that's a red herring. I live a separate life from my mum, you see. She's very busy. I go to college, and in my spare time I – '

She leapt up and danced around the room, then stopped, embarrassed. One result of her attending that class might come out – what she had done to Jim Betts, even though he deserved it. His plight had completely slipped her mind.

The struggle on her face left the two men puzzled. 'What is it, Karen? What have you remembered?' George gently took her hand. 'It doesn't matter how disagreeable. We have to know, for your mother's sake.'

His expression was haggard. On the wall a clock ticked softly.

Karen pointed to the drawing as the artist held it up. 'My Tai-kwondo class. He used to go to it. Wasn't any good. Clumsy, ugly man. I only spoke to him once or twice.'

'Name?'

'Can't remember. Give me a minute, it'll come back to me. If you can get a list of the people who attended from the sports centre, I'll know then . . . There has to be a list, we were all insured. But wait . . . I do remember he was boasting about inheriting a house. From his grandfather, I think. Said it was a mess. Could they be there?'

'It's possible.' Morris tried to hide his excitement. 'Did he say where?'

'Not far from the centre – Wandsworth, I think. And his grandad was eighty-three and dying, and that would be about a year ago. Is that any use?'

'Could be. We can get on to St Catherine's House. They may be able to trace recent deaths of men born in . . . what? Nineteen-fourteen or thereabouts . . . with addresses in that area. It would really help, though, if we had a name.'

The girl bit her lip and looked to George in misery. He sympathised. 'It mightn't be the same one anyway. Or he could have been using a false name.' He put an arm round her shoulders and squeezed. The natural gesture was fatherly and comforting.

The inspector excused himself and left the room. The artist continued to shade and tweak, then rubbed his eyes and lumbered out also.

George and Karen found themselves alone. He sat down heavily in a chair while she continued to pace agitatedly around the room, forcing her brain to recall more. Then in that irrelevant way which sometimes occurs to those under great stress, it came to her that her manners left something to be desired.

'George – thanks for being here,' she started, but he cut her short.

'I'm as involved as you are, Karen.'

She examined him for a long moment. 'You very fond of my mum?'

'Of course. If I could change places with her right now I would – I'd give anything to know she is safe.'

His voice shook. The passion in it wiped out the girl's remaining composure. She bent her head and wept, her hand on his shoulder. He touched her arm wordlessly.

At last she found a tissue and blew her nose. 'I can see why she likes you. I think you'd be good for her.'

'If she'd have me,' muttered George with feeling. 'I tell you, Karen, if – *when* – we get her out of this, I shan't take no for an answer again. But take heart. We're not done yet – '

The youngster's answering squeal made him sit up in alarm.

'You OK?' he asked anxiously, but she was already running for the door.

'Done yet – that's it,' she answered breathlessly. 'Got it. You're brilliant, George, you know that?'

He was at her side in a trice. 'What do you mean? What did I say?'

'Dunn – Graham Dunn, that was his name. That's him.'

Elaine shrank away and looked down the stairs. Her breathing was rapid and shallow. She bit the inside of her cheek, hard, to remind herself this was no fantasy, and tasted her own blood.

Cold metal was pressed into the back of her neck.

'I won't use it, Elaine. I promise. Not unless I have to.' The man was edgy: the blade trembled. 'Downstairs.'

Slowly, one step at a time as if uncertain of her footing, she descended into the gloom of the basement. She steeled herself against dankness, but to her surprise the place smelled relatively clean and was quite warm, as if a heater had been switched on down there for a long time. A few boxes and a rusty bike came into sight. For most of the way her view was obscured by the low ceiling, but as she reached the bottom step she paused and gaped in astonishment.

Every wall was covered in pictures and press cuttings. From floor to ceiling whole pages of newspapers had been carefully pinned, with articles marked in blue and red ink. Several were duplicates – he must have bought multiple copies of the items he liked. Many were in colour, whole articles from *Hello!* and *Woman's Weekly* and *Bella* magazines. Some she did not recognise but most were as familiar as her own name.

For the pictures were of herself; and the articles all mentioned her, or were about her, interviews and gossip pieces and reports of press conferences and photographs of her speaking or cuddling children or haranguing audiences. Her face, laughing or serious, mouth open, shut, close-ups and full length, smartly dressed mostly but with at-home interviews in which she wore jeans and an embarrassed expression: pictures by Sally Soames and Jane Bown, by male photographers without number, old poses with Mike and Karen as a young teenager, more recently from her election address with Karen alone – in fact that *was* her election address and there were four or five copies of it.

The place was a shrine. It must have taken ages to collect this stuff, though on closer examination she realised that nothing was more than two or three years old. The obsession could be dated, then. Where had he been before that? Hospital? Prison? Only he knew. Given his erratic reactions it would not do to interrogate him.

Her common sense told her that such practices were not so unusual. Around the world thousands of bedroom walls were covered in Elvis or Marilyn, Madonna or Brad Pitt, posters and montages and signed fanzine pictures. Fan clubs flourished for the most hideous pop stars or famous sports or film personalities. Even for politicians the phenomenon was not unknown – Che Guevara and Castro had adorned student rooms for decades, while Hitler featured behind many a locked door. Somewhere in the UK somebody probably worshipped Lady Thatcher and lovingly collected her memorabilia. For anyone in public life, for a celebrity who became an icon, it was almost inevitable. But herself . . .?

Bob was speaking. 'This is your sanctuary, Elaine. You'll be safe here. None of those horrible reporters – all the dreadful things they say about you. I will look after you, you'll see.'

Speechless and increasingly petrified she moved around the low room, examining some of the items more closely. On a small table was a large brown folder of press cuttings about her resignation: she surmised that he had not had time to pin them up. Then the far wall brought her up sharp.

On the left-hand side were full-page spreads of the demonstration at St Kitts, complete with herself emerging from the car and being escorted by the burly police officer to the door through jeering crowds.

The photographs did not flatter: to her own eye she looked supercilious and remote. In the background of one, however, a blue felt-tip circle had been drawn. Elaine wondered if Bob had seen himself and peered close, but it was the scowling face of a middle-aged woman.

On the right-hand side of the wall there were no pictures of Elaine. Only more lurid headlines about a murder, the finding of a young prostitute, dead and cut, behind a Tube station. Red ink had been scribbled liberally over the pages as if in commentary, and an effort had been made to obscure the murdered girl's features completely.

Elaine began to shake. She took a step back. Dunn was at her side and grabbed her arm with his left hand, gesticulating with the knife in his right at the wall.

'Both dead, see. That one' – he pointed at the St Kitts story – 'because she threw something awful at you. I didn't mean to kill her, it was an accident. But she deserved to die. And the other because she was a filthy tart with a nasty mouth on her. She called me stupid. And she wasn't nearly as pretty as you.'

The knife snaked slowly towards her face; she could see it flash out of the corner of her eye. Was he going to cut her? Blind her? Summoning all her willpower she held herself steady. Only a faint tremor betrayed her terror.

The knife slid under her hair close to her ear and lifted up a blonde curl. Dunn's fingers grasped the lock. 'Keep still,' he warned, and cut the piece of hair, letting it rest in his palm, weighing it as if it were real gold.

The knife came up again and touched the point of her chin, then lightly, so lightly, began to slide down her jugular. She could not see his face but could hear his rasping breathing. It was as if he wanted to demonstrate in the most violent way possible that he was in charge – not only of her, but of himself.

The knife changed hands. It rested more easily in his left, as though it were less dangerous there, nestling amongst her cut hair. Then her tormentor raised his free hand and placed it on her breast.

'Time, now.'

She swallowed. He was massaging her breast, hard. He must be able to feel her trembling.

'Wha – what do you want me to do?'

'Take off your clothes. It isn't cold. Put them over there.'

He indicated a chair. Next to it on the bare floor was a mattress with an inappropriately flowered quilt.

'Then lie down. And don't scream. Nobody will hear you. And if you do, I'll have to kill you.'

Chapter Twenty-Five

'Cup of tea, love?'

Short, stolid and pale-faced, PC Sharon Bassett held out a sympathetic hand. Karen rubbed her eyes and sleepily accepted the proffered drink. Its scalding sweetness roused her.

'Where am I?'

'Canon Row police station, where you were before. It's six o'clock. The cleaners'll be in here in a minute. Thought I'd better warn you.'

'Oh – yeah.' Karen dragged herself back into life. Suddenly she remembered why she had been asleep under a black police mackintosh on a sofa in the inspector's office. She jumped up anxiously. 'My mother – any news?'

The young policewoman shook her head. The same age as Karen, she had joined the Met straight from school in the footsteps of a father, brother and two uncles, determined to prove that a girl could be as effective a law officer as any man. The teasing in the station had been acceptable after the endless jokes at home. What was harder was the assumption that as a female she would have special treatment when promotions came up; and that when she did get her stripes it would be not be through merit. Yet all her mates came from similar backgrounds. It was most unfair.

That said, she gravitated naturally towards the more humane aspects of police activity which might have bored the men. An assignment to care for victims and their families was the kind she relished. Some people almost deserved what came to them, in her opinion. But nobody, not even a politician, deserved what had happened to Mrs Stalker.

She chattered encouragingly at Karen, who was attempting to brush her hair using a small comb and the inspector's tiny mirror. Sharon felt sorry for the girl. How long might this case last – long enough to make friends, perhaps? What would be its outcome? The hunt for Mrs Stalker was like looking for the proverbial needle in a haystack. But she must neither raise Karen's hopes nor dash them unnecessarily.

'They're chasing up the information you gave them. Having a name helps.'

She did not say that Dunn's police and hospital records, once unearthed, were altogether too substantial and alarming for comfort. The various episodes of unprovoked belligerence, the spells detained in secure units under the Mental Health Act 1983, the plethora of addresses at which he had briefly lodged: everything painted a picture of a deviant but cunning psychotic who had repeatedly evaded incarceration. Nobody had been able to curb or cure him; nor did he consider himself ill at all.

The search exercise had, however, been useful. Old mug-shots were being hastily copied, fingerprint records examined. But knowing *who* he was was not the same as knowing *where* he was; and there, so far, the investigation had drawn a blank.

'We'll find her, don't you worry.' Sharon spoke with an assurance she did not feel. The man and his captive might have gone to ground anywhere.

'Oh, yes, I'm certain of that,' Karen murmured, averting her eyes. It would not do in any way to undermine the efforts of so many people doing their best.

More robustly, Karen asserted: 'I'm sure of something else, too – my mum can look after herself. I wouldn't like to be in the shoes of any guy who tried to hurt her. She's brave and strong. She'd flatten him.'

The moment he arrived at the department, Fred knew something was terribly wrong. The greater intensity of security, so that he and his driver had to show their passes; the 'Red Alert' signs everywhere which had replaced the more usual 'Black'; the wary expressions on the faces of messengers and doorkeepers. It added to the unease which had nagged at him all night once he realised that Karen had not come home and had not phoned to explain.

Since he knew better than to ask questions he headed for his office but at the corner was intercepted by a grave Martin Chadwick. The two went up in the lift in silence, as if the Deputy Permanent Secretary feared the machine might be bugged.

On the fourth floor Fred was ushered into the Secretary of State's room. Two other men in suits whom he did not know waited respectfully at one side. An assistant secretary stood ready, notebook in hand. Bampton paced about in agitation.

'What's up, Ted?'

'We have a problem,' Bampton said gruffly and indicated the strangers. 'Police.'

The officers introduced themselves but Fred did not catch their details. He listened with mounting incredulity as the tale unfolded of Elaine's disappearance.

'Are we involved?' he asked.

Ted stopped his pacing and glared. 'Of course we are. The theory – one theory, anyway – is that she's been taken by someone with a grudge against this department. Could have a go at one of us next. So we're on our guard.'

Fred groaned. 'It's like the IRA back again, isn't it? God, how awful. I hope Elaine's all right.' The thought struck him. 'Her daughter – Karen! I share a house with her and she didn't come home last night either. They couldn't have taken her too, could they? Is she – ?'

'Miss Stalker is with us, sir,' the older officer said quickly. 'She's OK.'

'I didn't know you lived with Elaine's daughter,' Ted muttered suspiciously. 'How long's this been going on?'

Fred was not about to argue the loose morals or divided loyalties of the younger generation with Ted Bampton or anybody else. 'Long enough,' he answered curtly, then turned to the detectives. 'I'd like to go to her, if that's possible. She may need some support. May I come with you?'

'What, now?' Bampton began to protest. 'But we've prayers in ten minutes . . .'

Fred suddenly saw Bampton, alone and blustering, under heavy criticism for the disintegration of his team, the subject of whispers in the Commons Tea Room and bars, dismissed by the media as a failure. His staff had glided imperceptibly away as if the space he occupied had become contaminated. The Secretary of State seemed to have shrunk: in this imposing room he looked too small for the job. Fred, no longer so green and starry-eyed, understood why. Increasingly he realised he despised his boss for his ignorance, his insensitivity, his bad manners and his lack of humanity. Fred had heard too much of Bampton's cruelty towards Elaine to side with him. Yet he suspected that had Elaine stood up to Ted more vigorously that overbearing aggression might have been checked. Fred did not intend to make the same mistake.

The young Minister headed towards the door and motioned the stony-faced police to follow. Out of respect he attempted to keep the sarcasm out of his voice and was glad he did not quite succeed. 'Then I suggest you pray for Elaine, Ted. It might just do some good.'

Under the duvet, naked, Elaine shivered miserably. Her tied hands had gone numb. She twisted them carefully inside their bonds, but he had made too thorough a job of it.

In the distance a church clock chimed: she thought she counted six or seven. A small window high up in the wall of the basement indicated it was light outside. A car went past, then a bus. Slowly she stretched her limbs and wriggled her toes in an effort to alleviate the stiffness caused by sleeping on a mattress spread on the cold hard floor.

Not that there had been much sleep, though sheer exhaustion had made her doze in the end. Her fingers crept towards her chin and found the matted edge of the scar. It no longer hurt unless she pressed it. There would be a mark, a reminder, for ever.

If, that was, she came out of this in one piece.

For whatever her familiarity with the psychology of captivity, however much self-control she could exert, she was certain about one thing: Bob, as he called himself, was totally deranged, and she was in mortal danger.

Her inner voice had remained active through the night and now spoke urgently. *Figure him out*, it said. *There is some consistency in him: even if he's completely crackers, recognising it will help you.* For example, much of the time Bob spoke and acted relatively normally. His eyes did not roll and his tone was calm, almost dreary. He didn't froth at the mouth or show any other outward signs of his mental state, except for rubbing his hands together in an oddly compulsive way. His behaviour was methodical, as if he had figured out what to do long since and was following a set pattern to which only he had the key. True, he had threatened her with the knife several times and used it on her once – twice, if cutting off a lock of her hair counted as an assault, albeit trivial by comparison. And her bound hands would not let her forget she was a prisoner. But there had been moments when conversation had been possible. Bob in other circumstances might have been a tolerable companion. Provided he got his way.

Then the events of the previous night, after she had slowly come into the basement, came back with a vividness that almost made her cry out.

'I don't get it.' She had pointed at the massed press cuttings.

'You seem to be a great collector, Bob. Could you explain to me?'

He hesitated. He had expected screams and protests. He had pictured her in floods of tears, kneeling at his feet and pleading with him to let her go. The more abject and cringing her response the more he would have liked it. Women ought to beg men for it. That would confirm their status. Men were the dominant creatures. The female should acknowledge that fact.

Had she lashed out at him or tried to run away he would have been ready. If Elaine would not have him then nobody else would have her: on that his mind was made up. He would not willingly have marked that beautiful face, but had it proved necessary to stop her escaping to the arms of another man – any man, ever – then he would make the sacrifice. She was his. Nobody else's.

'It's all you, Elaine. I told you why when I picked you up.'

'I can see you're very fond of me.' She had made herself smile directly into his face. *He must believe that I am on his side. Only then can I win his trust.*

He twisted impatiently. 'More than that. I told you.' He raised the knife. 'I love you. And you love me. Don't you?'

Her voice faltered and her eyes were fixed on the blade. It seemed to have a life of its own.

'I don't know you very well, Bob,' she demurred.

He grinned. 'Plenty of time to get to know me. All the time in the world.' Then, in one of those savage mood swings which so terrified her, his mouth turned ugly and he shoved his face into hers.

'Like now. We're wasting time. Will you take your clothes off or shall I do it with this knife?'

She nodded dumbly. Bob seized the chair and sat down, arms folded across his chest. With revulsion she realised he intended to watch as she undressed.

Her tied hands shook as she moved to unfasten buttons and undo the zip of her skirt. He seemed happy to let her struggle awkwardly: perhaps that was part of the fun.

Do it slowly, her inner voice urged. *You are playing for time.*

She paused and looked sidelong at him. Bob gazed back, eyes hooded, then waved the knife lazily. 'Not enough just to undo them. I mean it. *Off.*'

'I can't get the blouse off unless you untie my hands.' He obviously hadn't thought of that. With an oath and an impatient lurch he rose and came to stand before her. She flinched as he touched her but he was too engrossed to notice. His stubby fingers had difficulty with the flex, as if he were unaccustomed to performing intricate tasks. As he breathed heavily she smelled him again: sweatier, more acrid than before. With the greatest effort she held back nausea. He returned to the chair, banged it into place and sat down heavily. She rubbed her wrists until he began to mutter at her.

In slow motion, every movement dragged from her, she slipped the blouse from her shoulders and stepped out of her skirt. The garments lay discarded by her stockinged feet. It was almost a relief to roll down the torn tights and throw them behind her. Then she stood upright in her slip.

Her body was trim and taut, but in her neck the tendons stood out and her eyes were wide with fright. The blonde hair framed her face in a tangled mass. Her bare arms crossed over her breasts in the lacy bra made them bulge and cleave. The chill air on her shoulders and calves, her naked feet, her toes on the cold floor, made her feel horrendously and miserably vulnerable. She curled one foot protectively over the other and saw his eyes glint at the movement.

'Very nice,' Bob murmured.

She risked another glance at her tormentor. He was smiling, with his mouth open. He licked his wet lips. Then he pulled off his shoes and planted his feet in their woollen socks on the floor. When he moved, his feet left a damp mark. The knife was in his right hand and held tightly. He sat, knees spread, leaning back and to the side to get a better view. His left hand slid to his crotch.

If all he wanted to do was masturbate then maybe he should get on with it, she thought grimly. She stopped and looked at him enquiringly. Without a word he waved the weapon and signalled to her to take off her slip.

There was only one way to do it and it would leave her completely unsighted for a few seconds. She bent and crossed her arms over her body, reached down and hoisted up the hem, then pulled the silky garment over her head, hiding her face. Now she could not see him, though she was conscious that he was shifting in the chair. The straps became momentarily entangled in her hair and she had to shake her head to free them.

The slip joined the rest of her crumpled clothes on the floor. There was to be no escape. The heater may have been at full throttle but every inch of her skin was goosefleshed. She swallowed a sob and forced

441

herself to remain silent. Shoulders bowed she stood before him, trying to control her shivering.

'Aahh!' The breath hissed out of him. 'You are so beautiful. If you knew how I've waited for this moment, Elaine . . .'

He rose, unfastening the belt of his trousers. He let them drop and kicked them away. Swiftly he tugged his shirt and jumper over his head, pulled off his socks and disposed of his shorts.

He was naked. The flabby body seemed grey and shapeless in the pale light. He was taller than her and much more thickset – at a guess a good four stone heavier, possibly more. Her inner voice noted with a desperate drollery that he was not well endowed: the knife was a great deal longer than his modestly erect penis. He would not hurt her that way, it seemed. Unless he used the knife instead.

He came to stand behind her and undid the bra hooks, sliding his free hand round and pinching her left breast and nipple hard. She winced in pain and braced herself. Then he slid his hand down and felt around inside her panties, sticking two hard fingers into her and exploring. The action made him lean his whole body against her back. The pressure of his rough chest on her chilled skin made her want to scream.

The inner voice was not necessary. There is only one way to get through this, she told herself. You can't simply ignore it and switch off – not if he keeps pinching and hurting. And it will hurt all the more if you resist. No, you'll just have to try the other tack. You'll have to pretend you're with somebody else. Someone you love and would want to make love with. Isn't there a fine line between good and bad sex? Between loving lust and this ghastly travesty? You must imagine you are with a real lover, somebody you *want* inside you. Like George. Only that will make it bearable.

She closed her eyes and exhaled, long and deep, as if his fondling were acceptable. He was nuzzling her neck and murmuring that she was lovely; the voice had an oddly soft, almost child-like quality. Perhaps there had been some gentleness about him: he had been a child once, and maybe had been loved. How strange, she caught herself, to be thinking kindly thoughts about a man about to rape you. *But if you think anything else, you will die.*

'Take 'em off.' He indicated the panties. She took a step away from him and did as she was told, then stood humbly, hands limp at her sides, head bowed, her skin crawling.

He pointed at the mattress. 'Lie down. On your back. Open your legs.'

As she did so he knelt beside her. 'Wider.'

It was almost laughable: he wanted to gawp. She kept her eyes firmly fixed on the ceiling and breathed as regularly as she could. Was he only going to stare at her? She could cope with that. Whereas a virgin or young girl would have found such blatant exposure the worst humiliation, since she had had to put up with being examined by strangers when pregnant, in a curious way this was not an ordeal. Though no other stranger had bent down close to sniff at her and giggled as he did so.

After several minutes he appeared satisfied. With a grunt he placed the knife out of her reach but within his own. One hand returned to pinching her breasts until she gasped: the effect of causing pain seemed to please him. His other hand he ran lazily over her abdomen and tested where her hip-bones rose as if committing her personal geography to memory. His fingers were stubby and not clean; several nails were ragged and scratched her. She kept as still as possible but tried not to go rigid. It seemed wiser to keep her eyes open, but terrified of confrontation she avoided looking him directly in the face. To judge from his ecstatic expression, from his point of view all was going to plan. She suppressed a shudder as he traced the dimple of her navel with the broken edge of his thumbnail.

Then his manner changed. He slid his hand further down and reached between her open legs with a sudden shove. The thrust was brutal and uncompromising: she cried out involuntarily and arched her back away from him. He laughed – a high, thin sound, as if from some other body or soul, unearthly and triumphant. Then he was on her and, fingering her still, thrust himself inside her. She clamped her mouth tight shut to stop from screaming as he heaved up and down on top of her, his distorted face a few inches from her own; as he tried to kiss her she wrenched away, so that the bristles on his chin scraped the small wound on her neck and made it bleed once more.

It seemed like an eternity, but it must have taken only a few moments until he uttered a deep groan, grunted once more, then flopped, his breath coming in short rasps, his eyes shut. At last he slithered off her and rolled on to his back, belly heaving. She hoped he might let her be and that she could remain unbound; but he had not forgotten their peculiar circumstances. He reached over her, grabbed the end of the flex and roughly re-tied her unresisting hands. And that, for the moment, was that.

She forced herself to count her blessings. She was alive. He had had enough for the moment. He could have humiliated her further, but

443

had merely sighed happily, given her a quick affectionate peck on the cheek and, almost unbelievably, rapidly fallen asleep. He did not seem interested in any further sex: he had wanted it only once, and straight, missionary style. She had survived, and she had respite, at least for a while.

He must think of her as a wife. Presumably he'd been with prostitutes; maybe he had had a girlfriend. But a wife he might be persuaded to treat with honour. Perhaps that was the knowledge she needed. She would wait until the morning and see if that might work.

She had not dared to move all night. Between her legs she could sense his stickiness and had forcibly to suppress the urge to vomit. Should she reveal her hostility and fear in any way, she reasoned to herself, she would become truly his victim, not only in losing her sense of self but in confirming to him his absolute power. Only if she managed to maintain her outward calm, and even make herself nice to this monster, might her chances of seeing daylight remain.

The clock outside chimed again. Beside her the heavy body stirred and she caught her breath.

'Bob, good morning.' She made her voice casual. His eyes opened.

With a swift movement he reached for the knife which lay beside the mattress and waved it above her face. His breath reeked, the stubble on his jowls was dark and rough. She raised her hands defensively but not too fast and brushed his arm away. 'There's no need for that, Bob, you must see by now. I'm not going anywhere.'

He relaxed at that but his manner was still wary. She continued, 'But I do have to go to the toilet and have a wash. You promised me a hot kettle this morning. Is that possible?'

With a grunt of accord he rose from the floor, collected his clothes and shuffled out. Elaine sat up and took stock. Her head no longer throbbed; her ankle, though wobbly, would serve. Her breasts hurt where he had pinched them, but not excessively. Her hands were still tied but a brief examination suggested she could use her teeth to untangle the flex if necessary. He had torn nothing, not cut her, not bitten or badly scratched her. Not touched her, indeed, during the night. She offered a quick prayer of thanks to whichever deity had so ordained that her captor's libido and technique, despite the knife giving him *carte blanche*, was distinctly limited.

A minute later Bob reappeared, steaming kettle in hand, and motioned her upstairs. She followed his lead and collected her own garments on the way. At the top of the stairs he undid her hands without being asked. She entered the bathroom and pushed the door to, then heard his steps clatter away down the stairs, as if he wished to respect her modesty.

With a fierce savagery she began to wash between her legs. At the smell of him on the flannel she started to retch in terror. With a small cry she fled to the toilet, where she allowed herself the luxury of being thoroughly sick.

It was going to be a beautiful day. The sun streamed through the dusty windows of New Scotland Yard and made its grey interiors almost attractive. Not the best weather to be working when golf or fishing in greener pastures beckoned.

The commander leaned forward, the braid on his dark uniform glinting in the sunlight. His rugged features were as well known as those of many MPs and rather more admired. 'You think you've found the address, then?'

Detective Inspector Morris flipped back the pages of a notebook. 'We traced deaths in Wandsworth over the last eighteen months and came up with sixteen Dunns of about the right age. It could have been a different name entirely, of course. But one, a Jacob Dunn, had an address which might fit: in Lysias Road. We're checking it out now. Can't be many places in that area to hide a transit van. It could be our breakthrough.'

'And he's real trouble, this bloke?'

Morris tapped a pencil on the pile of folders before him. 'Yes, Commander. He has a long history of violent behaviour. I've not the least doubt he would resist arrest.'

'But as you're well aware, David, if you want the Armed Response Group I'd prefer evidence that he uses firearms. Best of all, does he have a gun with him?'

The inspector spread his hands. 'We can't be sure of that, of course. But he is armed. And very dangerous.'

The commander knew exactly what was in the mind of his subordinate. He did not disapprove, but whatever decision was taken he might have to defend it. Especially if anything went wrong.

He pressed his fingertips together. Television training had taught him this made him look wise. 'I suppose we do have to take into account who the hostage is, don't we? I've had a call from the PM's office asking us to do whatever we can. Private information, that. But we mustn't take any chances.'

'Absolutely, sir.' Morris waited.

That was enough. The commander signed the piece of paper with a flourish. 'There you are. But David . . .'

'Sir?'

'Be careful. There are two people inside that house, remember. And maybe innocent bystanders around. I'm having no shooting gallery out there, understand? No pot shots, no heroes. Don't let anybody get trigger-happy.'

He wagged an admonitory finger.

'If we're going to have a dead body to explain later, do me a favour. Make sure it's the right one.'

Elaine sipped her tea and regarded her jailer out of lowered eyes. He had given her a clean sweater to wear on top of her blouse, 'round the house', as he put it. The blue lambswool pullover still had its Marks and Spencer tag intact. It was the correct size, a matter she now took virtually for granted.

On the shelf above the sink a small radio was tuned to Talk Radio. It was on too softly to hear clearly but Elaine was certain her name had not been mentioned. For once she was not big news, just at a time when to know she was the subject of a huge investigation would have been great consolation. On the other hand, a public hunt closing in might have put her life far more at risk than it appeared to be at present.

Bob was eating fried eggs on toast as if he had worked up an appetite. An old copy of the *Globe* was propped up on the teapot. That it was a week out of date did not seem to matter. In the middle pages he found an item of interest and pushed the paper over to her.

'One of your MP colleagues got caught good and proper, didn't he? What was he up to, four in a bed? Very naughty.'

Elaine glanced at the article. 'I know him quite well and he's not that sort,' she answered, careful to keep her voice neutral. 'It was a set-up. He invited some friends – or people he believed were friends – to dinner and didn't realise the woman had a tape recorder. I mean, who'd want to see their private sport all over the press?'

'Shouldn't carry on, then. It's all wrong.' Bob shook his head morosely and gulped his tea.

It took a considerable effort to conceal her disgust that this evil man, a rapist and killer, who had kidnapped her in a frenzied attack and might at the least provocation assault her again, should have moral scruples about the peccadilloes of an obscure backbencher in the supposed privacy of his own home. She bit back the words, 'Wait till *you're* the target. Then see how you like it.' He would probably relish the infamy as much as he was enjoying his breakfast – and, she realised with a bitter sigh, might in due course be paid handsomely by the same newspaper for his story.

At the sound of her sigh Bob looked up quickly. 'What's the matter? Tea too hot? You've hardly eaten anything. Do you want a bit of toast?'

It was futile to volunteer that what she most wanted to do was go home. The knife lay on the table top between them, casually placed next to the cereal bowl he had just emptied. It was joined by a vicious-looking bread knife, brand new, its bar-code label still stuck to the wooden handle. By contrast the broad-bladed knife which was his preferred weapon was older, its black handle well scored, as if it had been in use a long time and had been scrubbed more than once. The thought made her shudder. Yet the unreal air of domesticity in the dismal kitchen was, she sensed, a protection for her, to be preserved at all costs.

She pushed up the sleeves of the sweater. 'I'm OK, thank you. But I was wondering . . .' Her voice took on a slight wheedle. 'If I'm to stay here, it would be nice to know more about you.' He frowned. Hastily she continued. 'At the moment, you know everything about me. A real relationship, Bob, would redress that balance. At least a bit.'

He put down his mug and pondered. Beyond capturing Elaine and bringing her to his hideout, he had planned very little. There had been the determination to have sex with her, of course; he still wasn't sure that the events of the previous evening hadn't been a fabulous dream. But if it had been for real, and if he was right that she had secretly loved him all along, then tonight there'd be a second chance. This time, he smiled to himself, she would have to ask for it. On bended knees, as he had always imagined her, in a moment of abandoned passion. With her hands tied in front of her in entreaty, like those pictures of martyred nuns from his childhood. Only without her clothes. With her white skin glowing in the lamplight and her blonde hair falling over her face. Yes, that would be perfect.

'Bob?' Her voice was anxious.

'Mmm?' With a wrench he abandoned his fantasy.

'I was only wondering whether you've always lived here. You sound as if you come from my part of the world – the Midlands. Would that be right?'

He could not fathom why she might be in the least interested. Yet it was so pleasant to sit here with her, as she nodded and encouraged him. As if they were married, nearly.

For the next hour Elaine managed to engage her captor in trivial conversation, but gleaned a great deal of valuable background along the way. His interest in martial arts, for one, and his extensive and exploitative knowledge of the gaps in the community care system for another. It was one way to pass the time safely. The technique she had learned in advice bureaux – of prompting the constituent to confide while she took in not only the spoken words but the manner, body language, tone of voice and other clues – was extremely useful in this surreal context. For Bob clearly liked talking about himself. His face became animated, at least as long as the topics were anodyne. Only on the subject of those who had hindered him did his manner change.

'Did you find the doctors helpful at St Kitts?' she enquired.

'Yeah, they were all right. Bit weird. In some of these places the doctors have been there so long they're madder than the patients.' He chortled, an unpleasant sound. Then his expression darkened. 'St Thomas's, though. That was a bad place. Acute psychiatry, they call it, but it's only a ward with beds in. No treatment. When I made a protest they bunged me so full of Clopixol I didn't know what day it was.'

Elaine made a sympathetic gesture. 'Must have been awful. Do you still have to take tablets?'

He looked slyly at her. 'Well . . . I'm supposed to. But I'm better. Don't need 'em anymore.'

'Yes,' Elaine murmured, 'I can see that.' She sat up purposefully. 'Are you finished? I have to get on with the washing up.'

He looked at her with astonishment verging on gratitude. 'You don't have to.'

'Oh, but I want to.' She rose and started to collect dishes and cutlery.

'Well, look . . .' He stopped, suddenly confused. 'I have to go out and get some things – food and that. I was going to tie you up.'

Her heart skipped a beat. She carried on stolidly clearing the table and waited until she could reply in a steady tone. 'You don't need to. I'm not going anywhere. Where's the washing-up liquid?'

He paused, doubtful. His hand strayed to the knife: he picked it up and weighed it in his palm as if seeking its opinion. The menacing act served to remind him of his purpose. He spoke brusquely, as if denying some vestige of a better nature.

'No. I don't trust you yet. I'll be out for some time and you may try to escape. Downstairs, now. I want to be sure you're still here when I get back.'

It was useless to argue. This time he tied her hands behind her back and pushed her gently down the stairs before seating her on the chair and fastening her ankles, one twisted behind each chair leg. It took several minutes of grunt and strain for him to complete his handiwork, for his movements were clumsy. Nevertheless he achieved his crude objective of rendering her immobile. She would not be able to stand or stretch; if she struggled she would fall forward on her face with the chair on top.

'I'll leave the light on,' he offered charitably. Then he bent down, put his hand into her hair, pulled her head back, and kissed her sloppily on the mouth. 'Be good, now.'

His steps receded up the stairs and she heard the back door slam. She could not reach up to wipe her mouth clean: instead, in urgent need of clearing his spittle from her lips, she spat out as hard as she could.

The house was eerily quiet. Breathing hard and whimpering she looked around unhappily at the newspapered walls of the fantastic grotto. Her own image returned her gaze, Elaines in their dozens, smartly arrogant, untouchable, inaccessible. Her former face mocked her for her current impotence: the past, ignorant of the future, so merrily had assumed that such a thing could not possibly happen.

Yet the dead creature was in truth the one plastered all over her prison cell. Those photographs were relics of a life smashed beyond repair. She would never again be that person, for even were she invited by a future administration to return to government – which, given the manner of her leaving, was unlikely – the brittle certainties of that Elaine Stalker were gone.

She could not recover the same self-confidence and assertiveness. She harboured a sense of her own passing: it was time for the next generation to move in, to take the risks, and, if they wanted office enough, to pay the high price demanded. There would never be a shortage of takers, of that she was sure.

Merciful Christ, her inner voice chided. How could she feel sorry for her old self at a moment like this? To mourn the demise of a meaningless icon when death, stark and genuine, floated like a spectre in the air before her was outlandish in the extreme. Her current agonies demanded her total attention. It came to her as an overwhelming shock how desperate her situation was.

449

Gagging, she shook her head vigorously to rid herself of the sensation of that hateful hand on her hair. Again she hawked and spat, and tried not to speculate about what might happen on Bob's return. At least while he was out she was not being violated.

Only then, certain she was alone, did she throw back her head and howl in fear, until the tears slid in a despairing flow down her cheeks, and she could see no more.

'I must come with you.' George stood, his mouth set.

Karen went quickly to his side. 'Me too. I'm not sitting around here while you're out trying to rescue my mother. She would expect me to be there.'

Fred rose to his feet and nodded his concurrence.

The inspector gazed helplessly from one to the other. 'I can't have you there. I'm sorry. I need every man of mine to concentrate on the job in hand. The more bystanders, especially VIPs' – he motioned at Fred – 'the more my chaps get distracted. Not to speak of those in charge,' he muttered.

They look like the Three Musketeers standing there, he reflected irreverently: scared witless, but all for one and one for all. And I'm not d'Artagnan. I have to put my foot down.

'I'm a reserve Guards officer: I could be helpful. At any rate I know what to do.' George's calm dignity was impressive. Karen slipped her arm through his and stared brazenly at the inspector. Mrs Stalker's well-known features unnerved him. He turned to Fred.

'I'm sorry, Mr Laidlaw. I know you mean well but you'd only get in the way. We already have one MP in trouble. I can't take responsibility for another. And you're a Minister too. It's more than my job's worth to put you at unnecessary risk.'

Nor, the policeman implied, can I see what it has to do with you. Fred was not about to spell it out, but hesitated just long enough. Satisfied, Morris collected his cap, jammed it firmly on his head, picked up his mackintosh and headed for the door. Karen and George, moving as one, followed.

She must have fallen asleep. Her neck was stiff and she stretched it cautiously this way and that to free the muscles.

It was the clang of the yard gate which had awakened her. The van engine thrummed and was switched off. The kitchen door slammed, and she could hear his boots clumping about above; but it was not for some minutes that the stair door opened and the familiar baggy-trousered legs started their descent.

Time to be friendly again, though now that her ankle was stronger from this point onwards she would be seeking any opportunity to escape. A gap between Bob's wariness and her own alertness might blessedly begin to open. If he could be encouraged to relax and become slightly complacent while she kept her wits about her a whisker of a chance might appear.

There was still no evidence of police involvement. Probably no one had yet reported her disappearance, though it could not be long now. Bob had been happy for her to listen to the radio in the kitchen. The news had made no mention of her, but again, she remembered, that was not surprising: a news blackout was quite likely. There was no phone in the house, of that she was fairly certain, or if there was she had seen no sign of one. Yet she realised that if she allowed herself seriously to believe she was entirely alone the despair and self-pity so close to the surface would turn rapidly to panic and destroy her ability to help herself.

Any move would have to be before nightfall. She had no idea what was planned for her second night in their 'home', but it would be a miracle if further sex wasn't on the cards. This time he might be more adventurous, or more degrading. Instinctively she pressed her thighs together. Her feet, still bare, felt cold and dirty on the stone floor.

Bob had a carrier bag in his hand. The basement had warmed up as the day had proceeded and he discarded his jacket. He must have shaved upstairs and had combed his hair. He pottered around, went to the file of press cuttings and read them through as if to remind himself of his inspiration. Then he came to stand in front of her. He was looking pleased with himself as if he had a secret.

'Have a successful trip?' she asked with as much gaiety as she could muster.

He shrugged, but without being asked bent down to untie her legs. She turned her back as if it were entirely natural and he undid her hands also.

'I bought you some trainers. You lost your shoe. Got the right size,' he assured her. He dug into the bag and took out a cheap pair. She made herself thank him, and with some relief put them on and stood up. He was right: they fitted.

Then: 'I wasn't sure what you'd like to do this afternoon so I got a couple of videos,' he announced.

She feigned delight. 'I didn't know we had a TV and video, Bob. That's a good idea.'

He smiled proudly. 'We've got everything we need here, Elaine. I bought some chops for lunch. You like them grilled with a dash of Lea and Perrins – I know that, and I've bought some for you. Tonight if you're hungry I'll get a Chinese. Can't let my lovely lady starve, can I?'

Where was the TV? Obviously in a room she had not yet seen. 'I'd like to see your . . . our . . . video. Find out if I can work it. I'd like to help you.'

'Sure.' He led the way. His mood was lighter, almost jaunty. Over his shoulder he said, 'And I got you a little present. A token of how I feel about you, Elaine. Hope you like it.'

What could he mean? Her heart was beginning to beat faster. He had not waved the knife at her this time; in fact jacketless he appeared *not to be carrying it at all.* A step or so behind, following him with apparent docility, she urgently weighed up her chances: should she barge in front, give him a hefty shove back down the stairs and run for the front door . . .?

During their breakfast he had described his desire to keep fit and his attendance at Tai-kwondo classes. He had talked of his prowess, though there was no telling how much was boasting. In a struggle he might be a formidable opponent, as he had proved at the moment of her capture: a straightforward confrontation would not work, even were she briefly endowed with the strength of desperation. She put such ideas to one side. But she would try something, soon.

They had reached the top of the basement stairs. Sunlight filtered in from the cracked window-panes above the street door and made the dust dance in the air of the narrow hallway. Bob turned towards the front.

Adrenaline was running through every artery. It was as if an extra dose of energy had been delivered to her in preparation for what might come. Outwardly calm but increasingly excited, she concentrated on the prospect of viewing more of her prison.

He pushed open the door of the front parlour and pointed. 'There's my present. I've bought you some flowers, Elaine. I've put them in there to make it homely for you.' So that was it – that explained why he had looked pleased. Thank God it wasn't anything worse. With a slight bow and a smirk he ushered her in, so that she entered the room first.

It was all she could do not to cry out loud – not at the ordinary television set and video in one corner by the uncurtained bay window;

nor at the shabby but relatively clean furniture, the cracked leather armchair facing the TV, the sofa with a coloured blanket thrown over, the single bookcase with a few paperbacks; not even at the pretty blue vase containing a posy of fresh anemones on top of the television.

No – what she had fleetingly witnessed and which had dropped out of sight the second she moved towards the window was the unmistakable peaked helmet of a police officer behind the privet hedge, with a short-barrelled rifle in his hands.

'The flowers are sweet, Bob,' she whispered.

'That's our man, sir.'

'Correction: that's our lady. For Christ's sake, don't shoot.' Morris, on bended knee, spoke into his mobile. 'Sergeant Fowler – you in position yet?' A crackle startled him and he cursed, then half bent he moved twenty yards away, motioning the four men in front of the house to stay low.

'Sir,' came the crackle, its tone impassive. 'We have a reasonable view into the downstairs front room. Two people, a man and a woman. She's a blonde. I think it's Mrs Stalker, sir.'

'Damn,' the inspector muttered. 'We should have gone in before he got home. All very well waiting to make sure it was the right house, and the van confirmed it – but she was probably alone in there before, and she isn't now.'

'You weren't to know, inspector.' Crouched beside him George attempted to soothe but had come to a similar conclusion. He felt bitter and frightened.

'We need to let her know we're here, somehow.' The inspector bit distractedly at a hangnail. A young officer at his side began to make suggestions but George cut in.

'I'll go and knock on the door, shall I? Pretend I'm selling double glazing or something.'

'No! Don't be so bloody stupid.' Morris laid a warning hand on George's arm.

'Well, then, it won't do any harm if I simply walk past and glance in,' continued George coolly. 'He doesn't know me from Adam, but if Elaine looks out she'll twig at once.'

This time, before anyone could stop him, he had risen to his feet, thrust his hands into his coat pockets and set off along the pavement, head down as if deep in thought.

'Almighty Christ!' Morris grabbed the mobile. 'All units alert. Keep your eyes peeled. We may have action. Hold your fire. Suspect and hostage are in the front downstairs room of the house. Hold your fire, I repeat, unless you have target.'

Elaine picked up the heavy blue vase and raised its contents to her nose. She stood side on to the window. 'These are so nice,' she remarked, 'but anemones have no smell, do they? Though they'll open up beautifully by this evening.'

She allowed herself to chatter lightly as Bob knelt to fiddle with the video. There was movement again out there: she could see something out of the corner of her eye but dared not look directly. A black figure leaped across a rooftop opposite. In a trice it had ducked behind a chimney. It too was armed.

Her mouth went dry and her heart thumped wildly. If Bob had stepped close he would have spotted the pulse racing in her throat at once. Casually she stepped away from the window. They would not take pot shots into the gloomy unlit room, not if they were sure she was inside. The problem was how to get out, and whether Bob still had the knife somewhere, and how quickly he could move, and whether her ankle would carry her speedily enough to safety . . .

A tall man in a buff-coloured coat suddenly came across her line of vision, walking along the pavement towards them. He had his head bent and seemed lost in his own thoughts. As he passed in front of the window he raised his head – and looked her fully in the face.

'George!' she cried involuntarily, then turned in horror. For Bob had leapt to his feet, his face contorted with rage and alarm. He was shouting and grabbing at her. His fingers closed on her arm in a vicious grip and he started to drag her towards the door.

'No!' she screamed, and struggled. Then, pulling back her free arm, she threw the vase with every ounce of her strength at the window.

She had aimed true. It shattered with a tremendous crash, shards of thin glass fracturing and spinning everywhere. A tiny piece flew back and caught her on her mouth: she could feel the sting and the warm blood, could taste it on her lips. But she did not hesitate. With a fierce tug she tore her arm free and jumped for the gap, kicking away broken glass to place her foot firmly on the sill among the ragged flowers. Praying she would fall safely, she rolled her arms over her head, thanked God for the thick pullover and pushed herself forward. Then suddenly she found herself blessedly in a tumbled confusion of blood, crunching glass and dusty privet hedge – but at last she was out in the bright open air, being grabbed by willing hands and hauled to freedom.

There was a shout and the sound of running feet as she was hustled out of range. Behind her came a savage roar of frustration, pain and anger. As she twisted her head she saw Bob's hands emerge from the window, one on each side of the frame. He began to haul himself out, as if to pursue her. Her last image of him, of his face, showed the same crazed scowl she had seen when he had first forced her into that van – only this time he was unarmed, and she was no longer alone.

The police officer in the peaked cap raised his hand and dropped it, his mouth set in a tight line. From the rooftops and from prone black figures came a single volley of rifle fire. The noise cracked and echoed and stopped, then hung in the air. Her eyes were on Bob: she knew, even in the infinity before it happened, that he was their fatal target. His body was framed in the window, almost motionless, as if time had stood still. Then the bullets punctured his trunk with calculated accuracy. She saw the shirt rip in several places and the marks of his wounds appear, not spurting as in films but a dark ooze in each hole, for these were high-velocity weapons. He shuddered as each shot thudded into him; then his hands slowly lost their grip and his dying body slid backwards into the room. As the echoes of the firing reverberated around the terraced houses, the expression on his thrown-back face changed to one of amazement, as if it had never occurred to Bob that one day he might be killed too.

'Elaine! You OK? Where's the ambulance?'

'Mum! Mum!'

Pandemonium broke out. Police in flak jackets were everywhere: several leapt into the house through the broken window. An ambulance with a blue flashing light screeched from round a corner, then another. Elaine was oblivious. Instantly she felt overcome with tiredness. Karen was on one side of her, sobbing and laughing, George on the other, gabbling nonsense at her. With his handkerchief he wiped blood ineffectually from her cheeks and hands and picked gingerly at the pieces of glass which shivered in her hair like a fragile tiara. Behind him hovered men and women in Day-glo jackets – paramedics, she surmised, who hesitated to put blankets around her shoulders for fear of driving glass into her skin. Nobody but George dared touch her.

Then the world turned black. She heard a voice shout 'Catch her!' – and knew only that she was safe in George's arms.

Epilogue

'The carriage awaits, Ma'am.'

'Thank you, Michael.' The Queen kicked a corgi from under her feet, patted her stiff grey hair and stole a final look at herself in the long mirror.

The years had been kind, considering. Her face was lined and paler, but in her early seventies that was hardly a surprise. Why did they say she was so dowdy? That hairstyle had been the latest fashion and had even incurred adverse criticism as too flighty for a future monarch when first she wore it. Never satisfied, some of them.

Take the morning's papers. Full of carping remarks about the silly practice of a redundant old-age pensioner in a white silk evening gown – in broad daylight – weighed down with diamonds, driving around London in a lacquered horse-drawn coach to open Parliament. If only they realised how tough a job it could be. It was not her fault that the speech was boring: *she* didn't write it. Were it up to her, she'd much rather perform in a Hartnell dress and jacket with a matching hat. And sail up in the Rolls: vastly more comfortable than a draughty carriage, and fewer whiffs from the horses. But should she try to change one jot or tittle they'd scream blue murder about the loss of tradition. Damn their eyeballs: they were lucky to have her.

The equerry twitched. Quite right too: these things were timed to the last second. She moved back a few steps to the adjoining door and poked her head through.

'Right! Philip – are you ready?'

'Speaker at prayers!'

The cry echoed around the lobbies. The only ceremony at Westminster which is hidden from the cameras was under way.

Fred Laidlaw stood at the furthest end of the second row, correctly in his place as a junior Minister, bowed his head in reverence and tried to concentrate on the ancient words.

What amazing changes had occurred since he had stood in the Chamber at his first State Opening. He had been guided by Elaine Stalker on that occasion, he recalled, but he had not seen her this day. Then she had advised him, not entirely seriously, that it was better to watch it on television if he wanted to see and understand what went on. But that was not the same as *being* here.

The place was magic. Every stone breathed history, continuity, gravity. Its law-making had placed it for centuries at the bosom of the nation. What was said at that dispatch box really mattered: the phrases were recorded for all to read and would be consulted and quoted long after its utterers were dust. His entire youth he had fantasised that some day he might enter those doors, and still had to pinch himself that the dream had come true.

The famous names of his adolescence were largely gone, of course. Sir John Major was a luminary in the World Bank and had dropped out of politics entirely. His brother Terry still made regular appearances on chat shows and believed the audiences were laughing at his jokes. Michael Heseltine in retirement had lost all his hair; somehow the baldness had unmanned him completely. Bill Cash had been a bold appointment as Minister for Europe and to everyone's astonishment was in danger of turning native. Teresa Gorman had at last succumbed to advancing years, stopped taking the tablets and shrunk to a benign little granny.

Another old lady had, however, gained a new lease of life. Margaret Thatcher adorned both the Lords and the Order of the Garter: she and the Queen had long since patched up their quarrels. Or maybe Her Majesty simply found the baroness more entertaining than her successors. Neither would tell.

As for himself, Fred Laidlaw: to be a Minister, serving in a government he admired – wasn't that the pinnacle of a political man's ambition? He half opened an eye and surreptitiously gazed around. On the front bench a few yards below him stood the broad shoulders and well-cut suit of the Prime Minister. A good man, Roger Dickson, though a bit cold at times. It was almost as if, Fred mused, despite Dickson's having attained the highest position in the land, something disappointed him deep in his soul. Maybe power was not all it seemed.

Only one thing was lacking in Fred's life: the woman he loved. He mouthed, 'Give us this day our daily bread', along with his colleagues, but added under his breath, 'And please, good Lord, give me Karen as well, for ever and ever. Amen.'

It was not as if he hadn't begged her. Indeed he had bombarded her with marriage proposals, and repeated his offer after her mother's rescue. The whole incident, the danger which had faced Karen herself, the bravery with which she had insisted on accompanying the police, had served to underline his conviction that there was no other partner for him and never could be.

Was he such a poor prospect as a spouse? Surely not. He had a steady job with every expectation of holding his seat as long as he wanted it. His reputation in the House was growing, though it was recognised that he still had much to learn. He had made several speeches worthy of note. He might expect a modest promotion in due course, if not at the next reshuffle then the one after. Should his luck hold he might some day find himself as a senior Minister of State, or even on the lower rungs of the Cabinet. What more could a girl want?

His moral behaviour was impeccable; and that was no fabrication but the gospel truth. He had no affairs on the side, no strange proclivities which might shock or titillate readers of the *Globe*. On the contrary, he adored the girl and despite her refusals to marry him was faithful to her. Since she had appeared on the scene, indeed, he had had eyes for nobody else.

They lived in the same house and shared the expenses and chores. They slept in the same bed, mostly. They made love regularly and it was fresh and wonderful every time. They went on holiday together. Dammit, they were nearly married; yet still she resisted. Whenever he raised the issue she pushed him gently away with a friendly laugh, even as she wriggled her naked bottom at him invitingly. He had not dared mention the possibility of their having children. Damn women.

'Prayers over!'

Fred resumed his seat. All was well with a beautiful world. With a little cunning and a lot of hard work, if next year he was further up in the hierarchy he would be entitled to sit on the senior of the two front benches, nose to nose with Her Majesty's Opposition. And, if Fate were kind, some day, a couple of years from now, on his left ring finger there would be a wedding ring. On that he was quite determined.

'Ah, Jayanti, it is so beautiful.'

Pramila Bhadeshia lifted the box of Kleenex on to her lap and abandoned any attempt to hide the tears which flowed down her cheeks. At her side her husband frowned and fanned himself with the *Times of India*. He dared not turn off the television for fear of reprisals: the women in his household upbraided him sufficiently for his failures already.

His wife adjusted her sari over her shoulders. On the screen the Queen emerged from the Irish state coach, her expression bland, her hand held out to the Lord Chamberlain to steady herself. Pramila sniffed audibly.

Without warning the cameras switched to the waiting Lords' Chamber. Red and gold splendour blazed as the peers, caparisoned in similar colours, their wives in ermine and pearls, rose to their feet. The sound of trumpets filled the air.

Pramila began to keen loudly. 'Ai! Ai!'

'Oh, do stop, wife.' Jayanti jumped up impatiently. He had had enough. 'Are we to have this nonsense every year? I cannot return. You are never going to sit in a peeress's seat. You know the reason perfectly well.'

He stalked out of the room. In the corridor he beckoned to a retainer. 'I suggest you fetch madam another box of tissues.'

'Yes, my lord,' the old servant murmured with a bow.

Jayanti gazed at him mournfully. 'No, don't call me that. Especially not today.'

Mrs York bent towards the television set and gently switched it off. Slumped in his armchair, his eyes glazed with tears, her husband made no attempt to stop her. Nor could he.

She moved awkwardly since arthritis had set in, but at least she was more mobile than her husband. His stroke had partly been a consequence of Anthony's arrest and the newspaper furore. He had reacted so badly to his son's death. For months it seemed to her that it had been a matter of waiting till another disaster struck the family in the form of her husband's illness. When it came it had felt like divine retribution. She had relaxed marginally since; probably nothing much worse could happen to destroy them now.

Yet for him to be deprived of speech was the greatest irony of all, because he had been such a taciturn man who had found it impossible to express his inner feelings. They had never been a family that had talked much. Now he could not talk at all, paradoxically it had become easier to communicate emotions, such as his grief at the parliamentary ceremony, since words no longer got in the way.

Was it all their fault? Had they never understood their son? Had the family's reluctance to share worries set the seal on his fate? Perhaps that had been the nub of the problem. Had Anthony been able to articulate his fears in good time, had anyone responded with compassion and love, he might have avoided his agony, or at least been able to cope with it better. She sighed and touched her husband's hand, which trembled in response.

There was no way of knowing. It was too late.

'We can't upgrade you, sir. Business class is full.'

Jim Betts scowled. 'But you've just told me the smoking section's full in economy. How am I to survive if I can't have a smoke?'

'I'm sorry, sir.' The British Airways clerk dug deep into her training and contained her temper. 'It is only an hour's flight to Brussels. The plane is full because there's a big conference there tomorrow. You can have a cigarette in the lounge before we take off.'

Betts slouched away, his ticket and passport in his fist, muttering angrily to himself.

He knew about the conference: that was why he was on the same flight. He expected to see certain familiar faces, not least Ted Bampton, who had been pushed sideways to become Minister of Agriculture, with no prospects of a further Cabinet post after that. That meant Bampton would spend the remainder of his career negotiating fish quotas and debating food safety. The PM's office claimed, tongue in cheek, that it was a good move, but Bampton's morose face told its own tale.

Not that he, Betts, had much to sing about. He sought an empty space among the few smoking seats in the departure lounge of Terminal One and sat down gingerly. The bruises had long since healed, but he had been warned that certain parts of his anatomy were likely to be delicate for the rest of his life. He would have to be careful how and where he deployed them. He winced at the thought and rummaged for his cigarettes.

At that moment Bampton, briefcase in hand, wandered in. Betts half rose politely and proffered his pack.

'Thanks, I don't mind if I do.'

The two men puffed companionably for a few minutes. Then Bampton eyed the journalist.

'I hear you're going to be a regular on this trip, Jim. Is that right?'

Betts grimaced. 'Yes, I'm afraid so. The paper says it's a big promotion, but it doesn't feel that way. Though they are paying me better.'

'What exactly's your title now?'

Betts sucked deeply on his cigarette, then blew two smoke rings into the air above their heads. His eyes were full of sorrow.

'Me? I'm to be the group's Brussels correspondent. Big deal. Fourteen newspapers, mostly heavies and regionals. I'm to cover not only haddock and your goddam set-aside, Ted, but the Part-Time Directive and nitrates in tap water and compulsory paternity leave and equal pay for lesbian goldfish and the goings-on of Monsieur Santer. And how subsidiarity's working and the Committee of the Regions and, oh yes, I have to shadow Lord and Lady Kinnock as well. That'll be a bundle of laughs. Terrific job.'

He hung his head and continued in a lower tone. 'My boss said he was fed up visiting me in hospital. A five-year posting to Belgium should keep me out of trouble. On that he's probably right.'

Bampton chuckled. 'We'll have to keep in touch then, Jim. I was sorry to hear about your accident. They didn't catch the muggers, did they? How many was it – four? Five? Terrible. It's not been a grand year for either of us, has it?'

Martin Chadwick would be on duty after lunch when the Prime Minister rose at the dispatch box to start the more formal debate on the Gracious Speech, but for the moment he had an hour to spare, provided he kept a wary eye on the mute television set in the corner of his new office overlooking Horse Guards Parade.

To have been made the senior civil servant in charge of the Number 10 Policy Unit was quite a promotion after the mishmash of the Department of Health, Welfare and the Family, now fortunately no more. He smiled quietly to himself. Strictly speaking he was not the unit's head – that job was a political appointment reserved for a former features editor of the *Financial Times*, a friend of the PM's since his days at Tarrants Bank. But the position of the senior official was far more significant.

Politicians would come and go. Their reputations would wax and wane, mostly the latter. Whatever the crises, he had steered his masters serenely through them, always finding a suitable phrase to soothe and compromise, though whether that resulted in good government was not for him to say. His wealth of knowledge and experience, his tact and charm, his sheer *ability*, guaranteed him permanent access to power. He had served both the competent and the forgettable with the same diligence and would continue in that vein; he would be there long after the current bunch had been replaced by their bitterest opponents from the Opposition benches. Indeed, the more wet behind the ears his masters might be, the more influence it gave him and his ilk.

Whatever the future held for others, for Martin Chadwick it would be rosy.

At the far end of the same building there was a great deal of activity. It was such a squeeze to fit in any kind of decorating or renovation at Number 10. The place was so busy and, if truth were told, overcrowded. But needs must: new carpets for the Prime Minister's personal flat had been on order for months and had at last arrived. The housekeeper had insisted on no further delay. Mr and Mrs Dickson would sleep downstairs for a short while until the work was finished.

Meanwhile some of the heavy furniture presented problems. From the moment the PM had left that morning the two blue-overalled removal men had sweated and tugged; the result of their labours was an ungainly pile in an adjoining office, with the unpalatable thought that in a week's time it would all have to be put back again.

'That desk'd be easier to shift if we took the drawers out.' Arthur stood hands on hips, breathing hard.

Steve nodded. 'Right. Hope they're empty – don't want to be accused of nicking state secrets.'

Together they set to. The old central drawer held notepaper and oddments; others contained scribbles on curled-up bits of paper, an ancient copy of *The Economist*, half a packet of sugar-free gum, a faded wedding anniversary card. One drawer appeared to be stuck.

'Give it a tug,' Arthur suggested. He was the ideas man.

'Right,' Steve said again and bent to his task. Grasping the handle he pulled sharply. There was a splintering sound and the entire drawer came away. Startled, Steve fell over backward with the drawer and its miscellaneous contents on top of him.

He sat up and rubbed his shoulder as the two men surveyed their handiwork. Then Steve, whose eyes were still at the same level as the drawer opening, knelt and peered into the hole.

'What's this?' he murmured. 'Secret compartment, by the looks of it. These old desks have their mysteries, don't they? Let's see.'

He reached in his arm, grasped the tiny handle and pulled out a small wooden box. Arthur peered curiously over his shoulder.

'Something in here,' Arthur said. 'An envelope – must have been left behind. Could be hundreds of years old.'

'No, I don't think so.' Steve picked it up and turned it over. 'It's addressed to somebody alive and kicking right now. My auntie's MP, in fact. "Mrs Elaine Stalker", that's what it says.'

He straightened up, the letter in his hand, their immediate objective forgotten.

'Well, now,' murmured Arthur. He scratched his head slowly, 'That's a turn-up for the book. Should we give it to her? Or maybe it should go to Mrs Dickson? This is her desk after all.'

'Or maybe it should go to the *Globe*,' grinned Steve, and he put the letter in his pocket.

'Yeah!'

Karen Stalker leapt in the air and ran to her mother.

'Watch my hat, Karen!'

'Oh, never mind your hat. Or mine. Now you've done it I want to give you the biggest hug. You deserve it.'

Laughing, Elaine succumbed to her daughter's warmth, then smoothed down her new coat and adjusted the corsage on her lapel. The lone photographer beckoned her to turn in his direction. Self-consciously her finger flew to the scars on her neck and her upper lip, then with an intense shake of her head she made herself ignore them and smile into the camera.

'And George too,' cried Karen determinedly. 'The pictures can wait.' She reached to kiss him on the cheek but he put an arm round her waist and hugged the girl to him, his face suffused with joy.

'Golly! Do I have to call you Dad now?' she enquired in mock deference. 'You going to tell me what to do?'

'Get on with you,' he grinned. 'If I can't tell the new Mrs Horrocks what to do – and I've tried it, it doesn't work – I doubt if the next generation will take a blind bit of notice. Call me George as you have always done.'

In the background Betty Horrocks smiled indulgently. Tactfully she guided Karen out of the way to stand with her and Diane. The wind threatened to lift all their hats. 'Let them have their first photos together, dear,' she whispered. 'As man and wife. It's their day. At last, thank God.'

463

'They picked fine weather for it,' Diane remarked sociably. 'Pity to miss the State Opening, though.'

'On the contrary, it's a perfect choice.' Betty was pulling on her gloves. 'The whole country's attention is elsewhere, including the blasted press. Anyway, I reckon they've got their priorities absolutely right.'

'They make a handsome couple, don't they?' Diane clutched her handbag to her own solid body. Her tone was wistful. 'She seems to have got over that dreadful ordeal. What a business! Yet she's never breathed a word about what really happened.'

'She brushes it away with, "He's dead, so what's the point?" Sensible attitude, I'd say.' Betty began to hunt through her handbag. 'Come on, Diane, Karen: where's the rice? Quickly now.'

'I hope they'll be very happy.' Karen realised she was about to cry. She wondered if every wedding was like this, and whether acceptance of Fred's repeated offers mightn't be a good idea. Though not just yet. She wanted to prove herself first. He would be miffed when he discovered she had not told him about this event.

But then nobody knew. For it was, out of choice, entirely a private matter, and not a parliamentary affair.